The Reciprocated Silence

By the same Author

- Violence and Religion: Cross Cultural Opinions and Consequences
- Social Behaviour of Children
- Contemporary Social Science Research: An Evaluation of National and Non-National Contributions
- Spirituality and Well-being
- Chance and Probability: The Limitations of the Social Sciences

---

About the Author

Ralph Tanner has a B.Sc. and Diploma in Social Anthropology from Oxford University and a D. Phil in Law from Stokholm University. He has done fieldwork in Thailand, the Philippines, Guyana, Zambia, Zimbabwe, Tanzania, Uganda and Kenya as well as in Britain and Eire. He was Chairman of the East African Institute of Social Research and Lecturer in Comparative Religion in the University of London. He has published books on Murder in Uganda. Witchcraft killings and religions and successful change and a cross cultural study of the Roman Catholic Mass. He has co-authored books on the social ecology of religion and the environment. He has written numerous articles on the social aspects of religious change, translation and language use in religion, as well as on behavioural theories in the *Journal of Modern African Studies, Africa, Journal of the Social Sciences, Nordic Journal of African Studies, Antropos, Studia Missionalia and others.* He is currently working on studies of religious behaviour as a working misunderstanding and the commonplace nature of religious experiences

THE RECIPROCATED SILENCE

The Modern Individual and Religious Misunderstanding

R.E.S. Tanner

CONCEPT PUBLISHING COMPANY PVT. LTD.,
NEW DELHI-110059

ISBN-13: 978-81-8069-924-5

First Published 2013

Published and Printed by

Concept
Since 1974

Concept Publishing Company Pvt. Ltd.
A/15-16, Commercial Block, Mohan Garden
New Delhi-110059 (India)
T: 25351460, 25351794, *F*: 091-11-25357109
E: publishing@conceptpub.com, W: www.conceptpub.com
Editorial Office: H-13, Bali Nagar, New Delhi-110 015, India.

Cataloging in Publication Data--*Courtesy:* D.K. Agencies (P) Ltd. <docinfo@dkagencies.com>

Tanner, R. E. S. (Ralph E. S.), 1921-
The reciprocated silence : the modern individual and religious misunderstanding / R.E.S. Tanner.
p. cm.
Includes bibliographical references (p.) and index.
ISBN 9788180699245

1. Faith. 2. Religious life. 3. Psychology, Religious. 4. Religion and sociology. I. Title.

DDC 202.2 23

To Amoret in gratitude

Preface

Public religion and private spirituality are often assessed as a dialectic between public obligations and private needs and theological and institutional requirements. It may be that they function in parallel with only some paradigmatic connections which are as much cultural as religious.

This has become a pronounced issue when these two aspects of the ways in which human behaviour copes with uncertainty and distress loses its public ability to continually adapt to the processes of personal and institutional change.

The invention of literacy and the expansion of printing provided those who thought about these issues with the ability to organise and promote their views within religious institutions. This resulted in the production of both hard and soft orthodoxies in detachment from the beliefs and needs of their members who then often created their own combinations of public religion and private spirituality.

This combination of religious thought and literacy can be divided between the religions of the book, Christianity, Islam and Judaism with their precise thinking related to a single life and the Eastern religions with their less precise recorded thinking around a succession of lives and their absence of defined theological concepts. The third group are individuals and those in quasi-traditional societies whose public religion and private spiritualities have not been and are little affected by literacy and they cope with their problems in ways that are different to those of the followers of the ostensibly literate religions.

The result of this intellectual, professional and institutional detachment is the production of written and then printed orthodoxies. These orthodoxies in their current forms are not closely related to communal or individual needs. Believers were told what they should do by authorities claiming divine connections for their interpretations enshrined in print and administered by hierarchical authorities with some personal and institutional charisma.

Thus, it would seem that the three religions of the book with their bureaucratic structures have evolved hard orthodoxies which has contributed to the development of divergent parallel private spiritualities and the formation of religious orders, cults and sects. The generality of believers maintain their affiliations with their divine foundations within which there is a working misunderstanding. Neither party invades the religious practicalities of the other because believers have little interest in the theology behind their beliefs and practices and so continue to use their religion in ways that meet their needs within the passive assumption of conformity.

In contrast the Eastern religions despite a far longer literate tradition of religious thought have produced an enormous body of soft orthodoxies in which the absence of definitions and centralising religious bureaucracies left much religious influence dependent on personal charisma and social environments.

These believers similarly have little or no interest in the theological and philosophical backing for their beliefs so that they have produced an even larger range of public religious and private spiritualities. Within these faiths there is an even wider working misunderstandings within their soft orthodoxies between what believers actually do and the vague requirements of their faiths about what is considered to be divinely necessary. This allows for an easier adjustment to current realities.

Finally, there are the personal and communal public religious and private spirituality occurring in urban settings and quasi-traditional environments which have little connection with literacy. In this scenario there can be little misunderstanding since what is done relies on the social setting of episodic memory and current needs.

It would seem that secularisation has not become more than a form of political and social thought which has not replaced the general global availability and influence of public religion and private spirituality. Whether people live within hard or soft orthodoxies or in environments in which no religious orthodoxies exist, their need for both public religion and private spirituality continues.

This is an exploratory study of the working misunderstandings in individual public and private religious ideas and practices between formal, informal and personal orthodoxies which are felt to exist and how they do not appear to lead to any breakdown in their appreciated personal value.

This study will show that the amount of dissonance between orthodoxy and personal beliefs and practices is more a feature of the Western religions of the book than Eastern ones with their dearth of definitions and the faiths of quasi-traditional peoples with all people sharing a concentration on ritual performance and a dislike of abstractions.

Acknowledgements

This study is based on wide ranging participant observations in East and Central Africa, Guyana, Myanmar, the Philippines, Britain, China and Sri Lanka rather than from the detached and restricting data provided from elitist books and specific research projects.

Throughout I have been consistently helped by Christian priests, pastors, sisters, traditional healers and Muslim dignitaries as well as by students involved in comparative religion degree courses for Buddhism, Hinduism and Islam.

I am particularly grateful to the many Tanzanians with whom I have had prolonged discussions on religious issues in Swahili in which language I was fortunate to have become bilingual. More particularly to Ntemi Kapongo of Nassa, Ali Farahani of Kilwa, Nfumo Kabadi of Nyegezi and Juma Ndamulo of Mwanza.

In addition my thanks go to Professors King of Makerere, Widstrand of Uppsala, Wijsen of Radbound Universities and to Fathers J. Laishley and G. Croft of the Society of Jesus, Father J. Hendricks of the White Fathers and Chaplain J. Kenney of the United States Air Force.

Contents

1
Working Misunderstandings

It is probable that a global feature of all public religions and private spiritualities is that they work in the subconscious and indeed in the consciousness of all individuals without regard for intellectual and social differences but that the religious ideas on which they are founded are necessarily misunderstood.

The Social Bases of Religious Practices

Any general overview of contemporary religious behaviour and thought discloses not only the binary nature of these systems between thinkers and doers, but that there are parallel patterns of connected religious behaviour in many contexts. There is a marked difference between that part of major global religious systems that are based on literate frameworks enabling the creation of codes of conduct, required dispositions and preferred thinking and what people do under these folded umbrellas.

Secondly, there is a marked difference between the elitist conceptions of what should be involved in religious practices developed by full-time specialists and a few charismatics in comparison to the thinking and religious behaviour of more ordinary part-time believers.

Thirdly, the differences between the regularities required by religious organisations made possible by literacy and those who do not wish for or indeed cannot follow such regularities and wants religious system that are responsive to immediate needs and involve personal religious creativities.

It is not so much that some religions have a public persona which is not widely successful in providing conformity and binding on individuals.

The reality is surely not two desparate systems in which each is theologically and socially hostile to the other. There is rather a form of titular indefinable unity within which there are two systems. Each recognising the theological existence of the other and integrating into each other at some levels of social and religious need while remaining functionally independent for the majority of their religious practices and interpretations.

A working misunderstanding which applies as much to Buddhism, Hinduism and Islam as it does to Christianity and Judaism. The great majority of believers are provided with the nominal coverage of an overarching theological and philosophical system, a social as much as religious emplacement. This framework is available for latent comfort and support leaving the individual and social groups functionally free to pursue their own religious interests.

We have to recognise that the arrival of literacy has created systems dominated by secular and religious bureaucratic elites which in terms of their use in a religious context has probably not been as significant as administrators of these religious systems may have planned and thought.

So the religions which have put their doctrines into writing have provided for their believers this framework within which their faith should be expressed and through which they can fulfil their membership obligations. There are, however, distinctions between the 'religions of the book', Christianity, Islam and Judaism and Eastern faiths which are similarly based on sacred literature but without any disciplinary sharpness which is so characteristic of Western faiths. So believers in both these categories are functionally committed to their basic literature in different ways.

In addition there are the remains of earlier religious systems which were not and are not tied to literacy and contemporary individual systems of religious belief and practice which are nominally independent of any organised supra-individual faiths (Bellah, 1989). So outside these formalised faiths carried forward by special institutions and professional ritual providers and administrators, there are these quasi-traditional personal faiths which do not belong to the Great Traditions nor to the sectarian Little Traditions (Redfield, 1956). More particularly there are the private spiritualities, the so-called *sheilaisms* of contemporary urban-industrial societies (Bellah, 1989) whether in Amsterdam, Amritsar or Accra. Both these ways of worship are not part of this study simply because in their personal self-sufficiency there cannot be any misunderstandings.

There is, however, a further distinction between personal needs and practices of modern Christianity in its predominantly Western forms. Here there is the overarching theological and moral requirement that the believer has to have a proper framework of thought and behaviour for the core rituals to become appropriately active shown in the Roman Catholic phrase in Latin *ex opera operantis*.

For the vast majority if not universally whether as Christians or members of other faiths whether committed to writing or not or subject to institutional supervision, there is the belief that the performance of rituals, regardless of the performer's moral state has some beneficial effects even if it is only the accumulation of personally valued religious merit. This again is shown in the Latin phrase *ex opere operato*.

It is the persuasive overall feeling for almost all people in all faiths that the simple performance of a religious ritual has benefits for the performer even when this participation is entirely passive, regardless of personal moral considerations which dominates religious practice in all societies and within all religious cultures. This is the basic feature underlying 'the working misunderstanding' under which believers persist in their liturgical activities with a limited regard for its theological significance.

Performers believe that what they are doing is valid and so successfully meets their needs. Western theologians are at best doubtful that such ritualism can have any religious value without some active moral involvement. Eastern theologians on the other hand, see these practices as necessary for the current lives of believers but that their status can be improved on in subsequent lives;. What they are doing is inadequate certainly but no more than stages in spiritual growth within the belief in rebirth.

Fundamentally there will always remain the mysterious value of ritual, a physical performance which is and must remain outside social science created understandings. These rituals are directed at supernatural entities and the performers themselves judge the adequacy of the metaphysical silence with which their activities are received. The response to these rituals is certainly silence according to the assessments of the social science but it is a reciprocal one in the understandings of those carrying out these rituals personally or in participation in institutionally provided rituals.

There is the fact that the belief in the efficaciousness of ritual performance goes back into the mists of time in all known forms of traditional and personally created ritualism and fits in with human psychological needs. We can assume that these performances have had a high rate of psychosomatic success without much necessary expense in time, effort and economic outlay.

The social sciences in their evaluations explain away these activities rather than accept their social and theological reality. The participants see their religious experiences as a form of inexplicable reality about which no cultural or intellectual outsider has any right or indeed ability to evaluate.

While theology has this factor of overall applicability, the objects of devotion in practice have no such general characteristics. They are locally and personally specific. (Robb, 2008:124). The Virgin Mary or Krishna in one household or community is not the same reality as the Virgin Mary or Krishna in neighbouring households or communities thus having the same variable utility as 'ancestors' or 'tree spirits'. Each individual whether Hindu or Christian creates and maintains their own understandings with the supernatural entities of their choice which to their way of thinking is isolated from any forms of primary pragmatism. The increased devotion to the Virgin Mary in the community in which the Chilean miners were rescued is an example of such individual and popular response.

From whose point of view is there this 'working misunderstanding'. Certainly not from the point of view of those worshipping who are there on their continuing assumption that it is likely to work in ways that are a mixture of hope and the reality of personal perceptions. Human beings are logical enough to have assured their own evolutionary survival so it is reasonable to assume that what the social sciences see empirically as silence does in fact work satisfactorily enough to make the carrying out of religious rituals a feature of all cultures and in most private lives.

If there is a 'misunderstanding' then it comes from the assessments of those who are detached from the ongoing realities of religious needs. The fact that the social sciences conclude that this success is due at least in part the result of ill-defined propositions is beside the point as it is personally experienced as success.

The Social Realities of Contemporary Religion

As far as can be estimated religions have developed as a severely practical response to the problems of survival to the current position in which as a result of literacy and institutionalisation the theoretical understandings have become further and further socially distanced from practical religion, the predominant pragmatism of 'traditional' and 'popular' beliefs.

There is firstly an elitist core of religious understandings which produce the complexities of theology and philosophy which few understand and use to any extent in their worship. This provides for most a covert core of orthodoxy which the believers of faiths feel put their existence into some sort of orderly perspective. A recent Indian woman reformer wrote 'I beg my Western sisters not to be satisfied with the looking on the outside beauties of the grand philosophers and not to be charmed with the long and interesting discourses of our educated ones. But to open the trap doors of the great monument of ancient Hindu intellect and enter the dark cellars where they will see the real workings which they admire so much' (Ramabai, 1893:308). A harsh comment no doubt but it is hard to see any close connection between the sacred *puranas* of Hinduism, the Analects of Confucius and the Spiritual Exercises of St. Ignatius and the everyday practicalities of religious performance.

'While the higher religion at their most elevated and philosophical levels may provide a set of intellectual propositions that answer (in the religion's 'own' terms and which are not terms that need convince an outsider) 'ultimate questions', practical religion, religion at the everyday level has been preoccupied with other issues.... These ultimate concerns may be of limited consequence in the everyday life circumstances of those who, nominally embrace the teachings of one of the higher religions. The social significance of religion has rather laid in the provision of categories and symbols that facilitate simultaneously man's comprehension of his circumstances and his capacity to evaluate them to cope with them emotionally' (Wilson, 1952:10). Life after death or repetitive sequential lives are distant considerations for men and women who have today's problems to cope with.

Under these comprehensive but little understood intellectual coverings public religion and private spiritualities continue to flourish within these more personal misunderstandings to accompany rites of passage and to alleviate personal and communal distress and uncertainties.

The Nature of Theological Understandings

A misunderstanding starts surely from the assumption that there has been originally an understanding which has subsequently been misunderstood.

To what extent do members of the Roman Catholic Church understand its doctrines which are detailed in the Vatican II documents, the ex-cathedra statements of the Pope and in the catechisms widely available in the major languages. This same question must apply with equal force to Hindus and Buddhists which have documents but not from any accepted centralised source and also to Taoists and Shintoists who only have interpretations from obscure ancient sources. Only Islam has a simple list of the basic requirements in the Five Pillars of the Faith but beyond that they have only the interpretation of scholars of the Koran and the reputed sayings of the Prophet Mohammad. It would thus appear only in Islam can there be a clear coincidence between what is required and what is universally known to be required, but then Islam as a narrowly revealed religion is not involved in complicated patterns of background thought which are the basis of Eastern religion thinking.

Understanding would be that current members who state that they are Roman Catholics have kept themselves up-to-date with the official doctrines of their Church. Those who have done so are most likely to have been professional full-time members of the institutional Church. It is often the case that Hindu priests have little knowledge of the theological details behind their carrying out of lengthy rituals which they perform; they are as performance oriented as the simplest peasant worshipping at a village shrine. It seems unlikely that the laity would go through these time consuming activities in order to know more about the theological backgrounds to their on-going faith. They would be unlikely to get any satisfying return from acquiring such unusable religious knowledge in time and motion terms when their time is filled with family affairs and work requirements.

Whether they have misunderstood or not, they remain more or less active members of the religion, sect or cult as it provides rituals which they can use within their own interpretations of their personal value. But the changes that are always going on in any religion are now part of religious history and for contemporary believers it may remain a question of whether the rituals provide the emotional and immediate practical services which they know not just interpret as being to their advantage. It seems unlikely that no more than a very few are interested in how why their religion in its local forms came to provide what it does.

If the religion does not provide what its customers want in marketing terms then they lapse, but not necessarily into agnosticism. They will change their faith to another belief system or create their own individual system of belief and practice. In this sense it is difficult to talk of a lapsed

Hindu, Shintoist or Taoist for there never were any statutory requirements from which they could be said to lapse. For those that remain within Christian denominations with their different and changing theological legalisms it is a 'working misunderstanding'. There has always been a distinction between those offering a religious service for personal and or institutional purposes and those that receive it.

In non-literate religious systems the diviner or the spirit possessed provides a service dictated by some ill-defined cultural paradigms and their own experience of the spirit world. These practitioners always have to attract a satisfied clientele or they would go out of business. In many languages there is no word for 'belief' as that would imply for them the nonsensical idea of the absence of the divine (Bernardi, 1959). This traditional world may have had theological thought but it would have been related to the public need to cope with changing social circumstances and without writing it could not have had any specific identity. The system is self-adjusting within a belief in some unchanging realities. There can be no working misunderstandings in religious system which have never formulated their understandings in the first place.

With the development of literacy combined with the creation and professionalization of theology using languages or linguistic codes which required special learning, misunderstandings between the different levels of religious knowledge and practice appeared. They provided rituals and if you wanted to know more about these activities individuals would have had to undertake special training or go to consult the relevant experts. There does not seem to have been any programme to extend this knowledge to the general class of believers as there has always belief in the efficaciousness of the rituals rather more than what is behind them. If individuals feel the need to know more than they should seek it from the necessary professionals who have no obligation to bring these specialised and secret understandings to the laity and thus diminish their own importance. This remains the current way of working for both Buddhism and Hinduism as well other Eastern faiths which are perpetuated in languages which are no longer in common use or involve ideograms which require special learning.

So theological thought in Christianity became a way of interpreting religion which not so much was specialised but carried on without much interest in how their thinking might be received by their customers; it was not market tested. In its early days this did not matter all that much because the various ways of interpreting and using the rituals carried on as a very popular parallel continuing 'working' misunderstanding'.

Then for a variety of political and religious reasons the Western Reformation required the faithful to conform to theologically defined requirements rather than to continue to experience religious ceremonies as emotionally and socially satisfying. This led to a progressive decline in attendance at authorised services (Duffy, 1992). This paralleled Protestantism which from its start attempted to teach what people should believe in and practice rather than continuing a form of self-interpreted ritualism which the vast majority found to satisfy their needs with little or no concern for the restrictions and complex elaborations of literate theology. Outside the West Christianity was largely spread by Spanish and Portuguese missionaries in which converts covertly incorporated their traditional beliefs within the overt requirements of their new faith; an extraordinary amalgam of faiths which continues to dominate in Latin American Roman Catholic 'working misunderstanding' (Orta, 2000).

Then the Roman Catholic Vatican II Council in which decisions were dominated by Western theological thinking and a range of decisions which related more to the external relationships of the Church and what their believers should do rather than what they might want. In some senses it repeated the theme of the Protestant Reformation and had almost parallel consequences in a marked drop in attendance at church services and a loss of large numbers of committed personnel.

No other religion has a denominational structure except Buddhism which carries out periodic conferences about the nature of their practices. Even the Buddhist conferences such as the Sixth Buddhist Council held in Rangoon 1954 would not involve itself in the metaphysical stupidity of voting for unenforceable conclusions binding on Buddhists.

Thus, many Christians were faced with the alternatives of either lapsing from such formal dictated commitments or continuing with participation perhaps interpreting the core ceremonies as if they were the same; a return to their understanding of rituals as sacred mysteries in which there were no necessary social requirement of understanding. Private interpretations relating to whatever personal needs they may have had by emphasizing to themselves its sacred mystery, which is probably an essential element in the understanding of all religious ceremonies.

When any system of religious understanding is based on some defined theological exactnesses it is this that trips up cohesion and makes consciously or not, a behavioural necessity for a working misunderstanding; it is the system of cognition that makes this inevitable.

Christianity in its cognitive duality of body and soul is an example of this as it would seem that such a concept is probably not accepted by non-literate quasi-traditional societies and is certainly not the bases of Eastern thought. The Chinese considered the Dao, the mode of action of Heaven and Earth to be Unitary.

How in fact can a religion work with a functional agreement between theory and practice if there are cognitive differences between those that live a religion behaviourally without thinking about both the whys and wherefores of what they do and those that think about it in what can be seen socially as cognitive isolation.

The difficulties of Christianity in China between these two cognitive approaches would make a working misunderstanding a necessity for the retention of faith. 'The Jesuits concluded that the Chinese were materialists since they considered finite matter and Heaven to be all of the same substance. The Chinese literati for their part concluded that the Jesuits were materialist since they deprived the universe of the invisible form, turning it into finite matter directed from outside and lacking the spontaneous intelligence that all creatures display' (Gennet, 1985:203).

On the other hand, the detailed discussing of the mental imagery of the Melanesians has been usually carried out from the superiority of socially distant literate theologies and a self-defined superior civilisation which make it a functional confrontation of superiors and inferiors. The Chinese situation was different as their intelligentsia met Christian thinking head-on and usually considered it to be ridiculous; they had thought about such things and committed their conclusions to writing at a time when Western societies could have been classified in terms of Melanesian 'primitiveness'. An early letter states that the superiority of theWestern teaching lies in their scientific calculation capacity while their inferiority lies in their veneration of a Master of Heaven creating everything which does not merit serious discussion. This Chinese attitude parallels those of Western missionaries and perhaps covertly by social scientists in Papua New Guinea confronting the complexities of ancestor worship and their cargo cults (Clark, 1992). It is hard for most intellectuals to accept that a metaphysical idea can have social and theological status before it is recognised by outsider intellectuals.

The Workings of Faith

The catch phrase 'working misunderstanding' was originally used to describe the religious practices of the Roman Catholic minority of the five million Tanzanian Sukuma (Tanner and Wijsen, 1993) living south of Lake Victoria. This 12 per cent are now mainly born into that faith rather than adult converts despite well over a century of effort by the White Fathers, a missionary order so named because of their costume.

All religions even the ostensibly simple tribal cults with no seemingly substantive beliefs and nothing committed to writing, all have the same basic characteristics. They provide on the one hand, round the corner and out of sight ideal systems of belief and morality which it is reasonably safe to assume that no one has ever attained. On the other hand, they have developed systems of immediately realisable ritual and belief which attempts to cope with their experienced difficulties and hopes and which in their estimation has been so successful over the centuries as to insure the continuation of what Christian outsiders may assess as theologically questionable religious behaviour.

In all cultures we have seen the development and maintenance of religious systems which have kept a functional balance between ideologically impossible ideal objectives of which the most extreme is the Buddhist aim to abolish the self at which only a very small number of the laity attempt to attain (Spiro, 1971). There can be little doubt that there are many contemporary martyrs in the major faiths who have died for the reality of their beliefs and that this idealism is a necessary but perhaps background part of believing.

The vast majority of believers whether Christians, Muslims or Hindus find solace and satisfaction by fluctuating between high rates of religious observance over festivals and pilgrimages to centres of devotion combined with daily devotions and reactions to adversity and periods of religious inactivity. Seventy million who are estimated to have attended the last Hindu Kumbh Mela on the Ganges river, the two million who annually go on the Muslim Hajj pilgrimage to Mecca, and the four Christian pilgrimage sites in Europe with attendances of over a million are all attending as individuals with their own reasons for being there ranging from religious tourism to undergoing their own ecstatic experiences.

In addition large numbers attend repetitious rituals such as the five brief daily prayers of devout Muslims and those that come to Roman Catholic Sunday celebrations of the Mass and lengthy Coptic ceremonies in which celebrants are hidden and out of the hearing of participants crowded outside by the small nature of the churches and inside screening behind which their liturgy is carried out.

Enormous numbers find help and satisfaction in being in sacred surroundings and having performed for them rituals of which they have little informed understanding, in linguistic codes with which they are not conversant and often cannot hear for reasons of echo, distance or infirmity. They are all ostensible believers in the religion to which they nominally adhere but get their needs fulfilled by praying for relief from their misfortunes in reciprocal silences or just from what would appear to be unthinking participation which for most is just being there at the required times.

This is indeed a working misunderstanding in which the major faiths provide rituals in support of what they have institutionally and theologically have defined as the background to their ceremonies which believers utilise within personal creative thinking which may have little to do with any formal theological precepts.

Much of the dissatisfaction of Western Roman Catholics has been over the celebration of the Mass in vernaculars and this was thought by theologians to make the ceremony more relevant to participants, rather than in Latin as a specifically sacred language. No other major religion has made such a change to make participants more involved and it does seem that unintelligibility has always been an appreciated and indeed necessary part of global religious experiences. Even the shamans and diviners in quasi-traditional religious systems usually speak in glossolalia which has then to be interpreted for the understandings of those who have come to them for help. Generally, religions avoid using language which would be directly understood by those attending their ceremonies. There never seems to be any idea that general authoritative understanding was a necessary adjunct to their successful involvement in rituals.

However, by what standards are we to use in referring to intelligibility. At the level of theology it is clear enough that very few of the faithful have enough interest in such intellectual exercises. Once it is accepted that religion is mainly an emotional experience, then there is not much value to be found in making Christianity an exercise in learning except as part of a rite of passage for entry (Lewis and Tanner, 1998). Only a minute proportion of these believing populations will have attempted to read the *Bhagavad Gita*, the *Analects of Confucius*, or the *Dhammapada*.

If an individual at their level of social and intellectual capability feels that there is meaning enough to justify their presence at a religious ceremony, then that ritual is functioning adequately enough. At this level the sight and sound of a ritual are equally important and they may have equivalent successful functions for the diplomat, ditch digger and a Down's Syndrome girl.

Perhaps here we are considering not meaning in the sense of intelligible wordings but sacred sound. The Sukuma would certainly see their religious understandings to be better expressed in their own language into which the *Bible* and some standard prayers have been translated, but not necessarily for it to be in writing. Most would think and dream in their own natal language or more probably in a linguistic code. To such people celebrations of the Mass in Latin would not have been functionally different to the use of their own glossolalia in divination and just as efficacious.

The current use of the national language *kiSwahili* in Tanzania may have range of commonplace economic and political usages without any religious intelligibility according to their social and mental understandings. These people are mainly subsistence farmers or short-term wage labourers and much less uniformly literate than Europeans who may but do not necessarily have any higher standard of practical literacy. Neither peoples will have the time to look for and appreciate the finer points of modern theology. What is done at the altar is more important than the theological reasons accounting for what the priest is doing there.

The Reciprocal Silence of Faith

While many believe that they have heard from, seen or in some convincing way experienced the supernatural, but from the social science point of view there is no evidence of this other than the convictions of those who have had these widely occurring experiences. In fact these experiences are relatively common and if they are believed to be true they will be real in their consequences (Thomas and Thomas, 1928:572). Of course, many of these occurrences are explicable in terms of widely accepted social science categorizations of psychological abnormality, but many are the experiences of people whom their own societies consider to be socially and mentally normal. It is this majority that should be accepted as those who are involved in working misunderstandings.

It may be that religious thinking and behaviour in how it is carried out is not all that different to other human interrelationships. We relate to the supernatural as we do to humans by initiating by range of activities from which we expect reciprocity, so that there are not too many counterintuitive aspects to these beliefs. It is only going to be different in fringe ways from human interrelationships in which connections are only likely to be responded to for the simpler communications.

Of course, these people have no means of knowing whether their approaches in prayers and ritual have reached their objectives but a high proportion feel that their approaches have been reciprocated. The objectively assessable silence is not accepted as such by most if not all believers. What we do know is that a high proportion of those carrying out ritual activities know rather than just feel that it has been successful in terms of their needs. It is a reciprocated silence.

The fact remains that this assumed reciprocity cannot be assessed by social science methods in what are one sided approaches in which the definers define the terms of their own arguments. What is important is the almost global assumption that this reciprocity of silence does exist and that both in the past and in the present in all cultures it is virtually religiously universal. We should start with the fact that if something is believed to be true regardless of the extent that the social sciences may explain its origins, it is going to be 'scientifically' real in its consequences.

The Composition of Religious Behaviour

The Chinese, Indian and Japanese Christians have a faith which has been present within these societies for several centuries despite periodic persecutions. It has to be seen as a relatively recent appearance there in cultures which have written religious and philosophical documents for other faiths which go back for well over a millennium. By any standards these religious writings are elitist and are written in linguistic forms such as Pali and Sanskrit beyond the comprehension of average people and in the case of Mandarin with its system of separate ideograms for anything identifiably distinct in its meanings, they cannot be read by educated Chinese. They can have had no more popular appeal in the past as in any contemporary Christian theology.

However, Christianity has to be assessed as having been implanted in and continue in societies with enormous populations practising and believing in long established divergent faiths subtended from these obscure written ideas. In these societies we see an almost total lack of uniformity in religious practices which certainly have a vague eschatological background but an overall concern for an immediate return on religious activity responding to their current difficulties and anticipated recurrent needs. Rituals in pursuit of this immediate return can be seen as normal and that in such contexts complex theological perspectives are a form of deviance and their ostensible connection to contemporary practices is a further example of a working misunderstanding.

However, the contexts in which Christianity and Islam expresses themselves will carry within them substantial elements which come from their pre-existing and contemporary culture; the language used must carry with it ancient meanings as well as customary obligations. It would seem that to be Chinese and a Christian would involve necessary working misunderstandings which cannot be theologically unscrambled except by the use of ambiguities.

Participation as an End in itself

If we look at religious practices in historical perspective as well as in the ways that they are used in proportion to a universe of available populations, there can be little doubt that what is seen and practised as normal is the use of ritual *ex opera operato*, that performance brings its own return. These elitist theologies in all the major religions provide a background feel good factor of a vaguely sustaining nature while the latter provide for the immediacies of personal need and the hope of self-interpreted help from the inevitable reciprocal silence. It is certainly a bipolar situation which is heavily weighted against specific theological conformities.

Some contemporary examples supporting such an interpretation of involvement in ritual as an end in itself. A Sunday Mass at the church of our Lady near Mexico City which contains her image miraculously imprinted on a cloth has the altar rail pilled high with flowers. There is a massed standing crowd in constant movement. Some of whom have approached the church and interior on their knees. It would be hard to make a case for anyone paying attention to the celebrating priest in anything more than just being there for the carrying out of as ritual when the priest's actions are both distant and inaudible. The congregation is not so much in constant movement like an ant heap but a crowd composed of deeply involved individuals. It is a demeaning categorization of those people coming to the altar with blood stained knees from crawling there as mere socially explicable ritualism.

In a Taoist temple near Kunming a nun in front of an alcove with deist images sprays a moving queue of men and women passing in front of her as they made small coin donations. She did not appear to speak to or look at the people as she sprayed them with sacralised water. In a Beijing Buddhist temple a man in a business suit standing in front of a Buddha statue rocking backwards and forwards with three burning incense sticks in his right hand while talking into a mobile phone held in his left hand. At the temple of the Jade Buddha in Shanghai during a ceremony involving a procession of robbed monks, seated vendors continued making and selling votive offerings, while visitors continued making incense offerings to iron bowls in the courtyard in front of the ceremony. The complex interpretations of these activities would appear to be in conformity with the involved perspectives of the social scientists involved, rather than accepting the obvious that it was in their ritual actions that those involved saw value.

Participation for a Purpose

Attending a ceremony in order to accumulate merit sets the background for ritual devotions to have greater emotional and pragmatic usefulness. These ceremonies or at least how people utilise them are not directed at some general divine power. We see that in most religions the majority of attention is not paid to God or *Brahma* but to some lower deity or metaphysical power who has some more personal connection with petitioners; a diminished social distance which make these superhuman figures more humanly understandable and perhaps more personally interested in those who address them. This is the case with Hindus and Shintoists with their multiplicity of local deities and the traditional understandings of the Tanzanian Sukuma who accept that there is some overarching ultimate power to whom they pay little attention in their propitiations of the nearby ancestors and spirits which are disturbing them. Actions which diminish social distance is a fact in all metaphysical relationships.

In their difficulties they appeal to a power with whom they assume there is already some personalised connection and on whom they can rely for some favourable reaction to their appeals for help. This is created by putting the supernatural force under an obligation to help because of the offerings and promises that have been made which accompany their social behaviour. These appeals are initiated by individuals on their own initiative at centres of devotion acceptable to them in places likely to create supernatural reactions. In general people needing self-assessed immediate help aim their rituals at supernatural sources which they consider are already obligated to help them.

At the Meiji shrine in Tokyo, the national centre for Shintoism there are racks outside on which there are posted personal petitions to the spirits and indeed this is a feature of all temples in Japan, some written in both Japanese and English. On the footpath leading to the prehistoric Long Kennet tomb in the Wiltshire county of Britain, an oak tree has a number of petitionary objects hanging from its branches. This is a common feature on trees considered to be sacred in Cyprus and Crete and in the East where the Lord Buddha was considered to have reached Enlightenment under the sacred fig tree *Ficus religiosus*.

The Cenacle Sisters in Britain run a Crusade of Prayer and in a recent year received over forty thousand petitions by post requesting prayers for some personal anxiety. The shrine dedicated to a little known saint near to Nijmegan on a weekday has several hundred petitioners lighting candles and making personal appeals for help while attendance at regular Sunday devotions has been falling in numbers.

In Thailand there are innumerable factory produced shrines on apartment verandas, in gardens, outside hotels, offices and police stations as well as hand made ones beneath forest trees, in front of which petitioners can be seen leaving offerings and making petitions. Some of these shrines do not appear to be specifically Buddhist. Many Japanese homes have domestic shrines *butsudan* which can be ordered from a manufacturer's catalogue. In Nairobi, Kenya hundred attend services for the laying on of hands by priests of the Legio Maria Church, a breakaway sect from the Roman Catholic Church which practices a ritual which accentuates pre-Vatican II liturgical forms using Latin without any knowledge of its meanings.

There seems little doubt that beyond the unknown numbers who keep their prayers to themselves, very many feel the need to put them into physical form and to accompany this with physical presentations; there are many petitions on boards in Christian churches just as they are outside Shinto temples.

The Naturalness of Religious Disorder

We find that quasi-traditional societies in their religious activities which are not based on institutions enabled by literacy, will have some conformity to cultural ideas but that uniformity could never have occurred. If any uniformity is found this is likely to the creation of the social scientists need to categorise and produce their conclusions in an orderly professionally acceptable form.

We need to recognise that historically religious ideas and practices would have had besides the presentation of an authoritative basis, a dialectical structure in which individual and communal religious activities would have had an unstable competitive element as people would have seen that some rituals were successful and some failed. The sense of certainty combined with instability.

Thus, it would seem that religions have always been part of and provided a dialectical process for diminishing the hardships occasioned by demographic and social change. There could never have been more than a formal assumption of stability as the inaccuracies of memory and changing demographic, social and psychological circumstances would always have insured ritual variations. There will have been slow changing cultural conformities but few recordable uniformities.

The Range of Working Misunderstandings

Our enquiry looks at cross-cultural religious ideas and practices in terms of their versatility, universality and persistence. Secularism, the disappearance of religion among some people in some situations which was widely anticipated by the social sciences as the inevitable consequence of the spread of education and scientific understandings, seems to be no more than a minor issue in some situations. There should be an acceptance that these religious aspects of human understanding and behaviour have their own ongoing self-sustaining reality.

Public religion and private spiritualities can only be seen as isolated and identifiable specialised activities by the exclusion of economic, social and political factors which surround and deliberately or not influence these activities. The Ethiopian anchorite seen meditating in a cave above the Coptic monastery at Debera Libanos was beside a path and he had to be fed as well as participating in the services of the monastery half a mile away. The bones of the Saints in a nearby cave were in boxes which had at one time contained Italian imports. Buddhist monks in Myanmar and Thailand have daily begging rounds to get their food donated by secular households but their bowls are of secular manufacture. Religious communities such as the Shakers often die out because of social factors influencing recruitment and external support but not because their ideals were wrong.

Any religious system which has become institutionalised and basing itself on written traditions has to provide an effective broadly based social as much as religious service in which there is a working misunderstanding, an unconscious disconnection between what is required by orthodoxy and what the individual is doing or a conscious awareness by individuals that their practices are not what their religion requires. For this to continue requires some sort of practical bilateral tolerance for all those involved. At the base of these faiths there are often written principles, pivots around which formal adaptation has to manoeuvre (Rappaport, 1979). These principles may have little relevance to personal religious activity. In effect theologians have to come to terms with the almost universal fact that for most people the performance of ritual which has some formal internal and eternal authenticity, is all that they want and indeed that is all that they expect from the faiths in which they believe.

The analysis of religion and its institutional continuation together with the analysis of the permutations of behaviour and thinking involved, is always carried out by intellectuals whether they are theologians or social scientists. These specialists are haunted by the need to put religious activities into as broad a social environment as possible because they hope that their social science and religious message can have the potential to be globally and relevant in some uniformity.

These thinkers with their macro-preoccupations are not professionally and personally happy with conclusions and indeed applications which in effect say that while there may be supra-community and supra-individual ideas, these do not dominate religious behaviour. What happens, however, it may be thought to originate, is both locally circumstantial and individually situated. These experiences and understandings are not shared with anything like the required accuracy for any assumption of culture wide applicability except insofar as it is ill-defined and ambiguous. How many Christians can list the ten commandments, Buddhists the Patimokha's ten requirements for Buddhist compliance and the Five Pillars of the Faith for Muslims and of course for Hinduism, and other Eastern faiths there are no such statutory requirements and as we will see among the Jains no one, even the experts, is all that sure as to what they should do ritually.

There are many examples in which the intellectual overview of what is required fails to coincide with what people actually do; their functional requirements.

A code of customary law was produced for the Sukuma after considerable consultation with knowledgeable elders, but each specific case coming into their local courts was found to have circumstantial factors which altered or at least modified these carefully worked out principles (Cory, 1953).

Arthur Ransome the popular writer of children's books as a British Foreign Office official was in 1919 sent to Galicia to find out the ethnicity of the rural population. Groups of peasants on being asked whether they thought themselves to be Russian, Little Russian or Polish usually replied that they were 'Orthodox'. On being pressed to state their ethnicity they answered safely that they were 'local'(Ransome, 2008).

Whatever bureaucracy required or recorded became a working misunderstanding.

A Professor of International Relations (Coker, 2008) comments 'when it comes to the task of understanding the world and our place in it, we may perhaps pay too much attention to the grand themes, and too little attention to the particular. If we were to take the local more seriously and stop scanning the world through binoculars, we might recognize that the global is only as strong as its power to shape the local for the better'.

A further analytical division is usually made between Eastern, traditional and Western religions may be an artificial one created by theological and philosophical terms which are used to describe them. These conclusions implicitly seemed to consider linear thinking to be superior to its lateral alternatives. It may well be that such an approach is detached from giving adequate attention to actual religiously connected behaviour in its lateral ramifications which falls beneath the glass ceiling of theologically acceptable behaviour.

On any analysis we find that Christian, Hindu, Muslim, Shinto and Taoist believers demonstrate their religious needs in individual ways and in the context of their primary groups and neighbourhoods. There will be some lowest common denominator with unspecific cultural parameters. In any global analysis the Eastern and traditional religions with no definitional orthodoxy which could be enforced through institutions and literacy, we will find that all religions are functionally hierarchical and polytheistic and invariably individual and circumstantial.

We may find that that the heavily institutionalised religions of the book have in their modern forms been a deviant form of religious behaviour and the demand created New Age sects and cults replicate the diversity of Hinduism, the saint cults in Islam and widespread spirit possession events are all similar in function, the hopefully immediate relief of human distress.

Social science data can usually be faulted on methodological grounds and even more so when related to religious behaviour; they look as if they were praying and indeed say that they were doing so, but we cannot know whether they are actually praying and how far are the recorders free from their own biases. There is also the theological inferiority given to any carrying out of ritual as an adequate end in itself which undoubtedly is the overwhelming framework within which people carry out their religious devotions.

What we have in religion is on the one hand working misunderstandings between theological parameters and what believers actually do within them, and on the other, is the sustaining reality of contemporary performative religion. This work is a study of the underside of religion which has few of the intellectual and religious attractions which might have been anticipated from studying the foundations of the great religions. It is an investigation of the gap between what is required of the believers and what actually happens, the almost universal working misunderstandings.

2
Acquiring Knowledge of Religious Understandings

The finding out of the religious behaviour of others much less the reasons and misunderstandings for such activities involves metaphysical issues which can have none of the relative clarity involved in the study of agriculture and disease. The investigative methods used can always be scientifically questioned and each research project underlines the inadequacy of its predecessors' methodologies and conclusions particularly when the results have been quantified rather than qualified.

In this pursuit of information there are three separate factors to consider. The ability of the researcher to collect information, the amount and quality of the information about religious practices which has been gathered and lastly the backgrounds of the providers of information. In each of which there is the persistent existence of rather than just the possibilities of working misunderstandings within the parameters of professional skills and its qualified absence as well as the possibility of conscious and unconscious deception.

So it is not so much that the social science methodologies which have to be explained and defended in every evaluation of research into religion and its peripheries but how such individual practices and thoughts in their constantly changing personal environments can be recorded but how such activities assuming their personal reality can be fitted into some larger social and religious categories.

To disentangle these difficulties in an Israeli situation is only overtly more difficult to finding out the same religious practices in Mumbai, Manchester and Melanesia. In every cultural setting there will be the highly educated and the mentally handicapped, the immigrants, the devout fundamentalists and the political activists and many other categories. Any methodology for realistic enquiry has to be elastic to the requirements of personal interrelationships and the inadequacies of writing and any attempted quantification.

To what extent can we state that there has been an individuals or collective misunderstanding in the fulfilment of religious obligations and ideas in what is assumed to be related practices. Apart from the fact that there may be in some situations clear written statements of religious orthodoxy, in every other situation there are likely to be differences in the quality and quantity of the data collected and as well the ongoing changes between individuals and the social environments in which they are living and to which they will always be reacting in different ways. This is always a behaviourally unstable situation in which any conclusions has to be both tentative and involve misunderstandings.

Researchers are always Part of What is Researched

Social scientists by the simple facts of choosing, observing, recording and writing up are part of what they are researching. As professionals aiming to replicate the methodologies and status of the 'hard' sciences they do not like accepting the reality of this factor and they do their best to cut out the more obvious and self-admitted biases. They are usually not very successful in this because they like to think that they have always achieve the necessary detachment to make themselves feel secure as social scientists in which neutrality is a professional requirement.

In most cases this is broadly easy to achieve because it is obvious that they have little in common with the people whom they are observing except their common humanity. They pride ourselves on their secular detachment and they have little difficulty in separating ourselves ideologically and emotionally from Roman Catholic men in Manila whipping themselves on Good Friday, spirit possessed Swahili women in Mombasa, Kenya and a Buchwezi initiation ceremony on the shore of Lake Victoria in Tanzania.

But are they all that detached from seeing such behaviour as personally valid ways of metaphysical experience but slide into thinking that this is not the way that 'our' people at home behave. They are probably to some extent psychologically or physically revolted explaining away such activities in terms of psychopathology or the pressures of cultural environments. The illusion of detachment is easy when what is being observed is so obviously different obscuring the fact that there will have been important metaphysical issues behind such peculiar and indeed intellectually interesting religious behaviour.

They are probably poor evaluators of any behaviour which is extreme in terms of their own socialisation and professional training whether these social scientists are by birth or naturalisation British, Belgian, Bengali, or Basuto. In addition because of their prolonged education they have increased the social distance between 'us' and 'them' so that they see these activities as in some ways dehumanised. Moreover, the social science tools with which these social scientists work come from Western intellectualism based on the European Enlightenment. This is a culture based system of evaluating human behaviour.

The Biases in Detachment

There is another aspect to the difficulties of detachment when they are observing behaviour which is part of their own experience and understandings. They all have very decided paradigms as to how marital relationships should be conducted, how their children should be brought up and animals treated. Such activities are shared whatever their cultural backgrounds and regardless of their prolonged education in institutions a long way from their homes. The hot-house intellectualism of all higher education institutions is a long way from the behaviour which they see repeated at pilgrimage centres and temples in Europe and Asia and the initiation rituals of traditional societies and in the fraternities of American universities.

It is in religion that there may be the greatest difficulties over detachment. The Muslim social scientist visiting the Mohammed Ali mosque in Cairo and the Roman Catholic one attending Mass in a hut in the highlands of Burma or in the cathedral at Cuernavaca in Mexico is having to move their evaluations between personal and professional dispositions. In such situations it would seem more than likely that they are as one with the others there who are worshipping; an emotional link which can come as easily from distant socialisation as from any current religious practices. This sense of unity comes with the realisation that they may be more in tune with the people they are observing and that there may be much more conscious and unconscious sharing than they would have comfortably admitted to ourselves. Both Muslims and Roman Catholics will always have worldwide opportunities to encounter their fellow believers in both worship and research.

They look at these day to day activities and religious occasions through the mirrors of their own experiences and their own expectations of reasonable behaviour. These are the people with whom they share television programmes, political rights, social services, public transport and those that are praying or avoiding praying next door to them in church, mosque, temple or synagogue. To all intents and purposes they are as much 'us' rather than an arbitrarily or necessarily defined as 'them', because they are behaving so very differently to these observers.

Situations with Social Distance Factors

Thus social scientists have to accept that they are unable to distinguish themselves at all clearly from people with whom they may share public and private religious beliefs and practices despite the wide social distance separating them in their everyday secular life. So when they study these religious activities social scientists become aware that they are part of what they are working on or at least emotionally on its fringes.

Public religious behaviour or private spirituality are both aspects in which social scientists are interested. It is unlikely that any social scientist does not have some personal behaviour or mental processes related to metaphysical issues which are on the edges of what they are observing in others. It is indeed possible that there is no such thing as a totally secular individual.

There is in this the official doctrines and rules of the religious institutions to which they belong even if the affiliation is nominal. Then there are the religious behaviour and ideas which they admit to believing in and practising which is unlikely to be a replication of what they are required to do for full affiliation. Lastly, what they actually do which is likely to be a personal construction of metaphysical ideas and practices of which a high proportion are likely to be definable by social science as magical which was the conclusion about the English character (Gorer, 1955). Abstract ideas and the practices devolved from these hidden activities and thoughts which have little pragmatic accessibility, are possibly part of the behaviour of all people.

In this there is the fact if not the difficulty that they are recording what are aspects of their own behaviour which brings us to the subject matter of this study. Many people including social scientists practice systems of belief which they have created themselves from within their own social and personal environment and culture or more likely borrowed from other cultures. Most of these practices will be outside the orthodoxies of the 'religions of the book' which lay down in some detail what is required of believers to which there is at the least some ideological affiliation but yet not brought to the point of any overt conflict with what they proscribe.

A Sharing of Understandings

There is thus the final approach in which these social science researchers realise that they themselves are experiencing what they are in fact researching about religious thought and behaviour. The recognition that in their own religious beliefs and practices there is a satisfying and self-created gap between the upper level precepts and practices of the religious institutions to which they are even only vaguely affiliated as Christians, Jews or Muslims and what they as well as their co-believers actually do. In this there is a functioning contrast, a working misunderstanding which in their own ways satisfies both the higher abstract and lower popular dimensions. This is not quite so obviously the case with Buddhists, Hindus, Shintoists and Taoists for whom the precepts of their faiths have been much more loosely defined if indeed they have been defined at all to whom the range of options available to them can be identified.

So we have a methodological difficulty of researching into religious ideas and practices which are part of overt orthodoxies but are also part of the social scientists' own covert behaviour as Westerners or as professionals brought up intellectually to see behaviour in social science terms which originated in the West (Suinn et al., 1992).

There is no reason to suppose that these social scientists are any better able to understand their own behaviour in this context than that of other people who may well be similar to themselves in cultural understandings and religious socialisation. Researchers can always reach professional conclusions why Mexican men carry cactus on their shoulders in Good Friday processions or Japanese hang their requests to their gods on boards or trees at shrines. In this research they now have to reach conclusions which they have to apply to their own understandings because they are part and parcel of the one behavioural universe in which perhaps working misunderstandings are integral part.

The Non-Discursive Nature of Religious Experience

While much of what we do and believe is the subject of personal doubt and public discourse, the private and public rituals with which we express our religious devotions and doubts have a certain isolating quality.

Informants are ready enough to describe and discuss their business practices and even their marriages but they are much less ready or perhaps unable to describe and discuss their religious experiences. They produce commonplace phrases to describe their emotions because they do not have the intellectual capacity or vocabulary to do otherwise. The religious event seems to be far from any possibility of adequate expression.

Thus, informants may reject specific certain religious practices and by implication the beliefs tied to them as they may no longer wish to carry them out as part of a general move towards disbelief or part of changed personal circumstances but this is not usually the subject of private or public discourse. Similarly, the positive religious experience is kept in personal privacy; the six individuals in a London suburb who recently had independent visions of the Virgin Mary only told about these experiences to their parish priest.

Thus, there are built in difficulties in the social sciences attempting to research any behaviour which relates to metaphysical ideas and their expression. If the social scientist attends a celebration of the Mass in Sri Lanka as much as a spirit possession ceremony in Tanzania and write down a summary of their observations for analysis, this changes the sense of the whole which is the point as far as the participants go. Social scientists pick the event to pieces in their attempts to understand what is going on by this piecemeal methodological process and from their professional training this is the only acceptable way to proceed. In this process they now appear to have lost the meanings which believers know they have experienced and have gained from the whole event.

There are parallels here to theology in which the leaders of religious thought create the intellectual rather than emotional support for the institutionalised faith systems which they themselves have created or contributed to their maintenance. A recent study of Islamic devotionalism has suggested this (Havevi, 2008). It is not the way that participants understand or rather experience their religious needs rather than their understandings. The Belgian as much as the Basuto on being asked why they do this or that in a metaphysical context are likely to reply that this is what we have always done and that if you want to know more than it would be best to ask someone more involved in such questions such as a diviner or a priest.

It is very questionable whether more than the smallest of small minorities approach their understandings of the rituals in which they have personally participated by any such analytical process. No doubt theologians and liturgists can explain when asked what is the meaning of what is done but it will be largely for their own professional benefits. The drip down effects of a ritual are in how it is experienced by participants rather than what is the intellectualised meaning of what is being done. In this sense what is happening within a crowd attending but neither hearing nor seeing a Coptic service as much as a rain-making ceremony are having a personally valuable religious experience. Similarly, in Usukuma in which the propitiatory rituals have been more or less invented by the diviners involved has to be seen as much as assessed as working misunderstandings.

The Possibility of Inappropriate Intellectualising of Human Behaviour

Whenever the social sciences have quantified the results of their research into human behaviour the big percentages have always gained attention as the answer to what has been investigated; an assertion of behavioural clarity rather than an acceptance that it is an abbreviated categorisation of behavioural complexity. There is a drawback to this because the approach has been devised by upper level intellectuals looking down at what they often describe as 'popular' religion. By this phrase they relegate the religious realities of the vast majority of mankind both to an intellectually second class status and to a collective simplicity.

Wittgenstein (Budd, 1989:4-5.21) wrote about grammar in terms which are relevant to the social science approach to analysing behaviour 'The description of the grammar of a word is of no use in everyday life; only rarely do we pick up the use of a word by having it described to us; although we are trained or encouraged to master the use of the words, we are not taught to describe it...The meaning of a word is its use in language'. Theological understandings of religious behaviour and experience have parallels to the learning of a second language which starts from mastering its grammar and not from its emotional and metaphysical relationships.

Putting this understanding into social behaviour 'The (Swedish or Sukuma) farmer's knowledge is experiential... he uses his knowledge like his hoe. He is in a sense not mentally aware of it. His knowledge is his self-image and this self-confidence as a community member' (Fuglesang, 1984:42).

Social scientists are achieved members of the upper intellectual level of their society and their approach to the behaviour of others is a reflection of the superiority which comes from prolonged education and their attempted professional detachment from the subjects of their observations. In this they consciously and unconsciously put on one side the fact that in any consideration of metaphysical matters they are part of what they observe and there are few reasons for supposing that their understandings are necessarily superior or indeed inferior in relevance to those of the factory worker, financier or those defined as intellectually subnormal.

In this context it is prudent to remember that contemporary psychologists in their study of cognition cross-culturally have generally concluded that the notions of superiority and inferiority should be rejected and that no value, status or hierarchy should be assigned to either cognitive behaviour or to individuals or groups (Mishra, 2001). From one perspective an inversion of values has entered the evaluations of the social sciences in its attempt to exclude the observer's own attributes in their assessments while often requiring the objects of their research to complete tests and narrate events based on their individuality.

The Compulsion to Overt Symbolisation

To have a fleeting idea in the mind is no doubt satisfying as part of a process but it lacks any power until it is embodied in a public or private act. In this there may be little distinction in its personal value whether the performance or participation is public or private. The meaning is created by those involved whether they are suffering from Down's Syndrome or have just completed a well received treatise on Greek Orthodox theology; it has equal value to those involved. The emotions of the former will be regarded as cognitively handicapped while the latter will be overwhelmingly regarded as incomprehensible by the vast majority of Greeks. The fact that the average educated Italian or Indian will neither understand or wish to appreciate either viewpoints has to be accepted as an almost 'natural' social state.

The institutionalised liturgy provided for the localised Buddhist and Hindu will usually tend to provide an ambiguous paradigm within the boundaries of which everyone will add their own interpretations and needs without much regard to the ostensible purposes of the liturgy as defined by theologians. There is always the need to perform and to perform in ways that are personally significant and fulfilling any number of individually significant functions.

The lighting of a devotional candle for a Roman Catholic in front of a statue of the Virgin Mary, bowing before the seeing 'eyes' of a statue of the Hindu Goddess of smallpox Karni Mar or ringing the bell at a

Shinto shrine to alert the spirits of the petitioner's arrival are commonplace religious activities. These are all repetitive acts ticked off as such by the social scientists, certainly classified as magical because it is not scientifically accepted that there will be any assessable reactions from the 'Deities' to whom such appeals are repeatedly made.

Any institutionalised liturgies provide relatively specific frameworks of meaning but nevertheless ones which have accepted authority which in their ambiguities and inexactnesses provide hand and mind foundations on which individuals can build their own satisfactions and needs at that time. However, much the social scientists may categorize these into definable simplicities at whatever level of intellectual understandings they are examined, they will always be both complex and individually specific and more specifically temporary.

As there is a perceptible but sectional shift in social environments from predominantly collective ascriptive social environments in rural environments to ones which are more based on achieved individualism in urban and industrial settings, there is an even greater need to accept the individuality of religious practices. When an estimated seventy million attended the last Hindu Kumbh Mela on the Ganges there is an almost irresistible need to lump this enormous quantity of human activity into simplistic social categories. Even if it were possible to have the basic principles of Hinduism defined by some accepted centralised authority which cannot be done, we have to accept that everyone of these millions have their own reasons for being there. We can also see that this rushing into the waters of the Ganges at an astrologically determined time may not be quite so much part of any working misunderstanding since they were conforming to the ambiguous generalities of Hinduism. We may then have to accept that misunderstandings can only occur when the principles of a faith have been in some way accurately defined and enforced; these are atypical options rather than working misunderstandings.

With this development or perhaps the persistence of an already existing individualised religiosity which must have been the main feature of all pre-literate or current non-literate rituals apart from the possibilities that rituals occur in the behaviour of the higher primates (Huxley, 1966), then a greater attention has to be paid to individual religious creativity and practise.

Onto these varying rituals have come the literate rigidities of institutionalised Christianity which has perhaps functioned for some two centuries. Despite the decline of this form of worship more obviously in

Western Europe than in North America, there has been a parallel growth in individual religiosity or perhaps a continuation of a pre-existing individualism. In the assumed context of an increasing secularity, individual rather than group needs still occur and have to be coped with outside any possible or potential impersonal social security or communal help (McGuire, 1988). Personal needs have to be reacted to and they continue to be both the focus and site of personal rituals. While much of this personal and private ritualism will be individual creations, many will tend to see what they are doing to be part of an approved devotional system of which the social scientist may well find no more than nominal correlations. This is the main arena in which from a social science rather than theological perspective, there are working misunderstandings.

Symbols sanctifying Matters of Importance

While everyone has created and maintained a mass of symbols of great personal importance some expand in significance by becoming attached to matters of what is seen to be as fundamental to both individual and group survival. Thus, we find popular symbols attached to birth, marriage and death, to changes of status, to the maintenance of order and the overall prevention of disaster but highly varied in their actual form of use.

It would be impossible to define whether a society, group or individual first articulates what is important and then attached symbols to these occasions or that these occur in unison. They may have a potential lateral potency to which matters of importance become lineally attached.

It is individuals who create this popularity by which they pick and choose what they feel is a support and a solution to their private concerns and it is religious ones which predominate. The crucifix dominates both as a protective amulet and as a tattoo for people from a predominantly Christian environment and the Koranic calligraphy or material derivatives in Muslim ones. Among Buddhists there are often complex tattooing covering large areas of the body and the attachment of shrines to both trees and business premises. Whatever they are, they cluster round the disturbances of experienced or anticipated change; a necessary accenting of personal anxieties and their probable rather than possible resolution.

Working Misunderstanding as an Historical Process

Prior to the introduction of literacy primarily for its bureaucratic uses and its wholesale extension to every sphere of communication through printing on paper and computer screens, working misunderstandings cannot have existed. Individuals and groups created their religious rituals and understandings relying on unreliable and variable memories as reactions to immediate or serial needs. Such rituals either worked in the opinions of participants relying on their memories and were repeated in forms which would have varied in some respects from what had occurred before. Alternatively they would just have disappeared in much the same way that genetic mutations dropout of human behaviour when they have failed to find a functional slot in which they could prosper.

Then came the period in which religions became institutionalised and under the control of a specialised literate minority which has occurred for several millennia. However, it has only been a few centuries in which this has had the structure and ability to attempt to enforce these practices on their constituents; the age of religious instruction and the learning of how to be a believer in 'the religions of the book'. The period surrounding the European Reformation in which intellectuals and theologians were able to develop systems of religious ideology and behaviour which ecclesiastically outlawed the ways in which most people had seen and practised their religious ideas and needs (Duffy, 1992).

It is in this period of perhaps no more than a few recent centuries that people have found their literate based religion unwilling or unable to provide the help they needed or to adjust quickly enough for their very immediate needs. So religion prospered on two observable levels, high level ideas and a range of public practices principally around cyclical and linear rites of passage and low level private practices. It seems likely that throughout history the latter have always been much more extensively practised than the high level forms requiring time for thinking and administrative commitment. They have never been prepared to admit the marketing factor of popularity or to intellectually and effectively merge their theological thinking and liturgical forms into a single religious entity.

Then in the last two centuries in European institutionalised Christianity has failed to gain or retain any popularity and even the 1851 English census of religious practice had only about half of the adult population participating in public worship. The growth of the ways in which individualism prospered from internal migration, social mobility and the growing awareness of almost worldwide alternatives combining with personal creativeness has contributed to a reversion to the individuality of pre-literate religious practices.

This is a situation more applicable to the socio-religious situation in the Northern hemisphere in which most Christians, predominantly Roman

Catholics saw in their liturgical participations no reason for dissatisfaction. Then the Vatican II Council reforms resulted in a general decline in all public participation in Roman Catholic official rituals from decline in the numbers of priests to people attending the obligatory weekly celebrations of the Mass. This certainly contributed to the growth in individual private forms of spirituality.

It seems likely that most Christians in all forms of adherence pay little attention to theological and ecclesiastical issues. It would not be correct to see what has been happening in Western Europe and indeed America (McGuire, 1988) as a working misunderstanding as much private spirituality is quite independent of theological thought and liturgical practices. Contemporary practice relates more to 'Sheilaism' (Bellah *et al.*, 1985) named after the individual who considered that she had a religion which did not related to any Church. In this era of post-modernity private religious practice has shown the greatest growth because of its convenience to a migratory society and in its self-creativeness its adjustable nature. We can thus expect that working misunderstanding as an explanation of religious ideas and practices to continue in Western urban industrial environments.

However, in Africa, Asia and Latin America the situation is different and religious practices there appear to be more related to pre-Reformation Europe. The Christian metropolitan Churches particularly the Roman Catholic Church as much as Islam is presented through the theological thinking and publications coming from Rome, Medina and Cairo and are valued for their assured superiority. However, most believers have a nominal adherence to these precepts and practice parallel systems, regularity in the one and reactions to emergencies in the other. These people feel that there are few conflicts in this. Social scientists socialised in the post Enlightenment thinking of the Western world and professionally trained in a secular perspective different can see this as a 'working misunderstanding'.

The Framework for Analysis

Any overview of religious ideas and behaviour shows two basic problems which come from predetermined values. The social scientists who study these activities are professionally agnostic so that they would approach religion with the same methods as they would use for evaluating economics and politics. They would be viewing religious at best with tolerant interest but with some underlying feeling that believers have some underlying intellectual shortcomings to account for the lack of rationality in their behaviour.

There are also those theologians and other committed persons who start from the opposite dimension of seeing such religious behaviour as rational and who would see the agnostic social scientist as similarly lacking in the necessary intellectual capacity to appreciate the realities of religious thought and behaviour.

There is also the factor that whatever results come from both these assessments of religious ideas and behaviour they are not usually directed or formulated with any idea of general distribution or understanding. In reality they are produced for the approval and support of their professional colleagues whether theologians or social scientists. 'The factual realities reported as findings of a given investigation do not inhere in the research process as such. The factual realities must be organised and put together by the observer. Only the observer's intention.... provides the apparently rational account of the social order' (Johnson, 1975:187).

There is also the noticeable top-down pyramidal approach in the analysis of religion in which thinking and behaviour is implicitly if not explicitly assessed against the standards set by those who have been divinely or at least spiritually inspired and the texts of the great religions which form the basis of their theologies and philosophies and their succeeding theological and religious legal interpreters; the tip of the pyramid.

This means that any observations and conclusions are likely to be part of some scaling of inadequacy according to these peak standards rather than in terms of partial conformity. It avoids any approach which comes from the needs of potential believers. Overall this may mean that the professionally and intellectually elite social scientists are usually assessing religious behaviour in terms of the conceptions of another elite rather than 'average' thinking and behaviour.

So what is observed and recorded is always filtered through some conscious and acceptable biases or unconscious ones which come from the various socialisations to which these observers have been subjected to as they pass through their professional lives. They are not and can never be detached observers of social behaviour and certainly not in considering ideas and behaviour as indefinable as the supernatural. 'Much has been written on how values shape the choice of a research problem and the analysis and reporting of it—values which the researcher has learned in some social class, ethnic or other biographical context...Audiences help shape the direction of social science research both in the direction of particular research endeavours and overtime, in the context of the researcher's careers' (Warren, 1980:306). This important factor that data on religious ideas and behaviour is presented by professionals who have their own personal agendas. From start to finish these assessments are in the framework of 'us' and 'them' rather than tinged with the possible inevitabilities of 'we'.

Our approach is to look at religious ideas and practices in terms of what are mainly popular activities as we consider what a million do at a shrine or who hold a practice to be religious are the most important and prolific factors to consider in evaluating the extent of working misunderstandings. We look at the base of the pyramid of religious ideas and behaviour as it is this vast expanse of mainly non-literate emotional involvements that supports or absents itself from the more abstract and intangible theological and philosophical pinnacles.

The Ideological Bases in Analysis

There is the basic factor that those who evaluate religious practices and commitments are either social scientists with a built-in commitment to a detached and agnostic evaluation of all secular and religious behaviour so that their approach to the assessment of walking and worship start with a commitment to the same professional methodological detachment.

The other group of assessors of religious behaviour are theologians and those holding positions in religious institutions who are similarly committed to a viewpoint supporting forms of religious faith to which they are professionally rather more than emotionally committed. They would look at walking and worship as starting from totally different bases. In these senses both groups are not unbiased as they enter their evaluations with pre-convictions which they consider to be both morally and professionally valid and necessary.

So there are methodologies for the collection of information about religious behaviour and commitments which are ostensibly neutral or at least aimed at neutrality but which are in practice collected by theological or social science outsiders who know that they are socially distant from the majority of the people whose religious ideas and practices they are observing.

On the other hand, these people from whom they get their information are both individually and communally insiders. These insiders are to a very large extent less educated and less intellectually aware of what is involved in such professional appraisals. These insiders are similarly biased as they would consider themselves to be bound by their religious beliefs and practices and they are also aware of the social distance which separates themselves from these outsider enquirers.

From these perspectives there are biases which affect how data is both collected and interpreted. The social scientists will not give any particular value to the intellectually inaccessible religious convictions of many of the pilgrims who go to Banaras, Lourdes and Mecca. On the other hand, those with religious commitments may leave out the social factors in which some of those same pilgrims are really tourists, conforming to family pressure or see in public religious commitment financial and political advantages. It would seem to be more likely that a Western pilgrim to Assisi would be carrying a guide to its architecture than the writings of St. Francis, while the pilgrim to Mecca and Banaras would not be interested in such non-religious issues.

Religion and spirituality for most people is a necessity at some level of general understanding and irregular practice. These are not matters to which they have given much thought and nor would they be able to express them coherently in response to the questioning of outsiders. Most people most of the time give little thought as to why they do what they do, much less how they behave in emergencies or in religious ceremonies, or whenever their emotions are involved; an analytical frame of mind is a rarity. Social scientists are no more likely to do this for their own beliefs and practices than street cleaners, factory workers, business men and women and society hostesses. So now let us look at the four methods of recording putting religious behaviour.

What can we actually know with any degree of confidence about the religious behaviour and commitments of those who are in fact strangers according to the categories within which social scientists box people together for bureaucratic and research purposes. The available methodologies cannot provide information about covert understandings; they are in the physical position of praying but are they praying. We can read the documentary proof that they have fulfilled certain religious obligations but this may be in order to get access to special education for their children or in fulfilment of the requirements to gain access to an inheritance.

Finally, only a minority of individuals are able and willing to talk or write about their personal commitments and understandings, so that the voluntary provision of data may well be as deliberately or unconsciously inaccurate as accurate. We have very little evidence that might support what these people may overtly or covertly think or behave in both religious and secular situations. There is always the factor that the wider the attempted coverage, the weaker the data. There are always methodological difficulties in getting information about religious ideas and behaviour of which only a proportion are visible or indeed readily available to those who want to understand these activities.

Observable Data

Seeing what is going on in front of the observer is the easiest method of researching religious behaviour but this is a crude and inadequate way of assessing faith and reasoning. Consciously and unconsciously observers pick and choose what they see and record. As outsiders they are more likely to record what is strange to their own understandings; in a seminary their attention will be caught by the sounds of the talking in tongues of one individual during the recitation of the key Christian Lord's Prayer; the researcher will not pay as much attention to the hundred others who continue in silent prayer. Observing cannot even begin to be described as a scientifically acceptable process and to assume its accuracy is a form of personal conceit.

It is true that one can often know how many people attend a religious ceremony as they may be counted at the door as for a football match or by immigration controls when foreign pilgrims enter Saudi Arabia for the Hajj. We can calculate how much these participants put into the local economy by their spending, how many beds are available for pilgrims at Lourdes, the amount of transport used in and around Mecca and the number of animals slaughtered there for the fulfilment of Islamic obligations and the number of bodies institutionally cremated in secular facilities at Banaras. These are all surface assessments which tell us almost nothing about why they are participating except in the primary senses that these involvements are probably in some part undertaken for religious reasons. In essence these calculations are no different to calculating the number of animals using a water-point or the numbers of people entering a market to buy fish.

The most highly trained social science observer of religious ceremonies will only learn the 'where' and the 'when' but not much about the 'how' and almost nothing about the 'why' for the thousands if not the millions of individuals involved. We may want to believe or indeed assume that those attending a religious ceremony have the fulfilling of their religious needs as their primary objective. We just do not know from seeing individuals participating whether they truly praying or just resting and what about the Muslims and Taoist in Delhi and Shanghai who were seen to be using their mobile phones while ostensibly praying. How many going on the obligatory Hajj to Mecca are just ticking off a religious obligation in a list of religious communal rather than personal necessities.

Whether it is deliberately done for a certain time at a certain place or the result of the accidents of the observers just being there, observation must always be flawed because it deals with a slice of behaviour taken out of context. The attendance at Mass at St Thomas' Mount near to Madras and going on a pilgrimage can only be understood if this behaviour is seen in the context of what went before and what happened afterwards for each of the individuals present. We need to know how people behave even if they are not fully aware of how a religious event has been slotted into their lives.

Observing a religious ceremony tends to be related to the timing of its start and finish as when the priest comes to the altar and when he leaves and this is to be expected as these timings are posted on the church's notice board. This timing approach is confined to the religions of the book and a clock for the timing of prayer is conspicuous in some mosques. In other religions it is hard to know when a ceremony starts and finishes as in most quasi-traditional ceremonies which starts when 'enough' people have turned up to make an implied quorum. A Hindu ceremony in a temple in southern India which lasts seven days will have had different levels of involvement for different categories of participants; it seems unlikely that anyone will be in attendance from start to finish; a shift system operates for all those involved. Much religious activity and certainly spirituality is slotted into daily activities and churches, mosques, synagogues and temples may be empty or full quite irregularly. In Tallinn the Orthodox Cathedral was full on a weekday morning with an elderly priest holding an icon for participants to kiss and providing blessings for them, but there was not a service going on. A mosque can contain people resting in its shade seemingly asleep and services in small Coptic churches in Ethiopia have few people inside but large numbers in the surrounding courtyards. Such approaches show the social as much as the religious pattern of behaviour. These issues raise the question of what constitutes attendance at a religious ceremony; the Orthodox Jew rocking backwards and forwards in prayer throughout a flight from London to Zurich is certainly being religious but what of those who attend Mass in a cathedral because of the beauty of the singing.

A single observer is always looking in one direction at a time and indeed his or her ability to observe is related to varying degrees of concentration and how long they are able to be observing. Those observing a religious ceremony are usually facing the focus of attention so they are seeing the backs of other participants or the minority who are facing the other way and the situation prevents them from turning round. What the researcher can observe is often dictated not by what they want to see but what they can see without becoming insensitive to local ideas of appropriate religious behaviour and their own need to be as inconspicuous as possible. Possibly only a single observer watching a single person carrying out a religious ritual under-cover would provide harder data but the status of this biased observer would still be modifying the observed 'realities'.

Having a number of observers does not mean that they will be seeing the same things and coordinating their writings is difficult as few if any see the same things in the same way. Their minds are always being diverted and of course their personalities may guide what they look at and see. The official orthodox focus of a ceremony may not be the points which participants find stimulating. There is always the factor of what the observer or indeed participants can see when the ceremony is shrouded in incense and poor lighting or so noisy that it is impossible to hear what is being said or sung by those officiating which is possibly evidence that these rituals are not important for intellectual understandings. While there may be an orthodox focal point for the ceremony the researcher will also be interested in those who are ostensibly on the fringes of the ceremony, seated at the back, trying to keep their children quiet, hanging around the church door and providing off the scene backup. Much behaviour is certainly connected with religion but would not involve behaviour which Westerners would think appropriately reverent. Such instances show the difficulties of recording religious participation which comes down to a problem of classification of what they think they are doing in relation to local rather than more general orthodoxy. We just cannot know to what extent they are conforming to what are public or private orthodoxies.

The researchers are always handicapped in their physical ability to observe and the fact that they do not receive the training in observation which would be given to doctors and detectives. They may have been up the previous night seeing another aspect of the ceremony and indeed when a Hindu ceremony goes on and off for several days, so that exhaustion may cloud what they see and indeed what they are able to record. The priests in such lengthy ceremonies may work on their own shift system but the researchers cannot afford to be away resting when they may not know if some critical activity might take place. In Pangani, Tanzania attending the recitation of the whole *Koran* by four simultaneous readers working from a single lamp in an overheated room over sleeping children who were to be circumcised the next morning, does not make for observational accuracy then or for the next morning's ceremony. Human observations are idiosyncratic for social, physiological and psychological reasons. The 'I was there and, therefore, I know' statement has to be treated with great caution as memory is a transient quality under constant ongoing modification.

Observers are faced with the difficulty of reaching conclusions about what numbers of people do for most of the time at religious ceremonies for which there is a known liturgy. The ceremonies of the Coptic Church in Ethiopia are long and what the priests are doing is hidden from view behind a curtain. Those outside the curtain can only hear mumbling and even if they could hear anything distinctly it would not necessarily lead to any greater understanding since the liturgy is in a specialised Amharic religious linguistic code. So it is not altogether surprising that numbers of those attending are asleep and in some cases lying down to do so; while these may be extreme cases it is certainly not infrequent. We have to decide what part such forms of observed attendance have in the religious understandings both individual and collectively of both participants and theologians.

Indeed we have to assess whether theological understandings have much part in the thinking of those attending religious ceremonies when it is carried out in specialised linguistic codes even in the national language under conditions which pay little attention to even the possibility of participants hearing and understanding. At the pilgrimage shrine of Katagarama in southern Sri Lanka of some hundreds of women attending a Buddhist day of spiritual devotion addressed by a prominent monk using a loudspeaker, at least a third were lying down asleep. The Hindu couple being married in Mombasa, Kenya were told what to do by the officiating Brahmin and it was unlikely that they understood the long Sanskrit prayers which were said over them. This situation of incomprehension was even more likely to occur in Chinese Taoist and Japanese Shinto ceremonies in which not only is the language specialised but the ideograms in which it is written require specialised learning so that even highly educated men and women cannot know what is written and would need to have these texts translated for them. If they believe and have benefit from their attendance it would seem unlikely that it is related to status than religious understanding.

In many ceremonies we have large numbers of people seen to be doing the same thing at shrines which are the centres of pilgrimage. There is little evidence that they are carrying out their devotions in such machine like automated ways and their participation has to be individually understood and evaluated. Any recorded observations are inevitably taken out of these contexts and are abbreviations from the basic individualism of all religious practices and spiritual understandings.

Is the use of machinery any more reliable? Cameras and recording machines only record what they are pointed at and are valuable and reliable records of only that. School children being photographed in the mithrab of the Ali Mohammad mosque in Cairo and for relatives and attendants at a wedding in the Azores being photographed round the altar after the priest has left, tell us about the limited and transient sacredness of places in which religious ceremonies take place and how people group themselves on such occasions. These are semi-religious slices out of the surrounding social environment.

Much the same would apply to the use of security cameras which are common enough in public places such as school playgrounds and public squares outside cathedrals and mosques where religious activities may occur. However, their use for research has the additional difficulties of how such a mass of continuously recorded data can be processed. Hundreds of people are doing thousands of different things in different personal contexts during a religious procession. The result of the use of these machines which are so attractive to the researchers and are often part of their basic field equipment is that they are likely to be overwhelmed with data. They have so much tape and video data that it would require large numbers of assistants to view and listen to what is available. Going back to listen or view this historical data would require the allocation of time competing with more immediate needs.

It would also require new methodological techniques to cope with mass data and mechanically varied viewpoints. Even then with such a mass of recorded observations these researchers are no further forward as to why people are there in the first place and what they personally experience. We are still left with the crudities of assessing mass participation which would put under the one category of both devotion and indifference.

The conclusion may be that observations are doubtfully valuable as it creates the impression of scientific accuracy. The greatest handicap may be that the observers are convinced that what they have recorded as their personal observations are correct. This is more so when the observers have had inadequate experience of watching what may be strange or predominantly monotonous ceremonies which go on for hours in languages which not only the observer but none of those attending understand. Neither social scientists nor theologians receive any training in observation which should be part of their professional training so that they observe noisy and silent behaviour with the same attention.

It seems unlikely that observation can rarely be more than a very limited activity which gives confidence to the researchers that having seen, they are beginning to understand. It is not a scientifically valid method in the context of religious ceremonies for understanding why people need and use particular religious ceremonies. Their value may be confined to the needs of administrators of religious institutions and their ceremonies who have to plan pragmatically for their efficient running. Days of prayer organised by the Cenacle Sisters require the supply of food and the disposal of waste as well as the provision of first aid and lavatories proportionate to the numbers coming but these dedicated women had difficulty in accepting that these issues were in their own way just as essentially religious as their interpersonal contacts. All religious institutions just as much as secular ones have budgets and to keep within their provisions if they want to avoid inefficiency and chaos. There is also the basic importance in observation to have the personal physically ability see and hear what is going on which can be related to the age of the observers and their height and physical abilities.

Participant Observation

All social science field work starts with some form of participant observation as they enter the community in which they are going to work. Whatever their backgrounds this is going to be a new experience which is going to have a primary influence on their thinking. Whenever they enter situations in which they are not familiar, there will be culture shock proportional to the social differences. Even the 'half and half' national researcher who has returned to their natal communities from living abroad, is going to be immediately struck by the changes which have occurred since they were last there.

It is one thing to accept the need for the fullest possible participation in the researched community or institution, but it is another thing to actually do so. Joshi when he wanted to work with Hindu farmers found the villagers amused at his lack of physical stamina (Joshi, 1979). Many religious ceremonies impose strain on both participants and observers.

It is clear that for every degree of involvement which opens up a new channel for information gathering, the researcher takes up a specific role which on the one hand, provides them with some new and previously unknown area of understanding but at the same time imposes restrictions. The Tanzanian Sukuma have so-called dance societies which have ancestor spirit connections but by attempting to belong to the Bugisu one, the researcher is excluding himself from the Bugaru one and of course the researcher would be unlikely to take on the appropriate facial markings.

An unmarried German researcher in India lived with a Hindu family in which all the women observed *purdah*. This made it impossible for her to move around freely until she made friends with a child welfare government official who acted both as her language teacher and chaperon (Bellwinkel, 1979) which would have still restricted the social situations in which she could participate. However, hard she may have tried to avoid disturbing her hosts Hinduism is a pervasive religion so she would have been upsetting their religious understandings of purity and impurity all the time in their sexually segregated eating and socialising.

In a strange way most social science researchers want to be socially invisible for professional reasons and yet be able to collect information as a person but whatever they do and whether they are nationals or non-nationals they are always someone to whom a role has been applied. In some cases they have no choice in what they are by age, sex and ethnicity but in other matters they can choose their roles by selecting what they want to be accepted as and how they can go about doing it since the role of researcher would almost always be unknown.

There are serious methodological issues in using the data from the point of view of some form of participant observation. It is always the observations of one person at one place and at one time and, however, long that participation may be in that community, it is participation in parts of that community observed sequentially.

So the basic methodological problem in observation is that it is restrictive and no researcher can observe what she cannot see. This leaves reliability to those who live in one part of the community as a round the clock resident and perhaps not living in a separate house or tent. Observations received second hand from informants are even more suspect as they have already been filtered through their personal conscious or unconscious biases which from the point of view of reliability is more likely to have the characteristics of formalised role related lying (Salamone, 1977). Whatever form of participation occurs the researcher takes on a role even the minimalist one of just being one of a crowd among thousands, and it is always a restricted role controlled viewpoint. It may lead to some intuitive rather than conclusions as to the nature of working misunderstandings in particular contexts that can be validated.

It has to be accepted that any form of participant observation is ego-centred and it cannot be otherwise and thus carries with it all the problems of such social centralisation. As in any cultural setting one sees what one is culturally trained to see and what one is physiologically capable of seeing. A literate Swahili Muslim hospital assistant in Mombasa, Kenya on being asked to write down the genealogies of all the people known to him took months of persuasion before he started to record the matrilineal rather than only the patrilineal connections as he was committed by his Islamic understandings to see just the one system of social and biological connection. The researcher whether participating as man or woman would see behaviour from that one dominant perspective.

It may be more methodologically sound to be a sole observer with a known role in a highly structured environment like a hospital ward or a school class-room or one in which there is no restricting structure such as a railway station, market or airport in which the control is one of the area through which there is a behavioural flow (Baker, 1998; chap. 7) in which the observer is undifferentiated among the many who are present. A trainee for the priesthood was asked to record over a period of months any unchristian behaviour that he could see in the London rush hour public transport, but he recorded none as that was his charitable viewpoint; he saw the best in all that he saw.

The range of acceptability of a researcher being in a community and more specifically in a family in which they seek to become a full-time round the clock member is likely to change their hosts in overall ways as well as in relationship to particular day-to-day issues; one may be differently accepted in different seasons by different people since the family members are not one but to have different roles. This odd person who wants to live with them for reasons which they will treat with some scepticism, will go through a scale of partial acceptance from being seen as a stranger, guest, potentially trainable childlike adult, simpleton unable to do the simplest of tasks known to their children at an early age to being a straightforward nuisance, an ever-present nuisance and a handicap on their usual way of carrying on who has to be endured (Briggs, 1970) for financial and status reasons; the researcher as a paying lodger is an asset but may bring disadvantages if the surrounding community does not like being 'spied' on by a stranger.

If the researcher expects to become one of the community which they are researching then immediately their self-sustained and understood status of an educated and detached intellectual disappears. They become just what they are in their host's terms by age, sex and property. They may be given classificatory kinship roles which must inevitably be daughter or son and this of course is immediately qualified by the material benefits which they should be provided for their classificatory fathers and mothers. It is not a situation in which researchers can sit on personal property and say that it is mine and mine alone; their limited stocks of tobacco, personally preferred food and petrol in their transport will soon be exhausted.

In such situations the researchers are not renting social space in which they can expect to be left largely alone to carry on with their mysterious research activities. They cannot dictate the conditions of their residence in this way unless there is already there a well understood role of lodger who then is clearly not classificatory kin. Living in a family or religious community means sharing their work since they are sharing the cooking fire and their religious ceremonials. They may not have either the ability or the degree of commitment or stamina to sustain a strange way of living for long periods. It is no doubt upsetting to be treated as a daughter or son and then to find that one cannot live up to the social and religious obligations that go with such roles; being kin or a novice does not allow time for writing up notes when there is work to do in which the family or community expects participation as a matter of course.

The bilateral adjustments which would have to occur are probably virtually impossible to solve except at a peripheral level; the social science researcher cannot be that and a full-time participator at the same time if either role is to be performed satisfactorily. If they become truly absorbed into these cultures as classificatory daughters or sons then they will be addressed in the peremptory tones appropriate to their roles. They will not have been addressed in this way since they were in primary school and they will have long grown out of any form of kin related subordination in their own professional careers and personal lives. Overall for a variety of personal and social reasons it is perhaps prudent not to attempt full time participant observation.

Self-Reported Religious Activities

No individual however well trained, conscientious or self-conscious is able to report on their own behaviour in ways which are not biased from the simple fact that their minds do not function mechanically. They are partly creatures of habit, mood and are swayed by constantly changing personal experiences and indeed by their own philosophical and religious commitments.

Social scientists are reluctant to accept that there are few if any social reasons for people to tell the truth to strangers or indeed to record in writing their religious thinking and activities. Informants are worried about the subsequent uses of what has been written or recorded as this recorded data is quite out of the control of either the writers or the collators. Those filling in a form about their religious activities are either acting on trust or obeying an instruction from a superior to which they may have only half-heartedly agreed.

Why indeed should individuals give away personal and private information about themselves unless it is already common knowledge or they get some social return within their understanding of normal reciprocities. Most people have been brought up to be cautious about giving any information away to anyone certainly not an outsider unless they are going to profit immediately in some way from the disclosure. It is not only charitable but optimistic to think that what people say or write about their religious thinking and behaviour is related to some pragmatic quality of sharable truth.

Most people in most cultures would probably admit that they adjust their opinions to their current needs and that would include the people they are talking to in their social lives. This would apply more particularly to questions asked by researchers and other outsiders from whom they can probably expect no return. The Ayatollah Khomeini, the supreme Shia leader of Iran when the Shah's rule was overthrown, is reported to have said that what he may have stated last week would not necessarily be the same as what he might say the following week. What might be considered to be the truth is very flexible in how it relates to social circumstances.

The frequency of religious participations are usually exaggerated in order to make the writers look better in their own eyes and to show conformity to the norms of the religion to which they belong. We are not certain as to what constitutes participation in their own understandings since it may involve simply standing outside the church door which is not participation according to most theological understandings but why then are they there at all. On the other hand, it has to be considered religious when some are observably possessed by what they think to be religious when some are observably possessed by what they think to be overwhelming religious emotion regardless of psychological explanations.

The answers to questions posed in person is a social interrelationship in which the person questioned is reacting to the questioner as well as the questions asked. In a research situation this is usually between people coming from two totally different social worlds. They are intellectually different, of different ages and almost certainly look and smell different. There can be little assumption of trust which would come from some shared aspects of identity but a shared religion is certainly an important link. However, much a nominally Hindu researcher may wish to disguise his caste status, but gossip will soon make his status known and his lack of conformity will soon be a subject of unfavourable comment or he may be required to act as a Brahmin.

Most people having working vocabularies which do not contain many words unless there is a professional necessity to have a large one as in the knowledge of local plants and their medicinal uses if they use them in their work. A Tanzanian Sukuma or southern Indian Tamil might well know five hundred plants while having a very limited vocabulary of words connected with religion largely used by people in communities outside their own. For most natal speakers of English it is said that they have a basic vocabulary of about five hundred words. This means that for most people most of the time, they do not have the linguistic equipment to express themselves in phrases that carry what may be complicated ideas and personal and emotional meanings. This inability in most societies for all men and women to express complicated religious feelings and understandings and even more their inability to write about such matters leads to variable understandings and misunderstandings which are usually not sorted out prior to interviews or by the administration of questionnaires. We have to conclude that the ability to write about personal feelings is likely to be possible for very few literates with specialised motivations and abilities.

In fact, attempts to reach agreement with informants on the key words such as religion, spirituality and health when their cultures may not even have words for these concepts, will almost always lead to a multitude of intellectual and social difficulties even basic misunderstandings. The five million Sukuma use the Arabic word *dini* for religion probably referring to Christianity and Islam rather than for their own traditional beliefs about ancestors and unrelated spirits for which they have no collective word. These linguistic differences may make it nearly impossible to assume that those writing and talking about their religious practices and spiritual beliefs have even remotely similar meanings to those carried by the researcher's own socialisation and professional aims and understandings. A question to a Japanese as to whether he believed in God, got the reply asking what God had the researcher in mind. This was a sensible answer when there are reputed to be over a million named transcendental powers in the Japanese cultural and religious pantheon of gods and goddesses. Much the same reply might be expected from a Chinese when a recently purchased religious poster in Shanghai depicted no less than twenty gods and goddesses.

So the self-reporting of religious participations and spiritual beliefs is suspect because of the absence of details about the circumstances and motivations in which such statements have been made and their inevitable circumstantial impermanence. Whether they have the linguistic equipment and intellectual or emotional capacity to make such statements as perhaps no more than one in a million have such abilities. There is always the more basic problem as to whether both parties are in fact talking or writing about the same thing as this is totally different to talking about the concrete realities of cows, crops and children.

There are also striking differences in the amount of talking which will be given in reply to a question such as 'what do you do' asked of Roman Catholic priests in Zambia and Zimbabwe. This resulted in differences between fifteen minutes from one priest who thought such a question was an intrusion on his privacy and professional status to fourteen hours from another who saw the answers which he gave would give his views a wider publicity. We can reach different conclusions from the answers given by these two priests as individuals but what their relevance might be to any wider understandings about the works of the Roman Catholic Church there would be highly speculative.

A few people will like the opportunity to discuss religious understandings with someone whom they consider to be a knowledgeable outsider of equal intellectual status to themselves. This was the case with Victor Turner and the Ndembu diviner Muchona the Hornet who was isolated from his local position. In these discussions and so could talk freely to this interested and interesting outsider.

There is also the problem that occurs when the information acquired is so clearly contradictory. The Japanese according to opinion polls appear to be the most secular people in the world with 65 per cent claiming to be without religious beliefs. When asked about observance 75 per cent pray to Shinto Gods at the New Year although only 21 per cent affirm that they believe in their existence (Reader, 1991:5). In such situations the answers cannot be tied to anything more than circumstantial and variable 'truth'.

There are alternative methodologies which might avoid the potential unreliability of mass questioning and overall replies from informants about whom virtually nothing is known and who have no felt need to cooperate with the enquirer. By reducing the number of informants and the specific issues into which enquiries are being made, it is possible to know more about the backgrounds of informants. A study in the Netherlands used fifteen informants with different religious understandings and associations with whom there were in-depth interviews (Wijsen, 2009). This was an attempt to counter intolerance by bringing people together to pray in an environment which had no specific religious associations. This approach using words and phrases allowed the researcher to find out the backgrounds of the informants in some detail and to put their remarks into specific correlations related to their personal, social and institutional orthodoxies. The use of this expensive methodology in terms of time and money reduced the unreliability of information by relating it both to the personal backgrounds of informants and their relationship to a specific project.

Inferred Religious Behaviour

Even the most experienced social scientist in reaching conclusions from their field work are likely to go further than might be justified from what they have learnt. As researchers they are people who have absorbed the attitudes and career needs of their professional colleagues and the atmosphere of scientific secularism of universities which were founded in the beliefs and practices of the European Enlightenment. The intellectual environment in which social scientists are trained whether in the East or West or in Africa is in a methodological tradition of secular questioning. It is an almost automatic professional response to the fact of religiously motivated behaviour that there are ample social and psychological explanations and that the supernatural is not a necessary explanatory factor.

While they may not intend to depress the religious practices and spiritual understandings of the people and organisations they study, this is certainly their effect on religious thinkers, administrators and theologians to whom their conclusions are presented. The social sciences are not seen as supportive unless one of their own carries out such enquiries starting from this basis of religious commitment which explains 'in' religious behaviour rather than 'outing' it into secular conclusions. An example of this would be the Western nun who investigated the ways in which Zairean nuns might develop their culturally based vocations without breaking the vision of their European founder (Burke, J.F., 1992).

Their views are often combined with an unconscious feeling of superiority in their analyses which may come from their academic and professional detachment and from any direct responsibility for their conclusions and the ways in which they are reached. The situation has been summarised by Moberg 'The immediate practical problem related to this subject.... is to convince religiously unbelieving sociologists (and others) that they should leave the door open to the possibility that man (i.e. every human being) has a spiritual dimension of ultimate commitment and concern even in modern secularistic societies... the situation pertinent to science and man's spiritual nature is not a battle between 'pure science' and 'religious bias'. Rather it is in every instance a case of science plus biases *versus* religion plus different biases' (Moberg, 1967).

It is a big methodological leap from observing religious behaviour to making statements about the reasons for such behaviour in one social setting much less to extend such conclusions to more than the one community in which they have been working over immense cultural and social distance barriers. Researchers in the social sciences find it difficult to admit that they have been working from inferences rather than hard data and from an absence of definitions about the matters on which they have been working.

For others who produce results from well recorded and more easily available data, there are always these limits to such speculations. The Vietnamese and other Asian cultures have the general concept of 'hungry ghosts', the spirits of people who have not been buried with the appropriate ceremonies is not enough to explain action and reaction within one conceptual circle. When the social scientist goes beyond this primary explanation which is sufficient for those reacting to such beliefs, is to provide explanations which those involved do not consider relevant and certainly not understood by them, raises issues related to intellectual and assumed cultural superiority.

These researchers take a leap from information that has been quantified for institutional reasons. There is also the factor that the results may have had little to do with the research objectives because that was the way in which it was sorted and recorded. It would be unwise to infer from this the nature and extent of beliefs of individuals and whole communities. They must surely be tentative at best in showing the range of known possibilities leaving aside the inevitability of a further number of unknown ones, for which there is some preliminary evidence. Much of these results are tautological in which the proof provided by the data are used as its own proof.

Who is to know among the millions going on pilgrimages who are no more than religious tourists and those that are there for more predominantly religious reasons. We know in Japan that a rising proportion of the elderly and of Chinese in Taiwan go on pilgrimage tours which in the former cases fill up the gaps created by loneliness and the latter are combined with shopping. Then in mainland China millions go to temples on their annual feast-days which involves going to the opera being performed within the temple compound, eating new food and listening to the music with perhaps a ten-minute visit to the statue of the God(s) in the temple largely taken up by standing in the line to get in. The feasting held at a Cretan chapels in honour of its titular saint perhaps unused for the rest of the year, Myanmar pagoda festivals with gambling and the annual parish fetes in England, are thought by their participants to have a religious focus even though what goes on is almost entirely secular. The secular minded would see this as no more than secular entertainment and those of a religious pattern of thought would see the same activity as religiously motivated. It is necessary to be modest even charitable in conclusions when so much is outside the ability of anyone to evaluate with any degree of accuracy.

Data Based on the Requirements of Scientific Methodology

Since the social sciences from their title, deal with what can be pragmatically assessed from public behaviour, private spirituality rather more than public religion is both based on metaphysical assumptions with which they can never agree since they have no physical reality.

So the social sciences are left with 'relic' data which varies from what is clearly a religious fact that a mosque is a religious building and a wooden shrine under a tree has nothing to do directly with forestry. The inanimate connection is clear and that is as far as it can go without metaphysical speculations which may or may not be related to do with individual perceptions. There are no Christian objections to using a cathedral for a concert or having a tea and souvenir shops inside the nave but no one has suggested that mosques and temples should have such usages. So we are left with an enormous range of activities which have religious components and here the social sciences enter the disputable field of correlations in which a religious connection has to be admitted but cannot be proved.

There are parallels here to a clinical examination of a patient supported by laboratory data which is the end of an abbreviated story coming from its own design. We have already shown that the resulting facts no matter how internally accurate they are, may give explanations that are no more than accidental coincidences as to the cause of death or the incidence of the incidence of certain behaviours. Medicine claims to prove that a disease comes from certain practices after very careful epidemiological enquiries which exclude as much as include other causal factors. In Papua New Guinea there was an incurable degenerative disease named *kuru* after the valley in which it occurred which affected mainly women and the researchers concluded that it must be caused by a gene carried only by women (Glasse, 1967). Subsequent social science research showed that often women ate uncooked parts of their dead relatives for the religious reasoning that it would retain their spirits within the lineage and that this was responsible for the disease. In such a serious matter involving many deaths it might have been guessed that there would be religious correlations. This disgusting and revolting custom according to Western cultural standards was not given any serious attention as a religious issue. It is possible that even missionaries may not have been aware of this secretive practice. Pilgrimages spread disease and religious emotions just as shaking hands in a Christian service to demonstrate charity are potentially dangerous to health. The Russian Skopsi men who castrated themselves were clearly performing a religious act and just as clearly the mass suicides of all those in the Jonestown sect were not religiously committed. The lessons which can be learned from these extremes example are complex of which the principle one must be that the results of research may reflect the attitude of mind with which the matter is approached.

Science prefers collective data which has pragmatic bases acceptable by other researchers from which individuality has been detached as much as possible. In the consideration of the *kuru* case the religious satisfactions which these people got from this practice were not evaluated possibly because no one involved spoke their language well enough to understand their point of view nor would they consider it reasonable and acceptable behaviour. The individual in their understandings are unconsciously as much as consciously holistic, the social scientist has to take a partial approach if they have scientific ambitions to accuracy. Such extreme examples prove little beyond the extreme and attractive situations in which they occurred. It would be difficult to define extreme religious behaviour as working misunderstandings because they are often literal personal interpretations.

Since it is difficult to assess working misunderstandings except in relation to orderliness and its related hard facts such as a marriage ceremony in a church but Hindu marriages can occur anywhere and a marriage of Buddhists is only peripherally religious as the only religious feature of this civil ceremony is the feasting of and donations to monks.

There are thus an enormous range of activities which can be correlated to religion but not with any scientific exactitude but this certainly does not entail a necessary understanding. There are religious ornaments, picture and gestures which are clearly connected at some time and by some people to religion and to that extent they work. Whether there is any working misunderstanding is not a matter that can be decided in the absence of hard data.

The Excess of Divided Information

Once we leave the over-personal debatable evaluation of an individual's religious ideas and practices which are holistic and look for the wider correlations which connect with this in any social environment, the problem is not the absence of information but a surfeit of possibilities for investigation.

In a Western context there is much psychological data related to religious ideas and practices which despite their accurate statistical elaborations must remain of questionable as there is little reason to presuppose that what information an individual may provide verbally or much less in writing will be as accurate as a DNA calculation in a laboratory over calculations of religious endogamy rates.

Why do we assume that the information that an informant can and will provide is an accurate reflection of what they do and feel about their religious ideas and practices. Social scientists hope that they are getting accurate information and that makes them predisposed to believing in the information that they get. This information may indicate no more than trends in how people feel that they are behaving or ought to behave in that situation.

There are even greater difficulties in accepting written information in which informants are trying to express complex ideas and behaviour with very limited vocabularies and so there are bilateral misunderstandings in any use of language. In any society there are few who can explain an emotional issues although they are certainly universally moved by the important experiences affecting them.

There is also the factor that social scientists are not so much highly literate as committed to getting as much as possible into writing and seeing that this is professionally essential. Even in the most universally literate society people do not feel any compulsion to put their everyday activities into writing much less their emotional involvements. They prefer to talk and this is easily transferred to the use of mobile phones but they do not write except when there are more or less socially or economically compelled to do so. We should accept that social scientists may be just as unable to express metaphysical ideas verbally much less in writing than a literate Bengali farmer.

So writing in every sense of the word is a minority activity, time consuming and inadequate for expressing much more than commonplace needs. Social scientists possibly get satisfaction from the accumulation of data as they have this to show for their efforts without regard to the fact that it would not pass as evidence in hard science and probably not in any Western-based legal system court of law which regards hearsay as unreliable.

It verges on the ridiculous for people to be asked to grade or enumerate their ideas and activities which might be necessary for the examination grading of answers by professionals with serious doubts about its accuracy but not for religious activities and it is certainly not an everyday practice in any society.

There is also a quantity of information about the physical consequences of religious activities (Reynolds and Tanner, 1995) but this is also from the simplistic primary point of view. People catch diseases from going on pilgrimages and the same would apply to going on package holidays. We do not know why they have put themselves at risk in both situations. We know that monastic life and meditation significantly lowers blood pressure but so does sitting quietly doing nothing.

So what we have available is a very large quantity of information collected by social scientists and other professionals that is predominantly presented not only in an elitist form but under a cloak of what is really pretended accuracy when it should have been presented in inferential forms. It has perhaps elevated much of their conclusions to a higher professional status than the reliability of their data justifies.

There is also the difficulty that in the evaluation of religious ideas and activities much is related to idealistic conceptions of what behaviour should be rather than what is actually happening. This methodologically limited presentation should not be accepted as providing acceptable evidence when it is isolated from personal or at most neighbourhood values. This approach which in a religious sense lacks charity, makes it virtually inevitable that everyone is falling short of the religious status to which they aspire or at least nominally committed. There is also the basic fact that almost universally whether they are Hindus, Muslims or Shintoists, believers are satisfied that the performance of personally created or orthodox rituals is sufficient to bring about the real possibility of getting what they want.

An ideal system in terms of the religions of the book, Christianity, Islam and Judaism are provided with definitions and so the result of this recorded and defined idealism are inevitably records of shortcomings. So we have examples of what people should believe in the textbooks of canon law of these three faiths and in their denominational subdivisions. Social scientists look at these textbooks of required behaviour with the professional satisfaction of having something of substance to work from and by which to evaluate the shortcomings of all religious behaviour. Social scientists and theologians have almost always top down perspectives.

When we come to religious classics exemplars of what believers should aim at such as the works of Saint John of the Cross, whoever wrote the *Bhagavad Gita*, the meditation manual of Al-Ghazali, the Dialogues of the Buddha, these are accepted as exceptionally valuable. But they were written in the linguistic codes or specialized languages of their writers, classical Arabic, Latin, Pali, Sanskrit and subject over time to a variety of translations into other languages by parallel elitist groups with the doubtful assumption that an abstract word in one language can be correctly translated by equivalent words in another with which it has no philosophical affinity. It has been suggested that even Mahatma Gandhi, an influential political and religious figure first read the *Bhagavad Gita* in English, not in Hindi much less in Sanskrit. These theological and philosophical classics are known to and used by only a minute fraction of those who think they belong to these religions. In this sense we can conclude that misunderstandings are inevitable.

At one end of this scale of comprehension and utilisation comes religious writings which are no longer understandable by almost all the people who are alleged to be influenced by them. Even when the language has its supposedly comprehensible and commonplace forms it may not be understood as in the religious documents distributed in Taiwanese temples. Certain basic factors are referred to as religious mysteries which have to be taken on faith, and in this what are the definable differences between the beliefs of what Mary Douglas referred to as the 'bog' Irish, the simple faithful there or in Banaras or Berlin and the sophisticated understandings of theologically trained in Delhi or Detroit. Mysteries which are indefinable cannot be related to behaviour except by inference.

Whether these studies are done with the intention of informing fellow religious professionals and social science elite outsiders, they are top-down evaluations in which the theoretical background has to a large extent already been predetermined negatively or positively by these elitist foundations.

If these assessments of religious ideas and understandings were done bottom-up and assuming that these elitist understandings have only marginal influence on the ideas and religious behaviour of believers, there might be a better grasp of social reality. Of the seventy million who are estimated to have attended the last Kumbh Mela how many can we estimate will have had any knowledge of the Hindu classics and the current thinking of the Hindu theologians in Indian universities and *ashrams*. Those involved are indeed only able to account for their presence there in the simplest of dogmatic phrases which for them are enough to express their personal experiential realities.

Surely a more reasonable if not rational approach would be to take religious behaviour and ideas from what is popularly practised and to see the thinking of theologians and philosophers for what they are in social science terms, deviance. They should admit that orthopraxis in the thinking and practice of people who define themselves as Buddhists, Christians, Hindus and Muslims is normal and to attribute religious behaviour to other standards is creating categorical deviancy.

These elitist paradigms do not provide much theological and religious dignity to popular practices as they come from the elitist social science and theological frameworks within which religious ideas and practices are assessed and even more so because they are not assessed in referential terms.

The Usefulness of Inexactness

Since there is both individual and social environmental variability whether or not the social sciences are able to collect accurate information is really irrelevant because there is absence of uniformity when research is directed as these quantified sources. The accuracy of sources reporting in collective terms on issues which cannot be defined suggest that these averages have the overall characteristic of rarely if ever being applicable to any individual. When such averages are presented to the people about whom they were created, the usual response that this may be your view as an outsider but in this or that situation we will react in different ways; in other words your paradigm may be correct but is not really any use in how people as individuals utilise rather than think about it if indeed they do think about it in any way that is separated from particular situations. Whether individuals are tied to formulas or informal religious behaviour they probably accept in some subliminal way that there is a hinge of exactness, a lurking sense of trustworthy certainty about which they know little of which their religious behaviour is felt to derive but is not tied to in any practical sense.

There is a necessary ambiguity in the forms of more organised religions that imply certainty without in fact providing it which at the same time allows for much variability in individual religious behaviour without losing the implications of this lurking background certainty. Hinduism retains its popular hold without having any definitional foundation without individual Hindus being able to illustrate this except by religious practices which show that they are not Muslims and even that is debatable as in India there is considerable sharing of devotional sites.

It is outsiders, the researchers into religious behaviour who formalise these inexactnesses into conclusions about variability as if it was some form of failure, while individuals hold to their own personal day by day certainties, a moving staircase of major and minor changing realities. The only certainties in this are the individual's concept of themselves as separate individuals. What is reality may be philosophically debated but there is a personal reality about all religious experiences which probably escapes definition.

It may be that the assumption that certainties exist in all varieties of behaviour including religion antedates the European Enlightenment and comes from older Greek thinking and this has become a feature of the religions of the book, the ongoing processes of logic, the construction of definitions and the dominance of those who are in fact religious lawyers.

The Eastern religions have always avoided the dead-end of singular exactnesses and the futilities of debating in religious terms what is a fish and what constitutes cooking. The Buddha himself is supposed to have said that it was better to divide a monastery than argue points of religious difference since such metaphysical difficulties are never reconcilable by debate. In such circumstances a compromise is a loss of the religious realities in which the protagonists initially believed.

Exactness is something which is available for the measurement of supposedly inanimate objects. However, in all animate activity and in particular human behaviour, any statement of exactness raises issues not so much of that particular factor but the extent to which it does not apply so that it has the immediate function of exclusion. The inexactnesses of the Eastern religions having nothing to do with the existence or not of literacy and they do not have any such exclusivities except by providing an illusory dialectic of stability which the Western religious systems have pushed into the dichotomous reality of binary alternatives making exclusion much more socially divisive.

Inexactness seems to be a valuable religious attribute in terms of its functional utility of providing theologically acceptable realities in individual environments. It would be both prudent and more reliable to apply this same indistinctness to social science approaches and their indeterminate conclusions.

In any attempt to assess and indeed to pin down what appears to be working misunderstandings in religious thinking and behaviour, we are inevitably faced with the use of data obtained by methods which fall short of scientific requirements. It is perhaps almost ridiculous to approach religious issues with such hopes of accuracy anymore that it would be possible to reach conclusions about absolutes in literature or art.

The purpose of religious research is to produce representations of personal realities that are as reliable as possible (Philips and Jorgensen, 2002:182). It would seem that the methodology most likely to produce acceptable results is dialogic research in which those involved and their biases are accessible to analysis. The working together of researcher and informants on a common problem within some temporally acceptable parameters. If we accept the unreliability of verbal and written statements made in the assumption of possible detachment, it would seem that only in discussion can any researcher have access to social and religious realities. It is virtually impossible to distinguish social realities and their cognitive representations (Philips and Jorgensen, 2002:196).

It would seem that only in dialogic research which is inevitably small scale because of the costs in time and funds, that there is any realistic possibility of assessing the personal extent of working misunderstandings.

Any expansion in scale will progressively detach conclusions from this individual reality.

As Wijsen (Wijsen, 2009) concludes for his Netherlands study of the possibilities of religious tolerance 'we must be conscious that validity as a term comes from a different language game that of positivist epidemiology and quantitative research, claiming that scientific statements are true if there is a correspondence between reality and representations of reality. But if we accept that there is a dialectic relation between social reality and cognitive representation of reality, our representations of reality are never mere reflections of reality'.

Despite the methodological effort which has gone into collecting data about religious thinking and behaviour, what we end up with is a patchwork of information of which little is related to individual social environments; it comes out of social darkness. Social scientists extract whatever they can from the data they collect but it is difficult to conclude that such data has any cross-cultural or cross-community relevance apart from a necessary assumption of the uncertain reliability of solicited information. We need to examine how individuals gain their religious information and what factors surround its persistence and variability.

3
The Acquisition of Religious Knowledge

In the last chapter we discussed the methods available for investigating the possibilities surrounding the hypothesis that religions continue to exist because there is a working misunderstanding between what religions impersonally require and how individuals personally interpret and put into action their religious needs. We will now look at the particular problems which researchers will have to face within themselves and in the public and private environments in which religiousness will occur.

Bias and its Cultural Background

These seekers into the religious understandings and those that practice their faiths from whom they are separated by many social distance factors, have a number of commonplace demographic and social biases that prevent social science enquirers from having the impersonal detachment that is a professional requirement.

There will always be in the background the culture of enquiry which draws the researchers into the insensitivity of detachment, the legacy of Comte who thought that all social behaviour would eventually be explained in pragmatic terms and with this the expectation that methodology would provide the keys for the final understanding of religious as much as secular behaviour.

More prominently there is the cultural split between high level Eastern and Western cognitive perceptions and the lower level of popular practice; that between these high level perceptions and the quasi-traditional ones of non-literate peoples and the equally non-literate ones of individuals everywhere. There is not the even methodological agreement about how social scientists should carry out their enquiries.

However, the most difficult form of bias to overcome must be the ideas that come from within the culture in which the researchers have been socialised and it is within this that they remain psychologically whatever they do privately and professionally.

Researchers who have grown up within cultures influenced by the three religions of the book would be inclined to see public religion and private spirituality in terms which do not strain these boundaries and to see religious practices in terms of education and need. They are not likely to experience revulsion. They would start research in such communities or personal environments with a certain personal intolerance of the short-comings of others but with no particular tensions. They would almost by definition have no difficulties in researching there the nature of working misunderstandings.

These researchers are not going to be disturbed by Western religious art and architecture because it is explicable in their existing artistic evaluations and they are not likely to be confronted with the public ritual slaughtering of animals by orthodox Jews and Muslims; these more objectionable features of these faiths are not publically exposed to or experienced by these researchers.

However, the Western or Westernised researcher moving out of this restrained cultural environment with its theoretically understandable religious abnormalities, comes up against the visually created tensions of the inexplicable. They see the symbolically discordant polytheism in Chinese, Hindu and Shinto temples and the popular iconography of religious art in shops and kitchens, the public killing of goats in a Kolkota Kali temples as well as the seemingly noisy disorder of public religious activities. They are not only culturally revolted but find it inexplicable that any rational person can worship a Goddess with six arms with a necklace of skulls and a God with an elephant's head.

In reverse we can surely surmise that the Easterner and those coming from quasi-traditional predominantly non-literate environments, visiting the buildings or attending the ceremonies of the religions of the book will have doubts as to whether anyone can worship in such emotionally arid environments without any emotional stimulation. West Indians on migrating to Britain have often commented on the coldness of Christian worship there.

The social scientists of either sex come into the research of religious practices with a number of deeply rooted preconceptions of what is personally reasonable to them and what is not acceptable for which there must be pragmatic explanations outside any peripheral supernatural influences.

The Problems from Memory and Observation

However, much the researchers read up their interests there is always the need to see and hear more unless it is a purely literary approach. They go out to see and think that they see and record accurately but in fact that they do not. What they see and hear is dictated not only be biological capability but by social training as to what they should see and hear. They are socialised to accept that speech has to have meanings so that in hearing glossolalia, the speaking in tongues of those possessed, there is the conclusion that it is nonsense, not that it is a form of religious behaviour for which there could be rational and religious explanations.

Observers can of course record what they see and hear on the spot but that is an obtrusive and alienating activity and of course while the researchers are writing, they are missing what is going on in front of them. There is also the fact that a sentence is an abbreviation of activities which might more correctly require a book to describe inadequately. Human behaviour goes on while the researchers write and even if they have learnt short-hand they will miss much. We expect much from writing but it is always an inadequate reflection of the realities which it is describing.

So most researchers will write up what they have seen and heard much later after a delay of some hours within which other activities will have taken place. Memory becomes a factor and that is as unreliable as observation as it is not the unlimited retainer of all that is passed through the brain.

Short-term memory is poor and a large proportion of what is seen and heard is lost within a few minutes. Much of what is remembered of the religious activities at which they have been present, will be the parts that fit into the patterns which they are looking for from the nature of their socialisation and what they have learnt professionally so far. The pattern that temporarily holds and manipulates information as we perform cognitive tasks. A number of memory files holding partially processed information until some of it moves on to another location for long-term use (Smyth *et al.*, 1994). Much may be remembered that slots into pre-existing requirements or to existing cultural preconceptions.

Memory is often related to areas of self-chosen expertise. The observer of a ceremony who has existing interests in child behaviour, music or hysteria, will note and remember events that relate to these interests or matters that are so culturally discordant to their socialised sentiments that they get retained often for years whatever may be their overall importance (Ericsson and Lehmann, 1996). The Western researcher seeing spirit possession for the first time will retain this memory indefinitely. Matters of lesser interest will not be retained at this high level of remembrance.

While some social scientists are experts in particular fields of knowledge and are likely to become more so over their years of professional work, this would interfere with the noticing and memorising of religious activities and ideas which have a holistic background to their creation and performance. They rarely have the expertise for holistic perceptions which go into the training of detectives and general practice doctors.

The Factor of Uncertain Religious Knowledge

Religious knowledge if it is not written down and used for instruction and conformity, has little reality other than the immediacy of contemporary ideas and their connection with current practices; in such communities it is no more than a dimension of public opinion.

Where it is written there is the factor that it may have been learned at one time and as they grow older we have only what people state that what they currently remember of what they may have been taught at sometime in the past. What we are being told as the religious knowledge of individuals is usually what they consider to be relevant to their current situation but most will be eroded by time and inapplicability.

Unless they are involved in religious affairs beyond their participation in rituals, their religious knowledge is likely to be scanty indeed as for most people in all religions it is not something that they consider to be necessary for getting what they want from their participation. Indeed questioning people about their religious knowledge will often get the reply that it would be better to ask professionals who know about these matters. Questioning anyway is perhaps not a realistic way to find out about personal beliefs since it is usually considered bad manners to be so direct and it reminds many people of police procedures. This exposure of their ignorance of the more formal aspects of their religion would not relate at all to the value of the experiences that they have had from a pilgrimage or from passing through the sight of a Hindu *sadhu*.

So researchers are collecting as data scattered bits of religious knowledge which only in part will come from religious learning. This may have been based on the formalities of learning to recite the *Koran*, to know the Christian catechism and to be able to read the Torah. However, most of what is learnt about religion will come from bits and pieces on the fringes of institutionalised religion, the satisfying 'superstitions' associated with faith. Researchers will always find it difficult to distinguish between these different levels and environments of social as much as personally experienced religious realities.

The Binary Nature of Religious Knowledge

It is not only that social scientists and theologians start their understandings of religious thinking and practices from what they can read about particular faiths from the comfort of a chair. It is that much of their understandings come from what has been described as the sanskritization of Hinduism (Fuller, 2004); that the only genuine religious knowledge and subtended practices come from sacred writings and that all the rest of so-called religious activity is superstition.

Writing creates the illusion of static facts to which it is easy to attach binary patterns to which religious believers are assumed to conform or dismiss. The social reality may be that the mass of believers may not know what has been written and very likely have not read it anyway or have forgotten what they read or been taught. These believers will have a range of reasons why they should not pay much attention to these writings anyway as they do not think that their need for religious involvements are much related to what has been written by the elite of their faiths, much less the largely unintelligible sacred writings of their faith.

We consider this approach based on the literacy of the elite to be biased as it bars the majority of mankind from being considered religiously motivated as it imposes a static quality on whatever religious knowledge is acquired. Further than this it constricts the range of knowledge that is acquired and considered by those involved as being religious.

The fact that this side of religious understandings and practices is based on sacred or sacralised texts which cannot be easily changed and in which they are perhaps too specific in what is required when the environment in which they were written has changed. It could be argued that only the doctrines of the Latter Day Saints, the Mormons, have doctrines created in a modern environment but these modern institutions have constant problems over reordering their theological thinking to meet issues which did not exist for earlier generations. Thus, researchers will always have to be contending with writings that not only are static productions with no built-in flexibility, but are out of date even according to those who think about such issues much less those who implement their faiths in accordance with immediate needs rather than because of studied reflection. They forget that most do not give any attention to religious matters which are not of immediate personal concern. So while researchers concentrate on what has been written about the faiths of others, men and women will have their religious thinking and activity dominated by interpretations and needs which make up their private spiritualities.

Thus, the more important religions base themselves on texts which are needed for the acquisition of correct knowledge and this imposes a static character on faiths which crystallize into orthodoxies. It is certainly correct that any religion has certain basic qualities but these are interpreted in varying environments and through the workings of individual cognition.

So the other half of the binary nature of religious ideas and practices comes from the acquisition of knowledge which is more social than religious of which only a small part can be specifically related to the learning of sacred or sacralised literature. A high proportion of religious knowledge on which people may act is acquired along the way from personal experiences rather more than from teaching.

Knowledge and Literacy

The social sciences attempts to understand religious knowledge in its social realities is in some ways handicapped by literacy. What is written and propagated is assumed to have a certain religious as well as social stability and it is easier to start any study of the acquisition of religious understanding from this basis rather than from anything so evasive as personal knowledge and behaviour.

While it may be the key to the understandings of what is known about a religion, this will vary with the degree of involvement of such written elements will have in religious practices. Methodologically it is the easiest way of finding out the extent of formalised knowledge. Researchers accept that their own reading is both tiring and time consuming even when it is a necessary part of their professional life. They should accept it will be even more tiring and time consuming for others who are perhaps less ready to be intellectually stimulated. It may be that the majority of mankind get through their lives quite adequately without reading and writing at all. This would certainly be so for most

Indians and Chinese who if they have to use a document would get a specialist reader to do it for them.

The significance of literacy in religious knowledge is probably limited to the top of the pyramid of religious involvements and correlated to intellectual capacity and if these people that researchers find it easier to relate to. It seems likely that religious writings are of little significance for religious knowledge or needs where it is written in languages which are no longer spoken such as Sanskrit for Hindus and Pali for Buddhists and Chinese and Japanese believers as the calligraphy requires special learning. An amulet containing a religious quotation is equally effective whether the wearer can read it or not or even knows what is written.

Then there are religions which have never been put into writing such as those of the American Indians and African ones south of the Sahara; these still find no need to put their current practices into any literate form. No one would gain by the effort except when the ideas of a sect catches on and it becomes institutionalised like the large Kimbanguist Church in the Congo with its own extensive religious literature.

So we must look at the acquisition of religious knowledge and understandings which may initiate religious behaviour with the reality that except for a limited number of sophisticated intellectuals reading and writing may have little part in the acquisition and maintenance of individual religious understandings outside the limited range of observable orthodoxies.

The Possibility of Archetypes

The general idea that the individual is born with archetypal patterning, some instinctual imaginative predispositions within the mind which has come out of human evolutionary and ethological past and has been present in human thought since Plato's dialogues with Timaeus (Macdonald, 1997). Jung (Jung, 1959) thought that the concept of archetypes, ideas from the primeval past was the basis of mankind's universal capacity for creating myths and with this the whole range of backgrounds for religion and imaginative literature.

Whatever the biological carrier, it would seem that individuals carry within them some predisposition for imagery which is beyond and beside any pragmatic needs for survival. It is not surprising that there is little agreement of what this is except that imagination remains unexplained and universal in all cultures and at all levels of intellectual capacity. The symmetrical scratching in pieces of ochre found in a South African cave dated 75,000 years BC long before archaeology has identified human social existence is evidence of this capacity (Lewis_Williams).

It is certainly clear that children have the capacity to assume magic and that people and objects can be made to behave in irrational ways and this can be seen in the ways that play is invented and toys take on superhuman abilities. It may even be that a self-limited rationality is imposed on these amorphous ideas by the necessity for survival but that this is subordinate and secondary to these earlier predispositions. It seems likely that this magical understandings remain in the adult mind and partially accounts for their use of ritual so that working misunderstandings have no rational difficulties.

Childhood has been seen as a period in which the individual is free from the pragmatic necessities which envelop adulthood so that their imaginations have a freedom denied to adults, even those adults such as theologians who are professionally isolated and supported in order to think. In developed countries the length of childhood is extend by law for far longer than in subsistence societies and in situations of urban poverty. In these situations children are put to work in support of their families almost as soon as they can walk. Some South American cities have almost feral groups of boys who live almost entirely outside adult support and influence. In these environments it seems unlikely that these children will have much opportunity for imaginative thinking.

It has been suggested (Gopnick, 2009:238-47) that in situations where they are free to imagine 'children really do put us in touch with important, real and universal aspects of the human condition'. However, as a professed agnostic psychologist with children she may have read too much into the imaginings of some children.

The Childhood Acquisition of Religious Practices

We can be certain that a child's ideas about the mystical world which comes to be labelled and socially segregated as religion are at least in part socially created and psychologically constructed but the distinction is difficult to formalise.

If we take the position that there are stages through which a child develops and which later form part of their religious understandings there are problems over its general applicability of such imposed scales and classifications, when a majority of children are brought up in marginal subsistence communities in which levels of development may be truncated.

We can presume that Piaget's stages of moral development was based on research with very specific children from within a Swiss culture which has had no violent social disturbances for several centuries and probably from within stable families, a rare universe created by the persisting Swiss political neutrality.

There may indeed be some micro-cultures which are sufficiently stable over generations to justify the attribution of a system of moral learning such as the Amish and early Mormon settlements in Utah (Eckensberger, 1994) but in non-literate communities very little can be segmented out as specifically religious. In a Muslim village on the Tanzanian coast in which everyone follows fasting between dawn and dusk in the holy month of *Ramżan*, children remember this as a time for parties and staying up late and not as a month dedicated to religion. It may be that children experience religious practices as part of their usual pattern of existence and not as something theologically separate.

It must be rare indeed for anyone from infancy to adolescence which after all is a long period in developed societies and significantly shorter in subsistence cultures, to live in a socially stable environment. The implied stability of primary groups in subsistence and traditional communities must be largely an ideological fiction. These idealised communities will always have the tensions of rivalry, demographic replacements, anger and distress as a constant background to its seeming placidity. History and folk memory will only retain major communal distress.

Every child will pick up odds and ends of religious practice rather than a consistent and isolatable body of knowledge against a background of illness, marital instabilities, sibling rivalry, neighbourhood tensions, fears and longings from television and a wide range of influences from the macro environment. Enormous numbers of children grow up in deprivation and malnutrition in single parent families in which they are involved in the needs of survival rather than having a privileged and benign childhood at which in adulthood they look back on with pleasant memories.

While there is a tendency to see the acquisition of religious knowledge in the more formal terms of education, what is deliberately taught particularly in Koranic schools where the memorizing of the whole book is usually the sole aim of the process. Some Christian denominations aim to teach their children the basis of the commitment through a catechism with theological explanations for each point. Buddhist monasteries provide postulants with teaching of basic requirements where entering the monastic order is a rite of passage for men in Buddhist societies. This means that men are much more likely to learn some basic Buddhist doctrines denied to women but it is women that feed the monks daily on their begging round and who predominate in worship at pagoda shrines.

While this is a taught process it is not one that is closely institutionalised except among such closely integrated communities as the Amish in which the Bible is the basis of their lives. It is more likely that the bases of religious understandings occur in early childhood before there is any attempt to teach the young and if there has been some measure of formal instruction, its details are likely to be progressively forgotten. The lives of adults are flooded with additional information which will have direct relevance to their current situations. At the same time there will be the acquisition of ongoing religious understandings as they are faced with new situations. While individuals may continue to feel that they have an underlying commitment to being a Buddhist, Hindu or Roman Catholic it may not be tied to any extensive knowledge of what these faiths may or may not require. There is little stability in religious knowledge.

The Confined Environments of Childhood

Most children are brought up in specific narrow social environments in which the parameters of their imaginings are provided and restricted by their surroundings. There must be very early visual and audible absorptions while lying in cots and prams and more specifically from being carried on their mothers' backs while they work in their fields and in market visits as well as their participation in rituals; there will be no isolatable categorisation of these activities. They are more socially involved than in the mother-child isolation of urban living in which the door of the house limits experience. In most societies the young child is never alone and is fed on demand. In Western societies this must certainly be uncontrollably broadened by the ubiquitous television often left on as a pacifiers when their mothers have other preoccupations which isolates this form of socialisation from social realities.

We can conclude that children grow up covertly absorbing behaviour from their immediate domestic surroundings. It is in this process of growing up in a confined environment they are going to pick up patterns of behaviour related to religion without any explanations. It is just what goes on in their personal live-in situations. Before there can be any question of understanding the child has visual and tactile awareness of her or his surroundings which comes from consciousness, and some of these acquisitions will later become part of their religious understandings. In a London Roman Catholic parish some children think that the parish priest is God and in orthodox Jewish households they will learn particular systems of cooking and food consumption.

Firstly the child is likely to find very soon that they have amulets attached to their necks or waists which are not connected to feeding or comfort so would not be experienced as having any existential importance. It could be that fingering a cross with its hard edges will provide different and lasting impressions to those of other shapes and transferred to other arbitrary contexts.

Then there will be awareness that comes from contacts with their mother's body such as a selection of amulets round the neck from Christianity and Islam and on the arms and wrists that are connected with ancestor propitiation. Her face may be scarified, her hair plaited and her body tattooed which could later be seen as connected to religion.

The child in Hindu and more orthodox Jewish families learns not so much that specific foods are provided, but that cooking is done in special ways which are seen later to be not only exclusive but to be related to religious requirements. Although as a young child they will experience priorities over adults, they will certainly see that families do not eat together but divided by both sex and that the provision of food is in terms of relationship priorities (Appadurai, 1981).

The Individuality of Religious Knowledge and Practice

There may be a tendency to see the individuality of religious ideas and practices as an adult phenomenon as a result of environmental factors and personal dispositions but it is likely that these predispositions are based on childhood experiences which are both environmentally confined, quite short in length and initially dominant. Adulthood is a long period with innumerable transient overlaying experiences.

Social scientists tend to seek the uniformities in human behaviour not only because there is some assumption that human beings have rather more than some persistently shared characteristics. They perhaps do not attribute to others the extreme individuality which they give to their own beliefs and practices. Also because researchers do not usually have the time, funds or methodological capabilities to study individual childhoods. The reality may always be that researchers are not so much time-tabling their work but are more or less forced to do so within the parameters of their professional lives combined with personal and private obligations, their employee status and shortage of funds and time to explore behaviour which in social and psychological reality cannot have categorical boundaries imposed on it.

The child grows up with individual perspectives of which some have religious relationships but what knowledge is acquired and under what circumstances would be virtually impossible to find out without changing the very behaviour which the researcher is trying to observe. Except in the most detached sense of being an inconspicuous participant in mass ceremonies, the researcher will always be interfering in the behaviour for which they have the professional aim of being detached.

Acquiring Religious Knowledge in Subsistence Communities

In these communities which exist annually on the margins of survival religion is part of all that they do but it is not recognised as a separate sphere of activity except for a few part-time specialists. The children are units of production and as soon as they are able they contribute to the family's productivity by bird scaring, taking animals to water, weeding and generally making themselves useful. They are fractionated adults from whom they are separated only by the social rituals of biological and social age-grading.

Children will pick up a situational morality only marginally related to the diverting ceremonies which for them will be breaks from the monotony of farming. They will learn to be participants by watching and imitating and as far as the observed rituals go, there can be no teaching or explanations as their adults have not been given explanations and, therefore, cannot pass this on.

A researcher who can never be more than a fringe resident can see much of what goes relating to the public religious behaviour and infer its significance. We know that Evans-Pritchard never learnt to speak the Nuer language nor were the Nuer interested enough in this stranger to talk much to him through a despised outsider interpreter so he watched from his tent. From his lengthy observations he was able to produce a substantial intuitive work on the Nuer religion (Evans-Pritchard, 1956).

We do not know with him or any other researcher to what extent his Roman Catholic beliefs to which he was a convert, may have contributed to his careful conclusions. This does not detract from the fact that an outsider can reach conclusions which are likely to be just as valid as those obtained by someone speaking the language but who would still be socially distant.

Acquiring Religious Knowledge in Inclusive Communities

All communities if they experience themselves as such recognise acceptable strangers but it may take years for newcomers either as researchers or residents to be accepted. Margaret Mead was certainly accepted by the Pacific Island community in which she researched on and off for decades but she was always socially distant from them although those people recognised the material benefits of their long association with her and wept at the news of her death. Researchers will always be seen as outsiders on a scale of tolerated and tolerant acceptability. They will always have to accept that they start and finish within this scale over which they have little control and that wanting to be one of 'them' is an emotional hope rather than a possibility. The researchers starting from wanting to find out the religious ideas and practices of children there will be an experiential gap which will always be a far greater gap than with adults as they are threatening by their overall size.

While most children are brought up in families which do not have religious issues taught to them as a matter of course, some live in geographically closed communities in which their religion has created a distinctive way of life which is quite distinct to the way of living in the surrounding societies.

In the East African coast almost all the villages are completely Muslim but there would be little to socially distinguish one village from another. Children acquire knowledge of a way of life that could be called Muslim but not in ways that would distinguish their way of life from anything surrounding them. Children in Indian villages which are predominantly Hindu will pick up the intricacies of caste behaviour very early in their lives when it combines residence and use of water and the particular places of worship which they can use without harassment. It may be acceptable to talk to people of another caste on a field path but not at a well or on their veranda. Children will be faced with the realities of these ongoing religious practices rather more than proportionate changes as they age.

The children of Mormons particularly in Utah where they are in the majority, may not pick up much of their theology but will certainly learn early on that there is no smoking and drinking in their families and that the health of Mormons is better combined with lower rates for social upsets of divorce than those in other faiths because of their religiously inspired practices (Troyer, 1988). Much the same would apply to the less numerous and less geographically concentrated Seventh Day Adventists (Fraser *et al.*, 1991). In some cases the researcher can live there with the agreement of the community along with the biases built into their own lifestyle. There is also the fact that in most subsistence communities they are there to find out something about which their neighbours just as much as the researchers are not sure.

Acquiring Religious Knowledge in Exclusive Communities

Certainly there are closed patterns of living which are ostensibly Muslim but not distinctively so in the ways that the Amish (Hostetler, 1993) and Hutterites (Hostetler, 1974) are distinguishable from their neighbouring communities. There are other relatively closed communities such as the geographically isolated polygynist communes in Utah which usually are short-term groupings. The Amish and the Hutterites have rarely refused opportunities for research on their lives which they see as both religiously and materially superior to that of their neighbours and the surrounding society in general. They may even see such research as likely to explain to outsiders the benefits of their way of life rather than to expose them to serious criticism. On the other hand, polygynist communities will see researchers as representatives of a hostile surrounding culture and thus are unlikely to accept their presence. In these communes there are few children who grow up and remain where there is no record of a successful way of living over generations. This is not the case with the Amish and Hutterites who provide a satisfying way of life from which there are few dropouts.

As with most subsistence communities their children are rarely alone with on demand feeding. Their education is aimed at what they would need in Amish communities and they have successfully challenged the State to retain an education system attuned to their lives rather than one encouraging the children to see the outside world as providing better opportunities for personal development.

Their education is aimed at an ability to read the *Bible* as the source of guidance for the creation and continuation of a quite specific way of life which has provided them with a high standard of living from farming. Parents are responsible for the training of their children, not the schools, who learn by observing and imitating their parents (Hostetler and Huntingdon, 1971).

The Amish and Hutterites have been able to develop and maintain over a number of generation systems of Christian belief and practice which has provided enough material benefits to retain their children there despite a pattern of behaviour at least for the Amish which the outside world considers slightly absurd and a tourist attraction. The opportunities for research into the religious practices of exclusive communities rests in part on whether they are overly defensive to researchers coming from what they experience as a hostile surrounding society. In such communities it may be more difficult to find working misunderstandings as there is a continued effort to relate the metaphysical and the social into lives that are materially successful.

Acquiring Religious Knowledge in Slum Communities

Researchers inserting themselves into slum environments face greater personal difficulties than working in village communities. If they do more than commuting into their research area, they will have to accommodate themselves to a range of difficulties over hygiene, diet and personal safety.

Whether in Lagos, Nairobi and Lima, indeed in the majority of rapidly expanding urban communities the majority of children will grow up in overcrowded poor quality housing in which survival is more tentative than in agricultural subsistence communities from which their families may have migrated; a personal exchange of living conditions within the same culture of poverty.

In these predominantly matrifocal single parent families Christian children may well grow up with subconscious devotion to the Virgin Mary, the Taoist Goddess of Mercy and whoever is pictured on their walls combined with a realistic recognition of male transient dominance.

Children may well be more involved in insuring their own survival in seeking petty jobs at a very early age and in some Latin American cases live in independent feral groups. They are unlikely to get any deliberate religious teaching or regular participation except from public festivals and pictures on the wall. In Mexico they are likely to see the shrines to new cult to Saint Death and to be attracted generally to its correlation to the realities of their lives as well as to public religious iconography (Carmichael and Sayer, 1991). In such situations there may be the dominance of working misunderstandings as those people will have little formal relationship with the required beliefs of their faith.

Acquiring Religious Knowledge in Schools

Researchers into religious ideas and practices are in a better position to do so in schools and universities because these communities are relatively static within their age grades as well as being socially distinct. These researchers have an accepted status superiority and the pupils are already available for testing of which procedures they already have had experience.

Formal schooling has no ethological origins and most children pick up the realities of social life from watching and copying. It is often assumed that a denominational school will implant religious values into children but schools are dominated by secular needs once they became separated from religious elitism.

The major religions where they have political power aim at goals which would be disruptive to the needs of social communalism and survival if they were achieved by a majority, the school as such regardless of its religious affiliations teaches competitive individualism and to some extent institutionalises envy. A child in school is progressively separated from family obligations and contributes virtually nothing to its needs particularly in subsistence communities. Religions may promote and idealise the family but schooling progressively separates the child from this idealisation. Whatever the overall tolerances taught in a denominational school, it is still an 'us' and 'them' situation as in India and Northern Ireland where the political system subsists on religiously supported communalism. The researchers are never inter-denominational as they are committed to one side or the other.

While religion may be taught as a required subject in the syllabus particularly in Muslim Koranic schools but even there as in Pakistan these '*madarsas*' are now teaching secular subjects to balance the failures of the national school system. Some schools have a religious ethos but this is unlikely to provide sufficient religious knowledge to override its more dominant secular characteristics; a rigidity of behaviour not occurring at home, artificial grading, parallels to factory administration and timings and the impossibility of teachers being responsible for out of school behaviour. Most children learn the parallel social system which manipulates the official one of their school. Certainly subsistence communities are competitive but it is muted and they do not have the statutory licensed competitiveness of modern societies which starts from the moment that a child enters their school in which their progress is repeatedly publically graded.

What Muslim children will learn is that their faith is comprehensive and makes no distinction between what other societies regard as secular and religious activities and provides a unified legal system which dominates nations which are constitutionally Islamic such as Saudi Arabia and Pakistan. But even there children may well remember religious festivals in the context of parties rather than prayer. To the observer the festival week for the patron saint of Assuan in Egypt was predominantly a social affair filling the streets with secular distractions and excitements for children. Little was known about the saint concerned.

It would seem that schools whether they are denominational or teach religion as a secular subject in their curriculums, that children and adolescents would learn that there is a wide gap between practice and idealism but that does not appear to have affected the persistence of religious devotions. This is particularly so as comparative religious teachings would inevitably highlight the popularity of religious devotions in other cultures. It may be that any form of religious teachings would mute the realisation of the persistence and reality of working misunderstandings.

The Adult Acquisition of Religious Knowledge

It seems likely that only a small proportion of children receive specific religious teaching and that this is mostly stressing regularity. The majority will build a personal picture of religion from general archetypes and individual imaginative creations. Beyond this their perceptions are likely to come from their personal involvement in festivals whether in traditional non-literate communities or the more general ones of the Christmas of Christians, *Id al Fitr of Muslims*, the Hindu Holi and the Chinese and Japanese New Year.

Are adults likely to be better informed as certainly an enormous quantity of religious literature is purchased by Christians and Muslims as well as Muslim rather than Christian broadcasting from state controlled companies. Sermons on Friday broadcast by Cairo radio were not listened to in a coffee shop and seemed to have resulted in louder talking in order to be heard. Indian television broadcasted the *Mahabharata* and other Hindu epics in serialised forms and these were not only very popular but influential in adding to Hindu political ambitions with politicians using religious symbolism in their public behaviour. So if there is any adding to religious knowledge it may well be the result of such popular presentations as the Guyanese soldier reading the Christian New

Testament in picture book form with bubbled dialogue. The acquisition of religious knowledge is always predominantly by seeing and hearing often in convenient or indeed accidental situations rather than reading. Even secular television provides images of religious activities as news which keep its relevancy as popular practices in the minds of the viewers.

For any adult to learn more about his or her religion beyond what might be called surface trivialities, would involve the use of time and such learning to replace other activities. A small number will be included in professional training programmes in Islamic centres in Cairo, Mecca and Zanzibar and a range of Christian denominational training centres for careers in religion.

It seems possible that only in the processes of conversion in the deliberate changing affiliation from one religion to another that there is likely to be any deepening of religious knowledge and a serious attempt to minimise working misunderstandings. While some may convert from emotional situations, such as the instantaneous roadside conversion of the Christian Saint Paul but only a small proportion of those who came forward as converted at Billy Graham's American evangelical rallies followed this up; for most it was a one off emotional reaction in an environment staged to provoke such reactions.

In India there have been mass conversions of communities of Outcaste Hindus to Christianity, Islam and more particularly Buddhism for social and political reasons under the influence of their leader Dr. Ambedkar. There is little evidence that these converts acquired or indeed were required to acquire any new religious knowledge beyond a change of status which removed them from their theological supported caste subordination within Hinduism.

In Indonesia the government despite its Muslim majority decreed that a religion should be recorded on everyone's identity card which could be anyone of the major world religions. This led to the conversion of large number of uncommitted traditional peoples to Christianity rather than Islam although a catechist commented when some asked his advice, that it really came down to whether they wanted to continue to eat pork or not. There was no increase in religious knowledge in this Indonesian situation.

There were the so-called 'rice Christians' in China where conversion provided some protection from starvation as well as some opportunities for material advancement. The social science conclusions that these primary explanations are the end of the story would be incorrect. Certainly the Communist government in China saw Christianity rather than Islam as a narrow imported religion and thought that removing foreign missionaries that their numbers of believers would fade away. However, numbers retained their faith and they re-emerged after the relaxation of the Cultural Revolution and who became the nuclei of expanding Christian communities; an expansion of the more practical aspects faith without any necessary increase in religious knowledge.

There is a widespread feeling in Africa that to belong to either Islam or Christianity as overarching religions correlates with modernity but this has resulted in the growth of parallel religious systems in which there is overt conformity to these faiths but the covert use of quasi-traditional practices to cope with misfortunes. Children will experience two sets of practices rather loosely divided between public and private religious activities which may or may not lead to experiential difficulties. A clear example of working misunderstandings on either side of these parallel rather than alternative systems.

We can see that in both these situations, mass conversions for reasons which may not be principally religious and in the practising of a faith which does not meet the overall needs of believers and a measure of cross-conversion occurs. This may mean that there is always a movement between religious systems in terms of their situational appropriateness. This is the Japanese practice since individuals do not affiliate for life-time religious commitments.(Miller, 1992). This would be another level at which working misunderstandings are an ongoing reality as religious knowledge is not seen a major factor in their pragmatic practices.

Overall it would seem that religious knowledge in the sense of authorised doctrines is not a major factor in religious understandings. Believers assume that they know or rather that they know enough to support and validate their religious needs. But this religious knowledge that can be learned in some specific form which can be normatively assimilated as doctrine is confined to Christianity, Islam and Judaism. Elsewhere religious knowledge is too diffuse to be acquired in any direct sense and is acquired largely through social proximities in daily life; it is thus almost certainly a working misunderstanding.

Those researching religious behaviour rather than ideas recorded in writing by the major institutionalised religions, will always be faced with the elusive nature of the individual's public religious and private spiritual behaviour. They have to accept the limitations on what they can acquire and interpret from their socially distant positions and personal cultural predispositions. Whether we are considering the religious practices and knowledge of the majority, the popular aspect which is globally dominant which is certainly a working misunderstanding or those of the religious professionals, knowledge is always poor within the pragmatics subtended from largely inaccessible individual beliefs.

Multifaceted Religious Availability

While much attention is paid to the fact that in most if not all contemporary societies many religious options are available within their geographical surroundings or through electronic transmissions, there is the suggestion that this is a specific feature of modern life.

This may overstress the overt importance of institutions in all major religions and not just the religions of the book which visually dominate cities and countryside with churches, mosques, synagogues, pagodas and temples. It may be that all countries have a similar high density of these occupationally exclusive buildings which suggests that everyone has to be aware of the religious alternatives on offer.

It may be correct that Westerners have now become more aware of what is available in the religious and spiritual market place because of education about other cultures, the mass media and religious entrepreneurs offering new forms of belief and practice.

This may not mean that there has been an expansion in the use of religious alternatives to those that are provided by the major religions. There have always been sacred places of pilgrimage and their use has changed from the near to the far and have thus become more obvious. Alternative holy places of worship have always existed. Pre-Reformation pilgrimages in Britain were very varied and some indeed were to shrines of saints who may have never existed.

A contemporary Tanzanian Sukuma belonging to no institutionalised faith may have a spirit house for his ancestors in his compound and a choice within walking distance of local diviners with reputations for connecting the problems of petitioners to spirit forces. Subsistence farmers and the urban poor have as they have always had a great variety of available verbal and visual symbols with religious connections immediately available.

A Roman Catholic going to the new cathedral in Liverpool would have the choice of a number of side chapels dedicated to special devotions which is a feature of most churches. Hindus and Taoists in any temple would have visually a variety of deities to whom they can address their petitions. Buddhism shows its varieties in the number of shrines in houses, offices, courtyards, field edges and under trees which have their dedications in the minds of those using them.

Travel is not something new and the distribution of blood groups show that it has always been a feature of social life in exogamous matings and in this there would always be the migration of ideas and their symbols. Both Buddhism and Islam have travelled widely and only Christianity has had a specific widespread missionary impetus.

Christianity is no different to other faiths in the diversity of their private devotions. 'Catholics always appropriate the religious culture available to them in different ways. They negotiate with their religious tradition as it is marked out like all traditions with a certain 'givenness' by which some avenues....are imaginable and open and some are not. Their faith are not religion *a la carte* as if the number of cultural systems were unlimited' (Baggett, 2009:41). Individuals in their personal spiritualities pick and choose what they want to use devotionally but it seems rare for someone to move too far from the parameters which are easily available to them.

It is certainly correct that those who are less institutionally committed to a particular religion because of their employment, schooling and status, will zigzag between alternatives which come into their social orbit and appeal to their immediate needs and intellectual dispositions. However, some alternatives are ruled out because of their socialisation. It would be impossible to an American Protestant or an Iranian Shia Muslim to see Hindu worship of the Hindu Goddess Kali with her necklace of skulls as an alternative, but all might be attracted to a different system of meditation. But the dissatisfied Protestant brought up in a tradition of bare meeting places and a fundamentalist code of discipline might be attracted to the simpler dictates of Islam in their undecorated mosques.

Conversion to Christianity or even ascription by birth in cultures which have a long historical tradition of their ancestors as existing realities as would be the case in sub-Saharan Africa, China and Japan, make it unrealistic to expect such beliefs to be obliterated by conversion. So it is that Christian worship in such cultures have initiated devotional practices related to the souls of all the deceased in individual families souls rather than just all souls. For Chinese Catholics in Chicago there is a side altar devoted to these real presences and in Tanzania there is a basket on the altar in which the Sukuma can put the names of their ancestors which they wish to be remembered on All Souls Day.

It seems unlikely that the availability of more and varied religious alternatives are anything new. Dissatisfaction and need have always provided individuals and not just those with exceptional needs and abilities, with alternatives from their own creativity dictated by their emotional needs rather than their institutional availability.

What has been described as 'Sheilaisms' (Bellah *et al.*, 1985:47) after the American nurse who stated that she was religious but had no specific affiliations, is nothing new as it has always been a feature of traditional faiths which did not have the institutional permanency enabled from literacy so that their demand centred rituals are always different within the thinking that they are permanent. It seems likely that what Bellah calls 'expressive individualism' has always been a feature of individual spirituality in both imagination and its symbolic forms which makes working misunderstandings probable and more religiously acceptable.

The Unsettled Nature of Religious Practices

A settled belief and *its* supported practices is a reasonable possibility in societies which are socially settled and have been so for a number of generations such as the American Amish with their distinctive farming lives. In their case it is attractive to expect religious and social stability and to a certain extent they have been able to maintain an enviable pattern of successful living clearly attributable to the practicalities of their religious devotion. There has been such influences as mobile phones and the rise in the price of petrol which have provided strains and as well as support for their ways of living.

However, settled lives in ambiguous sense are a social and philosophical fiction produced by institutionalisation of some dominant features of urban and industrial life with its factories and schools and the scientific need to find quantifiable facts. Within the overemphasis of regularity in social science thinking, no one's life has ever been so regular as to establish it as a framework for thinking and behaviour within which a settled and overall pattern of specific religiousness can be established. Individuals may even have the idea of the stability of their thoughts and practices but that is similarly a self-sustaining and useful illusion.

It often seems that there is an underlying similarity between the practices of public religion and private spirituality in less economically developed societies and those of individuals in highly developed urban and industrial ones. The need for these and the accompanying metaphysical thinking are very much reactions to experience within the parameters provided by socialisation and the immediate environment. The use of the saints in Christianity, gods and goddesses in Hinduism and Taoism, ghosts in Vietnam and Japan and spirits and ancestors in sub-Saharan Africa.

The theological background to these beliefs and practices may have little to do with what people do within these paradigms. Their practices may have little functional difference to the requirements of household and daily work maintenance (Wuthnow, 1989). In all types of societies these spiritual entities have settled 'homes' but this aspect is not much used except for teaching about faith in literate religions and for most people not much more can be obtained from them except disparate and plausible data from persistent questioning. The answer that a person is a member of a particular faith is a rather modern reply to a bureaucratic question which would be more properly answered by what they do in times of adversity which is outside the normalities of social solutions.

One is struck by the fact that the 'newer' forms of religious practice in Western societies emphasise looser connections, diversity and negotiation with practical activity taken precedence over organisational position and rules so that symbolic messages and their individual interpretations prevail. Institutionally they do not carry out tasks but engage in performance and they do not speak about status or roles but talk about searching among options and presenting themselves in the best light (DiMaggio and Powell, 1991). These evaluations of trends in American religious practices seem comparable to those of the millions of Tanzanian Nyamwezi and Sukuma who do not have nor never have had any organised religion but they do have regular performances involving the spiritual in which the observer would be struck by the informality of these formalities; their almost do-it-yourself nature. No one involved in their ceremonies could explain what they have been doing and why except that this was what they feel as what they have always done which in analysis are working misunderstandings.

4
The Pragmatics of Religious Practice

Once religion became a separate and isolatable category of professionalized understandings it has tended to become a specialised form of thinking and behaviour dominated by detached thinkers, theologians, politicians and social scientists who keep religious ideas and behaviour under these theoretically distinct and isolatable categories. This obscures the fact that this approach and pattern of understanding is seemingly allied to and possibly confined to a particular ways of thinking in Western societies and in the three religions of the book.

For the rest of the world, the overwhelming majority in population totals, religious practices and the thought have developed from their ways of reacting to and relieving the immediacies of human anxieties and difficulties. Whatever may have been the possible ethological background to religious practices, it is these immediate needs which have dominated the practicalities of religious behaviour rather than eschatological issues.

There is always the problem that in the professionalization and intellectualisation of religious doctrine some religions have been less able to cope with the pragmatics of distress of their followers. In Malaysia there is an almost universal belief that malignant spiritual forces are responsible for personal misfortunes and that exorcism is necessary to rectify these situations by traditional healers. The Protestants have felt unable to react to this by accepting this reality while the Roman Catholics have allowed priests to exorcise this defined malignancy. The problem is now that priests are few in numbers and it has been left to lay Catholic Pentecostalists to carry out the frequent requests for exorcisms (Ackerman, 1981). In this situation the Catholic hierarchy are caught between specialist theological thinking and popular needs in their reacting to a very general form of distress popularly experienced as a reality.

Contemporary religious behaviour in any broad and humane understanding of the term should be seen in the context of the overarching shadows of new as well as old and inevitable widespread uncertainties. These are far beyond the control of individuals who may have folk memories of a more stable past for whom the politically and mass media propagated hopes of social development are now sensed as never likely to happen (Ferguson, 1999:165).

The Intellectualisation of Religious Understanding

We can assume that in traditional pre-literate societies the consumers of religious practices perhaps rather more than its ideas occurred within the paradigms furthered by their priests, shamans and diviners, so that they more or less got what they wanted. We can assume that neither preceded the other. People had difficulties which they could not deal with themselves and these specialists evolved to reduce these misfortunes. This was a simultaneous social process in tandem in which the latter provoked the former into seeing the possible advantages of their ideas and services. Seeking the origins of religion may be a pointless exercise in intellectual ingenuity.

We can presuppose that there has been a constant process of change, a reshuffling of hopes and opportunities to which individuals have dialectically responded. We know from history that there has been the repetitive appearance of new cults and sects some of which have grown into religions which have often foundered because of the restrictions of their own dogmatism and their limited social fit. It may be that the survival of any religion depends on covert uncontrollable adjustments rather than on overt authorised changes.

The systems and practices that survived were the ones which gave a general sense of satisfaction to enough people in that society. To give the title 'popular' to this general consensus is to downgrade the breadth of any system's intellectual coverage and it is this comprehensiveness which should be accepted. The intellectuals, the clever men and women who have always existed in every society have tended to personalize the dialectics of change. There are always thinkers in advance of the current pragmatisms of their societies who are prominent in producing new religious ideas in that social context. So-called primitives have as just as many possibilities of original thought as the most civilised of thinkers. History is sprinkled with their social and religious successes and failures.

The point has been made (Dronen, 2006) that there are parallels between Kuhn's idea that there are ground-swell changes in scientific paradigms and similar processes in religious thought. This has been suggested in Ninian Smart's mainstream of religions or world views as sets of beliefs and ideas, ways of approach which would be limited by transcendent and ontological dogma. This is illustrated by conversion as a long-term process rather than a blinding flash of change.

The surviving systems and practices were the ones that dealt with the immediate micro-problems of individuals rather more than the macro ones of communities, which may have temporarily unified people with divergent interests. The local specialists, the ever-present opportunist intellectuals whatever the source of their inspiration, usually did not go too far from what the people in need wanted, so that the explanations that they provided coincided with popular thinking. These contemporary religious practitioners who have little use or need for literacy and the examination of the writings of past thinkers, test out their solutions with their 'patients' and the people on whom they depend or depend on them so that the practicalities of their particular faiths inch forward in tandem with the support of local public opinion.

This was the integrated situation which must have existed for many millennia in which subsistence, the factor of assisting survival, must have been the dominant factor. All along thinkers who lived in their communities must have had ideas which they tested orally whenever the occasion arose. The paradigm shifts may not have occurred because of the intellectual cohesion of newly presented ideas but that some ideas caught on because they may have been explanatorily useful. More importantly these communities found that some of what was proposed was successful and some not. Whether these results were proto-scientific by accident or not, their placebo reality came to be accepted as social fact.

It could be that there has always been a preference in reacting to misfortune to do something practical rather than the passivity of acceptance and thought. Hence, the global extent of orthopraxis, the performance of ritual and the parallel predominance of highly adaptable and vague ideas on causation because any personal event had to be assessed in that social environment. In fact, the overall reality of working misunderstandings from the point of view of intellectualised theology.

Turner in his sympathetic portrayal of Muchona the Hornet, the Ndembu diviner who talked freely to this stranger about the restrictive social realities of his profession just as Kabadi the Sukuma diviner talked about the ins and outs of his work with a sceptical twinkle in his eye. But in their dealings with their clients they would never indulge in such socially dangerous digressions which would have undercut their professional standing and its mystical connections. In all societies there has always been a nucleus of sceptics whose views drifted into their societies and led to change. The diviners and priests are aware of public opinion and they have usually changed their approaches to coincide with what could be described as popularity.

But as the centuries passed and increasingly with printing rather than the literacy limited to a self and a socially segregated elite, the whole field of religious understandings in the West rather than the East became dominated by patterns of theological thinking and behaviour which appeared to set on one side the immediate needs of believers. Rather generally and more intensely in the last hundred years there has been an increase in the distinction between what people want, defined as 'popular' and what is given as theologically and ethically correct.

Not only in Christianity but also in Islam there has been an enormous growth in directive rather than reactive literature. There is little or no mention of the patterns of private as much as public religious behaviour which people use when they are in specific difficulties or find supportive in the generalities of anxiety. The lessons which could be drawn from the changes in popular devotions which were forced out of institutional practice by the European Reformation (Duffy, 1992) and correlate to the progressive decline in attendance at public ceremonies has not been learnt by theologians despite the increase in many forms of orthopraxis. An example would be the Jesuit priest in Bolivia who refused to carry out any public celebration of the Mass as he considers that the local Aymara Indians had only a magical conception of what is happening in that liturgy and the American priest who refused to pray for rain on behalf of the Sukuma as he was not a meteorologist. Yet there is ample evidence of the popularity of religious ritual; the growth in the numbers going on pilgrimages related to miracles, the *mantra* form of predominant prayer, the lighting of candles, processions and the public veneration of images and tombs. Religious behaviour has always been in constant adjustment to the needs of their constituents within the parameters of individualism and public opinion.

Popular Religion

Any study of popular religion almost inevitably starts from a number of top-down assumptions. The words popular religion and indeed spirituality have a range of semantic understandings which do not travel well not only between cultures but even within societies because of levels in intellectual capacity and theological knowledge. Whatever uses are made of these words it is usually done without any working out of predefinitions, or how these words are understood by the people to whom they are being applied with whom they may not have any shared social and religious understandings. In practical terms it decides in some ways how the researchers and thinkers in general are going to view activities which they associate with these words.

The distinction between elitist patterns of thought and popular religion dates back many centuries and certainly antedates 'modern' Christian theological anxieties on this issue. The Chinese philosopher Hsun-Tzu who died in the third century of the Christian era discussing the rites for the dead (Watson, 1963:110) made the distinction that 'among gentlemen they are taken as the way of man but among the common people they are taken as matters involving demons'. This is not so different to current Chinese views on popular religion taken by the intellectual elite as the spirituality of the rabble which allows the elite not to participate in such rituals as an acceptable much less a necessary part of their spirituality (Chan 1953. Chap. 4).

While many of the great works relating to religion are highly abstract some indeed carry orthopraxis into areas which Christians in general and not just theologians would consider not only irrelevant but quite distasteful. Westerners in thinking and reading about Islamic spirituality do not expect to find rules for lavatory use and the avoidance of the use of the left hand in many activities associated with religion. The writer has been asked on occasions in East Africa whether he was a Christian as he had been seen to cross himself with his left hand. Any researcher into religious behaviour is almost inevitably forced to confront the inevitability of ritualism about which the practitioners have in general given little explanatory thought almost as if it was unnecessary.

Attaching the word 'popular' to any religious activity immediately leads to its loss of intellectual status and any serious religious attributions. All connected activities have been immediately moved down-market so that medals and devotional objects generally are seen as religious junk without regard for their serious functions for the individuals possessing them. These functions are not seen as necessitating positive theological thinking rather than just providing opportunities for some implicit tolerance.

An example of the diminishment of popular religious activities is provided by a Christian fundamental statement (Pastor, 1994) that 'the phenomenology of popular religion may be regarded merely as the expression of a quest for existential security on the part of the popular classes in the face of a cultural and social situation of misery and backwardness'. There is no suggestion in this modern statement as to the possibility that such theological thinkers are missing the point that these seemingly commonplace religious activities is the behaviour which should be woven into substantive theological thought as religious realities.

It is not so much that popular religion has always co-existed with literate orthodoxies between which there has been peripheral dialectical interaction but that the former predates the latter out of which it has grown in detachment from the actualities in which the former developed.

Humans have always been functionally aware of the extent to which their activities are efficient enough to be worth continuing. Surely there is little reason to suppose that the approach of any culture to religious practices are any less or more subject to quasi-rational assessment than any other. What may have happened that in subsistence societies the range of occupationally related anxieties is limited as even chiefs and diviners have to farm; in such situations popular religion has to have a flexibility related to this limited occupational range.

As societies move up the occupational developmental ladder the anxieties may be broadly the same as related to death, disease and natural disasters, but they become not so much individually based which they have been all along while being disguised by communality but occupationally diverse. The British Census classification of occupations lists over ten thousand categories which are said to exist in British society, each of which are likely to have their particular anxieties, while the Bangladeshi or Bantu farmer would have in their communities no more than fifty different occupations about which anxieties can develop.

The binary foundation of rituals in subsistence cultures can no longer function. Individuality can no longer have its anxieties adequately catered for within neighbourhood categorisations. The result is that individuals develop their own popular rituals in personalised combinations, which go beyond the simpler individual rituals which preceded them.

It is not so much a theological struggle between literate elitism and popular sentimentality but the need for a simpler approach to what is shown in all religious behaviour rather than to concentrate on thought whether in literate institutions or non-literate traditionalism or personally created rituals. These popular pieties have the basic characteristics of being both direct and simple and are more or less aiding the search for enhanced functional ability to survive as long as rationally possible.

Of course, it may be possible to show that the millions who go on the Hajj to Mecca, Lourdes, Compostella and Banaras are not particularly intellectually distinctive nor conspicuously literate or well-versed in the theologies of their faiths, but this may not be the most important issue. What people do in their private ritualised spiritualities is by choice rather than by obligation. The fact is that unnumbered millions choose to spend time, money and hope in popular religious activities and that it is done to a large extent outside the institutional parameters of orthodoxy.

The Basic Reciprocity in Religious Behaviour

Religious thinking flourishes on theological abstractions which in practice usually have little relationship to what people actually do rather than think in any religious context. People whether they are from Paris or Peru in their religious actions assume that they can create and indeed maintain a reciprocal relationship with some aspects of the supernatural. They do not so much imagine but actively create a metaphysical relationship which mirrors their understandings of how their own social relationships can be created with people from whom they are socially distant. This relationship is only counterintuitive to a limited extent (Barrett, J.L., 1998).

It is not surprising, therefore, that in most religions at whatever level of sophistication, there is little attention paid to God as the ultimate religious source. People prefer to deal with lesser divinities who have personal characteristics which can be mirrored in their own social understandings. Named spiritual forces with whom they have shared local experiences, the patron saints of occupations and localities and the gods, goddesses and spirits assumed to have some shared interests in social continuations and not who are located in their neighbourhood.

People do not feel that these supernatural powers will do anything out of disinterested benevolence or indeed malevolence. The Chinese see the divine order as replicating their national bureaucratic system and should be treated in the same way by creating reciprocities which establish reasons for their help to be provided. Sacrifices and the performance of rituals create these necessary reciprocal links.

The Need for Redefinitions for Ubiquitous Religious Practices

Magic is a word loaded with definitions and practices which clash with theological thought when it is used to describe occult procedures attempting to control events; the procedures that footballers carry out to insure success for which there are behavioural parallels in every society for every activity between birth and death. A common approach is to divide religion and magic and to see the former as a development from the latter, more intellectually acceptable but still of little theological relevance.

A less predetermined approach would be to accept that human behaviour is divided between a limited amount of pragmatic activities and a larger proportion which are not but with no clear division between them. It is in this wavering division that there lies the area of working misunderstandings between the high intellectual ideas of religion and the practicalities of survival.

This has to be looked at in another way by noting that the performance of so-called magic, personal and public rituals relating to the supernatural to obtain some benefits has always been and continues to be the overwhelming form of activity by which humans react to their difficulties at various levels of cultural sophistication. It was Geoffrey Gorer in studying the English character described it as a culture preoccupied with magic (Gorer, 1956). The range of astrological publications in the United States is said to exceed the number devoted to psychology. There is no definable division here between developed and under-developed societies and people who are well or less educated. If the primitive mind does exist it is as likely to be found in New York as New Guinea.

It might be prudent to exclude the word 'magic' in religious contexts and to merely state that most religious activities are aimed at obtaining some immediate results while only a minority of such activities are devoted to less immediate personal religious development within equally unpragmatic eschatological presuppositions.

It is sustained by the fact that such performances are understood at whatever intellectual and situational level they are carried out; do this and that will happen which in the absence of pre-definition is just as likely to be fulfilled as not. It is in fact quite a pragmatically sensible way to behave when there are no primary logical solutions available.

In terms of what is done and understood by people in what is derogatively called popular religious behaviour, theology could be described as a deviant activity; whether in Buddhism, Christianity. Hinduism and Islam, their orthodoxies are not in any clear way related to the relief of individual distress in its generalities other than the institutional charitable activities of Christians and Muslims. Theology would appear to be a normative deviance created by a few and understood and utilised by even fewer.

It would seem that all societies have various degrees of religious behavioural latency. Some have overt religious practices which are conformist to orthodox requirements as with the Wahabi dominance in Saudi Arabia and less obvious but nevertheless pervasive nature of caste in Hindu communities as there are no religious police in India to supervise conformity. However, for most people in most societies religion operates at two levels; background and rather vague feelings, the theoretical understandings which might correspond in some respect to theology and the bringing these feelings into the forefront of behaviour at conventionally accepted important occasions typically cyclical and linear rites of passage and in relation to the intermittent but inevitable crises of personal life; a distinction perhaps between thinking and doing (Barrett, J.L., 1998).

It seems incorrect that what is overwhelmingly the way that religion is practised which conforms to the Latin phrase *ex opere operato*, that the performance of religious rituals have consequences independent of the state of mind of the performer, should be categorised as theologically having secondary status.

How does one upgrade the understandings of African quasi-traditional and Hindu 'popular' religious activities when they are already been defined as magical regardless of the fact that believers in the major religions in Kandy, Kengtung and Kyoto carry out their rituals in the same way and in a similar frame of mind in believing that performance is more important than theological understandings. The contemporary urban Japanese who rings the temple gong to announce his arrival before making his petition, is behaving intuitively and logically not magically. If these less socially distant spirits have some human characteristics, this is indeed logical behaviour and not part of primitive superstitions.

There first has to be a recognition that there is not just one Western defined system of cognition which applies to pragmatics but other non-material ones which accept as reality rather than just as possibilities, that ancestors physically affect their descendents, just as do the 'hungry ghosts' of the improperly buried dead and aborted foetuses which are as real for the Japanese and Vietnamese as the influence of saints in Christianity and Islam.

Then there is this almost universal belief in every society at the practical level of primary thinking, that the performance of rituals without any preliminary mental adjustments, understandings of their theological background or even of the language used, are influential enough in their lives to justify their continuance. In the overwhelming quantity of such thought and practice in all societies and groups regardless of their economic status and assumed intellectual capacity. This is justification enough for some Western theological adjustments. Eastern thinkers with a less finite eschatology involving an infinite numbers of lives in which the rectification of behaviour can occur, are little concerned with the detached niceties of distinctions between magical and religious practices.

If we look at Hispanic Christian religiosity whether in southern Europe or Peru we find that in practice it is closer to the ideas and practices of sub-Saharan Africans than to the theological models which the decisions of the Vatican Second Council endeavoured to encourage (Icoza, 1987).

The dominance of popular devotions, signs and symbols, a mutual interest in *darshan*, the seeing and being seen by the personification of the divine in statues, pictures, holy places, amulets and particularly in the possessed. These incarnational ideas of the unity of body and spirit must be a commonplace activity and understanding in most societies (Rodriguez, 1994), particularly Eastern ones. Spirit possession tends to be slotted into psychiatric explanations rather than being accepted as one possibly extreme form of inspiration which might apply equally well to artists, poets as well as mystics.

It would be prudent to use a definition which overlaps the aridity of that implied by contemporary northern Christianity and to use one that refers not only to the Hispanic Christianity of Latin America which contemporary American bishops recognise as requiring different liturgies but to Eastern and traditional practices generally. "Spirituality for any group of people refers to the 'inner space' or internal spiritual processes that allows people to become in touch with themselves as 'believers'. It refers to the area of life where the divine spirit touches the human spirit where the redemption appears as the person recognises the transcendent in her or his own life" (Ramirez, 1985).

Thus, it would appear that the overwhelming use of religious understandings is in the performance of rituals which are considered to have valuable consequences if performed correctly with religious motivation and which maintains umbrella assurance of their intrinsic value. Functionally, there may be little difference between petitioning prayer and the sign on a house to prevent the Evil Eye in an Amish community.

The Demand and Provision Factor in Religion

Magic since it is predefined derogatively for much activity directed at the Divine enables theologians to dismiss much such behaviour as demeaning to their idealism. This puts on one side that there is a demand factor in all behaviour which is voluntary in terms of the choice from the forms of behaviours available within all societies and in human creativity. Pilgrimage sites do not advertise their religious potentiality. The number of pilgrims grows as public opinion, the grape vines of religious gossip, suggest that attendance has had these benign effects. There was no advertising campaign by some Hindu organisation which resulted in the seventy million who came to the last Kumbh Mela.

The need for some way of reducing anxiety and distress must be a human constant and the Dawkins thesis that humans are only a highly developed mammal species with a necessity for overall pragmatism, can have little appeal to anyone who is not a committed and possibly somewhat inhuman pragmatist.

Even in accepting that the dividing line between secular and religious behaviour and thinking is always variable and indeed may not exist, it would seem that the religious need to perform religious rites is more universal than to think about the predetermining theological abstractions. Pilgrimages to sacred places would appear to be as popular as it was a thousand years ago even allowing for the increasing ease of transport. At the turn of the last century the annual Hajj to Mecca drew less than a hundred thousand as opposed to a largely air-borne two million now. Similarly, the last astrologically determined Kumbh Mela to the Ganges drew an estimated seventy million of whom not all were Hindus. Modernity has allowed the expansion of such fulfilments of religious needs not their diminishment much less their extinction.

Many Africans are Christians for the regularities of their social lives but resort to a parallel and demand created contemporary practices which is not just a surviving traditionalism. There are enormous numbers of these quasi-traditional practitioners, proliferating in urban areas where distress is less conforming to traditional understandings. Some Tanzanian communities are almost all Christians such as the Haya to the west of lake Victoria while the Sukuma to the south have not been greatly attracted to beliefs and rituals of either priest-centred Christianity or priestless Islam after more than a century of contact. The Sukuma are a sensible and pragmatic people and more would surely moved to become Christians or Muslims if they had assessed any secular or religious advantages from doing so. It would seem that their existing socio-religious system has coincided with the requirements of modernity or adapted to changing conditions more effectively than it did for the nearby Haya to their west.

Very few societies develop and maintain destructive behaviour and there is a constant pattern of adjustment in both religious and secular behaviour according to the same canons of rationality; that in terms of cost-benefit analysis certain behaviours pay off. The Sukuma are as hard-headed as Mumbai financiers in how they manage their lives. The Malaysian Archbishop has in practice accepted that spiritual evil in a quasi-personal form exists and can be exorcised. Tanzanians almost universally believe in the social reality of witchcraft and that certain people can transmit evil to harm others. The Christian Churches hold that this is credulous and primitive thinking which leaves affected people of necessity to take their own actions which in the case of the Sukuma led recently to the mass murder of more than two thousand suspected witches and wizards (Mesaki, 1992).

There is also the reality that for the Roman Catholic church in south India to enforce the abolition of caste in their public rites including cemeteries which priests are now obligated to do, would be to empty their churches. It remains a moral aim to which any sensible priest is going to refer to obliquely rather than to attempt its overt regulation in advance of public opinion in the surrounding parish society. Crude as it may be to see the believers in any religion as customers, this is what they are both in private spirituality in which they have always largely gone their own way and public rituals involving the expenditure of time and effort when there are so many alternatives accidentally rather than deliberately available.

A Scale of Religious Correctness

In terms of the frequency theological correctness is a pyramid with an enormously broad base of failure to conform but in terms of religious activities that parallel these high standards the pyramid is turned up side down. An enormous amount of activity at the base connected to some form of the Divine, entities which cannot be said to pragmatically exist, but which humans feel necessary to address with the rituals of private spirituality and public religion.

These two disparate sets of values are not so much the creation of immature and disorderly thinking but of the trained professionals both secular and religious who make these distinctions. It is doubtful whether the petitioners at the shrines of any religion make this distinction. It is a scale that appears to demean the popular and reactive behaviour of whole populations not just a majority, to create a supra-personal order in their lives and to petition for the help that they need to diminish the distresses in their lives.

If religious behaviour can be evaluated in terms of what believers want and what they actually do as a consequence of their beliefs, then this inverted pyramid is how the religious practices of nominally Buddhist, Christian and Hindu people should be considered as well as those who create and practice their own personal religions, the 'Sheilaisms' of north America (Bellah *et al.*, 1985:221) which are just as common in sub-Saharan Africa and Singapore. The amulets that the men and women of Ngara, Tanzania wear under their clothes are individually created for individual needs as they do not come from any shop or institutionalised religious source (Tanner, 1975). Those worn in England are just as diverse but show only combinations of commercial products. There are parallels between the tattooing of Shan men in Myanmar and contemporary British soldiers.

A more bias free approach which avoids any distinctions between religion and magic, would be to divide data between what is required by the orthodoxies of institutionalised faiths and cultural insistencies which relate to the non-pragmatic long-term areas of behaviour; what people state that they do in these respects and what the social scientists may conclude that they actually in the short-term.

The Localization of Religious Needs

Religious behaviour centres on the needs of the individual and only expands to others when these primary needs and ideas have been inadequately dealt with and they have some shared communal misfortune such as a drought or they have the time, means and vocation to work for the good of others. For those to be involved beyond sight and sound connections there have to be magnified needs. A child's illness is a primary group anxiety, the illness of a wealthy family head involves many more and the absence of rain whole communities. In modernised societies there are few events that can religiously unify an urban neighbourhood when there would be a more general feeling that the state should come to their help.

Once forms of religious behaviour become not so much institutionalised but organised from writing, there is the inevitable split between what believers want and do and what they are required to do according to these static often ambiguous formalisations. Of course, some of these are explicit but the balance is more towards ambiguity and for most the effort of disentangling this for their needs is too difficult; hence local and individual ritual creativities.

This is not so much a failing to conform but that believers at whatever level of intellectual understandings act in particular culturally restricted ways without necessarily working out in advance what they might do. Any society provides guidelines, parameters within which people think and behave but how this operates depends on individuality, location and circumstances. There is little that can be classified as permanent in the fluctuating mixtures of conflicting factors.

This suggests that the particular forms of religious understanding and behaviour within the minds of a Burmese Buddhist taxi driver in Yangon would not necessarily be the same for someone in the same occupation in Mandalay or in northern Myitkyina. Each will believe personally that their work is under the influence of the spirits *nats* of Burmese cosmology, but which *nat* and what influence this has will depend on their domestic lives, their experience of accidents, their driving and hours of work.

Taking the parallel of drivers in Mumbai, Manchester and Manila, most have objects in their vehicles to bring good luck and to prevent accidents. The annual 'blessing' of vehicles in Japan has become so popular that some temples specialise in this and arrange mass rituals for cars (Ohnuki-Tierney, 1984).

These are certainly examples of religious behaviour which can be boxed to represent particular meanings and anxieties but there can be little doubt that when any practices which have been grouped are examined more closely, we find the localisation and individuality of all types of religious behaviour. What *A* does in location *B* under needs *C* will be different to what *D* does even though they appear to be doing the same thing as far as outside observers can conclude. This is the result of their necessary process of simplifying data on behaviour to make analysis possible by the exclusion of individualising factors too difficult to identify and codify.

This process of individualisation and localization is not just a factor of particular relevance to those in Western societies who are more ostensibly individualised by the surrounding political and social understandings and by urban and industrialising conditions, but a universal one. The avoidance of accepting that there will be similar understandings in Cambodian, Zuni and Zulu communities if only because those living there are just as varying in how they behave and what they experience as those who live in New York or Nuremburg. It is this individuality in covert rather more than overt religious behaviour which makes misunderstandings inevitable.

The Development of Chinese Propitious Positioning

Since the relaxation of the Communist embargo on 'feudal superstitions' there has been an increase in religious activities in the building or rebuilding of ancestors halls, Daoist temples, Christian churches and Islamic mosques. The forty year gap in which public religious behaviour was forcibly discouraged has left many of these religious groups without professional religious leadership. Yet out of the past has re-emerged much that are essentially Chinese patterns of thinking established centuries before the Communist ideology arrived.

An example of this would be the Chinese have belief for at least two millennia that the fortunes of individuals, families, businesses and communities could be assured if their living sites were adapted to the local currents of cosmic breath *chi*. To put this into practice constitutes the 'pseudo' science of *feng-shui*, the art of adjusting the features of the cultural landscape so as to minimize adverse influences and maximize advantages from a favourable conjugation of form. This is defined as 'the art of adapting the residences of the living and the dead so as to cooperate and harmonize with the local currents of the cosmic breath' (Chatley, 1917:45).

Expertise of diviners was of crucial importance in the sitting of the houses of the living and the tombs of the dead, so that no city was ever planned without the advice of a geomancer (Wheatley, 1971:419). Although no new cities have been created, it is clear that existing buildings in Beijing and Xian follow original orientations of those cities. The curved lines of Chinese gardens were designed to break hostile force lines. The commercial success of Hong Kong has been attributed to the urban planning of the British with earth banks, curved roads and groves of trees. It seems likely that when they are given the opportunity to choose the position of a house and its more important contents, it will be done in accordance with the advice of a geomancer.

Above all graves should be located in auspicious and favourable surroundings so that a benign spiritual heredity would extend to the children of the dead (Porter, 1920). It can be assumed that geomancers are employed by all but the poorest of families and during the Republic although without systematic training they were licensed and were responsible for determining the cause of death (Naquin, 1988:50).

The central cultural belief is that *feng-shui* has the topographical force of nature used for the benefit of mankind (Rawski, 1985:23.33). It also has the practical advantage of not involving a moral code which has added to its contemporary popularity.

The placing of graves is both a complex and expensive procedure and becoming a noted ancestor may have occurred in part by the dead enjoying an excellent *feng-shui* placement. It would involve competing with one's neighbours and for making statements about political alignments. In contemporary China in the Hong Kong region *feng-shui* laws been affected by enormous changes in the landscape where neighbouring buildings block the flow of wind and water around and through the tomb. Now that the tomb is both a political and religious symbol *feng-shui* cannot easily be abandoned (Watson, 1958:215-6).

During the peak of the Communist policy of communal farms, there were restrictions on the burying of family dead in agricultural land and the destruction of graves. With the growth of individually permitted individual farming on long leases, graves chosen by geomancers are reappearing in fields (Whyte, 1988:301). It is necessary to ask how long it will take for the dead to reoccupy the land so recently reoccupied by individual families (Hinton, 1983:764). In China today the *feng-shui* specialist is consulted over the construction of offices and hotels. Apart from planning restrictions *feng-shui* probably adds a further restraint against villagers from making unwise ecological decisions (Fan, 1993:45).

The geomancer works with an astrological magnetic compass centred in disc inscribed with concentric circles and a variety of symbols. It has retained its importance throughout the Mandarin speaking world and it is a well-established form of localised religious practices. *Feng shui* is a widely used system of adjustment to undefined spiritual forces in which the specialist works from a store of culturally inherited symbolic knowledge which they can interpret within the pragmatics of particular social realities with which they are confronted. They cannot just order that a block of offices should be reoriented but they are able to break the lines of disorderly *chi* in other ways. It is a highly adaptive system in which these specialists have the intellectual and religious ability to devise solutions which appear to provide their clients with some peace of mind. It is not a system of working misunderstandings as there is a conformity between the ambiguities of the indefinable concept and the ambiguity of its interpretations.

The Range of Adaptation

In Japan temples are virtually independent religious and economic units in which the resident priests are dependent for their own survival and the survival of their temples on attracting custom, the users. We see in many temples a combination of religious provisions such as concentrating on the social needs of the increasingly isolated elderly and their wishes for a death which will not involve dependency straining the economic and physical resources of their small families. Temple 'owners' combine these religious needs and their accentuation of the success of their particularised rituals with the economic opportunities for selling special goods. The equivalent of gift shops in churches.

In Ghana the Pentecostalist churches have reacted to the uncertainties in the lives of middle aged women without male support and the career anxieties of the new middle classes by providing appropriate relieving ceremonies. They have enabled a break with the old gods and with contemporary witchcraft for which the 'missionary' churches have failed to provide any effective response (Meyer, 1998) because they failed to accept such things as demonic control and spirit possession to be realities requiring effective and immediate help.

A parallel situation seems to have developed in the Netherlands where the Churches are tied to theological frameworks which do not allow for responsive change to help immediate needs. On the one hand, there is the diminishing attendance for church based ceremonies and a partial move into New Age cults church based ceremonies (Houthn and Mascini, 2002).

It is perhaps too easy to elevate religious issues into complex theological interpretations. The needs of ordinary people may be now as has always been the case that religious truth requires a relationship to personal experience. A more inward need to do something in response to distress; lighting a candle or incense sticks is immediately effective just as going on as pilgrimage is an effective act whatever the usually post-hoc reasoning may be. It would seem that theology in its institutional framework and its cementing in written documents, is not the medium for any rapid response to personal distress however widespread its forms may be.

The Realities of Survival

The answer to the significance of religion may be that individuals consciously or unconsciously recognise that there are opposed viewpoints on the reality of their lives. On the one hand, there is biological extinction in which their place and behaviour is no different to that of any other animal and which for some is a dreadful conviction as John Wesley, the Christian innovator who wrote 'if I have a fear it is not a falling into hell but of falling into nothing' (Weslsey, 1766) which would not apply to Buddhist and Hindus with their concepts of endless rebirths which certainly reduces the fears that death as total extinction. This fear of nullity is expressed even more poignantly by those who have had near death experiences (Blackmore, 1993).

The opposing viewpoint is that each individual has some part of a continuing existence which comes as part of their religious beliefs which tells them that they do not face extinction. Whatever the firmness or the laxity of their beliefs this is an immensely reassuring possibility. Religions provide for their believers a reduced fear of death not only with their ideas of after death existence but in their provisions of an orderly series of rituals to account for the passage through life (Reynolds and Tanner, 1983;174). This is particularly so in Eastern religions with their belief in a succession of lives providing opportunities for existential improvement.

While of course everyone expects to die it is not a matter of any immediacy but what is immediate are the distresses which faces everyone in the here and now. Even in societies which provide in their comprehensive social welfare systems for a proportion of these misfortunes, it is bound to be an inadequate coverage because of the individual range and quantity of what can go wrong.

Social welfare systems are the material manifestations of institutions which have ever lengthening rule books. It is not that they mean to be insensitive but bureaucracies are impersonal and centred on records and systematized payments and assessments. Other than paper there are no connections between providers and receivers; only in extreme cases are there person to person relationships. Consolation and emotional support in the vacuum of isolation can be provided by ways of thinking and behaving which can be personally initiated and for whom they have an existential reality. The multi-layering and many faced nature of religions as personally interpreted provide this in working misunderstandings; it is an uncritical reciprocal silence.

Religions at all levels and in all varieties provide individuals with ways out of distress which at a minimum provides them with procedures of psychological amelioration. Some religions have set procedures for this and others while failing to recognise any obligations to sustain an individual socially at least allows them without recrimination to create an unorthodox religious system which has occurred among the Buddhists of Myanmar (Spiro, 1967).

The Individual Nature of Needs

The acquiring of knowledge about individuality is both a necessity and one loaded with difficulties as whatever the methodology used there can be little accuracy of the information obtained from what are interpersonal relationships between social strangers. A detailed study of the philosophy of a single elderly Navaho is certainly a *tour de force* (Ladd, 1957) but it is an act of professional faith to assume that it has any general application beyond what must have been a very personal relationship and on the part of the researcher an imaginative one in the leaps of theoretical understandings between intellectuals of very different cultures.

The fact that a famine is a matter of widespread distress and yet it can be seen realistically as a whole series of individual miseries and disasters. Many Indians fled from Burma in front of the Japanese advance in 1942 and died of hunger in the mountains; a family that stayed together usually died together but a husband and one child had they gone on alone might have survived. In those cases it is their individual moral interpretations that killed them.

Distress can be categorised in general terms but it is always an individual experience in which religion as a resource will be individually interpreted and utilised. While the religions may see their objectives in abstract terms of moral goodness this may only be possible when economic surpluses permit. Certainly there are a moral elites who practice what they preach from martyrdom to the maintaining of international charities on the ground. Thinkers whose livelihoods are assured will assess needs and patterns differently to those who do not have this security.

For the vast majority it is not so much a question of misunderstanding the religious message which makes misinterpretations obvious but the realities of subsistence living whether in the countryside or in urban slums. The term 'rice Christians' for early Chinese converts in the face of persistent famines and the early availability of missions to feed converts but their descendents survived as Christians despite Communist persecution and the expulsion of foreign missionaries. It could be that misunderstandings of the religious message is related to Maslow's hierarchy of needs and has an almost seasonal and situational occurrence.

People who live in marginal communities depending on the weather, their relatives and their individually created networks of reciprocities are extremely long sighted in the arrangements that they may be able to make. In this it is not a question of misunderstanding the religious message but of understanding it all too clearly. The distressed Nuer man who downgraded the value of his sacrificial offerings because there had been no adequate return on his earlier expensive attempts to get help from *kwoth* is an example of widespread religious rationality. It seems likely that most people apply the principles of profit and loss to their religious involvements as they do to their material affairs.

In this respect it is wrong to see African and Asian subsistence farmers as all that much different to Europeans. The Sukuma family in difficulties which a diviner has divined, is making a necessary propitiation ceremony rather than one which is advisable, so that family members attending in proportion to their interests; women would attend in their agnatic relationships and not because of marrying into the distressed family. Of course, there is the attraction of a 'free' meal but even that availability will be in proportion to the size of the problem. An ancestor problem involving the sacrifice of a chicken is not likely to be seen as serious enough to bring together many extended family members as one that might have involved in the sacrificing of a bullock.

What makes it difficult to understand about the reality of this individualism is that it occurs in the social context of a relatively tight community in which individuality has to be disguised by public conformity however nominal. Whereas in the developed world self-interest is open and blatant, the reverse in so-called traditional societies is disguised by social finesse; necessary no doubt when an individual is known to have had visibly a good harvest and a herd of goats but success has to be just as circumspect when he comes to spend the money which he has hidden in his house or in a bank.

It is mistaken to see the extended family as a social welfare support organisation as relatives may only help when it is to the advantage to do so; quarrels between siblings over the distribution of inheritance is perhaps a cultural universal. But increasingly relatives in urban and industrial communities have 'touch and go' relationships and are less likely to feel any obligation to provide support. However, it is hard to imagine a patriarchal Chinese family in Penang which meets weekly in the house of the family head, not reacting to the personal crises of any family member without providing judicious material and religious support.

Even when there are community wide distresses over drought, it is still experienced in individual terms and coped with individually. Rain continues to be a preoccupation of subsistence farmers and the absence or delay in the blanket rain of a monsoon with perhaps national prayers for rain as would have happened in the recent prolonged East African drought, a combination of meteorology and religion. But in the central areas of Tanzania rain is often sporadic and local so that it may fall on certain farms and not on others not far away; a communal rain-making ceremony would disguise the fact that it is a collection of individually based petitions; my farm before that of my neighbours to whom I am not related but a sprinkle on the fields of my brothers.

The response to a general need for rain would have been in the hands of the chief who is responsible in the abstract for the religiously base welfare of his community. In Ushambaa, Tanzania when rain falls on one hillside but not on another recourse would have been made to the chief who had an overall distributive responsibility but then they were abolished by the one-party government who saw their powers as not only tainted by traditionalism and the indirect rule of colonialism but as an indirect challenge to their pragmatic bureaucratic political system (Feierman, 1990). This resulted in the emergence of a new group of rain-makers responding to an opportunity but they did not have the quasi-traditional legitimacy necessary to authenticate their activities. Missionary priest have often been reluctant to pray for rain because of its magical associations. So rain-making will in practice occur as a covert activity in reaction to personal as much as communal distress with its aggressive element of attempting to obtain some form of finite advantage at the expense of others whereas previously it was the responsibility of the chief to provide such ritual reassurances.

The Simplicity of Religious Needs

Both the secular and theological researchers into religious ideas and behaviour by the nature of their training and intellectualism tend to approach the thinking of thoseless intellectual than themselves from the written standards of the major systems of thought. They assess the activities of more ordinary people as falling short of the standards to which they themselves aspire rather more than relative to their own personal experiences.

While this is a legitimate approach it is one that focuses on a minority of what might be called thinking believers and only covers a small proportion of religious practices. It is perhaps more prudent to start with the assessment of what we have already suggested, are the more commonplace activities which relate to the divine.

People use the forms of religious behaviour which they have either personally created or have been institutionally provided for particular purposes. This behaviour which can be divided on a scale between reactions to immediate difficulties, the praying for a particular narrow purpose and at the other end of such a scale involving themselves in very long-term complicated attempts to reach specialised spiritual levels and eschatological salvation which can be seen in the social isolation of orthodox Jains who cannot move without insuring that they are not killing any living thing.

The primary purposes behind any particular religious act may be difficult to find out both because there will always have been multiple factors and the principal ones may be thought to be discreditable; to pray for the recovery of a sick relative or not to be killed in war are acceptable but not for winning the national lottery which must certainly be a common enough objective of prayer. Success in many areas of human endeavour has to be at the expense of others. In Taiwan with its predominance of small businesses there are cults which are dedicated to obtaining success over rivals.

The secondary purposes of religious activities are clear enough in the petitions for prayers pinned on the bulletin boards of many churches as in sacred shrines such as the Meiji temple in central Tokyo and on the branches of sacred trees in Greece. These are selfish requests which may not fit in with the orthodoxies of their faiths and so are requested anonymously.

The Crusade of Prayer run by the Cenacle Sisters in Britain received many thousand requests for prayers of which the vast majority were for the illness of other persons connected to the writers. These are practices which fit into Christian orthodoxies and so are publicly and individually made; they receive an acknowledgement of their requests from both these Sisters and from the proportional success of their petitions.

Finally, purposes in which individuals pray for abstract aims such as world peace or the victims of disasters with which they have no material or emotional connections and it is these that perhaps may dominate in theological thinking as without any question they are both morally deserving and impersonal and so are safe from criticism but there can be no assessment of their value as such aims as for example world peace have no pragmatic hopes of achievement.

These are artificial categorizations created by the social sciences, they are not realistic divisions. Most religious activities involve all three categories at the same time or in some sequential order either before or after the actual overt behaviour whether we are considering subsistence farmers in Myanmar, slum dwellers in Mexico City or professional men and women in Manchester or Mumbai.

The purpose of propitiation ceremonies in many quasi-traditional societies is the relief of misfortune which has been personally experienced by the person who has initiated the divination enquiry. However, people live in primary groups and those are usually part of extended families so it is likely that the person's misfortunes will be inseparable from the people with whom they live and on whom they are interdependent. In a study of a Buddhist temple in Japan which received the prayers of the elderly for which for 90 per cent were for an early death so that they would not become bed-ridden and a burden to the fewer relatives now available because of the declining birth-rate (Woss, 1993:195).

Even in contemporary more individualistic cultural systems in which people live in so-called isolated nuclear families, it would be difficult to divide their interests from whom they are clear related biologically and socially, At the macro-social level the prayers to the Hindu God Ganesh and Taiwanese spirits for business success are for the benefit of a family and at the expense of others.

But these divisions imposed in the analysis of the religious behaviour of others sets aside the basic fact that there is one unifying element. Almost universally it is believed that the carrying out of prescribed rituals will have the wanted effects irrespective of the personal religious and moral standing of those involved.

The Regularity of Rituals and Ritualism

Can we not presuppose that human ritual behaviour with its probable ethological base in the ritualistic behaviour of the higher non-human primates was both spontaneous and related to some immediacies. Further, that it has only recently become socially possible to have ceremonies repeated in more or less the same form by regulation required by the religions of the book rather than Eastern faiths. In fact this ritual what has become defined as religious behaviour has been a new practice largely created by specialists who are not in any fundamental sense sharing the individual religious needs of those for whom they carry out these ceremonies.

Regularity in the performance of religious rituals in traditional societies on the fringe of appearing regular since they conform to lunar and seasonal changes and the social necessities of changes through rites of passage which are themselves related to social as much as biological pressures. There can be no conformity of the rituals performed as it will always have been personal reactions to specific circumstances. Institutionally regularised ceremonies are on the other hand can be detached from such social motivations. Their advantages include the provision of a regular period of rest or irregular excitement in the monotonous regularity of farming and animal husbandry.

There will be rituals for both linear and cyclical rites of passage which will be contingent on social circumstances, the status of those involved and actions which just seem culturally appropriate at a particular time which people can attend but have no fixed procedures nor beginnings nor ends. They are regular in the sense that something like it coming under the same title has happened in the past and there is a cultural understanding that it will happen for which they have no explicit reasoning. For some ceremonies there is a build-up of social pressures as for the multiple circumcision ceremony at Kipumbwi for Muslim boys in which children were accumulating and to carry out such a ceremony for older children would be more expensive and less socially enhancing.

Similarly, the maintenance of contact with the family ancestors is irregular as the throwing of scrapes of food into the compound's ancestor shrine; the spirits of the water being placated by Sukuma fishermen spitting into the waters of Lake Victoria or Roman Catholics crossing themselves before the aircraft in which they are flying takes off. There is probably not much differences in the quasi-regularities of rituals among of Asian subsistence farmers and fishermen and factory workers in Singapore.

Any differences that appear would be due to the introduction of calendar rather than solar and lunar timings as well as literacy which has allowed religious institutions to formalize these ritualised occasions. Not so much that they ought to be carried out but that they should be done in a set form. Personal regularities have been exchanged on one level into depersonalized regularities at another in which participants have little ability to influence the form of these regularities except by absenting themselves or letting their thoughts wander into personally created working misunderstandings.

Thus, we have in the major religions what appears to be a compulsion towards exactness and regularity and to print this as the bases for a religiously necessary orthodoxy. This is paralleled in the way that the social sciences search for order and whether they exist or not to the extent that is envisaged, they find regularities, so it is regularity which they find in religious and social behaviour rather than the irregularities of individualism and personal need.

The difficulty may start with different understandings about the meaning of 'order' which may be specific to English and the Western sense of formalism derived from Greek philosophy and developed in the European Enlightenment; a form of behaviour which is both elitist and idealistic. It is certainly alien to the ways in which subsistence societies run their lives and has no part in the religious philosophies of the Eastern faiths.

The religious ceremonies of the Tanzanian Sukuma follow a sequence which is not in any sense predetermined and which follow their understandings of what should be done at that particular time. This may not and indeed will not be the same as allegedly similar ceremonies previously performed in the same locality; different people, different problems and different circumstances make for different rituals. Even if the Sukuma had written liturgies as those converted to Christianity would have available to them, the inputs would still be as different as those on whose behalf a Mass is carried out. Any sense of order disguises the fact that the inputs can never be the same whatever ritual similarities may occur.

Similarly Ssonjo ceremonies for their God Hambagao has young men but not older men or women becoming possessed and seemingly uncontrollable. It is not known in advance who is going to become possessed or how uncontrollable they will become. If there is order in these striking events it fringes on disorder.

In a ceremony in honour of a village God in south-east China (Dean, 1995) which will take several days and much longer in preparatory status related negotiations. Participation will involve mediums rushing about while possessed and Taoists pronouncing from their secret knowledge and specialised learning. There is similarly a sequence but a very loose presence of order; there is none in the Western sense of religious order.

However, is orderliness all that conspicuous in Western ceremonies. A recent Christmas morning Mass in a Roman Catholic suburban church was more disorderly than a Sukuma propitiation ceremony; there were constant disruptions from noisy children, people walked in late, the elderly were immobile and the priest's voice with loudspeakers varied from unintelligibility to periodic audibility.

In these types of ceremonies there were no more than sequences and a sense of anticipation. It would seem that the fact of individual distress and religious need is jumbled into what is interpreted as order without eliminating its disorderly base. Even the most orderly of ceremonies in which almost all eventualities have been thought out in advance such as the Coronation of a British monarch or a royal marriage celebration, nevertheless has every participant bringing to it a series of different thoughts and probably personal discomfort from the length of the ceremony.

Most people most of the time spend their lives materially and cognitively in a circumscribed social environment and they only have contacts with outsider influences intermittently and peripherally. Certainly they have 'touch and go' relationships with such people or their images on television. Most people without recognising it as a restriction have very few contacts that they could not anticipate in advance.

This way of living is as common in New York as in New Guinea invites the attribution of system. It is not a form of social life to which outsider cognitive styles can easily intrude except in the mythologies of explanation. An appendage of different intellectualisms provided by the poet or priest which has always been within the potential and available understandings of all societies.

However, when we examine social realities we find that it is in practice less of a system than the categorizations created by the social sciences. The Christian spiritual director or quasi-traditional spirit possessed diviner operate within broad paradigms within which there is substantial covert and overt negotiation. There are always negotiated elements in which these interpreters of the metaphysical will provide solutions which are in general acceptable to the individuals who consult them.

These lower order regularities (Rappaport, 1979) are always responding to a range of distinct and individual situations. There are always matters of concern to which individual religious behaviour is a partial response. Humans accept that they are always going to be individually subject to expected or unexpected distress. A whole range of situations which are normally expected to occur at sometime or another as well as abnormal events, even the mass sorrows of the Indonesian and Japanese tsunamis for residents, business people, tourists, fishermen and farmers was very much an individual experience; in this sense there is no distinction between a volcanic eruption and a motor accident.

Soft and hard orthodoxies can never react quickly enough to personal and communal distress without individuals creating their own responsive rituals within what they may feel to be their personally created orthodoxies within the parameters of the religious ideologies to which they think they belong. In such creations there will always be the working of misunderstandings of orthodoxies.

5
The Bases of Misunderstandings in Religion

Even allowing for the abstract nature of religious realities and its physical expression the three areas of misunderstanding are largely independent of each other and yet are a constant feature of both fields of thought and activity. Firstly, there are the misunderstandings created by institutionalisation and literacy. Then there are the misunderstandings of the social scientists and theologians who examine and comment on the religious ideas and behaviour of others rather than from their own experiences and personal understandings. Finally, there are the misunderstandings of individuals in relation to the dogmas of the faiths to which they belong and the socio-religious expectations of their social environments.

Working misunderstandings apply to whole range of secular and religious behaviour and institutions in which the ostensible primary functions are often modified or enabled by a range of secondary ones which are not recognised as a necessary part of what religious behaviour and its institutions set out to do. It is perhaps how any ideological systems is enabled to continue to function.

For a misunderstanding to occur there has to be something communicated sufficiently clearly for a misunderstanding to occur. Within societies which are predominantly non-literate at least as far as their religious understandings go, there may be few misunderstandings as the socio-religious principals around which the societies operate are paradigms which are indefinable and ambiguously utilisable. Sub-Saharan Africans have witchcraft and ancestors and the Chinese and Vietnamese have hungry ghosts. Within these paradigms the Tanzanian Sukuma propitiation ceremonies and anti-witchcraft precautions are in effect similar to do-it-yourself home improvements for modern Westerners.

The possibility of misunderstandings in such societies is minimal and perhaps confined to the few charismatic prophets who try to introduce culturally new religious ideas and practices.

In so-called literate societies in which a majority can read more efficiently than the sending and receiving of simple messages, the situation is different. These ideologically based organisations formulate their beliefs and lay down the requirements for membership. Individuals can define themselves as a Shia or Sunni Muslim, Mahayana Buddhist or a Seventh day Adventist so that now misunderstandings become an active possibility by their commitments into which they have placed themselves however nominally.

So we can conclude that in these societies which attract the attention of social scientists and theologians, the only orthodoxy may be created by their own categorizations and that these religious system work because misunderstandings cannot exist except in the thinking of the evaluating outsiders. To what extent are modern societies all that different when we go beyond the metropolitan faiths with their defined orthodoxies. The hinge for understandings and misunderstandings would be the element of institutionalisation of any beliefs and the degree to which these beliefs and practices have been institutionalised by literacy. A written dogma is an existential fact to which believers consciously or subconsciously react but not necessarily reproduce in their individual thoughts and practices.

The Misunderstanding within Religious Institutions

The institution keeps going while its constituent believers are not necessarily working for the same objectives. A common enough feature in large institutions such as a church is that at different levels of involvement there will be different understandings and misunderstandings. Any institution whether it is a monastery, school, military unit, civil service department or business have an official way of working and as well as unofficial system working within this. Further the attitudes and commitments of everyone involved will vary with demographic and personal factors as well as to inevitable reality of chance events and the formal structure of the institution. The Japanese recent pattern of lifetime commitment to a company with reciprocal obligations would not apply to membership of the Legio Maria Church in Kenya or in membership of a Sufi Brotherhood in Turkey.

Religious institutions have generalised objectives which are indefinable except in the case of specialised vocations such as care of the dying, the seriously handicapped, the training of the blind or lepers. The personnel have always to be motivated with status and salary satisfactions which is more difficult when there are no clearly defined objectives, although often there is an institutional safety net which guarantees lifetime employment and care in old age.

Although the religious institution does not have definable economic aims it has still many shared characteristics with secular ones which lead to conscious and unconscious misunderstanding about its religious objectives. However, loosely a religious organisation may be administered, it will have ranks, roles, rules and objectives, and above all it has to remain economically solvent. Its permanent staff have to be housed and fed as well as their old age and illnesses provided for and buildings have to be maintained. Charity is not self-financing and the difficulties of maintaining a missionary created superstructure with only national resources is a common factor in the voluntary organisations of newly independent states (Green, 1995. 2000).

Quasi-traditional societies have always had men and women who have shown that they had specialised links to the supernatural but they have always been responsible for their own subsistence and have been paid for their services according to their clients sense of the value of their advice by its results. There is no idea traditionally or in contemporary subsistence communities that it should pay for permanent religious specialists or their backing institutions when they may or may not have reasons to use them. The Christian churches retain a reputation for always wanting money to maintain plant and personnel which the laity have rarely felt any overall need to contribute to in the first place. Islam does not have this problem as the Imam at any mosque can be running a business and his relationship to the mosque is part-time and not related to the idea of commitment to a parish and its believers. By accident rather than design this pattern fits into traditional ideas of religious specialisation.

Religious organisations have ranked positions between the holders of which there will be misunderstandings as to their religious roles and certainly a disguised factor of acquired promotion. Even religious organisations which have broken away from Western support and created their own theologies still have this difficult framework to control. The Kimbanguist Church in Zaire has been influenced by the appearance there of the Salvation Army with its ranks, uniform and brass bands. The Vietnamese Cao Dai Church provide difficulties from their terms as not only have they a Pope and two types of Cardinals but a number of other ranks above that of simple participant. The Legio Maria Church in Kenya has more ranks rather than participant roles than the Roman Catholic Church from which it broke away. There seems to be as general need for position and status whether in secular or religious organisations. The Legio Maria has official status for such persons as the washer of the altar cloth and a Kampala football team had twenty five members of which twenty two had named ranks rather than just player positions.

We can see the consequences of status needs in the nationalisation of the missionary created Church in Tanzania. The politicians and national clergy wanted the self-determination of all institutions. Thus, the local Roman Catholic clergy got the status they wanted but not the economic backing to maintain the buildings and the specialised commitments which they had inherited and which proclaimed non-existent wealth to poor believers.

However, it is in religion that there is the widest distinction what the organisation provides in fulfilment of its orthodoxies and how its devotees interpret these requirements in terms of their own needs. There is always the degree of differentiating conformity or indeed whether they know much about their orthodoxies. It is in this there has to be a working misunderstanding within which the religious institution continues to survive rather than thrive.

There will always be a hierarchically dominant elite who maintain the closest relationship with the Divine however defined but this is often a source of misunderstandings when this is maintained or indeed altered by prophetic possession of those who are in effect rivals for position of religious authority. There is also the working misunderstandings from the fact that most participants believe that they are conforming even when it is obvious to others involved that they are not.

The Misunderstandings of Interpreters of Religious Involvements

The majority of these assessors of religious behaviour are not members of any religious organisation which would make them suspect of the abilities to assess any faith with sufficient detachment. They are outsiders in several ways for social scientists are overwhelmingly agnostic as a result of their professional training and tend to see the religious practices of others even within their own profession as evidence intellectual failings and religious behaviour particularly inappropriate outside their own status level on a scale of bizarreness. There may be an understandable inability to accept that the religious behaviour of others as genuine as indeed their own emotional attachments and this division is not usually accepted as a matter of personal and professional concern.

The views and assessments of these outsiders are those of people who see themselves consciously or unconsciously as intellectually superior to the people they are studying, even to the extent that they consider all their beliefs and practices to be misunderstandings of reasonable rationality. How can they see in any terms of intellectual equality the Vietnamese Cao Dists who believe that their faith comes in part from the spirits of the French author Victor Hugo and the mediaeval French nationalist Saint Joan of Arc who fought against the English. The Vietnamese who leave offerings on their doorsteps to help hungry ghosts, much less the Chinese who have built a new temple for the Black Dragon King are behavioural realities but not evidence of any other forms of reality.

While they will accept that there are exceptional individuals in their own societies who have 'genuine' religious commitments, there is undoubtedly a real inability to see that the enormous numbers with their 'bizarre' beliefs and practices, are not the victims of their own misunderstandings but have very real and genuine religious experiences. A lack of what the Christians would consider charity in how they view the beliefs and practices of others. It may even be that the majority of Christians may have actually experienced the presence of God or like the six in a London suburb who have experienced an apparition of the Virgin Mary and beyond telling their parish priest kept its personal significance to themselves.

The misunderstandings of those assessing the religious beliefs and practices are thus in part the result of their own incapacity to accept the individual understandings of others and thus downgrade their personal importance by grouping of patterns of behaviour which inevitably diminishes the centrality of these personal experiences and understandings.

There are also misunderstandings which come from the professional failings in the methods which are used in these assessments. Most of these assessors are come and go professionals who would be unlikely to stay long enough in the community they are observing to even become on the fringe of being thought of as one of 'us'. An Afro-American researcher into a store front urban church was not able to get any of the woman to speak to her about their religious activities until she became personally acceptable to them as capable of seeing them in terms of emotional equality. This took about a year of local involvement at her own time and money expense without getting any religious data.

However, in some cases as in Malawi the leaders of a more fundamentalist Protestant congregation thought that the Afro-American researcher was in fact a potential convert, a half and half religious status. So there is this important issue as how do those researched relate to these outsiders. While they may not see them as police spies, they may well think that they have or should similar characteristics as they are working for some overseeing religious or secular authority to whose ostensible wishes they may feel that it would be prudent to more or less conform.

When we consider the social distance between these researchers and the researched there may always be some unwillingness to talk about their religious ideas and practices. They may in fact be intellectually unable to express themselves on matters to which they have never given any thought until they were invited to do so by an obvious outsider. Religion for them may be no more than the experience of a emotional reality about which they have never given any explanatory thought.

What grounds do social scientists have for believing an individual when he or she states that they have particular beliefs and consequently perform certain required rituals at regular intervals the summaries of which they communicate to enquiring outsiders. These explanations may have little relationship to the orthodoxies of the faith to which they say that they belong. So what they tell the enquirer can be seen as an evaluation of their knowledge but not a record of their practices. Self-analysis is a rare ability.

We can certainly triangulate what is communicated with other data when this is available but this is rarely so except for detailed studies of single individuals. Thus, the data which is provided only constitutes 'truth' when it coincides with the predominance of available data and probably the degree that it coincides with what the assessor considers to be rational enough to be presented to professional colleagues. In such situations the fact remains that working misunderstandings are likely to be both an individual and a common occurrence of cumulative significance.

The reason for accepting such statements from an informant as 'true' for information relating to religion is a combination of factors which would apply to every piece of information in its behavioural isolation. That it would apply to a series of events reported by a series of individuals is a theoretical rather more than a methodological possibility.

Whatever the thoroughness of an enquiry into a fact which has an enormous amount of supportive data available, this is only likely to be available for socially prominent events such as the coronation of a British monarch or the annual Hajj pilgrimage to Mecca and the destruction of the World Trade Centre in New York by Muslim terrorists. There are always elements of doubt over individual participations and they may have little relevance to everyday religious behaviour.

The assessment of any human activity involving both organic and inorganic material comes from particular social environments which partially decides what happened then and there only. Thus, for the understanding of the religious ideas and practices of any individual we need not only a mass of information but that this is necessity for each event as there may be no reason to suppose that sequential units of seemingly similar behaviour will have the same initiating and consequential environmental factors behind them. Multiply this for groups of categorically similar individuals and we have to conclude that the proportional possibility of misunderstandings will increase dramatically.

There is thus an accumulation of factors which make it unlikely that these assessors will be able to get much information of the depth necessary for any understandings of what will always remain a personal and individually temporarily distinct activity. So while it may be visibly obvious that there is a particular religious activity going on, it seems equally likely that there will be misunderstandings about what participants think they are doing.

Overall the attribution of meanings and understandings may be entirely the construction of these outsider assessors exercising their professional expertise, who are likely to conclude that understanding in terms of the availability or absence of any accessible orthodox behaviour is just not likely to cover the individual's feelings. In Indonesia it became national policy *pancasila* for every citizen to have an identity card on which their membership of one of the state recognised religions was recorded. This led to large numbers of conversions to Christianity and Islam. In such a situation the question of misunderstandings of religious meanings is entirely academic as it may well be almost total and of no relevance to how these people have behaved or will behave in seemingly religiously motivated situations.

There are thus a number of background factors before any outsider should reach any conclusions. Firstly, these researchers may have got it wrong by misunderstanding what they are seeing or hearing (Boyer, 1990). It has been suggested that the researcher of the French Canadian parish of St. Denis made mistakes in his interpretation as he was not a Roman Catholic (Miner, 1939). There is the quotation in Livingstone's travels when the rain-maker said to him that he hoped that Livingstone did not believe that he was actually making rain (Livingstone, 1857:23-5). In some situations social scientists may be too credulous and optimistic about the reality of the data they collect.

It may not be just that these researchers will always have great difficulty in interpreting the religious ideas and practices of people to whom they are culturally alien in languages or linguistic codes and of whom they have only limited knowledge. How indeed can they know the meanings of what they are told which even the speaker may not be able to explain?

The Individual Misunderstanding of their Religion

In view of the complexities of any religious belief or behaviour whether among the Kung Bushmen of the Kalahari, Christian Benedictine monks and nuns, Muslim students in Qom, Iran or Cao Dai spirit inspired believers in Vietnam, it might be reasonable to think in minimalist terms of what they do understand of their faiths. In such an approach the Benedictine monks and the Iranian Muslim students can be assumed to know more of their faiths because so much has been written down with authority as the basis for their understandings. However, for others who do not have any need for such professionally necessary knowledge little is known so that it would require considerable study to find out anything substantive or indeed to accept that there are no substantive factors only generalised ones.

Understanding a personal faith is an intellectual exercise which few have the capabilities of achieving and indeed to do so at all. For most if not nearly all believers in whatever religion they belong or are categorized by themselves and others as belonging to a particular faith, it is an emotional and social experience which whatever its regularities, is unlikely to occur regularly. The peaks are likely to be remembered and appreciated rather than understood in a very personal way which is usually beyond their ability to explain.

The individual in cultures which have no religious behaviour which has been structured much less written down live in an environment in which misunderstandings can only occur in inter-relationships over matters of personal concern. It cannot seemingly occur in any theological sense that such people do not understand the religion to which they ostensibly belong. There may not even be a word in their complex languages which could refer to religion as a distinct type of behaviour (Chitando, 2005). Whatever religious paradigms exist they will be so loosely understood and interwoven with their socio-religious lives that to state that there have been misunderstanding is the result of what should be classed as the arbitrary classifications of outsiders who themselves are misunderstanding the behavioural realities of the people they are observing. A Sukuma subsistence farmer cannot be said to misunderstand his religion because what there is to understand in the first place are no more than reactive behaviour to some situations within some vague paradigms which would not distinguish behaviour by any arbitrary classifications.

Misunderstandings and the Growth of Scale

We know that in traditional small scale societies religion and the totality of social thought and behaviour were in some incoherent unity. If we assess that situation as a working misunderstanding it would be analytically correct from the outsiders point of view but both words in that phrase have no pragmatic existence. Such subsistence societies have beliefs and practices which almost inevitably fit into their primary need to survive; understanding beyond this supposedly blinkered view is not an intellectual necessity because their beliefs and understandings are self-explanatory. What can be called 'out-there' metaphysical reality is contained and explained more or less adequately in the functional fluidity of their socially contained thoughts and practices.

We know that the human mind has difficulty in coping with mass distresses (Fetherstonhaugh *et al.*, 1997) as opposed to those that arise from smaller numbers (Humphrey, 1981:21-2) and indeed individual difficulties for which all societies have evolved their partially successful reactive adaptations.

This would suggest that human capabilities are perhaps geared ethologically as well as ethnologically to small group living in which social and metaphysical relationships can be better understood and creatively reacted to 'in-there'. If this is so there would be a progressive proportional decline in the ability of those people to cope with the growth of the size of the problems with which they are confronted. We are a small group species with none of the mass society administrative genetic capabilities shown in some insect societies.

If we transpose this loss of personal ability to react creatively within the macro theological understandings of religion we are led to some tentative conclusions about working misunderstandings.

1. Religious and spiritual social and psychological activism is a

reaction to small group and individual situations.

2. Societies and individuals continue these practices because they are assessed as helpful or at least neutral to continuing social stability.
3. This activism as a necessary and seemingly efficient compulsion progressively declines as involvement of people and societies moves from an interior 'us' to an exterior 'them' about which little is known except some imposed categorisations.
4. Within the small group and individual the phrase working misunderstandings would stress the first word but this inverts itself as the number and variety of situations beyond their ability to hypothetically control increases.

But of course, if a religion is to retain mass appeal, individuals and families will restrict their objectives to narrow social and geographical circumstances for which they can foresee help from their religious practices and petitions.

The possibilities of retaining some theological consistency in the senses enabled and indeed demanded by widespread literacy must surely lie with the ambiguity of the religious messages. These have to be sufficiently attractive to retain believers in their widely different situations of need and thus provide individuals with a personally effective religion even if the religious message in theological terms has been misunderstood.

The Unawareness of Misunderstandings

For most people at whatever level of intellectual capacity and cultural complexities, not much understanding is needed. The Sukuma subsistence farmer just as the Mumbai businesswomen when asked to explain whatever their admitted religious involvements may be, are likely to reply in much the same terms that this is what we have always done or should do. A failure to conform is not misunderstanding.

Language must always be the greatest handicap on any individuals understanding of what they may be doing. Individuals think in the same natal language and linguistic code as they speak. While it is not impossible for an unusually talented individual in any cultural setting to put their language together in a way to express original thinking, for most people their thoughts are restricted by the structures of the language into which they were originally socialised. It is doubtful whether someone who is functionally bilingual switches their thinking when they change from one language to another as the situations demand.

If the language provides for the Divinity to be only referred to with abstract pronouns, the idea that the Christian God is a personality with personal commitments to his followers is unlikely to catch on. On the other hand, the culturally pervasive ideas in China that the Divinities are similar to the bureaucratic hierarchy with which they are conversant is ones that can fit into other religions and secular concepts. Similarly, the ghosts of Vietnam are seen in terms of human behavioural realities so they are thought to suffer from abandonment as these people would themselves feel in such situations. There are similar linguistic restrictions on English Christians understanding the influences of Christian saints in Italy when so much is the result of socialisation.

There is also the fact that meanings can be constructed by individuals as much as by institutions but they cannot be fixed in the understandings of anyone at any time because the retaining mind is subject to constant situational change (Toren, 1993).

This issue is one that pivots round the individual's capacity to understand and that may have little to do with what either a local cult in Cairo or California may require of its members much less with the understandings of a Roman Catholic in Beijing or Bamako in relation to the promulgations of the Vatican. So there will always be a number of background factors affecting this matter before we can even consider what the individual may understand or misunderstand. She may not understand what the requirements are of the religion to which she belongs and he may not have the cognitive capacity to understand what is on offer. Then there may be situations in which an individual cannot practice their faith as in northern Myanmar where a Roman Catholic might be able to attend a Mass once a year. The half the inhabitants of a Japanese island that became Christian and then were isolated from Christian contacts for several centuries remembered only that they should not marry their cousins which gave them a quite distinct genetic profile (Schull *et al.*, 1962) to their Taoist-Buddhist neighbours. It may be that the only fact of which we can be certain in collecting information about religious ideas and practices is that someone said something or wrote it down or that we saw an activity. Beyond that we are dealing with not much more than guesswork as to the 'real' significance of what has been happening.

The Malaysian Temiar elder on listening to a recording of one of their song ceremonies commented that it was far away and deep inside, the sound of longing, like the voices of the spirits from the mountains heard deep within when listening and singing. The Temiar have always lived in a world of strangely dislocated simultaneity. They graft their experiences of the disjunctions between modern and traditional life-ways, between forest and out of the forest presence, onto expressive techniques and performance practices addressed towards healing spirits (Roseman, 2001:126-7). How much of this explanation is the result of individual sophistication on the part of both men, the elder and the researcher.

It seems likely that most religious ideas and practices are as much within the cultural parameters of their cultures than with specifically religious ones. It may be that social scientists and theologians start their assessments from within the channels provided by literacy and their perceptions of the necessity for order and this provides a basis for the assumptions that dogmas should exist and from this the inevitability of working misunderstandings.

6
The Nature of Orthodoxy

In the examination of social behaviour the use of a term that implies that it has universal application is a dangerous methodological practice as it usually turns out that before the appearance of literacy and indeed the creation of dictionaries an abstract term has its definitions in the circumstances that it is used. The term taboo for prohibited action is an example of universality in a religious word but it has no such universality in the cultures from which it originated. In its Melanesian traditional origins it was taboo for men to enter the segregation hut of menstruating women and for women to be anywhere else at those times So it seems that this word is not a noun but a verb that depicts behaviour which is 'off-limits' (Keesing, 1985). It may be that abstract thought comes late into the construction and use of any language culturally and individually and even when the language has this capacity, it may be used by only a few who have this intellectual and linguistic capacity and the social need for such usages.

The Unity of Society and Religion

A history of religious ideas would disclose that for most if not all traditional societies there would not have been any separation of functions into discrete categories. There would not have been any possibility to separate agriculture and house-building from religious ideas and practices or study religion without involving marriage and illness. Even in such complex societies as developed in the Indian sub-continent the collective term Hindu was created by outsiders for their intellectual and bureaucratic convenience.

Religion as a specific category of behaviour and beliefs was the creation from a series of factors combining dominant and inspired personalities, the success and enlargement of the numbers finding their ideas and their embodiment in rituals helpful in their lives and the use of writing to institutionalise these beliefs for their social survival.

So it could be seen that religion as a separate category of behaviour is quite recent and this is centred on institutions for which specific names have been created such as church and mosque or borrowed such as the Latin origin of the word religion.

Thus, the word religion applies more especially to overt practices which have been or are related to specialised institutions but this still leaves the fact that not only in the Vatican State but in the Islamic Republics of Iran and Pakistan religion is more or less a part of every activity. Even in states with separate religion and politics, there is the support and control of religious activities. Religious charities and terrorism are supervised and checked.

Even when religion is defined as a separate type of behaviour it is some part of many secular activities and it has been generally recognised that it is going to be always some part of so-called secular life. Indeed secularism as a predicted consequence of education has failed to materialise; it would seem that globally God is back (Micklethwait and Wooldridge, 2009) in some form or another if indeed 'it' has ever gone away.

Religion as Total Experience

In some ways by providing or creating a term, the activity becomes isolated from its overall nature in the human brain and becomes broken down to what are thought to be its constituent parts. This means that whether we are considering the religious beliefs and practices of a Cambodian farmer or a Kolkata businesswomen, we are missing the most important part of their thinking which is holistic; no one divides up their personal experiences into the categorisations which are employed by the social sciences. The individual is the same persistent whole whether worshipping or working.

A person attending a ceremony which may not be specifically religious such as a wedding in Britain under secular rather than religious law, may personally classify it as an important occasion because a number of past experiences may have come together. The church or temple may have provided a religious atmosphere because it has been the place of prayer for many centuries, the lighting is 'mystical' rather than direct and the ritual may be indistinct and has become the background to personal thoughts undisturbed by what other participants are doing.

In such a situation duplicated in many different environments and accompanied by many different personal circumstances are total experiences in which it is not possible to disentangle and identify the specific religious elements. Other factors may contribute to any such holistic experiences; the comfort of the seating, a benign temperature and in terms of cultural expectations in the timing of the ceremony neither too long or too short or indeed that timing has no significance as their participation has 'drop-in' characteristics. Nothing can be isolated as specifically significant in the essential wholeness of these individual experiences.

The overall impression of the liturgical practices of the religions of the book is orderliness; the recent successful protests leading to the change of regime in Egypt has enormous numbers of demonstrators praying in orderly lines in Cairo's central square and the Hajj pilgrimage is conspicuous by its orderliness. For those there it was an individually holistic experience as nothing can be seen as exclusively religious, economic or political.

Even in this orderliness there are different dimensions. Christians can be possessed by the Holy Spirit and there is the quietness of the Quaker meetings in which the theme is silence until someone is inspired to speak and the noisiness of the Salvation Army's brass bands copied in Zaire by the Kimbanguist Church as well as the triumphant singing of the Mormon Tabernacle choir in Salt Lake City, Utah.

These environments providing holistic experiences are totally different to prolonged Hindu and Chinese ceremonies with their competitive noise and 'disorderly' crowds. Northern Chinese funerals accompanied by bands of hired musicians and the explosions of fireworks to ward off disturbing spirits (Chau, 2006:129-137). The Hindu millions from different sects who attended the Kumbh Mela have been only saved from disastrous safety and social disorder by the imposed regularities of the civil government.

The social science coverage of religious activity is perhaps preoccupied by what can be described crudely as the obvious. But everyone in these crowds of ostensibly worshippers is having their own indivisible experiences. This fact of holistic experience which is virtually impossible to interpret because of its environmentally fleeting nature contributes to its basis of working misunderstandings.

The Nature of Orthodoxy

A standard definition of orthodoxy is the holding of accepted or correct views; and secondly which are not heretical but this would apply only to situations in which views have been defined and institutionalised and of course heresy is a concept of Christian and European origin.

Such a definition would suggest that in many contemporary societies there are orthodoxies and moreover that this applies in certain situations and not in others when religions are thought of as distinct areas of individual rather more than social activity. Only in the simplest and isolated societies such as the Kung Bushmen of the Kalahari area of Botswana can there have been a form of over-arching social and religious orthodoxy within which everyone without exception conducted their social behaviour; there was in effect no escape from its control particularly as the outside world was persistently and violently hostile to them.

It may be that the requirement that an act or a symbol should have a meaning is a social science imposition; people may not have meanings for what they do or understand but have experiences which have meanings for them at that time and place; why indeed should anything have a meaning, a single explanation particularly associated with and required by the formal thinking created by the European Enlightenment, which is not only pervasive in scientific thinking but is an almost controlling element in how the social sciences approach human behaviour. In the study of behaviour it is difficult if not impossible to detach meaning from its expression.

A society or group may have an ideology, a corpus of ideas to which they are attached to varying degrees. It was found that among the West African Fang there were some over-arching beliefs to which they would all appear to agree but individually they had their own interpretations of how these ideas should be assessed and used in practice (Fernandez, 1965). It was the same among well educated Swedish Lutherans that within general theological agreements, each individual saw these principles in quite different ways (Stromberg, 1981). The more internally differentiated a society may be, the more these individual differences will be realities shown by the ways in which they illustrate their experiences. There may be some general pervasive ideas but they do not have the hard edges which would enable their use to be an accessible feature in a variety of social scientifically identified situations.

A self-imposed orthodoxy may exist in individual interpretations of their own social and religious activities which will rest as much on memory and self-interest as on any narrow sense of religious obligation. Orthodoxy in any sense of observable conformity to known standards must rest on the extent to which it can be enforced in an Islamic state as divinely decreed through an updating process of interpreting the *Holy Koran* or indirectly enforced by exclusive groups such as the biblically based Amish amongst whom the advantages of conformity outweigh what the outside world see as outdated restrictions on personal freedom. The Exclusive Brethren, a Christian sect in Britain, did not have the resources or the ideological practicalities to become and remain a viable and cross-generationally maintained isolated religious group.

The Eastern religions and their societies have avoided narrow interpretations as the practice of these faiths has been too introspective and individually isolated to create definitions from which wider ranging orthodoxies could be developed. It may be that orthodoxy can become an operational reality in monotheism but in practice this may prove impossible when as in Shintoism, the divine essence *kami* is present in every object. How in fact can a Japanese of whatever religious inclination and intellect become orthodox when there are reputed to be several millions of named deities.

Lastly, there is the basic factor that orthodoxy to be an influential and enforceable factor in social and religious behaviour requires not just writing but the institutions to record religious ideas and to propagandize what is recorded. So the many and various religious systems of many cultures can have no enforceable orthodoxies other than that brought about by their regular religious needs always under the changing influences of social environments and charismatic personalities.

Belief and Orthodoxy

To what extent is belief an essential component of religious practices. Most Christians as part of their public religious ritual recite a Creed which starts with the obligatory 'I believe', but what does this affirmation involve. In situations of religious tension and hope it may be said rather than recited with substantial situational sincerity and understanding, but on most occasions it is recited with no thought at all as to what it implies.

The word 'belief' can certainly be applied to any coherent system of understandings. It can equally well be applied to schools of philosophy and the self-assumed coherences of schools of art, literature, fashion and indeed cooking in which participants overtly but temporally commit themselves. The principle difference may be that religions are predominantly abstract and marginally material while these other systems of belief are predominantly material and less abstract.

Beyond the religious environment with which belief is particularly associated, it is in practice an attitude of mind that can be applied to anything in which individuals have invested some often substantial emotional capital in a reality which cannot be substantiated pragmatically.

There are of course committed Christians and Hindus as well as a wide range of theologians who can be sure to have worked out as adults, particularly if they are converts, what they believe in at that particular time. They have reached conclusions which have a central role in their public and private religious commitments to created realities which cannot be pragmatically proved to exist (Bell, 2002). But the Muslims in their everyday affirmation of their faith in Allah and his Prophet are in fact stating a fact not a belief. There are semantic issues here as it is not possible in Kenyan Meru to state that one believes in God because that implies that it would be possible to similarly say that one does not believe in God and that they say is just too ridiculous to contemplate.

While both Christianity and Islam have clear and limited orthodoxies, these appear almost rational objects of belief in comparison to the florid multiplicities of Hinduism and the appeal to amorphous nullity of Buddhism for which there may be no written formulated creedal orthodoxies.

It would certainly be a biased conclusion that beliefs are illusory as might be the conclusions of a rationalist in relation to the beliefs of Hindus as much as the understandings of Christians and Confucians. This is to segment the nature of belief to a predetermined religious context which is always socially situated.

Belief is involved in almost all human intercommunication particularly in situations that actively use or imply use qualitative adjectives such as 'good' or 'bad'. Successful communication has to accept usually without any pragmatic reasoning that what is being communicated is for practical purposes socially correct; doubt has often to exist out of the social contexts from which it was derived. In order for society to function it would seem that we have to assume the good or at least mainly benign intentions of those with whom we interrelate; no society could function on the basis of any assumption of generalised deceit.

On the other hand, most functions of belief systems will have no overt coherence but which nevertheless form the covert basis within which people operate their private rather than public belief systems. A Tanzanian

Sukuma propitiating his ancestors in an innovative and unrepeatable ceremony from which his relatives by marriage are excluded is not in any coherent sense conforming to a belief as a necessary precondition for such activities; the actions of his ancestors on his and his family's existence is a social fact and not dependent on something as socially detached as belief. This man has gone to a reputable diviner according to local opinion who has suggested in a dialogue that the problem can be eliminated or at least reduced by carrying out such a ceremony of propitiation. This man accepts the need for a ceremony which has no predetermined form which he has agreed to carry out in cost-benefit terms both as a socially reasonable creative solution and that it is within his means. Of course, there are elements of illogical belief but overall it is just as rational as the patient who goes to a scientifically trained doctor and does what the doctor tells him without any rational grounds for doing so since he has no knowledge of scientific medicine anymore than that Sukuma has of theology. We may not know or even suspect that much professionally accepted medical knowledge becomes quite rapidly replaced as out of date or ineffective.

Some aspects of religious belief are so globally common both individually and communally such as the existence of ghosts and Supreme Beings that it is questionable whether the term 'belief' is appropriate. The Sukuma men and women in social and biological difficulties is provided culturally with what they accept as a wide range of factual rather than belief options. Today this is made more complex by the existence of a wide range of imported patent medicines, the various forms of Islam and denominational Christianity. It is surely doubtful whether people in difficulties whether in Birmingham, Banaras or Bamako see the choices and solutions available to them as anything so narrowly specific as needing belief.

Meanings of Meaning in Aural Societies

While in societies in which there is a literate elite, it is possible to have authoritative if largely unknown standards which have been carefully thought out and institutionalised in print, it is possible to state that an individual is conforming or not to certain propositions provided in the wide-ranging check-lists of orthodox requirements of which believers may have little real knowledge.

However, for societies which do not see their religions in such literate terms and those which have committed nothing to the rigidity of printed theology, all that we can find out about their religious ideas and practices are vague generalisations. There is the very obvious fact of which they may be unaware that these are constantly adapting to situational requirements while maintaining the illusion of constancy.

In these non-literate situations the majority of believers particularly in the Eastern religions are not only theologically non-literate but indeed see no sensible or indeed necessary reasons for being otherwise. There can be no commitment socially or religiously to anything as illusive as an idea; both sides of the equation are implicitly acknowledging that relating metaphysical ideas to behaviour in any definitional sense is impossible or indeed the methodological impossibility of finding out the nature of such individual activities with any exactness.

It is possible to go further than that and to suggest that most people in so-called literate societies do not overburden themselves with the existing written provisions of their faiths to which they may formally belong. Of course, if asked they will possibly list some of these written provisions but pushed to explain these there is either a repetition of what they have learned as children or very garbled and inadequate explanations which they have learned subsequently. Most Roman Catholics might well reply on the lines of the English woman who said that what was required of her was whatever the Pope ordered. It seems likely that the major influence on belief and practice is the institutional and personal charismatic authority behind what is provided for the faithful in particular circumstances.

It is Islam with its Five Pillars of the Faith of most Muslims are likely to show a high proportion of accurate knowledge of these requirements as four of them are physically finite and allow for no personal interpretation of in-built ambiguities. Go beyond this and there can be no such clarity since they are the productions of individual legalists called *fatwas*. There is no finite clarity between Christianity and what its denominations require. There is no clarity at all in what should be believed and practised in Hinduism with its absence of any agreed religious principles and in the obscurities of Buddhism and Taoism in which popular practice appears to have little relationship at all with what the specialists state to be the basic necessities of these faiths.

So it seems likely that the majority of individuals in what they understand to be their religion have systems of belief and practice which are largely individual interpretations of what is provided by the broad paradigms of their commitments and cognitive and social limits imposed by their socialisation.

Both the quasi-traditionalists in Zambia and Banaras Hindu craftsmen are restricted in what they believe by the broad parameters of the culture in which they live and the bits and pieces of religious practice and ideas which they pick up as they progress through life. These may be closely connected to a particular religious system or no more than a vague feeling of affiliation within which individuals pick and choose as the situations require without perhaps realising that they are doing so.

If we look at the ostensible religious experience of the average Chinese attending an event such as the annual festival of the Black Dragon King at Shaanbei (Chau, 2006), it is hard to see that there is any connection between what is available in writing as part of this Buddhist and Taoist merged faith and what is done by the attending crowds. They may burn some spirit money without being able to read what is written, queue and bow in the shrine to the complex multiple images in the temple, shake the divination sticks and then go to an expert for interpretation. Very little that these people do has much to do with the religious possibilities enabled from their limited literacy or the highly sophisticated knowledge available in Taoist literature and in the assumed understandings of the resident priests there.

So these crowds of people are in a very broad way experiencing an event which is nominally religious in that it happens in a temple compound but which has a strong component of other secular interests like just having a good time as a break from the monotony of their daily life with its food and merchandise stalls, gambling booths and an opera performance. In fact it might not be useful to talk about religious beliefs in such a situation as no one is particularly sure who or what was the Black Dragon King but they come away feeling all the better for what they have participated in with its touch of the Divine.

In what ways are the meanings which participants have at the powerful curing shrine of Lourdes likely to be significantly different. Admittedly there is no gambling or traditional noisy opera other than the emotionally laden and impressive evening service dedicated to the needs of the sick and the sorrowful. Those pilgrims get to the shrine through a town created by the belief that the Virgin Mary had appeared there and is dedicated to making money from the million pilgrims who annually go there in hope. From observation and detached evaluations they come away all the 'better' from what they have experienced.

Thoughts and the Use of Symbols

In analysing religious behaviour the background discussion is often on its linear implications on the lines of which came first the chicken or the egg. Did the ideas and practices of religion in a particular cultural and individual setting come from the inchoate past along the lines of Jung's archetypal thinking onto which researchers have appended their explanations. This might well be the case with such people as the Tanzanian Sukuma and other peoples who explain what researchers' see as their current religious behaviour as no more than what they have always done.

This is then an ongoing process of interpretation and elaboration and since nothing has ever been recorded except the partial observations of itinerant social scientists and committed missionaries; there are on-going innovative practices rather than thinking within the unrestricting parameters of what we can accept as traditional thought. This seems to be the case with symbols explained and utilised by thoughts in which both together and independently may have had a long mutually influential but undefined existence.

This would seem to be near to Geertz's appraisal (Geertz, 1973:5) that "man is an animal suspended in a web of significance he himself has spun and I take culture to be this web and the analysis of it is, therefore, not an experimental science in search of cause but an interpretive one in search of meaning".

Although these symbolic phenomena are not explicitly acknowledged, they are relatively restricted both in their use and in their transmission, because participants have some form of implicit knowledge. More specifically participants understandings of their own culture would involve millions of unconscious assumptions which guide their conscious beliefs and practices (Lawson and McCauley, 1993:2-3). It would seem that any more elaborate awareness in this sense is going to be limited to very small numbers in any society; few think beyond their existential needs.

On the other hand, there are some forms of religious behaviour that have become standardised in both writing and use for many centuries. Theological thought, the charismatic pronouncements of individuals and the collegiate pronouncements of such meetings as the Roman Catholic Councils of Trent and Vatican II which have not created new symbols. There are certainly symbols which illustrate certain types of religious understandings rather than behaviour such as the star of David for Israel and the Crescent in the national flags of Israel and Pakistan.

In contrast to the tacit assumptions which govern the linguistic understandings of both Tamils, Tanzanians and Trobriand Islanders (Hutchins, 1980;120), there may be a tendency indeed a presumption that any religion that has bound itself together with written pronouncements is more influential in controlling the thinking and behaviour of its believers. This may not be the case when there is their tacit acceptance of what are dismissingly referred to as 'popular' religious behaviour. Many cultures have many parallel belief systems between which their people zigzag, not changing from one to another but running them all at the same time in a logical mess despite their seemingly obvious contradictions; logic is not a notable nor necessary characteristic of people who gain personally important satisfactions from their personal amalgam of religious beliefs.

So it seems that not only we cannot see the thinking that is involved in religious behaviour much less as having narrowly paradigmatic origins and developments in how they are utilised. The Japanese Shintoism has an undefined number of spiritual powers *kami* in their pantheon so that what an individual may be worshipping cannot have even the beginnings of any private consistency or public uniformity.

The balance of evidence seems to be that people in all cultures and at all levels of intellectual understandings have their own individual symbolic systems which operate to varying extents dependent on or independent of official or theologically delimited religious understandings. These persist regardless of promulgations about what should be thought and done even when these have been widely known for centuries. This is the relatively uncontrolled result of what they hear and see, a non-literate religious environment in which literacy has a minimal involvement.

Language and Orthodoxy

Language used in all forms of thought is in the linguistic code with which individuals are most familiar and find useful for these commonalities. It is prudent to remember 'the cacophony of social voices in language heteroglossia. There are no 'neutral' words .... or forms that belong to 'no one'; language is shot through with intentions and accents... All words have the 'taste' of a profession, a genre, a tendency, a party, a particular will or a particular person, a generation, an age group, the day and the hour (Bakhtim, 1981:293). We cannot know the individual forms of these cognitional languages and when they are fleetingly vocalised or limited by the restrictions created by writing, one thing is certain that this is not the language in which the reasoning leading to orthodoxies was expressed.

There is thus the split between the linguistic codes which can be classified as popular which are likely to be divided up by religion, education, neighbourhood, status and profession, so that each social complex has its own restrictive ways and indeed it will be restricted as well by the structure of the main language, majority understandings and the linguistic codes used in the complexities of religious thinking.

Generally, people have not felt that simple commonplace language is the appropriate medium for approaching the Divine or whatever supernatural entities they are trying to communicate with whether a monotheistic God, Karni Ma, the Hindu goddess of infectious diseases, a malevolent ancestor or local spirit. While there may be some who pray in simple everyday language, the repetition of prayers gives them particular repetitive ritual forms.

In general languages used in religious rituals are specialised and can only be understood by those who have had special training or who get understandings from mystical insights. This applies as much to the African diviner and the Pentecostalist using glossolalia as it would to the Sanskrit reading Brahmin or an Amharic intoning Coptic priest in Ethiopia.

The semantic meanings of such religious language may be irrelevant as participants in the rituals which they attend are using the ambience and these officially authenticated religious sounds as adequate for their personal needs. Putting these rituals and orthodoxies into a single linguistic form may be theologically sound in its aspirations to generalise and assist understandings but then it becomes a question of which linguistic code is going to be used for the propagation of orthodoxy.

The Roman Catholic change in Tanzania from Latin into Swahili is a politically justified change to a lingua franca to unite a tribal system into a national one, so that believers have had their understandings of orthodoxy change from Latin which they did not understand except as a form of glossolalia into a language of political dominances with Islamic overtones; it may be that for some of their unconscious adherence to this new and potentially understandable orthodoxy has less attraction than the previous mystically shrouded use of a specific religious language.

In contrast the Western thinking on religion is based at least in part on the European Enlightenment's stress on logical understandings and coherence which is certainly not a feature of Eastern religions with their accumulation of sacred writings and of course an impossibility for non-literates except through the intellectual creativity of outsiders. Theological thinking has this form but it seems both questionable and unlikely that regular worshippers and those who come to religious involvements as the result of personal distress are particularly concerned with logical form or indeed any form which relates to their secular understandings. Whether the Buddhist, Christian, Hindu or Muslim understand their faiths as logical constructs from sacred premises or rather more likely that the experience orthodoxy if at all as providing necessary ritual sequences which are as impersonal as Buddhist and Hindu *mantras*. It should possibly be accepted that if a religion wants uniformity of belief from their followers it would be best for them to learn this from exclusively religious languages than for the religion to provide these requirements in so-called vernaculars which have their own socially segmented understandings.

Deference in Religious Behaviour

Whatever orthodoxies may have become available in written form and the extent to which they are enforced by the producing institutions, the basic element underlying conformity is deference (Bloch, 2004). We habitually defer in religious matters as in other affairs to those whom we consider to be better informed or more charismatically endowed than ourselves as well as to those who are socially superior to ourselves by reason of age, generational position, education and institutional stratification. Whatever happens in religious practices deference is as well represented as it is in secular affairs.

In religious understandings just as much as in building and accountancy, there is a professionally trained elite, the institutional staff and theologians who interpret and reactively update religious doctrines. These are common in both highly literate environments as in traditional societies where certain men and women go through prolonged informal training as diviners before their expertise attracts public attention. Often as not we defer to these experts because of the charisma of office; it saves time. The Chinese philosopher Mencius considered deference to be the basis of propriety.

In religious affairs there are always some men and women who have or who are assumed to have some personal connection with the spirit world which can be brought into play when they are consulted as in spirit possession. There are also people with personal achieved religious charisma such as the Italian monk Padre Pio whose stigmata made him the subject of Roman Catholic veneration and a number of Hindu divines whose presence is thought to provide religious benefits by simply seeing (*darshan*) or being seen.

There are also those with ascribed religious positions such as the inherited heads of Sufi schools of meditative devotion and the Shia form of religious succession producing the Iranian Ayatollahs and the heads of such groups as the Ismailis.

While these forms of deference are all subject to social negotiation, the position is altogether different with the treatment of sacred documents. The words of Allah are enshrined rather than just written in the *Koran* which students in Muslim schools are required to memorize and recite. They become the vehicle for the exposure of the Divine message over which they have no personal control (Eickelman, 1978).

The relationship between some form of orthodoxy and cognitive understandings may not be close because it may be no part of what the individual wants from their religious involvement. In a close personal relationship it would be necessary to have some more or less accurate understanding of what is in the mind of the communicator; this is not necessary in religious communication because of its built-in ambiguities and because of the one-sided silence of these encounters. If the Sukuma diviner states that by reason of his or her spiritual connections something is occurring, it is not necessary to understand what has gone into making such statements any more than we question medical or computer diagnoses of what has gone wrong.

The Problems of Institutionalising Charity

It is reasonable to conclude that the complying with the requirements of orthodoxy in its individual interpretation is perhaps more possible within small communities in which active concern for others and the control of personal behaviour is aided by their sense of isolation and committed purpose. The Amish communities are inward looking and look after their own members even when they are severely handicapped and only use the outside world when someone's behaviour is dangerous for others.

Once a religion becomes successful in numbers it loses the face to face ability to make adjustments regardless of their individual relationship with the supernatural; it might be said that the top numbers in which religious practice is controlled by personal influence as a functional possibility is twelve. It institutionalises its success in schools, training colleges, hospitals and specialised projects but real influence and its conformity to orthodoxy is demographically restricted.

Each one of these institutions involves an outside world which would never have an identity of commitment to their religious ideals. The airfield for the Irish pilgrimage centre at Knock involves international air traffic control; the Kumbh Mela celebrations involve sanitation, crowd control, transport and arrangements for lost children; and the Hajj the control of disease. Whatever the interpretation of religious orthodoxy is in any religion it is diluted by invasive secular requirements.

Thus, Christianity and to a lesser extent Islam has taken on or developed institutional forms which are the inevitable result of accepting charitable responsibility for running hospitals, schools, and special projects for the care of the handicapped, elderly or disabled. A few Christian denominations avoid this by limiting their activities to spirituality and one to one personal charity and thus do not become entangled in the consequences of institutionalisation but it would be just as subject to secular law as in the ruling of the United States Supreme Court that school prayers in publicly funded schools were unconstitutional.

There are unavoidable structural consequences from what becomes the collective impersonal treatment of people. At the primary level the death of a single person is a deeply felt tragedy but at the collective level it becomes an administrative need to legally dispose of the bodies of those that die in hospitals and care homes.

For Christianity the degree to which Christians understand or misunderstand the physical realities of their faith can often be seen in the extent of institutional and personal charity shown by their denomination and its senior members and administrators. But the Jewish charities supporting a hospital ends its Jewishness before the scientific and administrative demands of coping with the sick; what rabbis do there and the religious disposal of the dead is always peripheral to the requirements of orthodox Judaism.

There are analytical difficulties in assessing this. At one extreme an individual can be charitable to the extent that it does not damage their own existence and that of those to whom he or she has primary obligations. A mother cannot be charitable to the extent of damaging the lives of their own children although there are exceptions to this as the decision of the two clergymen at Eyam in Yorkshire to stay in their village rather than spread the plague by fleeing with the result that they and their families together with a large number of villagers lost their lives (Daniel, 1966).

There is some sort of implied but nevertheless realistic cap to this level of individual charity shown by the tithing required by the mediaeval Christian church and the current obligation of members of the Church of the Latter Day Saints centred in Utah who give a tithe of their incomes to their Church. This has not seemingly damaged the lives of their continuing members and has provided it with substantial funds for the support of weaker farming communities but not of course for the provision of charity for outsiders. In Egypt there are numerous Muslim charitable trusts but there is no feeling that any part of these should be spent on the Coptic minority of fellow citizens.

However, once one goes beyond personal charity giving affordable donations or using spare time in such activities as hospital visiting, proving relief for full-time carers and voluntary service generally, charity becomes institutionalised and expensive. In charitable institutions such as hospitals, orphanages and disaster relief, the issues go far beyond the possibilities of any personalised effort or self-denial as might be shown by the celibate specialist carer who has no other obligations; there are time, personnel and cost factors which prevent the personal care which orthodoxy requires. Mother Teresa's communities of nuns cannot in practice provide more than minimal personal care for the numbers of terminally ill people 'dumped' into their care in Indian cities; a hospice catering for ten patients is a very different humane institution than one for a hundred.

Running any institution requires management and specialised skills as well as equipment to that used in secular surroundings. Even the distribution of famine relief requires the presence of men and women with logistical skills and perhaps even a deadened sense of obligation on being confronted with such massive distress.

Some major religions have long standing institutions caring for the sick and deprived in countries with wide ranging and efficient social services maintained from general revenue. The extent to which such institutions are demonstrably religious is not so much obscure as they are more related to national standards of nursing care and surgery. This may be no more than Jews preferring to be cared for in a New York Jewish hospital than a Catholic one but not in the expectation that the treatment would be specifically Jewish.

The costs for the running of such institutions are set by the surrounding secular societies offset to a limited extent by donations and bequests. A Muslim surgeon is just as expensive as a Christian one whether in Chicago or Cairo. So in order to comply with legal requirements the costs of such institutions are very high.

However, Christianity occurs predominantly in societies which do not have more than minimal social services and nothing like the level of revenue required to fulfil the political and economic aspirations of the public. The result is that there is a widespread dependence on charitable organisations which then have the much greater problem of funding.

Roman Catholic institutions in the Ulanga diocese in Tanzania (Green, 1995) have to be paid for and maintained largely from overseas donations rather than from payments made by a population of subsistence farmers. Those who benefit provide no more than 20 per cent of the running costs of the secular and religious services they use and they resent paying for medicines which they assume have been provided without limits by overseas charities. To subsistence farmers a substantial building implies substantial wealth.

This is the situation in a diocese which has been 'nationalised' with a Tanzanian bishop and a majority of national diocesan clergy who have inherited a nominally Catholic religious system with on-going institutions dependent on overseas aid which as in many other dioceses in ex-missionary environments which they have inherited but which they will never be able to run from local revenues.

In this situation in Ulanga the Roman Catholic diocese inherited with some subliminal enthusiasm a whole panoply of religious structures which in fact have secularised functions, and so finds itself running an underfunded business. It has to try to get from its nominal supporters money for services which they feel should be provided free. In popular memory it was provided free by particular missionary priests to their personal circle of clients.

In such situations it is not so much a question of Christians misunderstanding the obligations of other faiths which certainly occurs in the split between the institutionalised religion and the less structured traditional faiths. Here in Ulanga the institutional Church has found itself tied to a substantial physical inheritance demonstrating material wealth over which now and in the foreseeable it has and will have very limited financial control and even less to spend on charity.

It cannot be charitable with funds and materials which it does not generate itself and is never likely to be able to. So in Ulanga the diocese has to run itself more as a business trying to balance its books while recognising that it cannot be charitable in any Christian sense without radical restructuring and abolition of many commitments created by their missionary predecessors in what then was and still is a situation of welfare monopoly. The buildings and perhaps the visible standard of living of the Tanzanian priests and nuns suggest access to wealth which they do not have for charitable purposes.

So for these Pogoro Catholics there is the obvious fact of expensive buildings, well-fed priests in civilian clothes and more cars than are available for the use of government personnel and the limited redistribution of this relative wealth to the poor around them. The cornucopia concept of charity provided by Westerners has got worse since political independence combined as it is with overall deficit budgets over which the national politicians have little control; pride and overall institutionalised mendicancy is an unhappy combination.

On the other hand, the Catholic Bishops of the dioceses of Shinyanga and Mwanza are not faced with quite the same difficulties. Despite more than a century of evangelisation only some twelve per cent are Catholics within a majority of quasi-traditionalists. They are not saddled with a number of institutions with buildings and institutionalised charitable obligations that are expensive to maintain and keep going.

These national 'administrators' trying to cope with the possibilities of their own interpretations of the Christian message between the providing of the sacraments and the provision of charity or secular social welfare which the government is unable to do. None have the funds to go beyond the sparse provision of the sacraments and to go beyond this some diocese are more severely handicapped than others. They are caught between the new ideas of this written faith about mundane rather than eschatological obligations and what remains in their minds and the minds of their believers from millennia of traditional paradigms involving reciprocity.

A Question of Intrusion

We have so far considered orthodoxy in the context of the larger religious faiths which have been established for long periods which can be verified historically and which have an acknowledged written record of what they believe in and try to do. Even if we do not know in definitional terms what constitutes Hinduism, it has existed so long that in the background of current Hindu practices there is some vague shared idea of orthodoxy in which they feel they are participating even if they are not identifiably conforming; there is a certain conformist whole in their minds which those involved feel exists.

Hinduism has automatically expanded through the migration of people to religious based nuclei in Fiji, Guyana, West London, Singapore and Texas and not through the transfer of ideas. It would seem that all the Eastern religions spread by their birth-rate and their exportable skills rather than by conversion. They intrude physically because their temples are visible but not in their ideas. If there has been any ideological expansion it is in ephemeral New Age cults. Expatriate Buddhists and Hindus in practice just ignore any surrounding religious culture on a take it or leave basis. Except in the context of India, Hinduism has not adopted any public officiousness demanding specialised rights in other countries.

Christianity whatever its Eastern origins has developed a philosophical and religious identity within Western civilisation and from this core that it has quite deliberately expanded both materially and ideologically. It is now a long standing faith and whatever its denominational sub-divisions, it is reasonable to think in terms of reactions to a vague orthodoxy.

So with both Christianity and Islam we have long established core areas in which these faiths in some form of orthodoxy have existed for so long that it is reasonable to see the contemporary behaviour of believers in what it is considered to be their orthodoxies. In these areas they are not new faiths intruding on the unwritten faiths of bygone eras.

However, these two faiths have expanded out of these core areas either historically by conquest as in central Asia or by trade in Indonesia or more recently into sub-Saharan Africa by combinations trade and missionary activities. Their written and institutional orthodoxies have come up against unwritten and less institutionalised orthodoxies which have existed for just as many millennia as these intruding faiths. These traditional faiths have almost always been defined and treated theologically as inferior from which their believers are to be converted or covert themselves for reasons which are complex combinations of religious and secular reasoning.

In this situation there is a clash of institutionally unequal orthodoxies in which these newcomer and intrusive faiths come up against persuasive religious understandings which have evolved over centuries in other cultures. It is a clash in which the overt is in conflict with the covert overall usefulness of these other beliefs.

In this context it is not just the 'back-sliding' of believers who should know better but parallel systems in which what are considered to be traditional beliefs survived as practices rather more than ideas, the social heritages and psychological Jungian archetypes. They fulfil functions for which the newcomer faiths have failed from ignorance or theological reasoning to develop acceptable answers. It is invidious to see these covert and unwritten faiths as pagan practices even if there is no contemporary overt use of such a phrase when they are no more than minimalist expressions of fundamentally important usually covert understandings and needs of those involved.

In terms of time and motion Christianity in the countries of Eastern Africa is intrusive and the older faiths survive such as Buddhism was in China with the same results of older faiths surviving. This indeed is the situation in the contemporary explosion of religious activity there in which it is analytically impossible to disentangle what activity comes from which religious doctrine. This parallelism must account for the overwhelmingly Christian men and women in matrilineal Zambia who have adopted a patriarchal religion just as the matrilineal Yao in southern Tanzania who are nearly all Muslim have adopted a religion which overtly accords a lower status to women who are matrilineally dominant.

There thus seems to be a division between internal and non-literate religious ideas and practices which whether it works or not is the implicit understandings in the carrying out of the rituals of Eastern or Western external faiths which intrude on this basic individualism are working misunderstandings.

A Question of Change and Survival

When so much overt change is observable in economics and politics and is assumed to be both rapid, wide-ranging and irreversible, it is often forgotten that this should be seen in terms of its repetitiveness. The collapse of the irrigation societies in central Asia following the Muslim invasion, disease and drought in central America and the so-called Dark Ages following the collapse of the Roman Empire. There is nothing 'new' in wholesale change affecting both individuals and their social environment.

It would surely be premature to assume that the collapse or massive material changes in the circumstances in which people live, has extinguished basic patterns of thought, the archetypal unconscious ways in which people back up their survival needs. It seems likely that these not only survive but undergo relatively little change which ethologically are very short term. The Tanzanian Sukuma who in half a century have experienced population explosion, political interference in their ecology with the programme of enforced villagisation, drought and AIDS amongst a long list of influences outside their control have changed very little in their religious understandings and practices (Wijsen and Tanner, 1994) in their reactions to new or should we suggest persistent individually experienced uncertainties. Moreover, they have found these adjustments and the thinking on which they are based behind, more useful in the reduction rather than the resolution of their problems than that which is offered by either the socially detached formalisms of Christianity or Islam.

In reacting to crises the usual situation is of a single event in a form which has perhaps happened before such as droughts, floods and epidemics which come and go and for which there are established reactions common enough in China, Eastern Africa and India. But what happens when there are a succession of crises which become disasters of a prolonged magnitude for which there are no traditional solutions that can be even remotely connected to the religious understandings of previous generations.

The situation in northern Uganda for the Acholi is an example in which almost every conceivable misfortune has come to them so that their solution is to accept a form of spirituality which to the outsider appears to be no more than social nihilism. This tribe was created in this collective form by the British for reasonable and necessary administrative reasons requiring local government within determined boundaries where previously they had no form of government larger than the village and clans. In this social environment they did not have the means to deal with the tensions of modernity apart from the fact that the north had been left with no economic development. The traditional leaders in local government positions with their gerontocratic understandings were seen as no more than government agents in disguise. The generational conflict was made worse by inter-tribal violence and tribal political parties.

The neighbouring Karamajong who might be classed as habitual cattle raiders who had been armed by the government against depredations from Kenya had by 1997 possessed only 2 per cent of the cattle they had owned in 1987 which represented a capital loss of $25 million to a pastoral society with no other source of wealth.

Into this situation as in Zambia with the visionary Alice Lenshina, a woman became possessed of the spirit of Lakwena, reputedly an Italian who had died in World War One started the Holy Spirit Movement which promised both worldly gain and spiritual recreation through its Holy Spirit Mobile Force whose members believed that through their initiation they were protected from bullets. When this was defeated a relative who considered himself to be the mouthpiece of God and a political oracle started the Lord's Day Resistance Army.

Violence from the beginning a traditional form of hostility containing a some major messages which recruited its members by abducting boys and girls. They just wanted to destroy what system there was out of anger and frustration because they themselves did not fit into any system any more (Doom and Vlassenroot, 1999). So we have the unusual situation of a form of religious behaviour taking hold in which their sense of well-being if it can be called that is no more than self-destruction, but the initial stimulus was religious.

It is rather too easy to ascribe the existence of religious reactions which the outsiders may see as short-term difficulties and to denigrate the intellectual capabilities of those practising what are often described as merely magical but which are the continuation of millennia of useful thinking. It may even be that these ideas are often part of what is not an entirely unreasonable antagonism to the abstractions and failures of clinical medicine and political rhetoric.

Afro-Americans who have lived in the United States for several generations and are not recent Cuban immigrants with their Latin-American Catholic rituals, practice their own form of private spirituality based on a combination of Yoruba archetypes, their slave experience and the overall dominance of Roman Catholicism which contributes to their sense of personal well-being (Murphy, 1993). Certainly a reaction not only to public discrimination but also to the inability of the medical system to provide a trustworthy response to their problems. The widely known Tuskegee scandal of Afro-Americans with syphilis, left untreated in order to see how the disease progressed (Gamble, 1997), merely confirmed what they had experienced all along shown by the continued use of student groups for psychological experiments.

In all societies there is the accepted idea that the spiritual world can be communicated with and that some men and women have the aptitude to be channels of that latent and can be developed relationship. Whether this is in the possession by the Holy Spirit of many Christians, the nearness to Allah coming from Sufi regimes or the widespread spirit possession in diviners in societies as socially diverse as Korea, Singapore and Zaire, there are these widespread channels of what are accepted as usually useful communication with the supernatural.

While certainly some of these reactions are destructive and attract attention as such, it is more likely that the forms of possession, however, interpreted by social scientists are a valuable channel for religious changes and in this help people with their current lives. No doubt from the point of view of the social sciences and theologians this is a working misunderstanding of rationality and the workings of their mind. It is adaptation and as such has widespread and varied manifestations; it works and again understandings are implicit. This hinge of personal experience should be accepted as expressions of personal religious reality.

Against these backgrounds common enough amongst disadvantaged groups in all societies, some groups have always developed their own empowerments (Abrums, 2000) which all provide a sense of individual and communal well-being under poor, discriminating and perhaps inevitable living conditions. They would feel in their development of their own religious practices that they were their own creators of divine relationships which were and under their control rather than being subject to intrusive requirements of socially distant religious administrators. They are able to create and maintain this sense of well-being because they believed that there was a difference in intelligence and understandings which gave them their own powers of mind and body from way back in time. This was expressed concisely by a Zambian nun on leaving a Western order of nuns 'Your thoughts are not my thoughts and your ways are not my ways'(Hinefelaar, 1994:6)

7
The Social Forms of Orthodoxy

Any religious group that expands beyond the number of believers that can be personally influenced by charismatic individuals becomes institutionalised through their writings and administrative requirements; the larger the following the bigger the institutional structure surrounding their religious efforts. This institutionalisation designed to enable their message to spread further and to continue over generations and to help the putting into practice their religious message can both hinder and help.

In this there is a distinction between the different types of religions as to whether they are concerned with individual development in a single life, eschatological aims, personal extinction or absorption into the infinite. It would seem, therefore, that for most religions there appear to be no obligations to others except as a means to furthering their own institutionalised ends. Thus, it would seem that both Christianity and Islam in order to further their charitable obligations have found institutionalisation necessary in order to run hospitals and charitable trusts 'wakfs'.

This has not occurred to any great extent in Buddhism and Hinduism with their doctrines of *karma* and transmigration of souls. So whether these religions are working misunderstandings or not depends on individual interpretations and not on how they are administered for the general application of their charitable beliefs and obligations.

Christianity right from the start has recognised institutional and personal obligations for others for reasons that have nothing to do with kinship and primary associations. This started to be seen soon after Christianity expanded from being a small introverted sect in their care of unrelated plague victims in AD 263 Alexandria (Eusebius, 1890);

this was shown more recently by the death of Father Damien from leprosy in 1889 after his long care of segregated lepers in Hawaii. With institutionalisation there have developed over the years increasing difficulties over legal, personnel and economic issues.

Religions with No Orthodoxies—The Absence of System

If we look at ethological backgrounds to human behaviour in that of the higher primates we can see that their lives are in a vague sense systematic in that certain things happen at certain times because that is the necessity imposed on them by the genetic impulses towards their own survival as a group.

Quite early in human social development they developed ways of behaviour which were required by survival needs but were as far as possible independently controlled by social rather than individual needs to systematize their own lives and with it ways which attempted to control their own destinies.

This was made easier by the invention of time and then later the clock which enabled discipline to be imposed on both social and religious behaviour. The reality is that many individuals and their societies have not invented or used or even seen the need to systematise their religious practices. Regularity of religious behaviour would seem to have been imposed and not directly as a response to people's needs. When religious ceremonies are needed the performance starts when enough people have arrived for the rituals to be effective and this would depend on such factors as cloud cover so the passage of social time would be delayed. One of the attractions of Christianity has been that they imposed on subsistence peoples a weekly day off. The community in Melanesia which decided to go modern work-times were started and stopped by the ringing of a bell (Mead, 1956).

To what extent do systems exist naturally in social behaviour beyond vague regularities and more particularly in religion and the answer is probably not at all and that it is imposed for the convenience of believers and the administrators of religion. It exists globally parallel to the availability of cheap watches and literacy.

There are certainly known ways of behaving into which we are all socialised but what actually occurs is intensely variable according to the personalities involved and the social environment in which it occurs at that time and place. To have a religious system implies a certain institutional permanency in the details of behaviour over a significant period of time for a recognizable part of society. This requires not only clocks but the ability to read time before acquiring the ability to read and write. Thus to have a liturgical system require a combination of these factors.

There seems little doubt that humans have inherited regularities in their social and religious behaviour but not in the exactnesses of definable stops and starts but its general systematization spread from a range limited to a few literate specialists to societies in general. The fact that it is an imposition on human religious needs is shown by the conspicuous clocks and the loudspeaker enhanced calls of the muezzin to prayer from minarets in many mosques as if Muslims on their own accord were not able to pray within the required periods rather than at exact times.

If there is no literacy there can be no recognition except through socially agreed memory that what is happening today in a religious ceremony is what has happened previously. In fact in quasi-traditional societies their current religious behaviour is attributed to what has been done in the past while it is no more than an elaboration of their current socio-religious situation but it is not evidence in itself of any system.

This absence of orthodoxy that predetermines what is expected of believers and lays down a partially observed pattern of required rituals, handicaps both individuals and societies of much of their ability to change as change they must in response to the changing circumstances in which they are always individually and collectively confronted. The Melanesians with their complexities of small scale societies with different languages and metaphysical understandings have always had the trances, dreams and spirit possession altered states of consciousness which made religious change and flexibility the norm of which their cargo cults were possibly not an extreme example (Stephen, 1976). To a lesser extent that is what has happened to the religious beliefs and practices of the Tanzania Sukuma which have changed from concern for their ancestors to combating the malevolence of their neighbours and the evil influence of unrelated spirits.

A system requires some of the rigidity that comes with the creation of codes. Thus there is the system of the Hindu prayer *puja* ritual which lists some twenty or more elements that certainly does more than imply a system even if it seems unlikely that it will be followed on a daily basis as part of domestic life. A Sukuma propitiation ritual with no written basis has an undefined beginning, middle and end in which there are no obligatory elements rather than a feeling of the appropriateness of what is being done. The complications of what is accepted as orthodox Jain procedures for correct worship makes it inevitable that conformity is implicit and is in practice a working misunderstanding.

It may be that Western religions have created systems as part of their institutional approach to religious necessities of behaviour but that Eastern ones have never become obsessed with order as a religious necessity. Westerner have a pattern of thought about Eastern religions dominated by meditation at least by disciplined quietness; they are emotionally affronted by the ill-discipline of Hindus at their collective celebrations and of Mexican and Philippine Roman Catholics at their Good Friday and Easter Day ceremonies. However, the social sciences with their origins in the same pattern of thinking as Western religions have extended this categorižation of human behaviour to religion. They have endeavoured to show that people behave along more exact paradigmatic lines than is in fact behaviourally possible.

So it seems that modern religious practices are based on millennia of varied ceremonials related to immediate needs and environmental necessities within loose cultural paradigms of what should be public religion and private spirituality; what is in effect a moving staircase of working misunderstandings which accounts for the successful persistence of this behaviour and its dependent thinking.

Religions with Soft Orthodoxies

The great Eastern religions have had written theologies and philosophies for many millennia and so we must conclude that widespread literacy may not be a necessity but a contributory factor for the existence of their relatively unobserved orthodoxies with its narrowed requirements for those of that religious persuasion. These religions have not only the behavioural fluidity imposed by their *kaṛmic* perceptions but have the difficulty indeed the impossibility of defining belief and obligatory practice when there are multiple divinities and socially created multiple ways in which they can be approached.

Chinese Thinking and its Soft Orthodoxies

The patterns of thought which may be discovered in some small populations of Australian Aborigines or American Indians may be of value to philosophers but it is the ostensibly long lasting patterns which are likely to exist to some extent in large identifiable populations which are of greater importance to the understanding of religious behaviour. The background to the thinking of such a vast population block as the Han Chinese is complicated not just by this demographic fact but by the antiquity of its literacy and the fact that their system of writing has retained its ideographic uniformities as far back as written records exist. There are no Western parallels to this extraordinary continuity of a system of symbols.

We have in Chinese philosophical and religious thinking the opposite of Judaeo-Christian dualism. Their intellectual elite have a belief in a single spiritual materialism, the Tao having a single spiritual unity, approaching in some respects the recent Western concept of Gaia in which the world is seen as a single ecological system. This is shown in such overarching and continuing concepts as Yin and Yang and the *feng-shui* system for the placing of buildings, graves and furnitures.

The practicalities of Chinese spirituality are tied to a form of orthodoxy which Christians and Muslims would find both inexplicable and distasteful. Their metaphysical pragmatism is shown in the comments of the Emperor Shuwżhi (1644-61) on attempts by a Jesuit to convert him—"You are right but really how can you expect us to practice all these maxims. Cut out one or two of the more difficult ones and then perhaps we can get along with the rest" (Le Comte, 1896-1900:228). Chinese metaphysical enquiry which is the basis of all knowledge has been concerned with nothing but change and not any static and immutable realities (Shuming, 1929:112).

Chinese popular spirituality which views the higher world of the gods and goddesses as having the functional characteristics of a supernatural bureaucracy, making a similar distinction between lower 'field administration' wherein God-officials in both the earthly domains and the underworld each have a specific area of jurisdiction and the higher 'court' comprising the Jade Emperor and the other higher gods. This parallels the understanding of everyday experience of an invisible contemporary central government and local bureaucracies as separately organised reflecting earlier experiences of the traditional imperial government (Cohen, 1988).

So it would appear that contemporary Chinese base their religious practices on their existing bureaucratic realities for propitiating the lesser gods and goddesses with their local understandings whom they can hope to influence in some personal way by establishing reciprocities and hope for the best from the greater spiritual forces which have no local visibility or interests. There is no orthodoxy in this but practical deference for undefined divinities, as shown in a recent Shanghai poster showed eighteen gods and goddesses of which only the central figure of the Goddess of Mercy was identifiable. We know nothing specific about the

Jade Emperor or the Black Dragon King or why the latter's attendants should be sculptured in such humanly unrealistic forms (Chau, 2006:83).

In such a framework of thought it would seem that orthodoxy is conformity to some measure of political understandings and in this there may be little scope for any misunderstandings in their religious pragmatism. The success of the Black Dragon King temple and its survival in the hostile atmosphere of official disapproval of 'feudal superstitions', may be due to the local power holders astuteness in promoting international knowledge of its tree planting programme and its popular annual opera performances. Just as in other places overseas financial support for local industry has been connected to the rebuilding of local temples and ancestral halls. Atheism has limited social and emotional appeal and is certainly not connected institutionally to small communities helping the needy.

Nevertheless the orthodoxy of Chinese religion is difficult to establish since the Emperor as the Son of Heaven and the centre of a state religion disappeared with the 1911 revolution which abolished this religious centralisation however nominal it will have been in the religious lives of peasant farmers and town residents many hundreds of miles from Beijing. This event made clear that China and a single religion could no longer be identified as India was with Hinduism and Saudi Arabia with Islam. So the background to the religious thinking and behaviour of the generality of Chinese both on the mainland, Taiwan and dispersed populations in Singapore and many British and American cities will be a mixture of spiritual bureaucracy, indigenous Taoism and Confucianism and imported Buddhism, Islam and Christianity which have developed independently after the Communist expulsion of all foreign missionaries.

The contemporary Chinese Government which came to power in 1949 is officially atheist within a constitution that permits religious freedom and has tried since then to eradicate any overt expression of religious behaviour as superstitious and feudal. It has erupted violently against efforts by religious organisations such as the over-popular Falung Gong, meditative sect attempting to establish its rights to collective independence of religious thought. No doubt this was based on the memories of the disruption caused by the religious eruptions of the destructive Taiping and Boxer rebellions. There was the persecution and frequent imprisonment of religious practitioners and the wholesale demolition of religious buildings of all persuasions as well as ancestral halls during the Cultural Revolution.

The millennia during which Chinese culture developed has resulted in 'magic' coexisting with science as valid systems of meaning. "what the state refuses to acknowledge in these cases of fraud and guesswork....are only of secondary importance regardless of how they are known. It is the ability to imbue these facts of illness and misfortune with meaning for those who suffer from them that constitute the shaman's special contribution" (Anagnost, 1987). In this context the comparative newness and limitations of science and its relevance to enormous populations who are more concerned with personal illness. They see little connection between their daily lives and the wonders of the new Yangtse dam and that of the Shanghai innovative architectural splendours. Their vague cultural orthodoxies have a stronger hold on Chinese cognitive understandings than the recently politically promoted connected atheistic pragmatism.

Before Buddhism appeared in China as the result of monks visiting India and bringing back Buddhist texts, the Analects of Confucius from the fourth century BC became the code of proper behaviour sustained by the performance of rituals, classical humanism as a call from Heaven. It is difficult to see this pattern of behaviour as religious rather than as one which appealed among the elite's a sense of orderliness required for the rational administration of large areas and large populations (Brook, 2009). It is this which appealed to the current government with its growing interest in Chinese history.

Chinese religious activity has a known identifiable history of over three thousand years and this physical as much as emotional continuity has been the basis of what can be seen today; a framework of orthodox ideas rather than specific behaviour. The complexities of modern popular religious practice which has almost universally emerged following the ideological relaxation which came after the death of Chairman Mao, may have trends but nothing that can approach the orthodoxies of the Western religions of the book. It is more a question of the creeping expansion of religious generalities which may have little connection in popular thinking and practice with the classic texts of Confucius and Lao-Tże.

Underlying both Confucianism and Taoism is this concept of the 'Way', an orderly system of living predating its extension into religious life with a series of binary oppositions which are susceptible to innumerable personal interpretations. The way has no orthodox meaning and what "is understood to be the Way has varied over time as to how it is individually or institutionally interpreted; it is the course of change, the source of things, the rational of being, the moral norms of society, the guidelines for rule, the pattern of nature. Whether the Tao is transcendental or immanent, material or immaterial, above or internal to things are all topics in the current debate" (Lai, 2001:134).

Whereas both Christianity and Islam are inescapably religious in both thinking and practice, the bases of Chinese thinking, the classical formulations are ambivalent and are certainly not in any sense bindingly religious. There is thus an element of secular realism in their intellectual thought but this is virtually ignored in popular Chinese religious behaviour with its temple fairs, opera performances, spirit possession and pictorial iconography; not so much a two level systems but two separate ways of coping with living in which the intellectualism of Chinese thinking is not the arena of last or indeed popular resort.

The Soft Orthodoxies of Hinduism

Social scientists brought up and professionally trained within the Western pattern of pragmatic thought and the rather ostentatious display of its scientific achievements are likely to approach Eastern religions with some degree of secular disparagement. This is combined with some quasi-intellectual reverence for the classics of Eastern religion and philosophy which are considered to be both valuable and incomprehensible. It is difficult for Western predominantly secular intellectuals to take seriously a contemporary Chinese temple dedicated to the Black Dragon King or the Hindu worship of the four armed Goddess Kali with her necklace of skulls and a body smeared with the blood of her victims. There is in this an ongoing conflict between some kinds of intellectual minority status of orderliness and the social reality of the disorderly beliefs held by many millions.

The so-called popular religious practices predominate globally in forms which are not overtly related to written orthodoxies, and in which their intellectuals do not make theological distinctions other than gradations of association with the divine in which there are no time limitations. So this distinction has to be assessed partially as a division created by printing rather than literacy and the institutionalisation forced on the major religions by what are in fact secular commitments and legal conformities to their surrounding societies.

Of course, elitist intellectualism of much religious documentation and its conformity to global trends are important but it has to be accepted that such works are of peripheral influence on those involved in public religion and private spirituality. This is noticeable in Eastern religion and particularly Hinduism. What is likely to be the connection between its ancient sacralised texts—the *puranas* written in Sanskrit—and the seventy million pilgrims who were estimated to have attended the last twelve yearly Kumbh Mela in order to immerse themselves in the holy Ganges at an astrologically determined time. Whatever this mass of humanity got from this ritual which cost them time and money it is likely to be minimally related to these texts.

Hinduism is an ancient religion which has come in written form out of an ancient religiously polyvalent civilisation in the form of a large number of sacralized documents of which there are eighteen major ones with some hundred thousand stanzas. In addition there are the Sanskrit epics such as the very lengthy *Mahabharata* and the shorter *Ramayana.* This whole body of documents is related to the polytheistic mythologies of Vishnu, Shiva and many other gods and goddesses and the more abstract Brahma which has no connections with historical events. They do not provide any code of conduct except what can be deduced from the pragmatically unusual lives of these two major gods which is the basis of the two main devotional systems in Hinduism.

So this ancient faith which has the unusual characteristic of coming from birth to Hindus rather than by conversion, has no particular form or single founder but a long series of charismatic founders of movements of thought and practice. While these prominent individuals have emerged from time to time such as Vivekananda, Gandhi, Sai Baba and Sarasvati, they have occupied no centralised institutional positions of authority which would have allowed them to spread a form of orthodoxy with authority beyond their own circle of devotees and disciples. There was perhaps in Hinduism an understanding and a feeling that an orthodoxy would be against what is generally seen as the fluidity of Hindu practice and philosophy which has no beginning and no end. Those who have studied Hinduism for years have often felt that they are no more competent to make conclusions than they were when they first started their studies.

Hinduism has no particular institutional structure and in villages and towns there are both local and more general gods and goddesses with varying functions and a disorderly and changing hierarchy of responsibilities as well as purely personal and domestic devotional involvements. To most enquirers the most striking characteristic of Hinduism is the caste system and its modern modifications maintained through sub-caste endogamy and changed through hypergamy, the arranged marriage of daughters to advance the sub-caste membership of grand-children, rather than its earlier forms located in wide areas of caste conformity. Even the most important of contemporary Hindus are at a loss to define what constitutes the foundations of this enduring faith whose extravagancies are just as visible in west London as in Kolkata. Westerners are likely to smile indulgently at Mahatma Gandhi's statement that the core of Hinduism is the veneration for the cow.

There is a personal conviction in the biological inheritance of this faith rather than socialisation which accounts for much religious persistence and for its survival even among those who emigrate to Fiji, Mauritius, Guyana and South Africa radically altering what might have been their caste practices in India. While we shall see that Buddhism in its orthodoxy is clearly impossible to follow, Hinduism in its total illogically of thought and practice would just as clearly be impossible to follow. The intellectual finds it difficult to believe that there is any rationality in a religion which connects business success with the elephant headed God Ganesh. It no doubt owes its continuing successes to the satisfactions of its ornate ritualism under the cover of its seemingly incomprehensible theologies. It has an inherent imaginativeness which Hindus believe has a foundation in an authentic religious reality.

The Soft Orthodoxy of Buddhism

It is difficult to use the word orthodoxy in relation to Buddhism because initially there is the fact that virtually nothing is known with any degree of historical truth about the life of the Buddha and that the numerous documents such as the Dialogues of the Buddha attributed to him were probably written some three centuries after his death.

We also start with an initial difficulty as to whether the contemporary ideas and practices of what is called the Buddhist religion have any connection with what are considered to be the philosophical advice and non-religious procedures attributed to the Lord Buddha. These are summarised in the Four Noble Truths of which the last affirms the existence of a path leading to deliverance from the universal experience of suffering centred on the egoism of human nature. It is only through the abolition of self through morality, meditation and wisdom as set out in the Eightfold Path that the individual can achieve this personal extinction by absorption into the Infinite. A nihilistic process through an endless succession of soulless lives in which the individual or whatever it is that dies and is reborn receives no assistance from any supernatural forces which do not exist. It is usually agreed that a form of thinking and behaviour which involves the supernatural can be classified as a religion and if this is so then these basic requirements attributed to the Lord Buddha make Buddhism a system of philosophical thought and not a religion.

This absence of the supernatural would mean that the overwhelming majority of men and women currently within what is considered to be the Buddhist faith are prime examples of working misunderstandings. Their activities are clearly in contravention to the system of thought and practice initiated by the Lord Buddha and so the current practices labelled Buddhist are more an example of human religious versatility and need than any development of the original idea of eventually achieving secular detachment from any form of individualism.

Bateson (Bateson, 1911) summarized the teachings of orthodox Buddhism rather than specifically that of the Lord Buddha as materialism, atheism, pessimism, nihilism and egoism. In fact a series of foundational precepts which can have had few attractions for any human being other than those whom Western psychologists would define as profoundly disturbed, extreme examples of clinical depression.

By renouncing the social environment in which each individual lives the Buddhist aspires to detachment from reality. The widowed in Myanmar are reluctant to remarry as it would means attachment to another person and thus count against them improving their status in their next rebirth. Large numbers become monks in a monastic environment with few possessions and a dependence on daily begging round for food. There is their removal of body hair as moves towards a necessary depersonalisation. It is more a rite of passage than the trying out of a possible vocation for the monastic life.

As to the existence of any single Buddhist orthodoxy there is the division between the northern *Mahayana*, the Greater Vehicle and the southern *Hinayana* Lesser Vehicle form. Within each of these there have been and are different schools of thought initiated by charismatic intellectuals. There are no overall orthodoxies other than these two broad forms within which individuals can assess their own progress towards the extinction of their individuality. In the northern form some individuals, the *Boddhisattavas* have delayed their achievement of this extinction of individuality, their 'personal' Enlightenment, to help the progress towards nihilism of the less fortunate and the southern form in which individual are left to what they can achieve by their own efforts. Rather than adhering to any specific orthodoxy which Buddhist thought could interpret as a form of attachment from which detachment must be achieved, Buddhism in its socially observable forms would appear to divide rather than to attempt the compromises which would be necessary in order to create any overarching orthodoxy.

It would seem that only monks and to a lesser extent nuns have detached themselves from social life and who have formally renounced all worldly attachments could be described as actively Buddhist. Even this way of life could be described as a barrier to achieving Enlightenment and in Thailand only the monks living under orange umbrellas on the rubbish dumps of Bangkok could be considered as realistically detached from society. *Hinayana* monks have their conduct governed by a set of some two hundred prohibitions (The Patimokkha, 1966).

Without any realistic existence of a recognised orthodoxy the practices of the Buddhists of Myanmar have been divided into four categories (Spiro, 1971) between which these men and women move according to their psychological and social environment. Nibbanic Buddhism exemplified by monks of whom there are enormous numbers as most men spend a short time as a monk as a rite of passage to social adulthood, who have had themselves initiated into the preliminaries of total detachment. *Kammatic* Buddhism in which believers are involved in attempting to achieve worldly satisfactions. Apotropaic Buddhism in which the performance of rituals is carried out against the dangers of ordinary life and finally Esoteric Buddhism in which believers use magic to achieve salvation. Most Burmese follow an Esoteric Buddhism which is a system of magical ritualism to cope with the realities of their current lives.

While there is an absence of the supernatural in orthodox Buddhist faith in practice the Buddha himself is treated as an embodied spirit to whom appeals are made and with whom a relationship is maintained by regular offerings and by paying attention to the seasonal costume changes of statues of the Buddha. The Sri Lankans certainly worship gods and propitiate demons and very generally attempt the manipulation of numberless supernatural powers so that they have a spirit religion almost complete in itself (Gombrich and Obbyeskere, 1988). The Burmese have a general cult of the Thirty Six *nats* or spirits to whom a substantial amount of ritual is directed, just as the Thais have spirit shrines almost everywhere on the verandas of apartments and in the compounds of hotels, offices, factories as well as beneath specific trees in which the Burmese consider that there are different spirits in the tops, trunks and roots (Glass, 1985:116).

The Indeterminate Orthodoxies of Christianity

Certainly Christianity has its origins in the preaching and life of Jesus Christ but in comparison to Islam based on the more recent inspiration of the Prophet Muhammad, it has not developed any overall specific orthodoxy. It has a history of constant splits over points of doctrine rather than over the implementation of the Ten Commandments which do not have the attainable precision of the Islamic Five Pillars of the Faith.

Contemporary Christianity has no more unity than its name and both within single societies and internationally there are innumerable cults, sects and denominations which their participants call Christian. A study of South Africa (Barrett, 1968) showed that there were six thousand identifiable Christian worshipping organisations in that country alone. Moving north there would be the large Kimbanguist Church in šaire and the popular Kenyan Roman Catholic breakaway Legio Maria and other independent Churches, prayerful places in which to feel at home (Welbourn, 1961). The United States alone will have similar numbers of Christian sects and denominations.

Apart from the historical splits and the division between Roman Catholicism and Protestantism in the mediaeval Reformation, Christianity has never developed any comprehensive political, economic and theological social unity as has occurred in Islam which has the Prophet Mohammad ending his life as a secular ruler. Christ had specifically distinguished between obligations to God and to secular authority.

While Buddhism encourages splits rather than compromises over insoluble metaphysical issues, Christianity has repeatedly split because the participants could not compromise over doctrines to which they were convinced they had divine access. There are states which claim to a Christian basis for their political activities but whenever this has been used as a basis for legislation it has proved unworkable because of the variability of social behaviour and in practice only the state is involved as in legislation for crimes which do not have victims.

There are Christian sects which identify themselves by costume and physically isolate their practices in enclosed communities with varying secular involvements. Others with practices that discourage recruitment such as the Christian Scientists' avoidance of medical treatment or prophylaxis by immunisation and the Jehovah's Witnesses' prohibiting blood transfusions or require the handling of poisonous snakes in the southern United States. Others like the Church of England, the Anglican denomination which is based on ostensible doctrinal uniformity but is now in the process of splitting on the issues of homosexual clergy and women bishops.

Some such as the successful Mormons, the American Latter Day Saints base their beliefs and practices on the inspiration of a nineteenth century prophet and others like the British Methodists have faded as their industrial base of deprivation has disappeared with the comprehensive extension of the welfare state. There is also the fact that some of the basic requirements cannot be fulfilled such as the prohibition of covetousness and the injunction to leave all and follow Christ, both of which are similar to the unattainable extremism of Buddhist doctrine.

So there is the theological hope for uniformity with a single orthodoxy because of the moral scandal of a divided Church but the reality is that such an orthodoxy would exist without any means of enforcement beyond that provided by the individual conscience and their social and religious commitments. Whenever there is a denominational orthodoxy, belief and participation is always a working misunderstanding.

The Hard Orthodoxy of Communism and Religion

A political system with a well-organised and secular ideology as is the case with Communism is in practice millennial because it is based on the development and achievement of material benefits which in practice cannot be realistically delivered even within the life-time of succeeding generations of believers; it is a system based on secular millenarianism.

It is appropriate to discuss this system after considering Chinese thinking because of two predominating factors. The Chinese Government is ideologically atheist as a Communist state and has been since it came to power in 1949. Further the bases of what has been theoretically considered Chinese religion are decidedly secular with Confucianism as a code of proper behaviour, Taoism is based on the 'way' which is as secular as much as religious and Buddhism in its orthodoxy is a way of thinking and not a way of worship. What the contemporary Chinese are practicing as their popular religion now and before the 1949 revolution has little to do with the classics on which Chinese philosophy and religion are supposedly based.

All states under Communist control have put their hostility to religion into practise. Their governments consider religion to be 'the opium of the people' and as an immoral obstruction to material progress from which came various forms of persecution concentrating on institutionalised faiths with specialised 'priesthoods', such as Buddhism and Christianity. Priestless Islam and some Protestant groups centred on the reading of the *Koran* and *Bible* were better able to survive until the ideological relaxations following from the Russian Perestroika and the death of Chairman Mao.

The Russian state destroyed churches and temples or turned them to secular uses and made the study of Communism necessary in all educational institutions as well as imprisoning and executing Christian priests. The Chinese Communist party similarly destroyed or secularised churches, ancestral halls and temples as well as venerated graves on agricultural land for the extension of communal farms.

Communism's orthodoxy misunderstood human behaviour in the narrow functionalism of its material economics and its policy makers certainly misunderstood the limitations of what they could achieve in bettering the lives of their citiżens even if they did not go to the extremes of the Pol Pot regime in destroying the society both socially and demographically on which it depended. Whatever their successes in the relation to religion Communist regimes have changed some overt forms of religious practice but probably not more than changing overt public religion to covert personal spiritualities and its more secretive forms which it had always been practised.

Communist regimes failed to progressively improve the material lives of their citiżens to parallel the people's common knowledge of the material successes of the capitalist Japanese and Western societies. It became a relict faith with millennial objectives perhaps even with its eschatological overtones. Many realised that there could be no secular solutions to inevitable human suffering even with material improvements for which religion was considered necessary. Such regimes never achieved any working misunderstandings.

Islamic Thinking and its Hard Orthodoxy

Of all the major religions Islam is the least likely to have believers involved in what could be interpreted as working misunderstandings over religious beliefs and practices. In general terms it has a single code of requirements over which there is no exegetical dispute which in any way parallels the multiplicity of Christian denominational interpretations. The split between the minority Shia and majority Sunni is over the finality of the Prophet's message or its ongoing existence in particular successors but not about the principles of the Islamic faith.

There are several cumulative reasons for the simplicity of its orthodoxy. Whatever the sources of the Prophet Muhammad's inspiration, there was no great time lapse between its occurrence and its recording in writing, his biography contains historically verifiable facts in comparison to which Jesus Christ is virtually unknown and the exegesis of the *Koran* shows its contemporary connections.

Secondly, the Prophet started his public life with metaphysical involvements as the inspired creator of a new faith in a political vacuum between the domains of Byżantium and Baghdad and ended up at the time of his death as the ruler of a state. The only parallel to this might be Joseph Smith, the founder of the Church of Christ of the Latter day Saints, the Mormons when they first established themselves as an isolated settlement in the semi-desert wastes of Utah in the mid-nineteenth century after hostility had driven them from the more populated lands to the East. It prospered in a political vacuum just as Islam had established itself in a hostile environment between the controls of Byżantium and Baghdad.

In his lifetime the Prophet against the background of his personal inspiration and charismatic personality, was involved in some thirty warlike skirmishes, heading a migration of refugees and the administration of a group working for its own survival and having to solve such pragmatic problems such as a number of widows from early battles for whom there was no available family support.

The chapters of the *Koran* which are datable in reverse order, show the change in content from the abstractions of religion to more secular concerns. In comparison to Christianity and the Eastern religions the metaphysical is less obvious except in the various forms of Sufism devoted to spiritual exercises developed as a reaction to what these believers saw as the spiritually aridity of Islamic legalism.

Orthodoxy among all Muslims is based on the same foundations, the Five Pillars of the Faith which are not disputed by Muslim theologians or Koranic scholars. The affirmation of faith in the one God and the Prophet as his Messenger in a single sentence. The five daily prayers which came to be a clock related short repetitive formula, the giving of alms, the fasting between sunrise and sundown during the lunar month of Ramżān, charity and the pilgrimage to Mecca once in a *lifetime*.

The orthodox elaboration of the Prophet's divinely inspired revelation to meet the circumstances of a constantly changing social and political environment and events which could not have been anticipated, lies in the systematic elaboration of what might have been the reactions of the Prophet had he been confronted with these issues. These decisions were made by what were in fact rather more lawyers than theologians belonging to four schools of regionalised law, Hanafi, Hanbali, Maliki and Shafii systems.

These lawyers have monopolised the creation of on-going orthodoxy in matters which non-Muslim contemporary commentators would consider to be of secular and indeed individually private concern such as the prohibition of interest in commercial transactions and of various forms of private sexual activity and to the purely biological as menstruation preventing religious practices.

These lawyers have monopolised and indeed created a widening range of orthodoxy from what was originally required for the salvation of a predominantly pastoral people of whom a few engaged in inter-tribal trade and urban living. They make explicit what might have been the Prophet's decisions and classifying them in terms of approved, allowed, condoned or ignored as a matter of indifference to faith. In this they are assisted by the *hadith* the many thousands of sayings attributed to the Prophet each of which has a pedigree as to the degree to which it is considered reliable.

As a faith it has always been far less concerned with religious issues and their metaphysical difficulties as with its physical performance as part of a single lived experience. The outsider is certainly astonished to find in such spirituality handbooks as that of Al-Ghażali instructions as to how to excrete and clean oneself prior to praying. It is a religion in which not only are the requirements of orthodoxy widely agreed on without dispute but are extended to a whole range of activities which the contemporary or rather Western world would consider to be well outside religious concern. Examples would be women being prohibited from driving in Saudi Arabia and for them to wearing black smocks in Iran and the existence of a separate religious police force in both these countries concerned with the national enforcement of the public aspects of Islamic law.

Much that is assessed by moralists and theologians with a global perspective as having placed in a world of interrelatedness such as religious based terrorism, the persistent hostility and indeed killing of those of other faiths cannot be seen clearly as working misunderstandings since there are Koranic support for such behaviour. The appreciation of its orthodoxy is certainly widespread but in face of its limited theological ability to adapt, it has less latitude to continue as has the working misunderstandings in other less confrontational faiths.

The Elusive Nature of Orthodoxy

However, much religious institutions may propagate their orthodoxies and even producing statistics on the conformities of their believing members, this as any detailed study of religious behaviour must confirm, is really an illusion created by the organisation's method of laying out its orthodoxies and their method of recording. The Philippine Independent Church founded in 1902 has a check-in-system in which each member has a ticket with his name on it which he removes on attending a service and replace it on the board on leaving similar to the clock-in system of many factories. There could be no better method of the turn-style method of recording attendance but of course it can be individually falsified and tells us nothing about the relationship of people attending to the orthodoxy of that denomination.

Religious behaviour is as varied as the personalities and social environments disclosed by any detailed study. These are time consuming and expensive assessments and without any doubt very little is known in detail of what any individual believes and practices over any length of time; indeed a relationship to orthodoxy can fluctuate day-by-day.

While individuals may believe with complete sincerity that their religious ideas and practices have been consistent over the years, this is not only unlikely but impossible. Each individual is in a constant process of intra-personal physiological and psychological adjustment to ageing as well as conscious and unconscious changes to their social environment in which they are behaviourally caught. They are constantly moving targets for the social scientist.

While there will be misunderstandings within any study of religious beliefs and practices, there could also be the factor that many or most adherents to a particular faith do not understand its complexities. Their body of understanding is likely to be composed of a patchwork of information from social encounters and the bits left-over in memory from what they may have learned in the past. A Christian convert is likely to have gone through a course of instruction before baptism while a convert to Islam has to do no more than affirm in front of witnesses that he or she believes in Allah and the Prophet Muhammad. It is not known how anyone can convert to Hinduism since it can only be acquired by birth and it has no overall orthodoxy to which an individual could affirm belief.

Even the ceremonies of non-literate quasi-traditional religions are complex and few can remember what they did in the past nor why they did it and the only permanency will be in the photographs of the visiting anthropologist. Similarly the details of such faiths as Jainism with an historical background of more than a millennium are so complex that few can understand the reasons behind the intricacies of its rituals. Indeed most Jains in their regular worship may well think say to themselves that this complex knowledge is unnecessary for their faith. They would not see this situation as a working misunderstanding but that is what it is in functional terms as most would just assume that they are orthodox Jains, even though not all that many go to the extremes of veiling their mouths to prevent the possibility of swallowing an insect or brushing a seat before sitting for fear of squashing one.

Even the few who read the theological explanations of the faith to which they belong or have been converted to, cannot be said to necessarily understand what are the intellectual implications of the faiths to which they belong. Indeed it is a difficult question as to the extent that individual understandings are involved. A southern Indian community of outcaste Hindus converted as a community to Roman Catholicism as the local priest had effectively represented them in a dispute with the secular authorities. Many Outcaste Hindus became Buddhists in mass conversions because of their leader's, Dr. Ambedkar, own conversion. Numbers would have had little understanding of Buddhism and indeed their religious practices in its popular forms continued to be Hindu except for some changes in images and pictures. In fact, all that had changed was their religious classification from Outcaste within the Hindu system of socio-religious understandings to being Buddhist which excluded them from what they saw as a demeaning social and political classification.

It is not only that believers may not know the nature of the orthodoxies to which they have become subordinated by their faith. It seems likely that only in Islam is it possible to evaluate Muslims in terms of their adherence to a specifically defined orthodoxy; of the Five Pillars of the Faith only the first involves belief and the remaining four only require performance within that belief. To pray in a set form five times per day, fasting during daylight hours in the holy month of Ramżān, a single pilgrimage to Mecca and generosity to the poor on Fridays. To be a good Muslim does not seem to require any intellectual sophistication and only the difficulties and inconvenience of these physical requirements. This is simplicity itself in comparison to the requirements of denominational Christianity and to an even greater extent with the behavioural intricacies of orthodox Judaism.

Even comparisons are not possible with Eastern faiths which not only have not defined their principles by any centralising authority. Their theologians might even feel that a definition is a form of property from which they ought to be detached and which would detract from the aim of personal extinction or unification with the Divine at which they should be aiming.

As an example Jainism is a faith believed in by a cult-educated and relatively well-to-do Indian supporters with a long-standing literary tradition. The extent to which a large number of believers have committed themselves to a particular framework of thinking can be assumed to exist in some form but what it involves for ostensible individual believers is beyond factual assessment. What an individual may state or write down about their beliefs is subject to socio-psychological handicaps, so it has to be accepted as no more than a possibly inaccurate rather than accurate expression of a personal religious reality at that time alone.

As to what Jains actually do and in conformity to what is by no means clear in any collective sense. In attributing meanings to one part of the prayer process *puja* the flower offerings "people gave not entirely random but certainly very different meanings and in some cases the meanings were dramatically opposed" (Humphrey and Laidlaw, 1994). It was also recorded that Jains stating that they are performing a particular prayer were in fact performing quite different ritual elements. It would seem that it is the personal assumption of validity that is important rather than that they were doing this or that in conformity to some known or stated orthodoxy.

The Jain prayer ritual stems from Hindu origins using the same word *puja*, comprising acts which according to authoritative Sanskrit texts have to be carried out in order (Fuller, 1992:57-82). In any possibility of Jain orthodoxy there is thus the added complication of Hindu admixtures as Jain altars may contain statues of those who have attained release but also representations of those who are clearly Hindu deities such as Ganesh and Lakshmi; particularly the former whose connection with prosperity is particularly significant for Jains who are largely a business community as agriculture would involve killing insects and worms.

Fuller records that in a major Hindu temple in Madura only four of these required prayer stages were being used and that is in a prominent religious centre which has organising professional priests. In any carrying out of any lengthy religious ritual the conducting priest unless he is confining himself to following a written order of service on the altar before him, is unlikely to be following the conformities of any orthodoxy, much less in the case of the Madura temple in which a festival might last a week of more or less continual rituals.

Orthodoxy is also difficult to see as a religious reality when ceremonies are in practice open to anyone as in an Indian setting in which festivals are social as much as religious occasions for whole communities. The Islamic Moharram festival is an occasion for communal participation in which the excitement is shared with Hindus; how indeed could it be otherwise (Saiyid, 1984:113-142) in shared village and city environments.

A further case would be the sacred site of Katagarama in southern Sri Lanka where this nominally Buddhist centre has a Hindu temple and a Muslim mosque in the same compound. About half a million people come there in the July-August pilgrimage season in decorated cars and buses without any clear sense of religious focus. Buddhist monks there complain that the majority of participants had a pattern of worship that was more Hindu than Buddhist.

In the Asian context it seems certain that the sacred sites which are nominally Hindu, Muslim or Roman Catholic have pilgrims or at least visitors of all persuasions (Younger, 2002:26-40) such as the shrine to the Virgin Mary outside Shanghai. Among the many million Hindus who attended the last Kumbh Mela there were certainly many Christians, Muslims as well as agnostics who were there because of the business opportunities provided by such a concentration of people.

Then there are examples of whole communities usually of Untouchables who have changed religion as in the case of a south Indian community which became Roman Catholic because the local priest had represented them successfully in a dispute with the secular local government which can hardly have involved any commitment to Christian orthodoxy. Dr. Ambedkar commented that such Christian carried into their Christianity their Hindu caste practices so that there were Brahmin and non-Brahmin Roman Catholics (Ambedkar, 1989:456) such as there are in the much older Roman Catholic communities in Goa to which there may be few recent converts.

More significant are the mass conversions of Untouchables from Hinduism to Buddhism in which the change can only have involved the installation of statues of the Buddha in their temples and in the popular pictures in their houses. Amongst the people changing there can have been very little understandings of Buddhist orthodoxy as who would have been available to teach its doctrines to some two million who followed Dr. Ambedkar's well considered personal change. These new Buddhists and Christians by conversion will have defined themselves out of their Hindu status of being permanently inferior and by this achieved new political voting leverage for special consideration.

It would seem that orthodoxy to be even nominally effective has to have a number of contributing elements of which the most important are definitions which have been committed to authoritative writing to which there is institutional commitment and supervision. Of course, this cannot be the basis of any religious commitment when the culture is in religious terms non-literate and its quasi-traditional ceremonies are made up from memory within vague culturally acceptable paradigms and the use of valued objects where meaning is subject to constant personal reinterpretation.

But even in the Eastern religions whose literate origins are far older than Christian and Islamic ones have some idea of a written orthodoxy. Their sacred documents remain in the background without any popular appeal more as discussion points for a specially trained learned elite or as the assumed basis for the teaching of charismatic individuals. These texts are not liturgical manuals with any parallels to the exact and institutionally enforced regularities of most Christian ceremonies.

This evasiveness to the possibility of regularity is not the absence of the idea of or the possibility of a created orthodoxy and its enforceable establishment. The problem if it can be called 'one' is the seeing of orthodoxy in its Western framework as something allied to its retention as a form of property. Historically the surrounding societies were often already centralised and substantially institutionalised with their own bureaucracies. The absence of such frameworks in religion cannot be seen as related to any failure of the ability to organise but a matter of cognitive choice.

It would seem that the concept of orthodoxy is a Western one related to the so-called religions of the book and the availability and the commitment to writing is not in itself a predetermining factor. In the Western senses it seems to obscure and indeed want to obscure the individuality of religious practice and ideas, while elsewhere this individualism seems to be the basic and perhaps inevitable factor when as in Japan there are reputed to be several million gods and goddesses. In such a situation there can be no misunderstandings because initially religious understandings beyond personal ones are so diffused.

The Limited Functions of Orthodoxy

Theological orthodoxy is always readily available in the printed books of institutionalised metropolitan faiths. The fact that this is so easily available to believing populations who can read leads to some assumptions that they are important in any general sense; being able to read is not necessarily related to the reading of information which a religious elite considers necessary.

A person's doctrinal beliefs may have a surface relevancy to those reciting the creed as part of every celebration of the Roman Catholic Mass in which it is heard or recited from Pavlovian memory. It is certainly not a reflection of what they know and use about the sacred from everyday personal experience (Baggett, 2001:8). It may be that what is worshipped or believed is an amalgam of what is seen as plausible from social realities and which has personal emotional appeal as we see in devotion to the Virgin Mary in Western Christianity but less so in its Eastern forms.

Orthodoxy is always a top-down imposition from the thinking of specialists who are more or less inevitably detached from those who have subsistence survival concerns and who are more institutionally detached from inevitable distresses. It would seem that where there is orthodoxy there are inevitably misunderstandings.

8
The Consequences of Orthodoxy

In practice any orthodoxy is a social and religious wall holding back change until the pressure building up behind it forces it to change unless the religion has the institutional means of authorising or initiating change when the orthodoxy is too soft to need legitimising change as it constantly occurring anyway or failing to occur in those with hard orthodoxies. There is then a slow and reluctant process within which there is constant discussion almost exclusively in the major Christian denominations over adaptation. Islam has the means to change through authoritative figures issuing rulings *fatwa* on their own account. In practice the egalitarian nature of the Imam role inhibits charismatic leadership so that they are unlikely to go beyond what is likely to be approved by their fellow professionals and local popular support.

This area of conflict is not a conspicuous feature of Eastern religions which do not have public debates over the inadequacies of their theologies for contemporary needs. In these faiths without any understandings of what orthodoxy requires or theological thinking implies there is a constant process of individual and social religious innovation.

The Documentary Nature of Orthodoxy

We have seen that orthodoxy is enabled if not created socially by mass printing rather than by the invention of writing and that it is in reality a relatively modern creation for certain religions particularly those of the book, Christianity, Islam and Judaism. The traditional religions in societies which have not developed writing or indeed felt any need to attach their religious beliefs and practices to writing, have the idea of orthodoxy as an ongoing and ever varying social conformity rather more in neighbourhoods than in societies. What are appropriate religious ideas and practices move along the channels of public opinion which may be no more than the next market place, the wedding ceremony of another faith and gossip as to how others cope or seem to cope successfully with distress.

The Eastern religions have not created the definitions and institutional centralisations necessary for the appearances of orthodoxy despite having instituted literacy long before the creations of the systems used by the religions of the book. They have no behavioural forms which could parallel the orthodoxies of the religions of the book and their creation of the resultant categories of socially disruptive heresies. They have an open multiplicity rather than the more covert ones in religions of the book.

Social scientists or theologians when they look at religious faiths other than their own or indeed at their own absence of any definite faith, printed usually go straight to the printed ideas and commitments of religious organisations or the explanatory elaborations of their intellectual elites. They more or less start at the end of the history which dominates their understandings of what is now going on. In a social world of almost infinite behavioural variety, theological writings and the pronouncements of religious organisations, take on a behavioural reality to which social scientists tend to attach to religious communities which are socially intrinsically unstable.

Thus, the foundations on which they build their understandings of these great religions which we know as Buddhism, Christianity, Hinduism, Judaism and Islam are based on documents which are often difficult to read and understand and thus require special learning to do so. Printed objects have often become divorced from the social environments in which they were created, regardless of any attributed divine origins.

So the first layer of our understandings of these great faiths are documents which are stuck in the time and circumstances of their creation so that their meaning has become institutionalised and inanimate. In many cases the language used was not and is not in everyday use and has to be translated for believers by socially detached and emotionally uninvolved interpreters.

The Chinese may not have words in Mandarin for 'belief' or 'faith' because in their complicated language they may have no use for such abstractions. The meanings which they put into and take out of their religious needs and practices may only touch occasionally on the meanings which are attributed to their great thinkers and their classical writings.

In Christianity particularly enormous intellectual and administrative effort has been put into the creation of defined and printed requirements. They impose a sense of valuable emotional stability for many believers even though their actions on these meanings may have little relationship to what has been defined so carefully.

It is not so much literacy as such but the spread of what has been written through the growth of religious institutions which has created a distinction between sets of stabilised belief requirements and those that are required to believe in them. Early systems of writing such as the cuneiform literacy of the Assyrians do not seem to have used it for the stabilisation of belief but overwhelmingly for economic needs; writing could have been invented to facilitate taxation not to create religious uniformities. It seems unlikely that the hieroglyphs used in the temples of ancient Egypt were used to stabilize belief, but more for the creation of awe with signs which those who viewed them, would have been individually used rather than interpreted in their own culturally channelled and individual ways.

The Uncontrollable Nature of Symbolic Meaning

Institutions can define the meanings of their requirements but Victor Turner has pointed out that every symbol has a fan of meanings. A few symbols such as the cross and crescent have certain widespread primary religious significances but still have meanings for individuals and communities which have secular involvements. There is always the factor of heteroglossia in which the use of each word and phrase in religious contexts will have an ever changing spread of meanings related to the social and psychological circumstances of their users ranging from those who are mentally handicapped to philosophers. Although we may believe that there is stability in our own symbolic understandings, this is unlikely. A defined meaning may retain its exactness in inorganic chemistry but it can never do so when its individual reception will vary not only with intellect but with the social situation in which it is used. There is nothing that is not transitory in the use and understandings of symbols.

For any individual or community there is a limited range of time and of situations in which the meanings are sufficiently exact to be understood beyond particular contexts. There is little here that can be used in comparative analyses because it is likely that their survival rests of their ambiguities rather than any exactnesses of use and meaning. The taking of the wafer representing the reality of Christ's presence in the Roman Catholic Mass in the Philippines was changed from its reception in the hand to being directly placed in the mouth when it was found that it was not being swallowed but retained to give power to fighting cocks.

Christianity has the central symbol of the cross and its use in architecture, art and as a protective amulet and Islam limits itself to decorative calligraphy for the *Koran* and equally magnificent architecture. Here there is a confining symbolism about which it is reasonable to attempt some at least definitions of orthodox meaning.

At the other extreme there are the symbols of the Eastern religions which to the analytical Western mind with its binary restrictions are seemingly a difficult tangle to interpret holistically. Every temple or illustration is seemingly only a confusing clutter of symbols. Almost every popular Hindu picture on sale in every market has enough symbols to provide any analyst with a lifetime of work.

This means that for both soft and hard faiths theologians have virtually no control over what may be being represented and in what form it takes in the individual mind and in communal public opinions. Is this a theological issue or is it the carrying forward into contemporary life of the indefinable and infinitely variable complex of symbols in preliterate and non-literate religious systems with no orthodoxies. Scottish Presbyterians certainly limit symbolism in their meeting places while Peruvian Roman Catholicism verges on Hinduism in the complexity of its varied symbols which continue from their pre-Columbian cultural understandings.

The attempt of Christian Churches and Islam to keep control of its symbols and their meanings but this is probably an impossibility when the controllers in their specialised professional education are trained and socialised into a different religious culture to that of the people with whom they will be dealing with pastorally. The Muslim Yao of southern Tanzania in a patrilineal religion but who are culturally matrilineal base their communal emotions on a packet of earth brought from the area from which they emigrated. It seems unlikely that even with indigenous dominance of local churches there will be any better control over Christian symbolic meanings with the intrusion of better understood traditionalism and contemporary lateral mass media influences (Rappaport, 1976). The Sukuma bishop of Mwanza in Tanzania removed from the altar the shell symbol of chieftainship which had been put there by a highly respected and popular missionary priest with a reputation for adaptation but this action over a visible symbol would have been just a minor element in the mental imagery of any Sukuma. The fact remains that the meaning of symbols will always be uncontrollable as they are individually interpreted and environmentally variable.

The Distortions of Definition

Definitions are not in reality any part of everyday life so that except in hard science and in the legal requirements of developed states where they are bureaucratic necessities but they are very much a human creation enabled by literacy. There is an urban-industrial need for orderliness and predictability. In trying to find out the religious ideas and practices of people who are in this respect functionally and emotionally almost non-literate, who do not hinge their religiousness on reading much less on the comprehension of what is written, so social scientists have to rely on the instabilities of conversation and description.

The researchers in discussion with the vocal and cooperative intellectuals in the communities they are studying almost inevitably fail to find anything which can be called definitions; there is certainly a scale in which they will state that this is what we ought to do or have been taught to do but this is what actually happens citing each event as behaviourally different according to the social circumstances in which it occurs. Then of course these researchers find that there is the third category, what actually happens according to their detached and necessarily fragmented observations and understandings.

The overall complexity of religious ideas and attempts to simplify their meanings for the individual in writing can perhaps be shown in the titles given to specific pieces of music. Sibelius's Kullervo Symphony fourth movement is entitled 'the origin of fire' and Stravinsky composed 'the rite of spring' but he went so far as to say that his music had no meanings. But in reality those who listen to this music as they do in listening to Indian *ragas*, create their own passing meanings just as they will do when participating in religious ceremonies and listening to liturgical music and watching liturgical movements. This indeed is a complex and individual process to which there can be no single answer just as there cannot be for the individual any single meaning for a prolonged Hindu ceremony at Madura. This lasted a full week in which there are day and night seemingly both continuous and discontinuous religious activities with a multiplicity of foci whereas in Christian and Islamic more time-limited ceremonies there are the conducting priests or prayer leaders.

For most people a religious ceremony is more or less what they think they have always done and there is no need for meaning in any scholastic sense which goes beyond the experienced realities of that ritual. If the enquiries persists they shift the questioner on to the need to consult a ritual specialist who might be able to answer such questions. It would seem that whatever definitions appear are tautologically created by those who need them and that in their purposive general application there is very limited application and use as for most people meanings are subconscious.

To refer to non-literacy in any contemporary society as correlated to some form of intellectual inadequacy or laziness which distorts the realities of religious practices cannot be an explanation. Most believers do not base their participation on reading any written order of service and for Christians they may only refer to a book in order to sing the hymns which accompany a particular service. Both Christians and Muslims base their faith and practices on what they have learned by heart through socialisation and the written formulations of theologians are no part of this. There is little interest in definitions rather than in the performance of authoritatively provided liturgies or those authoritatively created by charismatic figures.

The original definitions created by and for a faith once it developed into the initial stages of institutionalisation, were for the relatively simple needs of small communities devoted to a new faith. The need for cohesiveness among the small band of original Muslims led to the initial definitions of what was necessary for those Muslims to do in order to survive as a group. It may be that their simplicity was related to an understanding of their limited social and intellectual ability to cope with complex theological definitions which the Prophet Muhammad knew had already splintered Christianity which indeed he may have misunderstood in thinking from her prevalence in prayers that the Virgin Mary was part of the Trinity. Muslims in Tanzania have been seen to petition the statue of the Virgin Mary and have inserted her name into the 'Our Father' prayer (Wijsen, 2007:222).

This early clarity soon outlives its functional usefulness and these definitions are no longer related to their original purposes and the circumstances in which the original prophetic utterances came about. Islam became a political force, Christianity and Judaism dispersed into isolated colonies of which only the former became connected to overt social and political issues in the Holy Roman Empire. What these religions meant became the centre of speculation and redefinition in intellectual structures which served not to guide the faith of untrained specialists but to burden them (O'Dea and O'Dea, 1983:61). The four schools of Muslim law and the intricacies of Byzantine and Reformation theology and their descendants attempting to create orthodoxies to cope with and appear relevant to such issues as organ-transplantation, infertility, the prolongation of life, homosexuality, flying and the use of electronic appliances on the Sabbath and their individual use in a global society.

Decisions that lead to definitions are made by groups of specialists, social scientists, liturgists, theologians and religious lawyers who do not have the primary and immediate needs and preoccupations for whom religion is not a profession but a personal experience. Even these negotiations over what constitutes orthodoxy in what would seem to be of limited relevance to ordinary believers with their personal needs involve covert factors. In East Africa the discussions about a proposed new edition of the *Bible* in *Kiswahili* and the precise wording of key phrases involved both Protestants and Roman Catholics. This was debated with great professional scholarship with reference to earlier texts and documents. It may have been the case that whatever agreements were reached these denominations would have been faced with the costs of reprinting. It was perhaps concluded that the aim of agreement was morally correct but should be accepted as a distant ambition best left unresolved (Tanner, 1975).

Another problem over orthodoxy faced by the Roman Catholic Church over the ordination of married Anglican priests who had left the Church of England over such issues as the ordination of women and the overt homosexuality of some clergy. Celibate priests are cheaper to maintain at a level possible from parish and diocesan funds. It was understood by these convert clergy that they would be allowed and indeed required to take up or obtain posts which were financially supported by secular or religious organisations so that their new role of Roman catholic priests would be independently economically viable. However, much priests may be needed for parochial duties these men could only be used for part-time duties for which there were no parochially support obligations from those they served.

It would appear that such rules had been created within these institutions whether they are secular or religious, and they are secondary systems by which these institutions are semi-officially worked so that they can be applied in particular situations. Amongst the Luhya of Kenya the Roman Catholic Church ruled that to accept polygynous, sororate and *leveritic* marriages would be retrogressive in a modernising society and converts in those relationships could be married in church but that they could not receive the sacrament in the Mass (Kurgat, 2009).

So theological issues with their conspicuous moral backgrounds have to be considered as interwoven bilaterally in a framework of thought that is overtly religious and covertly secular. Ecumenism, the unity of denominations such as has been achieved in the Protestant Church of Southern India, is a morally justified objective. However, for it to become an institutional reality, up comes such issues as the ownership and maintenance of buildings so it is often left as a peripheral joint activity for those who feel thus inclined and who have the time for increased religious involvements. Functionally the practice of ecumenism is within a new denomination and believers may not have the time and material resources to take on such additional morally respectable religious obligations.

There is also the problem once a religion becomes above involvement in specific communities or a particular way of living, fishing as distinct from finance, herding cattle as distinct from hospital work, there can be no close connection between doctrine and the realities of need. However, when a specific group has a narrow ruling such as the Jehovah's Witnesses prohibition of blood transfusions, it is often the case of obey or leave and losing the benefits that come from the membership of such exclusive communities. No general religious group can have such narrow rulings without providing for exclusions. Ambiguity becomes a necessity for institutional survival and the ways in which doctrine relates to specific needs becomes a matter of personal interpretation.

Difficulties over Defining Innovation

It is difficult to separate variations in religious behaviour from what might be seen as innovation if it catches on and becomes a common practice within some identifiable community. There are immense variations in all orthodox religious behaviours in the sense that however mnemonic a prayer or procedure becomes, the intentions behind their performance will be as varied as the psychological make-up and the social environments of those concerned. However, we have no means of knowing what these innovations and variations may be as the moment they are described a new environmental situation arises in which it then has to operate.

Leaving aside the specialised situation in which someone describes their own religious related behaviour, what is important is the extent to which these variations catch on to what others feel is appropriate for them in their personal environments; will it spread beyond the individual and the primary groups in which these variations occur. This process of catching on may mean it has received the active approval of some dominating group, the passive acceptance of the majority and the active disapproval of some who now withdraw from participation.

Some innovations however charismatic the initiator may be, are self-limiting because its nature would not attract and because of the hostility which it would create. An example would be the *Aum Shinrikyo* (religion of supreme truth) cult in Japan founded by Shoko Asahara in 1984 which declared war on all civil institutions and carried out poison gas attacks on the Tokyo subway in 1995 (Reader, 2000). Initially the sect attracted many Japanese within their national characteristic of being attracted to new religions, but its widespread violence diminished its influence. The California cult of Charles Manson and a small group of women followers who committed several ritual murders in 1969 (Bishop, 1971) was similarly not likely to catch on. The Doukhobors a Canadian Christian sect have blown up government property in protest at its control imposed on their practices but more disturbing for civil servants was their custom of taking off their clothes in public over any decision of which they disapproved (Avakumovic, 1977). These were not working misunderstandings but self-centred religious exclusivities.

Innovations according to the degree that their religious message comes up against the surrounding political structure will always be subject to constraints. Regardless of their atheistic policies the contemporary Chinese Government has always been well aware of the Chinese potential to have religious uprising such as that of the Boxers and the Taiping risings in which the latter was estimated to have killed 20 million. The Falun Gong an innovative sect with its own meditation systems, prospered until through their mobile phones they organised a protest demonstration outside the compound of the national leaders so that from then on the government's restrictions on them became persecution. Much the same occurred in colonial Northern Rhodesia where the innovations of the Jehovah's Witnesses started to oppose the legal authority of the state (Fields, 1985). In both cases conformity to what these believers considered to be their orthodoxies resulted in reactive suppression.

On occasions individuals follow what most people would agree to be the extreme and socially impossible dictates of their faith. A Jain diamond merchant in Mumbai together with his wife and son gave up their comfortable lives to become wandering mendicants. They had been living in an expensive flat lit only by oil lamps in which the floor of one room was lined with a mixture of mud and cow dung (Mehta, 2004:457). However, much this man's sanctity was appreciated by his wider family, friends and co-religious, this form of religious extremism is unlikely to gain imitators but it could not be defined as a working misunderstanding since it appears to literally follow the requirements of Jainism.

Innovations under charismatic leadership is easier to initiate if the proposed changes to a way of life occur in a social and indeed geographical vacuum. The Latter Day saints, the Mormons, subjected to persecution in the already occupied parts of the United States moved into Utah which was of little interest to white American settlers and had no resident Indian population. In this empty space they were able to initiate a religious, social and indeed prosperous subsistence life which would have been difficult to develop in any actively hostile social environment. They created an implementation of their new religious ideals in which there was no working misunderstandings.

There was a similar attempt by American immigrants in the People's Temple settlement in Guyana who had been given a vacant areas of forest as a block against possible Venezuelan expansion. This project lacked both the practical abilities and adequate religious cohesion to succeed and ultimately led to the mass suicide of all involved when it became inevitable that they would fail because of intrusive hostility (Hall and Gaslanter, 1989. La Saga, 1980).

Innovations in Religious Practices

No system of religious practice and thinking however carefully it has worked out its orthodoxy, can remain static as its forms are in a constant dialectic between the religious needs of individuals, their social environments and felt reactions of the spirit world to these changing situations; a reciprocated silence which all believers consider to be an important existential reality.

When and where the forms of religious behaviour are dictated to the faithful through institutionalised processes and are maintained through a literate overseeing organisation, the dialectic takes two forms. There is the external one in which individuals ostensibly conform and their internal reactions by which they append their forms of belief in ways which are totally personal and hidden; in this there is likely to be a constant covert process of innovation running parallel to the overt realities of physiological, psychological and environmental change.

The factor of Muslim prayer is static since it is invariable in how it is performed but what is the personal background attached to these prayers so regularly carried out. In contemporary Iraq where there is the ever-present fear of random suicide bombings is not likely to be the same as that for a business man in California, a student sitting her final examinations in Mumbai or a Yao subsistence farmer in southern Tanzania.

The second form is how parts of each society popularizes reactions to what the experience as the aridity of the set rituals provided by orthodoxy. What is derogatively referred to as 'popular' religion, tolerated and excused but not agreed to by the dominant theological elite. In this there are likely to be constant local and personal innovations not only in the fiestas of Latin America and southern Europe but in the more private devotions of 'Sheilaism' and the New Age faiths which are a feature of Western societies. If any comparison is made with Eastern religious practices the conclusion would have to be that the range of variety is so enormous that there is little that can be seen in relation to what are really not bilaterally interpretable non-existent orthodoxies.

There will always be the interpretations of individuals, families and communities as to what should or should not be done in the context of religious beliefs. Of course, where the forms of religious behaviour and thought have not been committed to writing, there is a much wider scope for innovation if indeed it can be called that. There is so much variation in interpreting the few overarching cultural themes so that the actual ritual and its relationship to the performers is always creative rather than innovative. Sub-Saharan African diviners just as those who practice in Moscow and Delhi will always be changing their procedures as a result of their own imaginations, the needs of the people consulting them, their wish to attract other patients by the publicity that radiates from new and successful forms of ritual, and what is offer in the surrounding communities. Reputed success will always spread along gossip lines. The Sukuma diviner who introduced walking on hot stones into an ancestor propitiation ritual particularly as it was watched by a visiting social scientist (Tanner, 1997) might have caught on but for the fact that it used large amounts of scarce firewood.

The fact that these men and women will have ostensibly got their therapeutic vocations from spirit or ancestor possession, the inner voices talking to them alone which always allows for the possibility of differing from what is done by others. The social acceptance of the particular reality of how each diviner performs successfully is evidence enough of its spiritual origins.

In addition there are the innovations created by charismatic personalities who have had a noticeable effect on the faith to which they belong but do not see what they are achieving as innovatory in any religious rather than political sense. Mahatma Gandhi who innovated the idea of passive resistance against the locally dominant government was successful against the British who were only organised to deal with direct opposition. This idea spread to the United States and was used successfully in bus boycotts and sit-ins against discriminatory legislation in southern federated states in a constitutional democracy. He was less successful in reforming Hinduism to abolish or even diminish caste discriminations and to prevent persistent and repetitive inter-religious violence which has been left to secular governments to be equally unsuccessful in diminishing when they are dependent on popular votes for their own political survival. His life's work for an independent India, disappeared in the catastrophic Muslim and Hindu communal killings when the country was partitioned to exclude the predominantly Muslim parts.

A prominent but successful innovation was Mother Teresa's leaving her secure position as a history teacher in India to found a new order of nuns to help the deserted and dying in Kolkata and which has now developed into an international order with thousands of nuns.

There are always large numbers of innovators in the forms which religious behaviour can take in any society but almost all fail to catch on as their appeal is too related to individual and circumstantial needs and does not look into the needs of a wider public. The history of any culture contains a long list of sects and cults which have disappeared or are in the process of dying out because they have not attracted members as the American Shakers.

It may be that the individual privacies of religious behaviour provide opportunities for innovation that get round the much slower processes of change in orthodoxies. A calling from the spirit world is a socially isolating event and such individuals have to work out for themselves how they are going to respond. A socially isolated individual under divine influence might have fewer opportunities for religious innovation than a shaman living on the fringes of Indonesian religious and political life. We have described how a minor Dayak woman shaman in Borneo (Tsing, 1987) rarely used conventional ritual chants but combined a new style of oratory with a rhetoric reminiscent of Muslim theology, national politics and radio shows. Despite using familiar phrases her speech was at the same time meant to be somewhat incomprehensible and she was enlightening her audience through this very mystification. These innovations may have had important consequences for communities on the periphery of major contemporary changes in linking their traditional spirit world to the evolving outside one. This may also have been giving them the spiritual basis for a new form of ethnic mobilization laying claim to ideas which would gain support from an existing state syncretism that overrode the local interests of an expansionist Islam. Her ideas slotted into an unconsciously receptive social environment.

An Innovative Poly-Parallelism

It is a common enough observation that in some West African Christian communities a high proportion conform overtly to the public requirements of the denomination to which they belong while covertly using their quasi-traditional faith in their emergencies but such practices may not be such a simple dualism but may be part of their holist belief systems.

In Sri Lanka there is a more complex adaptation to the deity Shanda at the Katagarama shrine (Obeyesekere, 1978) in an officially Buddhist country with a violently divisive Hindu as well as Christian and Muslim minorities. While this pilgrimage centre was generally neglected a century ago, it is now the centre of devotion for very large number of pilgrims both within and outside the pilgrimage season. No one questions the supremacy of the Lord Buddha but there has been a change in the nature of worship which has not come from the influence of any charismatic individual starting a new religious movement but from national needs for a political focus.

Sri Lanka is not alone among developing nations in having aspiration to universal education and political democratisation and an enveloping bureaucratisation which has produced a series of culturally desirable and legitimated goals for everyone, clear cut but virtually impossible to be fulfilled on any large scale when the commonest goals of all the educated is a white-collar job.

So the uncertainties of village subsistence farming and fishing have been replaced by the anxieties of modernity which is not providing what it is popularly supposed to provide. They need a way through the maze of equally available inequalities for which this devotion to the 'new' deity Shanda may seem appropriate. He is considered to be a resourceful deity who can overcome obstacles by normatively unacceptable means to whom politicians, businessmen and criminals can appeal for support, helping for all sorts of problems from getting jobs to curing illness. So Katagarama has become almost a national shrine in which people of all religions can go for help in a centre of devotion which has parallel shrines for Shanda, Buddha and Muhammad.

Adjusting to Political Realities—The Chinese Case

Churches as institutions whatever their moral claims to political neutrality or independence, have to adjust to the political realities which surround them and in this religions with priesthoods have greater difficulties than ones which can carry on independently by their reliance on the *Bible* or *Koran*. On the coming into power the new Communist government defined the Roman Catholic charitable organisation the Legion of Mary as a counter-revolutionary group and imprisoned priests for running such activities (Hinton, 1983:84). On the other hand, religions which have no fixed doctrines, no specified devotions and are not tied to any written popularly available documents, are relatively free to adjust by innovations. So we see in reconstructed Taoist and Buddhist temples different types of locally developed objects of devotion responding to local imaginative innovations only loosely related to what may have been worshipped in pre-Communist times. Those in the 'know' of those pre-Revolutionary rituals are dying out so that the religious field became open to reinterpretations. Local deities can be constructed such as the Black Dragon King without too much regard to any theological or historical backing, through whom ancestors can be venerated without the reconstruction of ancestral halls.

Christianity was seen by the Communist government as a foreign religion dependent on missionary personnel and finance and in expelling all foreign missionaries and imprisoning some who tried to remain, they seemed to have been confident that Christianity would disappear. This left the Christian Churches there with the alternatives of extinction or working out an accommodation with the new government dedicated to atheism but perhaps not so aggressively as the post-revolutionary government in Russia. A situation in which orthodox requirements had to be set aside in the face of immediate need for innovation such as *Bible* class being held in a McDonald's restaurant (Yang, 2005) rather than in specially dedicated buildings which would have required official permission.

This forced the Roman Catholics into a forced separation from Vatican institutional and normative control, divided Chinese believers into a semi-hidden group loyal to Rome and that line of Apostolic succession and a national Catholic church under the supervision of the government which severed all ties with the Vatican. Subsequently to the post-Mao relaxation of the government's controls over religion, the Roman Catholic and other churches have become revitalised with substantial increases in their numbers of active members (Liu and Leung, 2002). Certainly for Catholics this could be theologically interpreted as conformity with the intentions of Vatican II within the three 'self' movements—self-governing, self-financing and self-teaching (Ying and Leung, 1996).

Marranism—The Adjustment of Portuguese Jews

While it is not an exclusively Jewish characteristic, this faith has shown a distinctive resilience under persecution paralleling that of Roman Catholicism under Protestant domination. Spanish Marranism was initiated as a result of two waves of mass conversions from Judaism to Roman Catholicism in A.D. 1391-1414 and 1482. This resulted in these converts being treated as renegade Jews and not really accepted as genuine Roman Catholics. As a result of their partial exclusion from both communities they developed and maintained their own form of split identity with mixed Jewish and Christians notions of religion.

In the 1930s, Portuguese Jews (Yovel, 2009) were all official Catholics with their rites of passage for baptism, marriage and death all performed according to Catholic requirements but without any regular church attendance at Sunday Mass or other Christian holidays.

Yet on Friday, they lit candles to honour the Jewish Sabbath, celebrating the Passover and Yom Kippur with special Marrana rites which are neither Christian nor Jewish nor do they eat kosher food. Most of them venerate Queen Esther as their patron saint and they have parallel rites for some occasions as before marrying in church the couples are married 'properly' by a Marrana woman as well as a form of baptism which replaces circumcision. All these occasions are celebrated in a private and jealous secrecy which has become part of their ritual taking on religious values. They have no collective forum which acts to maintain these communal distinctions.

Under contemporary conditions these activities are hidden from Christians who know well enough what is going on in secret. However, now there are efforts to return them to the practices of normative Judaism and they similarly hide these practices from immigrant rabbis (Molho,

2001). Much the same may have occurred under Spanish colonial Catholicism and continue to occur under American rule in New Mexico as a means of retaining their specific Jewish identity (Hordes, 2006).

While the Marrana case started as the result of deliberate persecution and the forced emigration of Jews who refused to convert, this form of working misunderstanding is likely to be a feature of all societies in which there is a dominant pattern of secular and religious thought and practice.

Working Round the Definitions of Orthodoxy

A dichotomy as a defined contrast appears to dominate Western systematic thinking runs into difficulties in cultures and individuals which do not see most matters in such behaviourally simplistic ways. The Sukuma see blue as a lighter form of black and would certainly not see black and white socially in dichotomous terms. In a lighter vein on enquiring why the Tanzanian Hangaza could not queue in an orderly way, the anthropologist was told 'we Africans queue in a circle'; linear thinking is probably not so much rare as confined cross-culturally to a broadly similar limited range of behavioural needs related to accountancy and recorded law. While it is easy enough to see the performance of rituals in terms of binary oppositions, it has yet to be demonstrated that the creators of rituals or the participants in rituals saw them as contrasts rather than just particular ways of doing things embodying lateral holistic thinking.

A common dichotomy in religion perhaps dominating Hinduism, is the distinction between clean and unclean but these are never absolute categories and dirt is socially defined (Douglas, 1966). Menstruation is often defined as unclean and a reason for non-participation in religious rituals, domestic duties and sexual functions, but who is to know other than the woman herself. A menstruating Balinese woman entered a Hindu temple there but offset her pollution in her own estimation by concentrating on her personal prayers. Also in Balinese thinking menstruation was good or bad depended on whether it coincided with certain calendar dates of spiritual importance. A clash of values certainly but one which individual ingenuity worked around.

What of the members of a religion with defined orthodox requirements in which the issues become more complicated as it may involve repeated prohibited single acts in personal life while those individuals still want to retain their commitment to the faith to which they may be emotionally committed. Orthodox requirements may be ignored unless it is needed for the fulfilment of some other act involving public conformity such as marriage or baptism. A Roman Catholic may get on very well in having the support of his beliefs and public ceremonial conformity without having to make any publicly observable binary decisions over conformity with ordinary day to day activities. For such individuals this is a common continuing working misunderstanding when a religion has the institutional ability to supervise public conformity which provide emotional satisfactions to believers but not the private and personal paralleling the legal category of victimless crimes.

A similarly private matter to the unwritten but widely known Balinese prohibitions over menstruation is the Roman Catholic prohibition of artificial contraception well known to church members in the Western world. There are many practising Roman Catholics who break this requirement reasoning that their personal circumstances override this requirement. Homosexuality is a more difficult issue as it has more overt aspects and in some cases such people gravitate to a parish in which the priests are covertly sympathetic to these personal circumstances (Bennett, 2006).

Unless individuals are extremely scrupulous over their understandings of their own denominational commitments as fundamentalist Christians or Muslims, it would seem that most would allow their personal needs and interpretations to dominate. This enables them to work round these difficulties by blocking out the exact nature of their religious commitments.

Linear thinking runs into difficulties when it appears to have the rigidity of fixed alternatives rather than poles of contrasts within the range of which there are substantial variations. It may be that this rigidity comes not so much from the creation of scientific methodology but the more corrosive application of these principles to religious affairs for which it could never be appropriate any more than it could be applicable to the arts. The effects of the European Enlightenment are perhaps over-estimated while the ancient Chinese were pragmatic enough to have the credit for a large number of scientific inventions and yet when they did move their pragmatism into religion, it was not to work up definitions but to attribute to the divine many of the characteristics of their own long lasting and seemingly rational bureaucracy.

If as in Chinese each word can have its own distinctive written form, this does not mean that each word necessarily has exact meanings. Semantic inexactness may be a product of any system as reductionist as writing by which even the most complex of activities is reduced to a limited range of symbols.

A definition of a matter which is incapable of being defined because of its abstract nature is apt to be experienced as a restriction by those who attempt to apply it to their own feelings and understandings. It is perhaps in the nature of orthodoxies, the rules by which humans try and make their lives more orderly that however carefully it may be worded there are always situations to which it cannot be applied so easily. It will have to be interpreted and then reinterpreted to bring its application into at least temporary coincidence with actual events. Islam has particular difficulties over this because some national codes of law are based on the *Koran*, the literal Word of God which is not easily accepted for the contemporary interpretations based on the writings of a charismatic medieval prophet.

It is not only that the permutations of human behaviour for even the simplest of activities are innumerable but even the attribution of simplicity may be the conclusion of someone not actually involved. Individuals in their religious understandings are faced with issues requiring immediate reactions rather than cognitive working out of long-term coherent solutions. The hold of orthodoxy will depend on the degree to which the individual and the community is committed to a particular code of practice and not of thought which cannot be supervised.

What is in issue is how these immediate solutions to personal matters coincide with what may be their orthodox solutions. Abortion as a solution to a personal problem is almost as old as childbirth but now because of medical advances, the nature of media coverage from printing and electronics as well as theological involvement into the question of viability; it is a public issue tied into orthodox rulings which in its origin could not have had any such considerations.

Contentious issues which theoretically religious at the higher level of institutionalisation will always be required to decide on, create intellectual and theological confrontations. These are dedicated to the creation of solutions which may involve small groups of specialists at an interpersonal level up to international ones with political overtones. These meetings are dedicated in theory to the creation of definitions but inevitably end up in wordings which make the semblance of unity possible. The solution in theory may be no solution at all in practice but the lowest common denominator at which overt agreement by theoreticians can be reached. Certainly some of those who have contributed to these compromises would call such solutions working misunderstandings.

It would seem often that contentious theological issues and their attempted solution by conference confrontations are a particular feature of Western ways of approaching issues based at least in part on metaphysical concerns and the cultural need for cohesion if not logical solutions for what are almost certainly insoluble religious issues. This approach to theological issues is not a feature of Eastern religions which do not have the corporate structures which might enable such events and attempted solutions to occur and it would be difficult for them to decide who would be entitled to be present and who could they represent in which most would consider to be no more than personal views. These religions have never applied themselves to the creation of definitions; they have no overarching orthodoxies. Since they are based on the idea of successive lives for the individual, the Lord Buddha is thought to have opposed theological disputations as they would lead to compromises over what an individual might achieve for his or her own relief from the sufferings of individualism.

It would seem that often contentious and insoluble theological issues are sometimes the creation of dominant or dominating individuals or groups who have established some degree of institutional dominance. The Vatican II Conference convened to decide global theological issues for Roman Catholics was dominated by Western thinkers. This led with the best of moral intentions to the overriding of the thinking and practices of the majority of believers who believe overwhelming that the performance of rituals was an end in itself received little attention. Their representatives were a small minority of delegates which could not challenge the opinions of the dominate elite.

At a primary level a religious difficulty over practice rather than thought is much more likely to be tied into social relationships and such problems have to be solved in that social environment. If they do indeed have any knowledge of orthodoxy it will have to be worked round rather more than the social relationship being forced into conformity to what an outside orthodoxy prescribes which has little to do with the social environment surrounding particular issues. If these differences are pushed to extremes, then those involved are likely to move their thoughts and practices into different covert practices so that the overt clash is minimized.

The commonest solution to a difficulty over orthodoxy is to drop out of formal attachment to a particularised religion and to continue with varieties of personal attachment to the 'Sheilaisms' which occur in most societies with the universality of religious individualism and is not just a feature of modern American life (Bellah *et al.*, 1985).

This individuality in religious practices has become more obvious because there are now institutional orthodoxies in the three religions of the book which for some individuals require binary solutions of conforming or not; an imposed choice required by the widespread knowledge of what these religious commitments require combined as they are with a public measure of supervision and overt commitment. Of course, there have been written orthodoxies for centuries but they were the perquisites of priestly elites with their knowledge of their own particular circumstances. Mass printing has pushed the knowledge that orthodoxies exist into the popular consciousness of believers mitigated by weaker public opinion in each community which has only a nominal social identity.

In quasi-traditional situations assent or dissent is not in alignment with written requirements so no binary decisions are required over matters which are either covertly or overtly solved by some measure of observable conformity. A propitiation ceremony to reduce the displeasure of an angry ancestor for some publicly known distress within a family is certainly a problem for a Sukuma Christian. A refusal to comply with what a 'pagan' diviner has diagnosed in a dialectical discussion, would be socially disastrous; such an individual might devise some important reason for being elsewhere at that time or contribute to the cost indirectly. An immediate social need in balance with a far distant eschatological consequence.

This institutional development came from the mediaeval European situation in which the priest would conform to the practices of the community on which he depended and from which social environment he came rather than conformity to theological and politically motivated dictates of distant authorities unless he or she belonged who were able to carry on a corporate religious life largely independent of local needs. This creation of orthodoxies has occurred in the logical context of monotheism and it is perhaps difficult to think in terms of conformity when the objects of conformity are both multiple and ill-defined. A modern Chinese village has a newly rebuilt temple to which overseas but ancestrally related Chinese have contributed, contains multiple images and ideograms which would require specialised training to read. In such situations duplicated in Hindu and Shinto temples the individual is the creator of their own personal orthodoxies by bringing into their presence their own holistic individual understandings.

Concepts of Orthodoxy and the Innovations of Women

African traditional religious systems and their modern quasi-traditional practices do not have an ideological block on the participation of women. The principal roles are usually performed by men but there are woman diviners and participants in spirit cults often in leading positions when they have passed the menopause and in most propitiation ceremonies agnatic kinship gives them prominence. Above all women have predominated in becoming possessed and in acting as a channel for communicating with the spirit world and perpetuating the reality of its existence; it is this possibility which has always been expected of them. This process is not the manifestations of closed self-affirming systems of thought, but a provisional and contestable reading of events, moments in the course of a particular situation (Lambek, 1993, 385).

Once Islam becomes the dominant religion of a community, religious practices become rigidly segregated and women no longer have opportunities for public participation. Islam on the East African coast has been the dominant religion for many centuries but it is possible that the contemporary strains of modern change with the introduction of fundamentalism has made ideological Islam much more prominent. Whilst most communities which are on the fringe of Islamic orthodoxy may not have this segregation to quite such an extent, elsewhere the exclusion of women from overt religious participation becomes more stringent. Their religious needs are not being met and to them the public image of Islam is of a religion run by men for men. But men are to some extent restricted in the ways that they might seek new solutions to their problems. Thus, each sex is constrained in their religious behaviour and the men more so as their religious roles are public so parallel religious systems have developed with mutual exclusion and usefulness (Boddy, 1989).

Moreover, Islam which in modern terms has its expression controlled and channelled through men and which has discriminating rules on the value of women's evidence, their rights to inheritance and the passive recipients of divorce and so on, is likely to create situations in which defensive spirit possession is likely to occur (Bourguignon, 1976). The basic principles of most customary laws are always subject to variation in particular circumstances. The *Koran* and the Sunna has to some extent blocked women and their families from negotiating the outcomes in situations which are inevitably situational and changing. Thus, women in Eastern Africa, Somalia and the Sudan have developed spirit possession. Zar cults which are not only a product of Islamic restrictions on women's religious expressions but also as a continuation of pre-Islamic paradigms in a wide ranging situation for which Islam has not provided solutions. A woman who becomes possessed by a spirit is accepted as beyond the social and religious control of the men who are legally her guardians, whether as father, husband and son.

These Zar cults also have the social value of involving spirits from outside the immediate social world of the communities of those involved. These spirits are in some ways paralleling the wider social experience of Muslims generally as more are going on the Hajj pilgrimage and are involved in commercial activities over tribal and wider cultural boundaries (Lewis, 1986). In this sense it is part of pan-Islamism in which there is a dialectic relationship between the Arabic literate orthodox and the non-literate and between the town with its closer Islamic organisation and the surrounding rural populations. It does not make sense in economic terms to segregate women in agricultural communities as well as in constitutional provisions for equality.

As in religious developments elsewhere in Africa, the spirits possessing participants are often foreign rather than familiar and have distinctive requirements including musical preferences. One suspects that these cults have coalesced round middle aged women with particular talents in the larger towns who have undergone some specialised training. An elaboration of knowledge developing into organised systems of religious activities appealing to urban women from a wide range of socio-economic backgrounds who are drawn into them by their experiences of illness or misfortune while being under greater constraints imposed by Islamic segregation. Thus, richer women are correspondingly more intensely involved in expensive cult rituals for which their husbands have to pay. Whatever cross-sexual tensions may be ventilated here, an important element is conspicuous consumption in which wives test and demonstrate the resources of their spouses (Wilson, P.J., 1962a, b). Peasant women enjoy greater economic and domestic independence as well as more freedom of movement and a stronger kin support so such cults do not occur as frequently in rural situations.

In the knowledge and power that spirit possession provides in these cults these women have access to a wider range of cultural understandings than is provided for them by men or which men would admit they have need of in their lives. It is essentially an urban bourgeois phenomenon in the Sudan and is usually viewed there as an intrusive foreign influence (Al-Nagar, 1980). These Zar cult experiences are not a type of exorcism for emotionally disturbed women as it is more a form of religious commitment with a regular membership and rituals as well as an assertion of independence. As elsewhere women through their membership of these cults are able to exert pressure on their male social controllers in the absence of any other effective and more importantly immediate sanctions.

Zar possession gives women their own semi-independent power to deal with a range of health and social issues in a highly structured and elaborate way in which the control of these spirits can take up an enormous amount of physical effort and social energy (Kenyon, 1999). The members are not just filling in their spare time but are involving themselves in personally located and chosen religious relationships. It is now necessary to move onto the ways in which groups through the coalescing needs and stimulus of individuals are making challenges to orthodoxy.

Muslim Women Circumventing Orthodoxy

With global electronic mass media coverage which leaps uncontrollably into the thinking of people in even the most socially isolated community as well as economic and political change generally, women are increasingly aware that restrictions on their behaviour for religious reasons may be hard to maintain. Whatever the Islamic theological arguments it is a religion that subordinates women to the general and particular social control of men for which there is eschatological support with the *Koran's* depiction of heaven seemingly dedicated exclusively to male pleasure.

It would seem that women would have little opportunity to develop their own religious lives except when filtered through male tolerating support much less independently of this all embracing segregation with sexual segregation even in some cases with separate entrances to mosques.

In China, women have created their own mosques from which men are excluded as part of their yearning for approaching Allah and gaining a place in paradise as women (Jaschok and Jing Jun, 2000:171, 174, 189). The major factor controlling this movement for women to have their own mosques independently of male control, has been sexual equality not only as a fact of modern life in field and factory but their awareness that equality was also the public policy of the Chinese Government so that they would be sure of at least mild official support. There has also been the factor of the relaxing of the Communist Party's control of education which has put the Islamic patriarchy on the defensive against their discriminations. These men must also have been aware that almost all other secular and religious groups have open-door policies with no entry restrictions and in which the seating is mixed (Lambert, 2006). This is a movement towards sexual equality in the personal need to approach Allah independently of male control for which the women feel that there is no theological justification for which there is ample secular support.

In Iran women through professional work and from the fixed provisions of Islamic inheritance have used their financial resources for religious purposes to founding seminaries for women. There is the appearance of a new cadre of women religious experts who have preached publicly using loudspeakers as well as selling tapes of their views. In some cases they have so monopolised shrines as to exclude men. These are certainly innovative practices in Shia Islam which is monopolised by men and thus considered illegitimate by religious orthodoxy (Kamalkhani, 1997:62-3).

Some Issues in the Value of Orthodoxies

There is a distinct difference between the so-called religions of the book, Christianity including such denominations as the Latter Day Saints and the Seventh Day Adventists which have fixed places of worship and relatively stable congregations of worshippers. Then there are more individual, creedless faiths (Stark *et aL*, 2005) such as the popular folk religions ones of southern Europe and Latin America and the audience, privatized and client oriented religions of California and the East.

It is the former form of religiousness which has the greatest difficulty in maintaining the ideal types of systematizing the behaviour of their followers by the creation of orthodoxies. In this process they have become organisations which have the shared characteristics of all such social units created to further the manufacturing of cars and computers, the curing of the sick, the teaching of science, the practices of competitive sport, the national defence forces and legal and local government systems.

These religious institutions have hierarchies of authority, written rules, full time and maintained staff, a separation of their official and unofficial roles and the staff do not own the plant in which they carry out their duties (Weber, 1978:956-63). But there is a basic difference between the administration of religious and secular organisations. The secular institutions retain control because they have the physical and economic power to do so. While some religious institutions have the economic power to support their theologically based orthodoxies such as the Shia Ismailis and the Latter Day Saints with their ten per cent tithe on members and political power in states with constitutions or practices based on Muslim principles such as Saudi Arabia and Pakistan.

Christian Churches although they have the social structure of organisation their power to control is largely confined to moral strictures; their priests cannot be controlled in the same way as employees except by handing them over to secular control. This is shown in the delay to control the perversions of some priests in the Roman Catholic Church and indeed parallel scandals involving Buddhist monks in Thailand.

So assuming that there is a need for the defined conformities of orthodoxy and the limited ability to enforce it except in the restricted circumstances in which believers want that religion's services, it becomes rather more a situation in which there are consistently almost automatic deviations from this required orthodoxy.

This again is paralleled in all secular institutions despite their greater ability to demand conformity from their employees and participants. Thus, every organisation has an official structure whether church or corporation and their members have a second system, unofficial ways of doing things. The primary groups in all these organisations develop their own ways of circumventing officialdom and it is often felt that it is these 'subversive' practices make the larger structure work more or less in conformity to the official orthodoxies (Blau, 1965) as they provide the adjustments to local realities which the organisation cannot.

Whether orthodoxy exists or not, individuals are going to put together an agenda of their own religious ideas and practices from what is culturally available. A wider menu certainly than has occurred in the historical past, probably idiosyncratic combinations but rarely innovative. The vast majority of people particularly in the Eastern religions have always done this unhindered by anything more than the neighbourhood religious orthodoxies of the communities in which they live or the occupations from which they get their livelihoods.

The consequences of orthodoxies may be to limit the initiatives of full-time professional members of a faith and pushing innovation towards outside intellectuals and the creation of competitively divisive cults and sects. This is a feature of Christian institutional creativity with the thousands of Churches in South Africa and the Zar cults of the Sudan and Somalia. Hinduism and Taoism maintain their vague ideological unities while having so many divergent practices that their division into sects and cults is a pointless exercise expected perhaps by Western theoretical thinking because that is the normative religious behaviour almost the orthodoxy of these faiths.

The paradox must be that any religious institution has to create a system of rules which would enable it to continue to function administratively. The record of idiosyncratic communes in both Western and Eastern societies has shown that unless they are able to create a system of rules which are largely independent of charismatic individuals, enabling for them to be experienced as just as useful for succeeding generations, they disappear. The longevity of such long-lasting institutions as the Buddhist and Christian monkhood shows the necessity of occupational orthodoxies which have a ideological utility not too dependent on particular living charismatics so that it does not become more like a formula for division.

How in practice can you apply orthodoxy to any human activity much less religious ideas and behaviour? The Taiwanese of Shegaang town hold complex triannual 'Jiaw' celebrations (Jordan, 1976) and a social scientist tries to make some logical sense of this obvious physical event which preoccupies these people over the long period of preparation and actual activity. Linguistically the word 'jiaw' has no exact meaning, and there are differing amounts of knowledge among informants and contradictions between them and differing understandings of the knowledge which the specialists and 'ordinary' people do have and of course there was no homogeneity in either of these created categories. All exegeses are different from each other in degrees of elaboration which may be due to ignorance or rejection and then there are differences in the appeal of particular points. Belief in an orthodoxy is never a possible holistic unit of this behaviour.

The people seem to be unaware that according to the specialists the objective of the ceremonies was the placation of demons rather than the involvement of gods. Few involved themselves in the temple ceremonies which they may have used for private petitions and status rivalry which had nothing to do with the actual ceremonies. Most were more involved in inter-village rivalry over what they could show in the processions and the lateral economic advantages which would come from their involvement. The press took the view that the ceremony was in honour of the visit of the county governor. Whatever conclusions might be reached as to what went on, it would be inevitably faulted by those who did not take this approach. Any attempt to create an orthodoxy out of this jumble of religious and social creativities and needs would have been fruitless.

So the problems of orthodoxy remain predominantly in the religions of the book and whether their believers have misunderstood these requirements or not, they remain more or less active members of the religion into which they have been socialised or in which there is ongoing socialisation. For many Roman Catholics both before and after the radical changes in the form of ritual and the language used initiated by the Vatican II Council since their private interpretations have not been actively invaded, it is for them analytically a working misunderstanding and they remain ceremonial members of their Church. They are still able to get what they want out of the ceremonies by watching and listening without being intellectually involved. They do not see their involvement with the Divine as requiring any ongoing processes of self-education or enforced spiritual adjustment.

The alternative response of the faithful to these changes rather than as response to the earlier requirements of orthodoxy is lapsing from participation rather than purposefully adjusting to the much more invasive changes in the time honoured rituals in which they are 'done to'. This is a term which is peculiar to Christianity in which believers drop out of active participation while still considering themselves in some vague way still Christians. This has been very noticeable reaction among Europeans possibly initiated by the Reformation and repeated by the decisions of the Vatican II Council. This has not occurred so much elsewhere where the 'foreignness' of the rituals retain their emotional attraction.

There have been occasions in which the laity have sufficient cohesion to actively oppose liturgical changes of which they disapprove. A Paris parish refused to accept a modernising priest as they wish to retain Latin as the language of the Mass (Badone, 1990). In Spain there has been a long-standing opposition between rural and urban populations that the former are orthodox in their religious needs and that the priests with their upper class financial supporters are perverting the true nature of Christianity. This is not just a peripheral attitude but a deeply felt one which was reflected in the large numbers of priests who were murdered in the Spanish Civil War by Republican forces opposed to the invasion of General Franco.

While Muslim fundamentalists and the religious police in Iran and Saudi Arabia impose the overt obligations of fasting in the Holy month of Ramżān, electronics and the privacies of the home have made differences as there are some five hundred Arab satellite channels, new television serials and sitcoms, chat and reality shows with their episodes fitted into that month. While Islamic theologians deprecate this unstoppable trend it is indeed a working misunderstanding of the purposes underlying Ramżān and a way that secularity assists its modern continuance.

For the priests, the professionals of the Roman Catholic Church these changes were more profound as these decisions made it necessary for them to change their theological understandings and with it the diminished status attractions of the priestly role. Large numbers have left the priesthood to which they had previously publicly committed themselves by oath.

It would be difficult to apply such a term to the Eastern and traditional religions in which there are not sufficiently defined orthodoxies to make it possible to state that someone has 'dropped out' of Hinduism when it is not at all certain when they have 'dropped in' in any full participatory religious sense since it is not a congregational religion. The collective concept of a Hindu religion is very much a creation of outsiders wanting to have a collective term to distinguish those people from Muslims (Van der Veer, 2002).

Orthodoxies are perhaps institutionally necessary for certain types of collective activities which are predominantly religious. Otherwise they seem to be little understood and widely ignored or misinterpreted and thus peripheral contributions to the working misunderstandings underpinning the continuing experiential importance of religious faith.

9
The Range of Individual Changes in Religious Practice

Every individual always has choices in what they do in the public expression of religion and in their private spiritualities as much as in secular matters even if it is the negative one of doing nothing or what they have always think they have done. Choices are available to the individual in a range of situations within institutionalised control just as they are to those for whom more unrestricted choices are available. The correct way of coping with personal problems has never been defined or indeed could not be in the absence of literacy and institutionalisation and this presents every individual with a range of socially approved preferences. We now look at the patterning of religious behaviour which are part of putting individual choices into practice.

Conformity to Religious Norms

Conformity to undefined religious norms perhaps more than any other form of adaptation to changes which have occurred in the individual's personal experiences or in the outside world impinging on them, suggests some sort of permanency; it has a comfortable feel about it for those who consider this to be their preferred option. Individuals conform or think they are conforming to some provided pattern of religious behaviour. This provision is perhaps far wider in situations in which literacy is not an important factor but it is the preferred unconscious or conscious situation in all societies regardless of their social development. In most societies it pays off to conform particularly in subsistence ones with their networks of reciprocities but this conformity has no statutory backing. There is no ready return for being different except in the covert advancing of their own or their families interests. However, conformism is hard to define and even harder to observe.

Even overt observable conformity has methodological difficulties since it can only apply when there are specific requirements which should be observed. With the quasi-traditional rituals of some societies, it is not at all certain what their requirements are and even less certain who should be present and when and who should do what. Overall any uniformities are obscure, except when non-conformity became a matter of public comment because someone has deliberately abstained making themselves social as much as religiously deviant. There is always an actual behavioural elasticity within a theoretical conformity.

Then of course there are further analytical problems as to the extent that answers to questions which have a religious and, therefore, moral element in them are likely to be answered as correctly as the questioner hopes. Moral issues make explanations more difficult to uncover than those related to agricultural practices and particularly when these questions are asked by strangers with whom there are tenuous and biasing relationships. Few if any societies have sufficiently uniform practices to evaluate conformity except in terms of small and possibly exclusive social groups for narrowly defined objectives.

In the case of Christianity and Islam there are detailed ritual requirements recorded in writing and often official definitions on what is the correct behaviour of people committed to these faiths in what they should do or not do in almost every conceivable situation with which they might be faced. The Roman Catholic Church has manuals to cover most morally difficult situations (Davis, 1946) while both Judaism and Islam have their moral dictates sectionalised by their theologians in numerous volumes.

It is possible to find conformity where there is a single set of observable religious obligations. The Five Pillars of Islam enable very large numbers of Muslims to be seen to conform as except for the affirmation of faith the remaining four are physical largely public processes. It is ostensibly a straightforward system in which conformity or at least the acceptance of the obligations to conform, is overwhelmingly accepted. Some do not fast in Ramżān, pray five times per day, give to charity or go on the Hajj. In many Muslim societies there are many religious practices which are very questionable according to orthodox theological thought and yet are part of what are publicly acknowledged to be Muslim cultures.

But beyond these religious conformities which are perhaps much more social than religiously situational, it is what the family, village or organisation does to which individuals conform. In the return of mortuary rituals to Chinese village life after the abolition of collectivisation, the old conform to their pre-Communist concern for their ancestors while the younger ones conform because it is what their families are doing while they appear to regard such activities as superstition (Chen, 1996). It was what they do that is important not what they think and individuals conform because there are social and perhaps also psychological sanctions against taking an asocial line. In these Chinese villages performance took precedence over beliefs and it mattered little what one believed about death and the after life as long as the rites were performed properly (Watson, R.S., 1988:4).

A Rajasthan village in India (Chauhan, 1967) showed a complex pattern of Hindu devotional foci ranging from nationally recognised pilgrimage visits to village specific caste interrelationships and local rituals over marriage and death. They are involved in worship to twenty named deities of which only Lakshmi, Parvati, Shiva and Vishnu are of national significance. Conformity in such a situation is both situational and environmental and would have little to do with any religious literature and the views of any external theological elites.

Thus, conformity itself is not easy to categorise since there is often a gap between physical conformity to a religious requirement and being present for reasons which are not primarily religious. Its entertainment value as in the annual festival for the local saint in Luxor in which the religious component is minimal since most people are not sure when he lived or the fiestas of Latin-American Catholicism in honour of local saints in which the attainment and maintenance of status is important.

How does a believer conform when their religion has no particularised beliefs and practices above the family and neighbourhood level. It is really impossible to think and practice conformity to Hinduism as a religion rather than Hinduism as practised in Patna, Poona or Pallavaram. Within this faith there is a multiplicity of gods and goddesses and the influence of charismatic figures and above all the dominant religious practice of gaining benefits *darshan* from gazing at inert or living embodiments of the supernatural.

While Buddhism may be more exact in its requirements at least for the monks rather than for the laity who have developed complex ritual systems to cope with their own needs. The visitor to Buddhist or Taoist temples in contemporary China who see in the images displayed there a massively complex system of symbols to which it would be difficult to conform. Believers pick and choose within a framework which would probably include family rather than individual ancestors. It would seem that in these Eastern religions there is nothing specific above the family and neighbourhood level to which individuals in the mass could conform. There is a layered and local belief system in terms of the divinities and their responsibilities.

Then as individual Africans and Asians move into or just frequent the urban industrial environment occasionally or seasonally, conformity becomes even more difficult as there is so much more socially and religiously available is them. The wavering certainties of the village environment where certain religious alternatives have ostensibly been on offer as long as they can culturally and inaccurately remember, are changed. Their eliding social conformity disappears within new neighbourhood and extended family practices. Individuals are no longer included as a matter of course in all that is going on without being invited.

In this new environment individuals are included in religious ceremonies when they choose to do so from the many alternatives which are available. They have to work for affiliation, but there is little if any cultural training as to how individuals can get themselves included in new social and religious environments. Some of these underlying difficulties affecting conformism are shown in semantic changes from using 'we' to 'I' as individuals move out of a socio-religious environment in which religion is not a specific category of activity in which conformity is assessable to one in which it is more a personal feeling.

Where theological efforts are made to isolate religion as a specific category of human behaviour, conforming in the social sense can be attributable initially to religion, but this inhibits those involved from publicly attributing their conformity to other reasons; keeping in with a rich family, the availability of loans from a religious association, the opportunity of seeing a particular person or just being in crowds of people with similar undefined intentions as a relief from the boredom of subsistence farming and factory work. The range of reasons for conformity must cover virtually every social activity and remain largely hidden within their religious functions.

The attendance at Catholic services in Manila where late comers cannot get into the church and thus can neither see nor hear what is going on attenuates the degree to which this could be called conformity. On the other hand, in the Ethiopean Coptic services performed in small churches, the majority of worshippers must remain outside in their large courtyards; this is the accepted pattern of attendance since sinners stay in the courtyards and menstruating women get no further than kissing the gate-posts to their courtyards. This is a theologically motivated architecture in which ability to see and hear what is going on is obviously irrelevant and it is a duplication of Eastern and quasi-traditional ceremonies which have this same characteristic. While the researcher assesses participation in terms of nearness to the sacred focus and the ability to see and hear, those involved appear to feel participation in terms of their less tangible psychological and social involvement. How is it possible to assess participation when some seventy million people were present in some sense at the last Kumbh Mela and who just hoped to rush into the Ganges at an astrologically prescribed time.

In addition to this social conformity, there are always other non-religious elements involved and where the conformity is to some extent rigid, there will always be substantial elements in all involvements in religious rituals when the individual's thoughts are elsewhere. There is in this issuc the fact that individuals may conform for periods of variable length depending on factors which may not have any connection with religion.

Nevertheless there is in the idea of conformity, the personal satisfactions of thinking that there is in their personal religious lives a consistency for which there may be very little pragmatic evidence. In their own minds they are conforming in some way to the official requirements of their faith. There is thus an ongoing process of conformity to what is considered appropriate at any particular time and place; a subliminal as much as social adjustment to the processes of personal change.

Conformity to Pre-Existing Religious Modernity

It may not be correct to suggest that quasi-traditional religious practices must fade away or radically change under modern social and economic conditions. It is necessary to stress again that the particular traditional thinking and religious processes of the Sukuma have not needed conversion to any new religion in order to cope with their modern lives. In this respect the six million Sukuma living south of Lake Victoria in Tanzania may be an exception (Tanner, 1999, 183-193). These people with their own language and sense of tribal nationalism, have been in contact with Muslim traders for just under two centuries and subject to Christian evangelisation for more than a century and yet it seems likely that no more than 12 per cent are now either Christians, principally Roman Catholics or some 2 per cent Muslims. This is unusual by African standards in which most tribal communities are nominally overwhelmingly one or the other. The Haya, the predominant tribe to the west of Lake Victoria are predominantly Roman Catholic and provide most of the national vocations to that priesthood.

The Sukuma have a culture which is traditionally 'modern' in many respects without being forced to be modern by events outside their control. They live in dispersed households away from rather than near to their neighbours and except for a core of landholders perhaps as many as a quarter move every year which means that their relatives are widely distributed. Each Sukuma attempts to create a neighbourhood network of social and economic alliances based on current reciprocities rather than kinship.

They do not have any obligatory rites of passage nor any initiation ceremonies except for specialised societies involving social, religious and economic benefits for their members. Similarly, they do not have any regular programmes of religious activities nor specialised institutions or personnel for such purposes beyond the ancestor shrines in some compounds. Their religious activities are centred on self-made healers with self-defined supernatural connections to various sorts of spirits and the personal possession of protective amulets combined with individually created ritual behaviour.

Thus, the root metaphors of their lives fit into urban-industrial needs as much as they must have done in their environment of subsistence farming in an area of poorly distributed rainfall and uneven soil fertility. In believing in the influences of spirit forces and the personal malevolence of others with whom they are working and living, there is little in their religious understandings which have to be altered because of the changes which have invaded their lives. In conforming to their quasi-traditional patterns of religious thinking and practice, they have not had to make any striking adjustments to modernity in urban living and in industrial employment. They are doing well enough with what they have developed within their own culture despite poor rains and economic depression.

Retreating from Society into Religious Isolation

Forms of retreating from normal social involvements are well represented in deviant behaviour when individuals become addicted to substance abuse whether drugs or alcohol or when they suffer mental disturbances from so-called nervous breakdowns to schizophrenia. Nevertheless drugs have been associated with several kinds of contemporary religious experience such as the use of the peyote cactus by Indians in the Native American Church. Certainly drug induced 'highs' have occurred in many religious contexts but it seems likely that they are usually passing phases which are not necessarily consistent or long lasting.

Whether it is theologically acceptable or a misuse of the concept of a religious vocation, many adaptations of religion can be seen as attempts to retreat from everyday society with its economic, social and political difficulties. The urge to create as far as possible personal physical and social isolation in which relationships with the supernatural can be experienced intensely. While Christian and Buddhist monasticism is a group activity in which the individual is not isolated, in Hinduism and traditional tribal religions and their current quasi-traditional forms, individuals pursue personal relationships with the supernatural which in some cases involve bodily distortions. This form of religious activity has certainly existed in India in ancient times since Arrian records Alexander the Great meeting such people. Hinduism has large numbers of holy men, *sadhus*, who have abandoned most of their secular lives to devote themselves to the furtherance of their own progress to unity with the divine. They become totally dependent on charity, have no permanent home and few clothes. Whatever changes have occurred in Indian society, they have had to make few if any adjustments in order to continue their distinctive lives in isolation. While it is impossible to estimate their numbers they continue to be a very visible feature of Indian life. We cannot know to what extent these men have working misunderstandings of Hinduism but it is certainly an accepted and extreme way of demonstrating faith.

With meditation on the other hand, the withdrawal of the individual into silence, has been and continues to be a feature of all the major religions as well as some of the traditional ones which required periods of isolation as prelude to initiation into adulthood. But for most of these meditation systems, there can be only partial withdrawal from the support of society if they are not to die of starvation as would have been the case with the forest monks of Sri Lanka. However, much it is evaluated as personal development, it is a withdrawal from as much social life as possible and indeed this periodic organised religious experiences for Christians are described as 'retreats'.

There is a division here between individuals using their surplus money and time to support their own retreatism so that they are not quite so dependent on outsiders of which participation in *ashrams* in India may be an example. Then there are the retreatants in largely subsistence communities who are supported by people who believe that in doing so they are furthering their own supernatural causes. The extent to which religious rather than addictive retreatism is seen as a conscious or unconscious solution to personal or collective must vary with the social environment. It is consistently popular in cities such as Mandalay and San Francisco where there are meditation centres for the relief of stress by a withdrawal into peace and quiet and as a rite of passage for Buddhist novices in which even male members of the Thai royal family participate.

Retreatism must inevitably be part of a process of change both for the individual and in the means by which this is brought about since it cannot exist in isolation. A system of meditation or withdrawal if it is to continue presupposes a supportive social system and as this changes so does the direct or indirect support provided. Emotion is a circular process that begins and ends with the transactions and actions of the self in the social situations which bring it into relationships with others (Denzin, 1984, 54, 58.), while retreatism aims to exclude as far as possible the complications of personal relationships.

Spirit Possession and Retreatism

Although Western societies and their religions no longer overall accept the possibility that individuals can be possessed by spirits, there is in Christian fundamentalism the acceptance that individuals can become possessed by the Holy Spirit and this is shown by unconventional behaviour and glossolalia, talking in tongues. In almost all other cultures it is accepted that individuals can become possessed by the spirits of their ancestors or non-related spirits which have no kin relationship with the persons whom they occupy. In more theologically sophisticated environments, it is accepted that there are heightened religious states which are accepted as religiously acceptable without any agreed procedures for assessing or explaining this validity. There are also those who have become possessed assisting others who have problems which are supernaturally based.

Overall it is so commonplace, expected and socially acceptable that for some societies to do without these occurrences would seem unusual and for those who become possessed not to be classed as deviants or in some way mentally disturbed. Spirit possession can be seen as a way in which the possessed individuals are able to adjust to situations for which there are no other immediate ways available to them for getting relief. It does not provide anything strikingly new since it provides what is largely within their existing religious paradigms. Spirits exist and they are active in their relationships with humans in seeking their own ends by entering the bodies of the living.

In these circumstances the ability to fall into a trance can scarcely be a qualification for becoming a medium since almost all the people in those societies would have themselves seen or heard of people being possessed. Scepticism may be a faculty which is not separated from these primary experiences. The push towards possession may come from a variety of preceding situations other than mental psychopathology; a sense of vocation, a felt need for personal advancement, a sense of failure, persistent ill-health combined with a series of personal misfortunes or the ability to perceive the reasons for other people's difficulties and the ways by which they might be modified. To be a medium and not just possessed, involves these people in being socially acknowledged to have a useful and indeed successful connection with the supernatural which has been accepted by others as helping them in their difficulties. The career in divining has its origin in the ability of some individuals to help others. There are also occasions when individuals against their own inclinations are pulled into accepting powers which are thought to come from possession because petitioners feel that she has this power.

The relationship with and adaptation to the spirit world has always be one of constant change and not necessarily in the contemporary world as a reaction to some increase in tensions which have always existed in illness and misfortune. Possession can be part of a process for reintegrating a family, reducing personal guilt, getting one's own back in a failing marriage, even bringing home the spirit of someone who died overseas in World War Two or for the spirit of an unknown family member who died of starvation during a famine. There can never be any one to one correlation between a cause and a spirit possession and it is always a complex social situation in which the variables of cause and its amelioration are constantly changing.

While there are situations in which an individual is accepted within a limited range to have these powers, religious institutions may accept what happens as a social reality without getting involved in questionable theological speculations as to whether some phenomena are religiously real or merely the manifestations of some abnormality. There is perhaps a tendency to see tensions as a feature of individual personalised difficulties within the social localities of neighbourhood and family but this is not always the case. In a north Indian rural locality half the cases of malignant spirits infesting Hindus were diagnosed by diviners as being Muslims. (Kakar, 1999, 135-45).

What seems certain is that the possessed persons, consciously or unconsciously are in a state in which the normal processes of social communication and negotiation are put into another dimension. The possessed wife cannot be beaten or reasoned with as she is not herself and the negotiations have to be carried out with the possessing spirit through the offices of a medium. The roles of women in the contemporary world come into this as do the possible solutions because spirit possession gives them power which they do not have in normal social life particularly if she is isolated in an exogamous marriage with no relatives to support her living nearby.

It is also an area of social behaviour in which there is widespread scepticism about the ability of anyone to know what the spirits want. The premise of spirit possession is not one that involves any questioning of whether the spirits exist and are active in the ways diagnosed by mediums. The Kaso people of Sumatra, not so much distrust spirits but mistrust the extent of anyone knowing their activities and yet for them it was a method of making sense of some matters beyond their comprehension (Steedy, 1993, 35). The Zar spirit possession cults run by women in the Sudan, Somalia and the Swahili coast of East Africa cannot be seen as just a form of exorcism for emotionally disturbed women. It is more a conversion to a form of religious commitment and experience with a regular membership and rituals which was independent of the men who ran all the overt social, religious and political activities of their communities.

Coping with Evil Spirits and their Contemporary Activities

If a culture has a religious system which has involved spirits influencing the living and this can be presupposed to have evolved a long way back in time, then conversion to another newer and imported religion will involve religious attitudes of mind and practices overlaying the more primordial ones. It seems unlikely that conversion or being born into a faith which is not the one with which the culture has developed, will not remove the conscious or unconscious urge to use these earlier beliefs and practices. In this context we can understand such developments within Islam of the Zar cults and the mass spirit possession of Muslim women factory workers in Malaysia (Ong. 1985) and Muslim secondary school girls in Mombasa, Kenya (Faki *et al.*, 2010). There is also the covert paralleling of Christian beliefs and spirit possession often copied within the so-called independent African churches.

In all societies there are always wide ranging social, political and economic changes for which individuals and communities will always have developed ways of coping. Malay society has a long established system of spirit possession in which there are two forms, those associated with human beings and free disembodied ones. This in action was usually seen as human spirits affecting married women as a form of conflict management that disguises and resolves social tensions; an acceptable way of rebelling against authority without incurring punishment as the persons possessed were controlled by spirit forces outside themselves.(Lewis, 1971), which worked well in rural village settings. There is also the factor that spirit possession attracts the attention of social scientists as it is alien to their own socialisation and this gives prominence to this activity which is not all that common there in either individual or communal lives. In the case of individual spirit possession it has the elements of a case study for which there are fewer methodological difficulties than for collective or communal events.

In the 1970s Malaysian Government decided to actively promote the economic and social advancement of Malays as then much of the country's wealth was under Chinese control. This involved large numbers of young unmarried Muslim women becoming part of a new female industrial work force and which gave them a profound sense of status ambiguity and dislocation (Ong, 1985). In several factories and indeed in some urban schools involving adolescent women, there were outbreaks of large number of women becoming possessed by disembodied spirits which had no association with identifiable humans.

Of course, this dislocated production and although the managements brought in traditional spirit negotiators, they had limited success as they were not able to negotiate changes in the factory system itself which would have reduced the likelihood of these workers becoming possessed. The management and Western trained Malaysian psychologists saw these happenings as a survival of archaic beliefs and that those affected being both biomedically ill and psychologically deviant as individuals; they were ill rather than normal and not behaving epidemiologically as responses to the overall environment in which they were suddenly working. In practice this was a religious adaptation to cope with serious violations of the ways in which these young women who in their village environments knew how they should behave and how their lives should be conducted where they had been well protected from spirit attacks.

Conversely the possibility or indeed the threat of spirit possession as socially inconvenient if not disruptive, can be seen as a sanction against the self-assertiveness of young Malay women going into industrial work independently of their families and village society in which they were subordinated to male controls. In a roundabout way traditional values are hitting back at those who are seen as disrupting them (Ackerman, 1979). These young women were all Muslims and the Muslim system had no solution for these collective phenomena and it was not seen as necessarily against Muslim understandings which accepted the existence of evil spirits. It can be seen as a way in which these women coped with the conflict between public modernity and traditional privacies.

In the village settings the privacies around excreting and menstruation were well organised and suddenly these functions were carried out in the publicity of shared lavatories and locker rooms. Moreover, they were supervised by men whose actions were no longer controlled by village life. These women had lost control over their most private functions as well as over factory social relations; whether it was true or not their work was felt to be under male supervision over whom they had no socially controllable relationships. So disembodied spirits appeared in liminal places such as in the lavatories, prayer and locker rooms where they had sought refuge from what they must have experienced as the harsh working conditions in factories however benignly they had been conceived and administered by their employers. These spirits even appeared in the microscopes which became hard to use after long periods of optical concentration. It was not surprising that the lavatories became the focus of psychic anxieties and that spirits lurking in the septic tanks attacked young women who had been forced to break so many rules. In accepting industrial employment they had unconsciously overstepped the boundaries of their own subconsciously acceptable behaviour. Thus, we see here a way in which unorthodox religious understandings had quickly adapted to the needs of those whose lives had been both physically and psychologically systematically disrupted. Let us now look at whether the regular performance of rituals can be seen as a form of adjustment and whether there are any changes in their performance.

Adjustment by Ritualism

The mere carrying out of rituals for their own sake is usually seen and would appear to be a psychological abnormality only in its extreme forms whether connected to religion or not. Freud defined ritualism in an individual as an obsession but that conclusion seems to neglect cultural setting which defines such behaviour as a sensible solution to a variety of situations which are thought to be beyond any possible human solution. This is, however, very much a question of definition and clearly what is abnormal in one social situation would be quite normal in another. Social scientists are not particularly prone to attributing 'genuine' value for those involved or their communities in religious practices; too much of these definitions are reductionist in intent if not in fact.

Whether this is at all assessable as a change from normal practices is likely to be the conclusions of outside observers rather than of those who appear to have this behavioural pattern and moreover have developed this as a change from mere regularity. The dividing line between regularity and ritualism is by no means clear. Most religions both those based on literacy and those which do not pay all that much attention to the written word, see the repetition of core rituals as having both an essential and cumulative value; the Moslem praying in an identical way five times per day, the Hindu with their daily *puja* and the Christian daily communicant experience, are building up religious credits from these repetitive activities. Certainly all those who accumulate such ritual performances see it as an accumulation of religious merit.

The response to external and disruptive changes or internal difficulties is often an intensification of the carrying out of these rituals or the resumption of these practices from which they have lapsed. Perhaps there is a scale for attributing the carrying out of rituals to a mere ritualism and how an individual is situated on such a scale is decided by outsiders who have no personal experience of such problems and in their detachment may miss any recognition of the core elements in which individuals have gained satisfaction, achievement and cognitive conformity. The repetitious Roman Catholic Eucharist has many variations in its practices which are both personal and situational apart from the officially accepted ones. Even those who list the rituals which they have attended and calling the total their spiritual bouquet for the year, are not being as ritualistic as the prayer procedures of Muslims in which there are no permitted variations.

On the extreme end of any ritualistic scale must be the Buddhist use of their basic prayer *om mane padme hum* as an almost endlessly semi-audible cadence intoned, whirled into the air on prayer wheels or even printed on water. The Sherpa porters on Himalayan climbing expeditions adjusted to the continual religious polluting of their sacred mountains by chanting their *mantras* almost all the time so that this humming is the background to much climbing (Ortner, 1999:130).

The Use of *Mantras* in Hinduism

If ritualism is shown in exact regularities it would seem that it must be tied to literacy which can insure regularity when it involves more than short prayers. Vaguely repetitive rituals on a theme would not seem to come within the classification of ritualism. Christians have the Holy *Bible* but do not treat the book itself is any special way to denote its sacredness and it is the interpretations from the book which are treated as sacred. Muslims treat the *Koran* as the literal word of God and the book itself is treated with reverence in a special cover on which nothing should be placed. The holy books of Hinduism do not have this form of sanctity because there are many of ancient origin and there is no concentration of sanctity in any one book such as the *Bhagavad Gita* however popular its use and interpretations from it may be. Holiness in Hinduism is enshrined in short prayer *mantras* and which for believers have a transcendent reality especially when provided for personal use by a *sadhu*.

This form of sacredness has to be constructed from the fifty syllables of the Nagari alphabet and out of these particular combination of sounds all deities, power and realities are homologised. 'Mantras are not merely formulae that refer to a particular god or force but are in fact this god or force itself, so that to utter a mantra in the proper way as provided by a *sadhu* would be to manipulate a particular divine cosmic force'(Bakker, 1986, 72). It would seem, therefore, that in both Buddhism and Hinduism there is the repetitive use of short phrases to which are attributed great supernatural power for those who use them; certainly there is gross repetition but it has within each use a religious value which is not created by the individual. Believers carry out the normative dictates of their faiths in their millions cannot be defined as suffering from obsessive compulsive disorder. It is hard to see their use in a wide range of circumstances as a form of valueless repetition when the users see the words, perhaps even the sounds as enhancing their spiritual powers.

Personalised Rituals and Religious Protection

However, there is another type of ritualism which is only incidentally repetitive when assessed by outsider observers, in which their performance is considered enough to hinder, halt or change events which have already occurred, are occurring or might occur. The greater the difficulty, danger or disruption, the greater the likelihood of personalised rituals involving the supernatural. Very large numbers of religiously minded people feel that their relationships with the supernatural are enhanced by the wearing of objects which have little function beyond this except as decoration. In this it seems that the believers instead of going to a shrine for their petitions, wears a refraction of this divinity permanently so as to create a personalised shrine to which they are always attached. There is little functional distinction between an object worn for luck such as the ancient Egyptian *ankh* in contemporary Britain and contemporary crosses and amulets containing quotations from the *Koran*. Many walls have religious pictures on them and there is in this a strong element of Hindu '*darshan*'. The eyes of the picture watches them while the believers only intermittently catch this watching. The viewers and the wearers gain from this association and it is for them an element in their personal construction of stability. In more economically developed societies these may be mass produced and their personalising lies in their choice from the selections on offer outside all pilgrimage shrines of all religions everywhere. Christian shrines have objects on sale manufactured in Korea and the first mass produced Hindu coloured devotional pictures came from Germany.

Elsewhere people go to experts in the supernatural to create for them their own personalised protections and enhancement and perhaps they are felt to be more powerful because they are both different and personal (Cory, 1949. Colby, 1969). A survey concerning the wearing of non-Christian religious amulets by Protestants and Roman Catholics in Ngara, Tanzania (Tanner, 1975) showed systematic differences. The Roman Catholics whose churches were full of symbolic objects and had their own amulets on sale there, wore fewer than the Protestants whose churches were bare of wide ranging symbols, yet wore some under their clothes to be seen only by their fellow bathers.

Those who do not wear amulets or have religious pictures on their walls attribute unthinking ritualism to those who do. They do not allow to these people who are perhaps defined as simpler in their understandings, anything approaching the complex motivations and meanings associated with the symbols themselves. In many religions the symbols themselves do not change but change in the form of their presentations. Thai Buddhist pictures of the stages of human life show modern themes and pictures of the Lord Buddha have women devotees in clothes which cannot be classed as devotional. The complexity of Hindu symbolism shown in virtually any popular picture suggests that there can be no simple meanings attached to them or to their depictions and that '*darshan*' comes from the mass impact of these holistic complexities. It is from this that millions of Hindus gain comfort and inspiration and to suggest otherwise would be to diminish their importance for believers. Whether they admit it or not, they are acting on this assumption that proximity to the sacred in the use of symbols and that their use in 'decoration' is religiously useful.

Revolutionary Change and Personal Violence in Religion

We take revolution in the religious milieu to be any acts for religious reasons seeking to bring about changes by violent means; short-term activities seeking immediate results rather than creative changes with longer term implications and steady applications. Developments which involve the radical upsetting of existing institutions and patterns of behaviour. Individuals who believe they have received a communication from God and have personalities which make this believable are potential religious revolutionaries on a much wider scale than other forms of inspiration. Those who experience glossolalia see it as the manifestation of the Holy Spirit but this is a Western religious interpretation. Possession in the Eastern religious context is not usually related to any ultimate divinity although the initiator of the death creating Taiping Rebellion claimed to be the brother of Jesus Christ.

Almost all people possessed interpret this state in their local circumstances and while the messages they receive could be revolutionary, almost all are potential solutions conforming to neighbourhood norms and within cultural parameters. A communication from ancestors and particular spirits is harder to relate to a wider population than family or neighbourhood. Such communications from God is more a feature of Christian thought and the prophets who initiated independent churches such as the Kimbanguist Church in Zaire and the Latter Day Saints, the Mormons in Utah. They do not usually give directions that the recipients should continue doing what they are already doing. They are necessarily redirectional or the connection would not have been made. Whatever may be their predisposition to receive in the silence of their own minds these communications or indeed the popular acceptance that this person has seen or heard something extraordinary, whether they are believed or not depends on social interactions in particular circumstances. This may relate to their current social and psychological uncertainties and to this extent personal change is likely to occur but for many who receive and accept such messages it tends to be absolute and the preparation for martyrdom.

Modern occurrences of suicidal bomb carriers or the crashing of high-jacked aircraft into the World Trade Centre tend to be associated with Islamic fundamentalists who see their acts as giving them instantaneous access to Paradise, such acts have a long incidence in many religions. The many thousands of Shinto *kamikazi* pilots at the end of World War Two attempting to crash their aircraft into Allied Warships had many parallels of self-sacrificing individual violence at lower military levels. A Hindu blew up herself and Prime Minister Gandhi of India whose mother was killed by her Sikh bodyguards who in effect were committing suicide by doing so. Philippine rebels against the Spaniards adopted the symbolism of the crucifixion of Christ to justify suicidal attacks by which they hoped to bring about a transcendental millennial order (Ileto, 1979). Thus, while religions and their practitioners tend to be seen in group terms, these groups are made up of individuals who may make very different interpretations of what their religion means to them and the reactions of some to perceive or experienced persecution may well be to initiate self-destructive personal violence.

The Ambiguity of Religious Violence

Religions endorsing violence for religious purposes have certainly been a feature of the past with both Islam and Christianity. The garrison churches of the British army in India had slots for rifles in every pew after the Indian Mutiny 1857 and in the Yom Kippur war both Egyptian and Israeli soldiers were pictured at prayer. Currently in Afghanistan Taliban men are frequently photographed at prayer with their automatic rifles beside them.

It is not that there has been a sudden increase in religious violence but that there have been lulls in its extent with seemingly the Holocaust killing of Jews by the Germans as a more recent peak. The creation of Israel and their treatment of the evicted Muslim populations has tended towards another peak with the so-called Christian West backing the Jews with arms and money but this has a longstanding identity as Churchill visiting Petra in 9021 was greeted by a crowd of Arabs chanting 'death to the Jews'. There are numerous other examples of simmering inter-religious violence whether in the Balkans, Nigeria, Northern Ireland, the Sudan, Indonesia and currently bomb attacks on Coptic Christians in Egypt. This coordinated violence by individuals against other neighbouring individuals of a different religion are a constant erupting feature of their lives. In Northern Ireland recently the children of one denomination going to school through a neighbourhood inhabited by the other denomination have had abuse screamed at them by both men, women and children. The response of Pakistani-British adolescents in a British school on hearing that Islamic suicide terrorists had killed thousands of Americans in New York was to cheer.

Banaras has a long history of rioting between Hindus and Moslems whose lives are interconnected both socially and economically and have been so for centuries. The individuals in both communities are quite easily capable of violence against their neighbours with whom relations on other occasions have been personally amicable. Christian and Muslim Cypriots were quite prepared to kill each other and destroy their property and graves which social scientists within their communities would describe as psychopathic behaviour (Loizos, 1988, 634-53). Although violence has become more socially visible *via* the mass media, almost certainly it has been a constant feature of socio-religious activity.

It is not so much that contemporary violence based on religious premises and beliefs is noticeable but that it is usually classed either as an aberration at best or at worst a form of religious activity to be classed as globally unacceptable. If certain people believe that killing or being killed in a religious cause is giving them immortality as would be the case with Hamas suicide bombers in Israel (Rapoport, 1982, 4-5), by the killing of Communists in Indonesia (Cribb, 1990) or for Hindus and Muslims killing Communists in Bali and Indonesia as they were defined as atheists (Robinson, 1995.) then global public opinion unacceptability is an irrelevance.

The Failure of Secularity to Appeal to Individuals

This growth in violence correlated to religion can be seen as part of a response to the failure of the Western model of secular and socialist nationalism to provide the expected improvements in the overall standard of living of the people for whom they are constitutionally responsible. The model for internationally acceptable governments of the newer independent states has been a secular form of democracy in which religion is seen as a sub-national or communal activity which should have no direct influence on national politics except as a systematic handicap delaying the inevitable rational development of society. This policy of aggressive detachment has failed on a number of counts.

It has rarely been possible to separate what people want into separate religious and political categories. Every religious aim at whatever stage of economic and political development has a political dimension if it is to be put into practice and since political systems are based on moral values, then religion is again mixed in with all that politicians do.

Secondly, if religion is considered for whatever reason to be dominantly important for individuals, then democratic elections will reflect the religious needs of individuals. In India there has been a religious dimension to politics ever since the Muslim Moguls gained suzerainty and the British inherited this religious division and gave it legal form. It is not so much political independence but the democratic vote has had a statistical form related to religion which is reflected in Northern Ireland and the dissolution of Yugoslavia.

It would seem that religions in dispute are usually beyond rational negotiations since the foundation position of each side's negotiating position is based on religious beliefs which cannot be displaced without extremism receiving further embellishment. In this it is significant that in the 1991 Indian General Elections public opinion polls showed that the third most significant issue in the minds of voters was the Ayodhya mosque built on the site of the birthplace of the entirely mythical Hindu God Ram and its destruction by a Hindu mob which initiated widespread inter-religious rioting.

Thus, it is not difficult to appreciate that the mosque on the hill in Jerusalem, the third most sacred site in Islam, allegedly visited by the Prophet Mohammad is often at the centre of Israeli-Palestinian confrontations. In all of this quasi-rationalists who predominate in Western societies tend to see the activity of whatever faith as some type of deviance in a scale from the abnormality of segregated sects to the mildly deviant who are religious through some facet of character inadequacy. However, there are very large numbers of people who see direct and often violent actions for religious reasons as both acceptable, necessary and praiseworthy. This violence for which there are always appropriate supporting texts in sacred literature means that those who define themselves as deprived, are able to justify their violence in ways that are symbolically rational.

Islamic violence in northern Nigeria may not have been just the result of the sect founded by Mohammadu Marwa in 1981-3 which resulted in thousands of deaths initiated by unemployed landless young men to whom his condemnation of the affluent as unbelievers had an immediate appeal. It was more the result of the Islamic political majority combining ethnicity with religion and the imposition of an Islamic constitution on multi-ethnic and multi-religious urban communities (Lubeck, 1985). This deprivation in isolation might not cause individuals to react violently if it were not for the elite in many countries who have benefited from the secularisation and in which the majority suffer from unemployment, shortage of housing, the rising cost of living and feminist initiated difficulties over marriage and the changed status of women affecting the traditional values of dominant men who in Islamic societies have their status supported by God's word in the *Koran*.

Individual Changes in Religious Practices as a Result of Persecution

The persecution of a religion is perhaps most easily done by destroying the objects which its believers have used for worship and there has been no reduction in this method of attempting to change the beliefs of worshippers; the recent destruction of churches in Indonesia and northern Nigeria and mosques in Croatia are recent examples of private initiatives. Both Russia and China have gone through recent phases of destroying places of worship or converting them to secular uses on a national scale.

In reactions to this traditional religions and those which operate through cells of believers without special buildings or personnel trained in special institutions are at an advantage as private prayers can rarely be observed and holy books can be hidden. Reactive violence and migration are common responses. Sometimes conversion is the only possible personal response as with the abduction of many Hindu and Sikh women by Moslems during the partition of India and the impossibility of their return to their own communities after their religious and biological defilement.

The destruction of places of worship by the Chinese Communist Party as part of their efforts to create a single Chinese identity has possibly altered Christian practices more than those of Muslims who have no obligation to pray collectively. During the Cultural Revolution most mosques were forced to close down and many were badly damaged or destroyed and in July 1975 some Muslim villages were attacked by armed police. However, since the reversal of the national policy of hostility to religion, there has been a remarkable resurgence in Muslim practices (Dillon, 1999, 163).

Individual Creativity in Religious Practices

Personal creativity in religious practices is probably more widespread in quasi-traditional systems than in the main religions with their written orthodoxies and patterns of consciously or unconsciously teaching their young specific religious practices. In quasi-traditional systems those wishing to relate to the supernatural can use any of the materials available in their cultures and in any combination and even their glossolalia composed from the phonemes of their languages would not have the implication of verbal ramblings. Those involved in ancestor propitiation can authenticate their own collection of family related objects and their shrines can be in any form considered suitable. Diviners in their own imaginations can create their own reasons and methods for operating so that no two are the same in what they say and do even when confronted with similar problems. In most quasi-traditional rural and urban settings there is a well-functioning adapting and adaptable religious elite (Hatfield, 1968). These men and women can change with the times so that their prospective clients have a feeling that they are up-to-date within the forms of behaviour which are socially acceptable. In a general sense it is a religious free market in which anyone with a personal aptitude for relationships can become diviners and the creators of religiously loaded objects for those that consult them.

Those who belong to religious faiths with orthodoxies are more restricted in their personal innovations. One suspects that even within the mind there may be a narrowing of acceptable innovations just as there is in overt behaviour. These believers can rearrange what they do within orthodoxy but not all that much as with Roman Catholics over the rubrics of their Eucharistic ritual and even less so for the Islamic prayer rituals. The answer for such believers in many cases is to choose a cult or cultic practices related to particular persons or places which appeal to them within Christianity or Islam and with this often to accept the feeling that they may well be religiously deviant. Particularly with Christianity there is the possibility of changing denominations and cross conversions from traditional or one of the major religions to another faith which is not necessary in Eastern faiths with their enormous variations of religious behaviour in every locality.

Individual Conversion and their Background

Conversion would seem an easy option for those that feel that one religious systems of practices and ideas does not fit in with their needs, but that assumption comes without analysing the problems involved and at what level conversion has taken hold. We have already discussed the forms of parallelism by which individuals carry on different religious practices at the same time even when they appear to conflict. The extent to which conversion has involved no more than attendance at required rituals or has involved the much more difficult rearrangement of their social lives to coincide with new moral obligations perhaps designed in another age and for different circumstances must always be obscure. Few if any individuals change religions or enter one with its known orthodoxies without some conscious or subconscious cost benefit analysis within their own type of calculating intelligence.

The small number of those who do change as individuals are likely to do so after considerable thought and the acquisition of new theological understandings; a long process of conscious and unconscious change. Conversion is still a process with a measure of public recognition in which there are ceremonies of acceptance after a long period of education for Christians but merely an affirmation in front of witnesses for Muslim converts and both these religions are concerned with belief. Membership of Asian religions are either by birth such as Hinduism and probably Shintoism to which there can be no valid conversions or by invalid conversion. Orthodox Buddhism would see conversion as a form of reprehensible attachment as a handicap to the attainment of release from desire. The composite Chinese religions would not appear to have a formal structure to which individuals could be converted and to consist more of the correct performance of rituals in complex social situations of which the principal requirement would seem to be being Chinese.

Converting from Hinduism in which the social and the religious dimensions are so thoroughly entwined is much more difficult than entering Christianity which in most cases has established well separated functions. Millions of Hindu Untouchables have moved into Buddhism hoping that this would free them from their socio-religious inferiority. It has not done so but it provided them with the personal satisfactions of now having a set of beliefs which were independent of Hindu Brahmanical dominance, although they must have remained within the village and urban orbit of Hindu considerations.

It is important to recognise that to see conversion in simple functionalist terms is to trivialize faith and the faithful. Furthermore, that the so-called traditional non-literate religions have existed and developed over a far longer historical period than any literate religion seeking to replace them which in this context might well appear to be a narrower form of a hitherto non-existing or experienced adaptive orthodoxy. There is the fact that these long-term processes which are largely unplanned and blind, nevertheless have discernible and socially valuable structures (Mennell, 1989, 93).

With the Hindu Untouchables the penetration of Hindu ideas and practices must have been nearly total but in most of sub-Saharan Africa the penetration of Christian ideas and practices must have been low indeed. In Usukuma the proportion of priests and pastors may have been about 1:100,000 leading to a current proportion of Christians at about 12 per cent. The strictness of Christian social doctrines does not seem to have been a factor. It may be that the Untouchables have been part of Hinduism for so long that it is a part of their social lives as much as their religious ones and that even with conversion to Buddhism much social Hinduism would have of necessity survived.

The Sukuma on the other hand do not appear to have ever been much interested in religious ideas and practices above those related to personal protection; a modern view perhaps before it became part of Westernised secularism. They have never had any permanently active religious groupings above that of the family. It would seem that they were not attracted by institutionalised religion which had permanent sites paralleling those on which churches came to be built to which they were expected to go rather than have religious operatives conveniently near to them; all the more so as they have never been a particularly static people.

Monotheism was also not particularly attractive when the Christians did not develop rituals involving the popularising of Saints. The Sukuma knew all along that there must be a single Supreme Being but that in the practicalities of their relationships with the supernatural it was the lesser spirits and their ancestors with which they had to cope. The Sukuma religious system minimally was as multilineal and multifaceted as that of the Hindu pantheon.

Then when the quasi-traditional Sukuma and the Hindus at whatever caste level do worship, there is in their rituals an immense and satisfying variety. No Sukuma propitiation ceremony is like another and Hindu ceremonies are observably complex with their noise, colour and crowds so that the comparison with Christian ceremonies is limited. A Hindu ritual despite the singularity of the *karmic* theme has always a diffuseness that makes any such simplification illusory. Even the mystery and symbolism of the Roman Catholic Mass was gradually reduced as a result of the decisions coming from Vatican II so that even its Latin would no longer have parallels to spirit possessed divination and its talking in tongues; there were no longer unbelievable subtle words or edification by puzzlement (Fernandez, 1966. 1980). Then the final distinctions which go against Christianity and so to some extent against Islam, is the unavailability of its special directing personnel when and where they are needed. The practitioners of traditional socio-religious skills are always available nearby in both tribal and Hindu cultures.

While certainly there are Hindus who are punctilious in their devotions, for the majority religion is in practice an irregular affair relating to festivals which are not nearly as wholeheartedly religious as they are made out to be and to a lesser degree this would apply to quasi-traditional religions as well. But to most people everywhere contingent availability is much more important than regularity. Any subsistence culture and more particularly community has persistent and inevitable problems (Goudsblom, 1989) as well as those from unavoidable personal relationships and lastly from human institutional and political mismanagement, entirely new handicaps. Thus, for many their problems have always had local coping mechanisms built into them combining religious and social processes for which conversion to another religion would rarely be seen as a sensible long term solution unless there are other new advantages in educational and medical provisions.

Divination and the Anxieties of Capitalism

In sub-Saharan Africa diviners have concentrated on providing a service for mainly urban people in the ordinary difficulties of unstable subsistence living under conditions of rapid social and economic change which have adversely rather than benignly affected them. South Korea presents an altogether different picture of how their supernatural specialists cope with the worries associated with business (Kendal, 1996, 512-27). It is a predominantly urban activity which is carried on by young and dynamic practitioners rather than the ageing ones in the countryside following traditional ideas and practices, since the population is now mainly working class living in the cities. The main clients of these spirit diviners are the new urban class of small entrepreneurs.

These diviners are overwhelmingly concerned with the vagaries of the business market place as it concerns their clients' preoccupation with wealth and advancement. This assumes the characteristics of controlling luck since in China they bring into play the Spirit Warrior of Commerce or the supernatural Officials of Commerce. They make an immediate connection between honouring these spirits and quantified material success in which they also honour the spirits of newly purchased cars, televisions and stereos. The volatility of the market and the arbitrariness of success or failure are consistent with Korean perceptions of spirit behaviour (Kendall, 1985, chap. 6).

The whole range of these spirit possessions in Eastern religions is not one of radical transformation any more than it is in sub-Saharan Africa, but one of calibrating the various forces impinging on personal success with what is materially possible 'lived realities defy easy dualisms...are complex fusions of what we like to call modernity and magicality, rationality and ritual, history and the here and now' (Comaroff and Comaroff, 1986), but overall those who have a working and successful economic and social relationships with the spirits appear again and again to be more adaptive in Africa and Asia than in the western world.

Commonplaceness of Spirit Possession

The possession of the individual by a supernatural agency usually involuntarily but acceptable according to the social beliefs of the society and religious group in which it appears occurs in some form or another in all societies and is commonplace in some.

Even assuming that there was in the recent past some type of paradigmatic religious uniformity of which the lowest common denominator was always the real existence of spirits, its contemporary manifestations have changed. Spirit cults have proliferated the world over including New York, Toronto and various European towns (Behrend and Luig, 1999). Spirit possession represents adaptation rather than retrogression to some idea of traditionalism.

The disappearance of spirits foretold by Western social scientists has not taken place and these modern occurrences are not any replication of archaic ways but localized ways of coping with ambivalent and contradictory processes of modernizing. These modern spirits are not replications of any past uniformities but an organisation of diversity (Hannerz, 1990). These contemporary spirits can be interpreted as the quintessence of cosmopolitanism when there are West African and Brazilian spirits in Cologne and new Christian holy spirits in northern Uganda. Hitler, Mussolini and King Bruce as well as Korean, Italian and American ones appearing in the Holy Spirit Mobile Force in the Ugandan civil war (Behrend, 1999). In Central Africa there are aeroplane, engine, guitar and angel spirits and in West Africa there are thunder, snake, playboy and prostitute spirits (Luig, 1997). These Bori spirits among the Hausa have distinctive language and consumption needs which have no African background (Krings, 1999).

Since spirit possession has always been a multi-purpose and ill-defined activity it is not hard to understand how easily it adapts to changed circumstances while remaining within the traditional paradigm that spirits exist and frequently influence the lives of the living. A move which is often between dealing with annoyed ancestors to placating and identifying spirit motivations which have no kin affiliations.

In most societies whether African and Asian the activities of ancestors have been much reduced by the dispersal of families in internal migration, settling in new localities and exogamous marriages. In China the land-holding foci of particular families and the obliteration of family graves by the Communist collectivisation of family owned land, made family ancestor veneration a combination of physical difficulty and political danger.

The flooding of the Nasser High dam in Egypt caused the removal of the whole Wadi Halfa community and the obliteration of all their graves and commentators have described the wailing of these people as they finally left. Much the same emotional distress must have happened from the massive high flooding caused by the Yangtse High dam.

The national villagisation campaign carried out in Tanzania meant that for a majority the connection between family and locality had been forcibly broken. The enforced resettlement of many thousands of Tonga by the flooding of the Kariba dam meant the destruction of many ancestral and local shrines of which only a few were rescued. Their ritual leaders interpreted this as the abandonment of their spirits tied to their land and their self-proclaimed loss of power.

In these situations there is not just an accumulation of individual experiences occurring because of their separate movement but a collective experience of community shared by all. In such mass forced movements even when efficiently planned with some official concern for their overall welfare, there are still the same problems augmented by the additional ones of a new locality and new neighbours.

Amongst the Zambian Tonga a new type of spirit medium developed actively adapting to the powerful spirit forces in these new localities so that their menace would be turned into the protection of those living in these new communities. In this these mediums were able to expand their influence by their creativity often in competition with the numerous Christian churches and cults whose effectiveness were limited their eschatological restrictions (Luig, 1999). On the other hand, the official teaching of the Ethiopian Orthodox Church was that certain illnesses, mainly mental, are caused by evil spirits thus allowing their priests to be involved in exorcism. This is similar to the situation facing the Roman Catholic Church in Malaysia where the proliferation of spirit possession more or less forced it to involve catechists rather than priests to be thus involved in exorcism. Some African Independent Churches have integrated spirit possession and witch finding into their rituals just as some spirit possession cults use the *Bible* for divination just as some Muslims in East Africa use the *Koran*.

So we see that a traditional role of diviner has adjusted their own spirit possession and the treatment of others thus affected, thus they have changed their alignment themselves quite effortlessly to these new situations. It may be that the previous necessity of being possessed prior to practice has diminished with the decline of more stable communities leading to taking this role for status and economic reasons. There enormous numbers in virtually every urban situation means that there are a proportion of dropouts who are not successful in setting up a practice by reputation. Those that do succeed have a talent for reducing the stresses of those who consult them. They are not necessarily the centre of new localised cults and are not involved in reducing the problems of dislocation and the negotiation of new moral order.

So spirit possession in one form or another is common enough in traditional and quasi-traditional as well as contemporary urban societies to be described as almost a normal reaction to personal difficulties or distress and a means of personal fulfilment as well as an aid to help those who come to mediums for help. In Asian and African cities it is a form of psychotherapy more common than in rural areas (Corin, 1979). It is not surprising to find it present on the fringes of the major religions as well as their subordinate cults and sects as in the Islamic Zar cults in the Sudan and East Africa.

There are difficulties of definition and elaboration since in orthodox Christianity there are many that identify their own experiences as those of others as possession by the Holy Spirit rather than being identified with other figures from Christian history. The occasion in which individuals feel that they are impelled to take up a dedicated religious life could be described as a form of spirit possession. The Umbanda cult in Brazil although deemed peripheral to Christianity, has historical links to the Roman Catholic Church but had weak control over the slave population which retained memories of African religious practices under the cloak of Catholicism (Browne, 1986).

The Roman Catholic Church is ambivalent about the reality of anyone being possessed by the Holy Spirit but is also reluctant to dismiss such obviously deeply felt experiences as illusions. Islam without religion wide authorities have many people possessed in Sufi groups as well as those who are peripheral Muslims. It is certainly a form of personal experience that can be classified as a working misunderstanding within both hard and soft orthodoxies.

Spirit Possession and Change

There can be few studies of traditional and quasi-traditional communities which do not include some cases of spirit possession and some understandings of what those involved consider to have happened. Social scientists approach to these phenomena is in general explaining away the experiences of those people rather than seeing this widespread events as having served predominantly useful results which could certainly account for its cross-cultural frequency in both cults and in the major religions.

We have already suggested that the decision to commit their lives to a religious vocation could be described at least initially as a form of spirit possession. Also a number of fundamentalist Christians in their ceremonies consider themselves as possessed by the Holy Spirit and behave abnormally, producing glossolalia and falling on the floor. There is the occurrence in the *Bible* and its description in capital letters which they would not use for quasi-traditional spirit possessions.

Leaving aside theological distinctions it would seem that these two forms of spirit possession have similar backgrounds. An impulse outside the control of the individual takes possession of at least some part of their conscious minds and this is strong enough to initiate observably distinctive behaviour. The second form is when an individual considers himself or herself possessed of some supernatural power and that connection with a spirit is used in professional capacity to help others who come to them for help because of their reputation for efficacy.

The socially accepted implication of spirit possession is that those possessed are out of the everyday social controls and that this leaves them free to be the vehicle through which the s(S)pirit can transfer messages to those possessed. The Sukuma person possessed by a spirit would describe himself or herself as having been seized which suggests the involuntary nature of the event is socially accepted. This may well does in numerous historically documented occasions initiate change in those involved and according to their charisma influence others.

We have already described a Dayak woman shaman in Borneo (Tsing, 1987) became possessed and her interpretations of what she had been told by the possessing spirit, initiated a new form of spirituality. This provided her small tribe with a form of identity which they could maintain without clashing with the political policies of the Indonesian state that everyone should be identified by one of the six acceptable worldwide religions. She developed a new style of incomprehensible oratory reminiscent of Hindu theology, national politics and radio shows, enlightening her audience through this mystification, while her esoteric knowledge enabled her to build up a personal authority on conventional lines. This is an example of spirit possession enabling a community to adapt itself to a political and religious environment in which they felt peripheral.

Mother Teresa left a secure position as a teacher in Kolkata to start a community of nuns to care for the destitute dying which she saw in the streets. She would describe her new vocation as being called by the Holy Spirit and by her charisma and personal abilities she was successful in starting a worldwide movement. So we see that in very different cultural settings spirit possession enables change to be initiated because it is accepted as not the production of a particular individual.

There are other more personal uses of spirit possession as the Malaysian women factory workers who 'solved' their difficulties of being injected into a modern environment for which they were not unconsciously or consciously prepared. It is also the way that middle-aged women whose lifecycle status is in between their power being based on fecundity and that based on grandparenthood and family status (Kessler, 1977).

There is another aspect to the versatility of spirit possession. In some Indian cases 'the torrent of aggressive abuse, especially when it issues out of the otherwise demure mouths of frail young girls or women, leaves little doubt that we are witnessing a convulsive release of pent-up aggression and a rare rebellion against the inhibitive norms of a conservative Hindu society of which its gods are the most obvious representatives (Kakar, 1983:67).

Individuality and Religious Institutions

While individuals will always have the vagaries of their own personalities influencing them in their ways of expressing their private spiritualities, the objective field from which they choose what might benefit them, is always to some extent limited. Quasi-traditional people can choose to use anything of which they have knowledge which until quite recently was materially limited. The ritual sticks and arms of Sukuma diviners carry rings of skin from the sacrifices which they have instituted. Once they used bones and stones in divination but now some use the tops of Coca Cola bottles.

Individuals within the arenas of Eastern religions have an unlimited range of symbols which they can use in household shrines, pictures on their walls as in a corridor on the Indian mobile surgical train or carried in their pockets. These are all publicly and cheaply available from which individuals can gain religious benefits through '*darshan*', the individual combinations are unlimited and entirely personal. In fact to the Western observers with their background of agnostic monotheism and a dominating linear way of thinking, there are early assumptions of theological disorder if not psychological immaturity. But in both these cultural spheres individuals have personal choices under their own control and in the Eastern religions there is an almost unlimited number of religiously authenticated symbols from which to choose.

With the religions of the book, the choices are much more restricted. Christians concentrate on the Cross and Jews and Muslims on the *Torah* and *Koran* respectively and stylised calligraphy. Only in Latin Catholicism in southern Europe and South America is there are wide range of popular symbols. So it is in the institutionalised religions of the book that individuals are restricted in their public use of symbols and that this must contribute to the extent to which there are both individual and communal working understandings in part at least because of these restrictions.

10
The Misunderstandings from Language

Even in communication between persons who have the same social background and live together for long periods, there are difficulties over meanings between what sent and what has been reccived. When the communicator and the communicated are different from a wide range of social distance factors related to age, sex, education and intelligence there is little likelihood of automatic agreement on meanings.

When the communicator and the communicant are thinking, speaking and hearing from within different languages, it may rather be finding out what little they understand of what is communicated rather than any assumption of general understandings which may be engineered by the most dedicated and time consuming translations.

There are persistent difficulties translating into a natal language the religious precepts coming from different cultural environment and which are indefinable and it is this that we can find some of the origins of working misunderstanding both within and between cultures.

The Absence of Simplicity in Any Language

While physiological influences on religious behaviour tend to be finite and to that extent analysable with some one-sided exactness, the use of language is much more difficult to understand in contexts which do not have any primary interpersonal directness. Asking for a drink of water and asking about a propitiation ceremony have different semantics. We have already pointed out that there are no neutral words or phrases and that they all carry the intentions of their speakers or writers (Bakhtin, 1981:293) augmented by their body language.

Most speech introduces and terminates with short-term needs and is usually made easier by the accompanying body language of physical and social nearness. A single religious phrase with the sonic exactness of a Buddhist or Hindu *mantra* will be heard but understood or misunderstood in different ways according to their intellectual capacity, age, sex, education and an unlimited number of social environmental differences of those communicating. However, exactly it may have been defined theologically once it is taken into the mind of any individual it loses this exactness. It is indeed questionable whether the statement of a religious mystery can be understood at all except in hidden ephemeral personal terms.

Once speech goes beyond situations in which there is some necessary sharing of meanings from socialisation and social functioning, language becomes even more complex and this make misunderstandings not only possible but likely. The fact that what is communicated and what is received shares phonemes is rarely indicative of shared meanings.

Firstly, the mind works in extremely complex ways which we can presume are always changing according to the situations in which it has to work whether it is the thinking of a Brahmin priest or someone with Down's Syndrome both of whose thinking can be affected by immediate social situations. To put this thinking into words involves abbreviating these personal complexities and even more so when it is represented into the calligraphic symbols that are available. This is very limited with the Roman alphabet even with the addition of accent marks and the complexities of the ideographs of Chinese Mandarin which has no alphabet.

We have no accurate way of knowing the coincidences between thought and language spoken in situations beyond the simplicities of close personal relationships and domestic needs. There is always the fact that whether it is deliberate or accidental the translation of anything beyond the commonplace is an abbreviation. Pass me the knife has a limited range of misunderstandings except perhaps from competing sounds and deafness while 'do we sacrifice for rain' or 'go to take Communion' have greater complexities and difficulties in any social communication.

The analysis of language and the attribution to it of religious significances involves serious methodological difficulties. The connection between the workings of the individual mind and what appears in spoken words is a matter of deductive faith rather than of exclusive connections which can be validated. The fact that there must be conscious and unconscious connections between speech and the mind does not mean that any exclusivities can be discovered. We can only assume that the complexities of thought are modified by the restrictions of speech in the size and range of vocabularies, available body language and intelligence. Most English speakers have a working vocabulary of less than a thousand words with which to express their secular and religious needs and this produces phrases more suitable for telegrams. A highly educated Mandarin speaker might know twenty thousand ideograms in which he can express his thoughts. Further, that these difficulties are particularly likely in any verbal or written communication involving abstract rather material issues.

What is said in relation to religious understandings will always be distorted by experimentation as in the completion of sentences using key religious words. Asking Sukuma to make up sentences using the word God, itself a debatable concept in their thinking, would provide enough speculative information for prolonged theological debate. This and similar exercises are all leading questions forcing thought into predetermined categories created by cultural outsiders (Chafe, 1994:9-18) which Chafe typifies as public and private manipulation. Translation even of a work of fiction, involves the forcing ideas of one culture into the categories of another which we can presuppose has little or no natural coincidence.

Then there are social differences between speakers and listeners. Of course, people who are socialised into similar environments are likely to understand much that is said because their minds already have clues as to what is meant, but there are limits to this. Most professionals whether tool-makers or theologians have working vocabularies which aides their intra-communication. Men and women as well as the young and old spend most of their lives in different social worlds. Subsistence societies do not have a wide range of occupations but even between them there are likely to be limits on what is understood.

Modern societies do not have these relative simplicities which would nevertheless be complicated by linguistic codes; no 'tribal' language is quite as uniform as it would appear in the dictionaries and grammars created by outsiders. As social distance between speakers and listeners increases so does the possibility of misunderstandings. The professor and the peasant have a range of mutual incomprehension whatever their range of intelligence and the subject of discussion.

Religious language has the characteristics of being founded on metaphysical abstractions which have little reality outside the minds of thinkers who have put themselves into a social category of some professional isolation. Some attempt to put their thinking into words and others isolate their thinking in the unintelligibility of glossolalia in which they are communicating sounds which are attributed to spirit possession. Once religious language goes beyond simple injunctions, misunderstandings are inevitable; abstract words and phrases will always be difficult to pass from the speech of specialised thinkers into the minds of listeners who have different specialisations and contemporary needs from whom they are different by virtually every category that can be used. All that may be concluded is that they may share some dimensions of religious devotion to Vishnu or the Virgin Mary.

The Sharing of a Language

The sharing of a language cannot mean that there are automatically shared meanings for words or the ways that they are used and there may be several and indeed continuing misunderstandings between people according to the nature of their relationships. The sending and receiving of a verbal message is rarely if ever between people of equal social and intellectual understandings and environments. Communication in a religious setting is a social coming together of people from different social settings at extremes of secularity and religiosity. Most of the seventy million pilgrims who attended the last Kumbh Mela led secular lives and if they heard any religious speech during their attendance there will not have been with the intention of understanding. The only uniformity in their understandings is that they are participating in some parts of the same ceremony.

A study of the use of English and Somali showed that whatever language these informants used, it had different implications for social behaviour changing the equalities in their traditional understandings so that arguments about authority became relevant. The use of English seemed to make integration with other African peoples more difficult (Laitin. 1977; 296. 223)

Even between people of the same faith ostensibly speaking the same language there are social differences shown in linguistic codes. The Ndembu diviner and the interpreter of misfortunes in Moscow are using specialised linguistic codes which they have learned but the words used will always have fan of situational meanings. There is always the widespread use of interpreters in religious situations will explain the religious implications of what the Divine has said whether in holy books or in the detachments of spirit possession. Only in the first case is there any possibility of equivalent vocabularies but not of meanings and in all other cases the richness of each language is rarely shown when there is communication over social rather than intellectual divides. In these religious situations there are likely to be restricted vocabularies so that a fan of additional meanings is attached to each word by the personal use. This is the inevitable consequence of the use and understandings of words and grammatically forms over the social boundaries of particular language groups.

We can presuppose that the speakers of a Bantu language will have general thought patterns associated with that enormous group of connected languages from southern Africa to central Kenya. There is no reason to suppose that such Bantu speakers will have any easier understandings of a Nilotic language spoken in the southern Sudan than a Bengali Indian. These are not just extreme cases as there has always been substantial intermingling of cultures long before modern travel. A modern urban church rather more than a mosque or synagogue is likely to have culturally varied congregations and a sermon is likely to be proportionally unintelligible. A church for Japanese Christians in Seattle in the western United States was faced with the fact that the older members thought and prayed in Japanese while the younger ones did so in English (Duntley, 1999). To solve this difficulty the hymns are written in both English and Japanese and are sung in either language at the same time to the same tune; each singer remains within the social and religious understandings of their own chosen language. "The act of singing together took precedence over singing identical words when sounds are similar literal sense becomes less important."

This is not the problem of simpler misunderstandings which could occur in day-to-day relationships but the more complex ones that can go wrong within tonal languages such as Cantonese and Burmese. The effort of the speaker to make a correctly pronounced statement can go completely wrong and if the correct message is got over, this may be due to the listener getting the point from other clues which may be available in a religious setting of goodwill if indeed they can be read at all over cultural barriers.

Whatever we may conclude about the Safir/Whorf hypothesis it has to be accepted that the processes of thought in a Bantu language with its classifications of nouns and placement pronouns will not fit in easily to the 'similar' sentiments in the Romance languages of Europe in which verb forms and tenses are dissimilar. These differences must channel thought if not guide it into different patterns even if they do not effect certain cognitive functions.

The serious difficulties come when researchers are digging into the more important aspects of the lives of the people they are researching using the words that are heavily soaked in cultural, ethical and personal understandings (Tanner, 1993) as to what both parties like, dislike, believe in and implicate in their understandings. The reasons for the silence of informants on key events by which they black out the horrors of their pasts (Mayaram, 1996) is to often attributed to lack of intelligence and to deliberate evasiveness to intrusive questions. It is more likely to be because they see no reason to disclose their private thoughts to strangers in a linguistic form in which they have no acquired ability to express themselves. Some cultures such as that of the American Indian Apache are reluctant to talk with people about whose social background they are unaware as with a visiting Christian pastor (Basso, 1970).

There is always the fundamental fact that except for a limited range of shared objects, there is an absence of sharable meanings even between members of the same faith. When speakers and listeners talk, there is a process of largely unconscious negotiation for some mutually acceptable interpretation for that situation alone rather than any enduring processes of translation. The deeper believers penetrate into even their own rather than another culture, the greater the possibilities of misunderstandings. (Nida, 1958).

The listeners to anything spoken in a language or linguistic code other than their own is always committed primarily to their own cultural understandings of the sounds which are entering their minds. Even the simplest of nouns such as the word for 'bed' brings up the image of a bed in their own cultural settings and the word is not likely to have any image that can be used in the Buddhist setting in which 'high' beds are prohibited for monks. There is little agreement on the cross-cultural understandings of colour in religious settings for church decoration or the creation of vestments. Anglo-Saxons may prefer single colour combinations while African Christians prefer liturgically a combination of discordant colourings as may have been the style of church decorations in pre-Reformation Europe. Marriage has one meaning in English defined by civil law but among the Sukuma there are twelve different types of marriage with different definitive phrases for each (Cory, 1953). This would include widow inheritance by her deceased husband's brothers existing in Jewish orthodox law as well as in many traditional tribal societies.

When it comes to abstract words, there is little reason to suppose that listeners and speakers are even marginally aligned and great care needs to be used in using abstract words without attaching examples of their meanings in that context. We must accept that all languages are complex and in this there may be little difference between Norwegian with a long linguistic history and the language spoken by the Nuer, an underdeveloped cattle people living in the southern Sudan. It may be quite clear in English what are the generally accepted meanings of a commonplace religious phrase as 'I trust in God'. In the Nuer language for a start there is no such word that coincides with this monotheistic divine entity and when it comes to trust, there are five different words or root forms for trust in different situations (Needham, R., 1977:27); to believe, to trust, to agree, to follow the example of another, to impute, to highly honour and to acknowledge which shows the psychological and social sophistication of these materially simple people.

Many languages have no heritage of common meanings stabilised through detached abstract scholarship and encased in printing. There is little reason to suppose that a small amount of schooling over a couple of generations will change the variable meanings of key abstract words which are no part of the national educational syllabus or national broadcasting. Once words are put into print it is very unusual outside scientific writing and legal drafting, for an author to use words with exactly the same meaning throughout their writings. The ability to do so comes with computerisation and not many would consider it worth the effort except lawyers, Writing has come very late into many cultures and has restricted uses of which religion is an obvious example.

Since professional theologians come from cultures and institutions with complex literary traditions, there is always the feeling that their own literate languages are superior to the non-literate ones which are being used by most people in their interior and unspoken spiritualities. The fact that we attribute rain to meteorological causes alone while 'savages' believe that gods, ghosts or magic can influence rainfall is no evidence that their brains function differently to ours suggesting some semi-genetic psychosocial superiority. As Evans Pritchard wrote (Evans-Pritchard, 1934) that "the particular idea attributing rain to physical causes formed part of my culture long before I was born into it and little more was required of me that sufficient linguistic ability to learn it. (The savage) and I are both thinking in patterns of thought provided for us by the societies in which we live". It is wiser to remember that the use of all languages is overwhelmingly verbal and that only a very small part of human inter-communion is ever written down much less printed. So in listening to believers or communicating to them, it is always two thinking speakers of equally complex individualities at work trying to understand each other.

There is certainly no reason to suppose that any language is superior to any other within its own cultural environment and outside this there is much that any language cannot express whether we are thinking of English, kiSwahili or Hindi. There is even less reason to suppose that any language illustrates superior or inferior cognitive abilities. Any opinion on linguistic status is probably no more than the expression of cultural superiority, a form of intellectual racism. In fact the complexity of the verb forms of kiSwahili shows up the relative poverty of English in this respect which has to use a phrase to express the Christian concept of loving one another which in that language is included in a single collective verb form '*wanapendana*'.

The Categories of Interpersonal Language Communication

The most important issues, perhaps the most fundamental are those raised by language in religious based conversation and the variations in what is said in any language. A language can be divided into four schemas of which only the last is the most important for theologians.

Firstly, there is the language of the believers. No matter how many people use a particular language, there is never any overall homogeneity and every person uses that language in such a way that it is both individual and polyphonic. Each believer is speaking about their beliefs and practices in a form of their language which is founded in a particular cultural environment and individualised (Aarts and Aarts, 1982). There is no nor ever has been any linguistic homogeneity in any society except in cultural and political imaginations of those creating dictionaries and in the aspirations of religious orthodoxies.

Then there is the linguistic and cultural understandings of the listener and in this those with any degree of shared language and cultural understandings has an advantage over almost all those who acquire understandings through the learning of a second language regardless of their degree of absorption, shared faith, personal sympathy for the speaker and intellectual understandings of their host society. However, theoretically possible it may be to become a full member of another culture and its religion other than their natal one as an adult, it has to be accepted that no one can make this psychological and social transfer from one culture to thinking and behaving correctly in another so that in the uses of language the odds are heavily loaded against the cultural outsider. Learning a second language grammatically is not more than an initial stimulus to learning its social practices as the socialisation acquired through a language from birth cannot be replaced by what may be acquired through learning and patchy social absorption.

A national can often establish a reciprocal relationship by using a vernacular relationship term. Dua called other women by the term for brother's wife rather than sister as this relationship was regarded as sacred and to be suspicious of her behaviour would then rebound on them (Dua, 1979). However, the Westerner with their background of Christian individuality may not realise that the obligations of extended kinship go beyond the use of such classificatory terms and involves both social and religious obligations (Meyer, 1996); it may be difficult in such situations to retain the use of what the outsiders consider their personal property.

Finally, there is the linguistic code in which theologians and religious specialists communicate their findings to their colleagues and in the end the abbreviated and probably socially foreign language in which these ideas are spoken in public and published.

Talking to another and Understanding

In any situation in which someone talks about their beliefs and practices whatever their feelings of empathy, the question of language and meaning arises. A prominent feature of rapidly changing societies and the creation thereof provincial, federal or unitary states, is that these people grow up into and use layers of different languages, not just the local and professional differences in how spoken English is used which exist in Britain and India. We have already described how an East African intellectual may have had to move himself through five languages. It seems likely that any Tanzanian who wishes to be upwardly mobile as a Christian priest or Muslim imam will learn to speak at least three languages or indeed those who have religious relationships at the simplest level at least two. George Steiner has described how his mother appeared able to move within three different linguistic patterns of thought in a single sentence (Steiner, 1975). Whatever may have been the case in the past modern men and women are likely to move between several linguistic codes and even languages in a single day relating to domesticity, neighbourhood and business relationships. So at whatever level of understanding information is being passed whether from believers to believers as well as over the barriers of relative disbelief there are complex issues of understanding which are rarely resolved.

Even when social scientists and theologians are talking to their co-professionals, they produce their thinking in different ways. They editorially put emphases into their related information such as the initiating knowledge seeking behaviour, participating in some joint task, voluntary information which may now be taken up by others than their professional colleagues. Such emphases can also be attributed to conserve time and to bridge cultural differences between different types of professionals such as those provided by interpreters between Hindi and French (Hsieh. 2006)

The Layers of Language and the Believer

There can be little doubt that in the use of language the national believer has advantages over even the most assiduous of outsiders wanting to understanding the wider ranges of religious generalities such as the almost universal sub-Sahara belief in the reality of witchcraft. The religious intellectual will increasingly have to work and think in a major language of which English is the most necessary when the advantages may in some degree turn against nationals who may now be professionally using a language into which they have not been socialised. A Ruandan Roman Catholic Bishop prior to the Tutsi genocide referred to French as his natal language but it may not have been a dominant part of his thinking over the years of those horrifying events.

The nominal sharing of a single language does not necessarily mean a semantic understanding across the whole range of social and philosophical issues, but it does make for easier entry into any community if combined with a shared publicly practised religion so that going to Sunday Mass or Friday prayers opens some doors. But the visitors' speech is going to be the linguistic code of those with less or more education than themselves. In talking and writing an educated Chinese Mandarin speaker might have the ability to recognise and voice ten thousand ideograms, while a working man defined as literate might not know as many as a thousand with comparable deficits in what they can share in conversation. The educated in their natal languages may always tend to overextend their linguistic understandings and usages or at least to feel that they have better understandings of the language of their own speech. In fact it may be that however highly educated they may be, their knowledge may be more abstract while others may have just as wider range of language use but that it is more clearly functional. A herbalist in Zimbabwe and a carpenter in Zurich will have large professional vocabularies while having very restricted religious ones because they have no reason to acquire one.

Thus, the most important issues in religious understandings arise about the use of language, perhaps even the most fundamental one. In practice there are always linguistic codes involved rather than a single language so that it is an immensely varied scenario into which the believer or non-believer enters every hearing of religious affairs with the semantics and perhaps even the subtended philosophy of their own natal language fixed in their minds even if they do not follow any identifiable faith.

There is always a more practical difficulty in understanding what is being said. In any one to one communication there is the reasonable possibility of hearing and, therefore, understanding as interruptions can be avoided. Much religious language is public speaking and it is rare that the audience for a ceremony is silent enough to hear what the priest says. The Christian Eucharist ceremony is persistently interrupted by children and movement except possibly in monastic settings. In fact a ceremonial environment which enables listeners to hear what is said may be a rarity because the usual distance of speakers to hearers is not much more than ten feet and that is almost always exceeded in religious ceremonies. The use of loudspeakers in ceremonies may have the characteristics of intrusion into the solemnity of the ceremony by dominating private thoughts and discontinuity between the sound heard and the body and lips language of the speaker. Many Hindu public ceremonies are noisily discordant in which there is no intention to provide a silent background to enable hearing.

The Analysis of Languages used in Religion

However, carefully and humanely the analysis of behavioural data such as language may be, it is a dehumanizing process which removes the wholeness from human behaviour. Hearing poetry or prayer may be emotionally stimulating even if it is without much intellectual understandings but an analysis of what has been said and what it is supposed to have meant, is likely to deaden many such emotional feelings.

We have suggested that scientifically there are four ways of analysing any language, the sound level in phonetics, the morphology in the structure of its words, its set rules in its syntax and finally the meaning of individual words and whole sentences as used religiously. There is a tendency in the social sciences to seek for a meaning but this may be a singularly detached Western approach developed from the European Enlightenment. No language except the linguistic codes of the hard sciences was created or developed to illustrate exactnesses. They are the means to enable speakers to negotiate inter-communication and thus have built-in flexibility. Of these four aspects only the last is part of any formal understandings and of concern to those involved in religion. The natal speaker is unaware of syntax, they know how a word should be pronounced locally and they have no interest at all in how a phrase is put together. They know the ways in which prayers to a divine being or petitions to a priest should be voiced and how to avoid talking to their mothers-in-law. The classification of nouns and the use of introductory syllables have no part in the necessary language understandings of those who use such refinements all the time.

In the religious situation there is the language used by believers but no matter how many people are alleged to use a particular language and this is usually statement of hoped for social affiliation, it has no homogeneity. Every individual uses that language in an individualised way so it is both idiolect and polyphonic.

The listener who is hearing the words for professional rather than for religious reasons has to understand the phonetics, the sounds which are broadcast into their private individual or public collective ears. How the words are constructed and the set rules which have been found to exist in the formal understandings of the language which may be known only through the prolonged formalities of learning a language. The non-national in learning a language which is not their own learns these aspects. The national who has spoken this language from birth will have no knowledge of the formalities of religious syntax and certainly does not possess or feel that he has to buy a grammar (Aartz and Aartz 1982;6-7). Nevertheless under almost every social category the language of one natal speaker is different to that of another.

Then there are the linguistic and cultural understandings of the researcher and in this the national researcher with any degree of shared language and culture has an advantage over almost all non-nationals regardless of their degree of absorption in and intellectual understandings of the people with whom they are working. Lafcadio Hearn became to all intents and purposes a Japanese but he did not become one any more than Cushing became a Zuni Indian. However, theoretically possible it may be to become a member of a culture which is not one's own as an adult, it has to be accepted that they cannot make this social and psychological transfer from one culture to thinking and behaving correctly in another. At best the linguistically proficient foreigner zig zags between the achieved social requirements of immediate social use and natal reactions related to the ascribed relationships of age and sex. The odds must be always heavily loaded against the non-national and in particular the non-believer.

Social scientists in seeking to understand the inner significances of the religious understanding of people from whom they are culturally different cannot surmount several handicaps. Even if they visit these communities regularly and acquired a proficiency in that language to understand much of what is going on, they are not then bilingual. Most social scientists have a field experience of these communities for under two years in which they are never divorced from their natal language in which they think and write their notes.

Religious Speech and Misunderstandings

Since writing is historically a late human development and a discriminating one that overtly distinguishes between various levels of this specially acquired skill and related intellectual capabilities, it cannot be the primary means of acquiring and maintaining religious understandings and needs, hearing and sight must always predominate.

Whereas writing allows misunderstandings from the static base of a texts in which there is no behavioural variability, hearing and sight have no static function at all. It is inevitably ephemeral and lasts no longer than its echo. It can be recorded and then takes on the characteristics of a written text and this is an even more recent development than writing.

Hearing and sight then have only very short-term links between speaker and the spoken to but they are further handicapped by distance and surrounding factors. Unless there are special circumstances which allow a more distant voice to be heard without the complications of echo, once speech goes beyond ten feet the possibilities of misunderstanding intelligible sounds must increase proportionately. With this the hearer has to proportionately use their own social and intellectual creative understandings.

We do not know the proportion of speech connected with religious understandings which are within sonically uninterrupted distance. Christianity is practised under conditions of isolation in special buildings where the only interruptions will be from the restlessness of the congregation, inevitable repetitive echoes and some intruding outside noise so that its interpretation is predominantly a social one.

In some Eastern religions the levels of noise are so high that it would be impossible to hear anything said against the competition in Hindu religious celebrations of several loudspeakers. Westerners staying in Hindu *ashrams* have commentated on the difficulties of meditating amongst so much distracting noise. There are advantages in reading from a religious text which is noiseless.

Some Christian charismatics such as John Wesley had great drawing power for his open-air sermons but it is questionable how many may have intelligently heard what he said rather than imagining a content from their social difficulties and emotional needs. In religious gatherings in churches, mosques and temples much less in the open air before the introduction of the microphone, it seems unlikely that those who were present could have heard no more than a few isolated key words; they were listening with their eyes not their ears.

Mediaeval churches provided religious sound but not any appreciable intellectual message when the liturgy was spoken by the priest at the far end of the church and facing away from the congregation. This is still the situation in Greek Orthodox and Ethiopian Coptic churches and in the latter the celebrant is entirely hidden from the congregation behind a curtain so that only murmurings can be heard. The Prophet Muhammad said to have chosen the first caller to prayer because of his resonant voice but he was not giving out a religious message but only a reminder of the obligation to pray at certain times as anyway there were no clocks then.

If we divide intention from the realities of religious practice, it would seem that liturgical sound and liturgical meanings have only recently been allied by what liturgists and theologians had hoped would be a joint activity. A crowded ceremony in a prominent London Roman Catholic church has the music and the singing of the choir transmitted effectively but not the speech of the priests who were no more than a decorative element near the distant altar. Historically words were addressed to the Divine and not to congregations. It was enough for them to hear that the divine was being addressed on their behalf. They could hear the sound of the words addressed to the Divine and it was not necessary or even a felt need that they should know what was said. This is still the case in Buddhist, Hindu and many quasi-traditional ceremonies in which spoken words are in languages unintelligible to participants.

Even when religious rituals are held in the vernacular in what participants consider to be traditional ceremonies it would seem to be a matter of indifference what the operatives are actually saying only that he or she is saying what is necessary to show the listening spirit that they are fulfilling a particular obligation. An example of this indifference is that a Sukuma child can be named after an ancestor but the ceremony ends the matter and the child may not be called by that name ever again. The ancestors are known to be satisfied with the naming ceremony as the fulfilment of a divined obligation.

Overwhelmingly both currently and historically religious liturgical speech has not been provided with the aim of the listeners hearing more than socially and religiously approved sound. There will always be an inevitable gap between the voicing of orthodoxy and what listeners take into their minds. A built-in reality of misunderstandings of which there are important consequences.

The listeners probably feel that they are conforming to the requirements of orthodoxy and that they have acquired an entirely personal feeling that they are fulfilling what was required of them. Secondly, since they may not know what has been said and that is certainly the case in the public ceremonies of Buddhism and Hinduism, this may allow them considerable leeway in how they attain religious fulfilment; they get what they want without being constrained by having to understand what was actually said.

Thus, there are two levels in this working misunderstanding. When believers have heard specific words which they would not understand anyway since these are religious mysteries of which the main constituent is belief in what is essentially incapable of understanding. Further since they will have heard little more than sound in a specifically venerated situation, they are freer to interpret the fulfilment of their needs in ways that they feel are conformist without conforming at all in any orthodox understandings.

There is also the factor as to whether religious speech is directed at any human audience as we have already suggested and if so whether it is a behavioural necessity in religious terms for those involved to know what is being said in any active cognitive sense. Let us assume that the Divine will accept all that is said and that mental thoughts are as acceptable in a silent but nevertheless personal verbally constructed form.

Whereas a conversation between priest and believer in a one to one situation can obviously be geared to mutual understandings, but how can this be the case in any public ceremony. Any religious congregation in any historical or contemporary setting have always contained a wide mixture of people, even if only two people are involved they will not necessarily have the same similarities of identical twins. They will be different according to age, sex, education, marital status, ethnicity, education, occupation, social status and physical and intellectual capacity. At whom can religious speech be directed, except some sort of imaginary lowest common denominator likely to catch the attention of some desired segment as must be the case for television and radio audiences. Whatever is said is always going to be beyond the semantic understandings of the majority of those listening. Why then go to the trouble of producing a liturgy geared to the idiosyncratic diminishment of some hypothetical vernacular average when those involved will always reinterpret what they hear to accord with their own conscious or unconscious needs. This is what Roman Catholic believers did with the Latin liturgy and what current Buddhist and Hindus do with the unintelligible sounds of Pali and Sanskrit prayers.

The reality must surely be that the only wordings that can have any reasonable chance not so much as being intellectually understandable but as providing a series of approved sounds provided in an religious setting which allows mixed audiences to interpret in ways that they find satisfying. They can be seen as being be washed over by holy words whether they are dozing or seeking help for some personal distress.

The Absence of a Single Language

Most if not all societies are polyphonic. In Goa the ex-Portuguese enclave on the west coast of India has four languages in current use; Portuguese, English, Konkani and Swahili used by returning emigrants from East Africa and each is related to status and within any single language there are linguistic codes which similarly are related to status. A researcher investigating historic events within the living memories of villagers (Amin, 1995;5) found that his familiarity with the local Bhojpuri dialect "may paradoxically have accentuated the use of status markers in his conversations while at the same time have helped forge a community of purpose in his work". It is more than a learning process to sense the uses in which a language is used appropriately for public religious and private spirituality purposes.

In some cases the users of an official national language are seen as outsiders or thought to be supporting an outsider political viewpoint. A Chinese who is not a Han but who speaks Mandarin may see this as a political necessity associated with control from Beijing and would rather use his own language which is not the medium though which political control is exercised. Swahili is the national language of Tanzania but it is not in the same linguistic group as that of the Maasai. This *lingua franca* would be the natal language of the coastal communities and since it is a Bantu language it would have the potential to be intelligible by other Bantu language speakers such as the Angoni, Yao and Sukuma. But it would be a totally foreign language to the Maasai moving backwards and forwards between Kenya and Tanzania and other minority speakers of distinct languages. In large states there are minorities with their own languages such as Romany among the gipsy travellers in Britain, while India has states with their own languages such as Tamil linked to strong feelings of sub-national nationalisms. The use of a *lingua franca* for religious purposes may miss the sensitivities in the vocal sounds which a community or individual uses for their religious needs. It is a matter for speculation when a new language is used liturgically, how many years will pass before private prayers and indeed religious dreams more from the one language to the other.

In some countries composed of many different small community languages such as Papua New Guinea, the international and national language is Pigeon English. It has an unknown semantic content because it is assessed contemptuously by outsiders as not worthy of serious study and is often the subject of jokes about its 'quaint' phrases such as an aeroplane being referred to as a 'steam chicken'. Its usefulness for employment and business is undeniable but it is unlikely to be the language in which individuals think religiously, however, much it may be required of them in formal religious gatherings involving the *Bible* recited in that 'contrived' dialect or is it now a language?

How much in fact do national believers know of their own culture as it is expressed in language and in many social situations they have to learn to use a language in a new way as they may be only conversant with the language and behaviour appropriate to their own social circle. It is indeed difficult for the Westerner to stop saying 'thank you' repeatedly in cultures where such a phrase may not exist or if it is, it is used sparingly as it seems to terminate a relationship rather than enabling continued reciprocity.

In religion practice is always related to behaviour and only independent of it in book learning and in situations of social isolation. It may be more difficult for a national to learn the religious and social intricacies of a dialect as they may think they know and for non-national to put into practice the understandings that there are in social terms no single language. In Ireland a woman researcher who was not living in a family may have been in some danger from not knowing the appropriate behaviour to be shown by a married or unavailable woman. Some Protestant missionaries in pre-Communist China learnt their Mandarin from low status people and this specialised linguistic competence came to give them the low status associated with their particular fluency. The Jesuits learnt high status Mandarin which led to similar biases. To learn another language so fluently as to avoid making a long series of social and religious mistakes is probably an impossibility.

While non-national and indeed national believers and non-believers may be assumed to be of higher status economically from their material well-being than most of the people about whom they are thinking and whom they are researching. Their social and political status is ambiguous and constantly illustrated by their use of language and the language which is used to them.

Difficulties over What Language is being used

We have established that no known community has a single language which all its members use all the time and in the same ways. There are always fluctuations which occur in every natal language depending on who is speaking to whom about what and such specialised uses as that used in addressing spirits, important authorities and the poetry of songs. Thus, whatever linguistic form in which a religion presents itself, it will not be received in the sense in which was intended to pass on.

Even in states which have a *lingua franca* for official correspondence and in and legislation there are other *lingua franca* which have a limited but nevertheless almost universal use in restricted fields. kiSwahili as a commercial *lingua franca* is used from the East African coast and inland to Zaire and remains the military *lingua franca* in all three East African states, just as Urdu is the military language of India.

Any contemporary city contains minorities whose members speak one language at home and with friends but use the dominant language in business, school and with the local authorities. Calcutta, Accra and Kampala will each have dozens of languages in use at any one time. We have shown that in a Kampala housing estate (Parkin, 1971) kiSwahili was used by people wanting to show brotherhood, Luganda by non-Luganda when wanting to show deference to the dominant community, English when speakers wanted to show their own status and a tribal dialect to show exclusiveness. So the language which they might be speaking or hearing in a religious situation might be the consequences of a temporary social situation.

In contemporary Africa and Asia there can be few children who are not to some extent multilingual for special purposes. So social scientists by learning or using a single language may be underlining a special viewpoint or keeping themselves within a particular social environment. Language in any cognitive sense is unlikely to bond any religious community beyond the aural assumptions of religiously authenticated religious sound. In this aural uniformity there is a working misunderstanding between what is presented and what believers think they are doing.

Religious language may be used to express viewpoints and beliefs but its principal use is to relate to the supernatural in whatever contexts a culture creates. The fact that it is heard by those present at ceremonies does not create the necessity for it to be understood. It is enough that this is accepted as religious language or perhaps religious sound is better able to explain this situation. In this there is a working misunderstanding from the point of view of believers who only hear and see and in the social sciences interpretation that they cannot understand an indescribable mystery.

11
Literacy and its Religious Restrictions

The printing of any religious document is a media event and it has none of the sonic limitations of speech. There is a sharp division between the writer and those who pick up the written message about whom little can ever be known. There is an imaginary addressee which is the creation of the editor with whom a relationship is simulated (Talbot, *et al.*, 2003).

Whereas historically these printed words had geographically and institutionally restricted audiences, they are is now potentially related to globalization. First world texts are consumed by third world audiences as a matter of course. Its production is disjointed but under institutional control although the addressees are composite individuals in which their only control over what they read is to switch off their attention.

There are four print producer roles within which and between which there are inevitable working misunderstandings. The originator of the text about whom we often know very little, the author who generates the form in which the text is produced, an editor who coordinates the process of production and the receptors of the printed message about whom we can always know very little within the dimensions of personal deliberation and accidental encounters.

The individual always has choices in what they do in religious situations as in other matters even if it is the negative one of doing what they have always think they have done. Choices which are available to the individual in a range of situations within institutionalized control and to those in which more unrestricted choices are available. The correct way of coping with personal problems has never been defined or indeed could not be more than attempts in the absence of literacy and institutionalization and this presents every individual with a range of socially approved preferences. We now look at the patterning of religious behaviour which are part of putting individual choices into practice.

In Religious Situations are more than Attempts

Any assessment of the value of religious ideas and practices is faced with the fact that the limits of the information which they want to refer to is imposed by what has been committed to writing. The overwhelming presence of writing is so fundamental in its preconceptions that not only do we take it for granted, but we assume that it is a totally benign force necessary for mankind's development. If we aim to discern how the carrying out of any religion's ideas are related to literacy we have to see this difficult to acquire ability in cost-benefit terms. What do religiously disposed people gain and lose by reading and writing about their faith and what conclusions can be deduced from a form of symbolism which is only peripherally connected to the wholeness of any individual's religious identity. The gap between these aspects leads to the inevitability of working misunderstandings.

Literacy has long been associated with some form of liberation by which people are freed from backwardness and new nations would be freed from the cultural alienation and political dependency of old and new forms of colonialism in everything including religion. In general this has not occurred except among the highly literate minorities who need this skill in order to carry on their businesses and professions in international situations which requires both literacy and the knowledge of languages other than their own. For ordinary people literacy has been all but overtaken by the impact of radios, television and cassette recorders which require only biological ability to hear and see (Baumann, 1986, 6-8).

Literacy in any social context has to be seen as more than the ability of some people to read. There is clearly no such thing as a totally literate society and within a society which has had universal primary education for generations there will be both illiteracy of those who cannot read and write and non-literacy of those who read and write only as much as they need to or want to. Thus, literacy in a religious context is likely to be even more discriminatory than literacy in general. There has to be a wish to read for a religious purpose and a varying understandings of what may be provided in print. Further what they read as a stimulus to some forms of personal and group change in religious practices and ideas is likely to be highly selective and restricted to small numbers of people; a personal dialectical relationship between the individual's understandings of the texts and their personal circumstances.

What they read has been put on to paper in either writing or print and thus becomes an object independent of its author and loses the elasticity of spoken communications in which misunderstandings can be cleared up by further questioning and these interrelationships are always accompanied by body language. Reading slows down the processes of interpretation and cuts out whatever alternative explanations cannot be contained in the print. Thus, words spoken in any social and religious context and the same words written have different social existences; it cuts out interpretations based on the other senses. One of the most important aspects of literacy as it affects both the individual and the group in their religious practices, is that there is no longer any moment to moment feedback and moreover without any intention that it should be so. As a result of this those that are literate have placed themselves in a perspective without a behavioural context.

The written mode in the service of religion has far fewer resources than are available in any spoken language; it is not for nothing that it can be referred to as cold print (Gomperz, *et al.*, 1984). If the written prayer is to cover the same ground as the spoken one, it has to carry with it into the writing the syntactic and lexical meanings which cover the same ground. This requires very sophisticated acquired literacy in comparison to the spoken word in their natal languages into which people have been socialised from birth.

It would seem, therefore, that the written words used in religious rituals have great difficulty in serving the same personalised and emotional functions as their supposedly spoken equivalents. This is perhaps illustrated by Chipwya literates where the relationship between two speakers is unknown; the norm is to keep silent because the requisite mental framework in literate form does not provide enough information to make a reply possible (Scolen & Scolen, 1979). It may even be that in cultures which are tied rather specifically to writing cannot carry the characteristics of more aurally linguistic cultures. The Dinka language (Lienhardt, 1980,77-8) compels its speakers to integrate the moral and physical attributes of persons within their physical bodies. There is no disjunction between abstract terms and concrete imagery shown there in the indivisibility of their religion and social life which indeed occurs in most traditional cultures. But then this interpretation of Dinka thinking is the creation of an outside intellectual and we should accept that very few Dinka would understand what Lienhardt has written. Just as few

Westerners would understand the writings of their theologians and philosophers.

Printing and the Word of God

Putting into print the Words of God in any language raises a number of inevitable problems. Of course, it shares with the spoken word the question as to what these printed words mean or were intended to mean. But by the fact of being printed, they take on an independent existence; these printed words now have a material existence shared with cups and saucers.

Arabic and Latin and indeed many contemporary languages have no upper case lettering and so stresses to show importance are a matter for personal, social and religious interpretations. Once capital letters are used in print, they raise theological issues as to whether Jesus was the Son or son of God and indeed in the use of the word God at all which makes no sense to Buddhists, Hindus and Taoists. Dialogues between the professionals of any religion is inevitably carried out through the discussion of religious documents in which these capital letters assume fundamental importance; the use of lower case allows liberal interpretations of what may or may not be divine influences.

Then comes the longevity of print and its quasi-immortality according to the conditions under which it is stored and the quantity of documents printed, but religious documents tend to be treasured. Speech fades with the end of its sound and the inaccuracy of the memories of listeners. Memories are personal and their social and religious relevance depends on the status of the persons providing them.

Unless it is deliberately destroyed or decays, the printed religious word is always somewhere and can be hauled into discussions as more substantive than voiced opinions as validating a point of view or being used to enable or block change. Once committed to paper a religious statement has a life of its own. Overall is the fact that in writing a religiously based statement or one that is connected to religion becomes potentially a permanent thing, a series of objects relatively independent of its author; it can go anywhere and be seen by anyone who gets hold of the paper on which it is written. The print cannot say that it has made a mistake and would want to rephrase something which has been misunderstood.

Arabic is a concise language and regularly dispenses with the verb 'to be'. Haider a distinguished Egyptian writer, wrote a novel in 1983 containing a conversation between two exiled Iraqi communists which included the sentence "they still rule us with the law of the Bedouin's god and the *Koran*.... It was recently reprinted without the dots and indeed without using the verb 'to be' and thus caused an eruption of fundamentalist hostility; the circumstances of what the novel actually said was irrelevant (Haider, H., 1983). So written religious phrases can be developed to have different meanings from what was intended and from what was actually put into writing. Certainly in some circumstances religious writing is dangerous for both the authors, possessors and readers.

The change from non-literacy to literacy is not to be confused with illiteracy, the almost deliberate inability to read when there are adequate opportunities to learn do so. If literacy is no more than the ability to read laboriously, a time consuming process which is scarcely likely to be seen as a useful use of time beyond the needs of business and the recognition of figures. This minimal literacy seems unlikely to make any important changes in the religious ideas and practices of most of those people who are classed as literate.

It cannot be seen in isolation as necessarily a secularising process if only because literacy at least in the earlier stages of Christian missionary effort was always associated with *Bible* reading in Roman script and throughout the long association of Islam with Africa and Asia with the reading of the *Koran* in the more culturally restricting Arabic script. So the form in which literacy is learnt is often as important as the contents; the former enabling a wide range of secular reading and the latter restricting this new ability to a narrower range of new knowledge. The fact that basic religious works are written in Arabic, Sanskrit or Pali will reinforce the mystical significance of those languages which so-called minimal literates may possess in written form but cannot read.

It must be incorrect to assume or even to postulate that those who can read are cognitively different from those who cannot since literacy is a variable characteristic at best and even today only exists to a limited utilitarian extent for a limited number of people and of course for only a short period in history. It would seem unlikely that there is a different type of rationality to be found in print and pre-print cultures (Veer, 1994,80).

Then there is another factor in literacy; what is obtained from reading and what is understood. Even a statement in writing that a Moslem may marry four women at a time, hinges on the circumstances constituting a valid marriage and that requires interpretation. Quasi-traditional customs may have basic principles developed from paradigms created in distant times, but their application is always situational. Literacy adds to the difficulties of this interpretation as it puts a material fact into behaviour which is always relational. It does not solve them as anything written is difficult to relate to some social event isolated in space and time.

The religious ideas and practices of any individual are always in a state of change but at the same time they are always members of social groups as well as religious institutions and particular situations with which there is a dialectical process always going on. But once literacy enters the equation, the rate of change in religious matters acceptable to organisations rather than more loosely integrated social groups, slows down noticeably as decisions to change or not, go through the long processes of committee consultations and approvals.

On the other hand, much religious change starts independently of institutional approval and in forms which it cannot control through literacy. Thus literacy in languages which are shared by ordinary practitioners and religious specialists creates almost by accident the division between official and popular religious practices. In these circumstances much of known religious change takes place independently of official or theological approval or at best its tacit acceptance of practices and changes which it would be virtually impossible for them to control. In these senses writing creates working misunderstandings.

The Experience of Literacy in a Bantu African Society

Social scientists, theologians and philosophers through their higher education and better standard of living have been so detached from village life and high density living conditions in general that they do not intellectually hear and react to the connotations inscribed in key religious terms whether Christian, Hindu or Muslim. People at the grass roots do not seem to need critical theologians Africanization from above, as they have already synthesized traditional religions and Christianized it in their own ways and according to their own interests (Meyer, 1994).

What has been the experience of the now six million Sukuma of literacy that should make it important in its own right apart from religion. The analysis of the categories of tablets excavated at Ugarit in Iraq (Goody, 1977, 86) which was a society with an alphabetical language and a far higher state of organisation than anything reached by the contemporary Sukuma, showed that 59 per cent were to do with administration and business and 16 per cent were letters. Literacy for the Sukuma is largely related to the bureaucratic processes of government. It is quite clear that written trivia would not be kept and we only know this from the accidental recovery of such documents from the excavated rubbish pits in the Roman military station of Vindolanda on Hadrian's Wall dividing Roman Britain from the unconquered north. Such trivia anywhere might not involve religious matters.

The Arabs running the trading caravans from the coast to the Great Lakes in central Africa would have kept their commercial records in Arabic, but that would not have affected the Sukuma who acted as head-porters receiving a standard payment for each trip. At best the Muslim Arabs were incidental spreaders of Islam through their marriages to local women which would not have involved much spreading of literacy in Arabic. Their first experience of literacy as affecting them would have been the German colonial authorities and to a much lesser extent the missionaries who kept records of baptisms and deaths rather than of the rarer marriages of converts. Right from the start the Germans would have listed the Sukuma for tax, for work levies and indeed for every occasion in which there were administrative relationships. Literacy for the Sukuma meant being listed by name and moreover these lists were kept in books. Literacy enables bureaucracy and for most people this aspect of writing is not usually a pleasant experience.

So the Sukuma would not have seen literacy as a door to the outside world through religious literacy, but as the principal means by which outsiders, possibly even missionaries, were controlling them. Even nearly a century later, the main relationship between their independent government rather than the preceding British colonial one, has been through lists. They are on lists for tax, schooling, attendance at dispensaries, making contributions to development funds, membership of a political party and voting.

Those approaching a government official are first of all asked for their names and down it goes on a piece of paper or in a ledger. There is nothing in their experience of literacy that it is something intrinsically valuable and interesting except as a way out of subsistence farming and that is proving less and less possible with limited development, persistent inflation and government retrenchment. What they did see was that literacy was related to power and that power meant a higher and more secure standard of living. Thus, the main reason for schooling would not be any intellectual or religious improvement but the hope of becoming one of those who put other people on lists. Thus, for these people religious literacy would have been advantageous in contexts that were mainly secular and even in a religious context it may have been seen in terms of social advantages. The Sukuma have continued to practise their quasi-traditional religion without seeing any need for literacy to be involved. Priests keep ledgers and diviners behaviourally relate.

Literacy and the Creation of Change

It is too often assumed that there is a clear dividing line between literacy and non-literacy and that there has been a significant change in the mental abilities of those who are literate as opposed to those who are not (McLuhan, 1962,1-41.). There is little evidence for this because both sides of the equation cannot be precisely defined except in relation to a particular piece of prose and of course much depends on intelligence. In a psychological study of Vai literacy, the non-literates were not found to perform at lower levels than those who were literate in Arabic. English or Vai by task, logic, abstraction, memory or communication. It was concluded that there was no basis for any claim that literacy was a necessary and sufficient condition for any of the script related activities which were assessed (Scribner & Cole, 1981, 251).

Literacy in its widest sense could be described as a state of potential enablement but not that it necessarily enables. Religious literature may be bought but not necessarily read. Taiwanese, Chinese and Sri Lankans on pilgrimage visits to temples purchase religious literature knowing that they would not be able to read and understand these specialised religious ideograms and phrases. Buying such literature as religiously connected souvenirs is part of the conventional pilgrimage experience there as much as it is in Europe.

It is first necessary to establish whether individuals and communities are literate but for what purposes are they literate and moreover whether this literacy is used for repetitious religious purposes or as a vehicle for religious changes. There are thus four levels or aspects of literacy to consider. An assumption of the ability to read and write a simple message according to the UNESCO definition of literacy for statistical purposes, is not adequate for assessing its influence in religious practices and their potential for change. Understanding a single sentence may be as personally significant as the ability to read a whole sacred text. Such a standard would not involve any reading of accounts, poetry,an instructional pamphlet for admission to a religious group or a letter in idiosyncratic handwriting.

For literacy to be considered of importance for religious change, it would have to be tested against reading and minimally understanding a passage from the *Bible* in English or in translation, the Koran in Arabic or kiSwahili and Hindu or Buddhist texts in Sanskrit or Pali respectively. This probably means that this level of literacy is rare and that the influence of literacy in precipitating religious change probably correlates to discussions raised through those who are literate at much lower levels than would involve some thorough understandings of newer viewpoints available in print.

Such a formula cuts down religious literates to a small proportion of believers since much religious literature in Mandarin Chinese, Pali and Sanskrit has no correlation to colloquial usages. Many Moslems may be able to read the *Koran* in Arabic without being able to use Arabic in any other context or in interpersonal communication. Since the *Bible* has been translated into over three hundred languages by the British and Foreign Bible Society, we can assume that parts of it are widely known as it is printed in the same script as is taught in local schools. Thus, its reading requires no more specialisation than the normal literacy available in the lowest forms of elementary schools. Literacy taught through learning to read the *Bible* in school may have been part of learning in mission schools. This is unlikely to be the case in any schools learning according to national curricula in grant aided schools or in the national schools which have superseded them.

Biblical literacy is also helped by the fact that it is cheap to buy due to subsidies and its large size makes it even more of a bargain as apart from its religious value it contains many interesting stories related to traditional experiences. For people with low incomes it is a better buy than other reading materials available on the market. Above all the reading of the *Bible* requires no specialist training outside that learnt in schools and used for economics and politics. Secular and sacred reasons for reading criss-cross each other.

On the other hand, the reading of the *Koran* in Arabic outside the Middle East has no secular advantages and the ability to do so is a specialist skill of no value outside its Islamic context. Indeed, it would be a handicap to spend time on learning Arabic when the national or local *lingua franca* are in Roman script, away from the teaching of secular schools and the possibilities of secular advancement. However, in Pakistan what were initially Koranic schools have added secular subjects to their curricula because of the inadequacies of the government's educational system (Zaman, 1999). While it certainly not the intention of these schools to initiate religious change in Islam, it may well do so.

However, there is a close link between popular Islamic and quasi-traditional religious practices which keeps Arabic literacy under the control of small groups of Koranic experts whose livelihoods derive from their interpretive and helpful skills used in allying to some extent these two divergent religious systems; the creation of amulets using quotations from the *Koran*, using the *Koran* in divination and adjudicating on issues of marriage and inheritance involving Islamic law.

So Islamic literacy which is often no more than the memorising parts of the *Koran* is a dead end unless this ability to memorise leads to some individuals becoming Islamic scholars or local religious leaders. It is not known whether this ability to memorise leads to this choice of careers or *vice versa*. The hegemony of English and French in sub-Saharan Africa and English alone in India and Pakistan is overwhelming in government and socio-economic affairs beyond the regional level.

This situation is even more so for those who become literate in Sanskrit or Pali who have to be involved into this specialised learning quite early in life and these languages have no secular correlations at all. Listeners to these languages would have no means of knowing to what extent these recitations might be accurate or not since their appreciation rests on sacralised sounds and possessing sacred writings.

Literacy and Religious Change

It is necessary to consider whether literacy does have some particularised qualities which must almost inevitably initiate widespread rather than narrow changes in religious thinking and behaviour. To read and be intellectually moved is difficult to breakdown into a specific isolated process; the banality of a commonplace prayer may serve an emotional purpose at one time and not at another. It need not involve a particularly high standard of literacy as we see in the attractions of cheap romantic literature and the satisfactions from being able to read even to a limited degree may be reflected in an increased religious self-confidence.

A small vocabulary does not necessarily correlate to restricted understandings of religious events and needs since words at every level of understanding words are symbolic and whether they are dominant or not in that society as a whole, each has a fan' or 'spectrum' of referents, which are interlinked by what is usually a simple mode of association, its very simplicity enabling it to interconnect a wide variety of 'significata'. (Turner, 1967,50). This fan of meanings may or may not lead to leaps of personal understandings and they are just as likely to come from being able to read a dogma and not much more as to hear it once or repetitively.

It is hard to distinguish whether an important religious word necessarily grows in value from its existence in print by becoming a static object rather than a manipulatable value. Much religious thought is related to the use of growth words or ideas creating new sensitivities (Nisbet, 1969,3-4). and the possibility of personal and social change is in almost all Eastern and Western religious discourse; the end may be static but getting there is through prolonged processes of ascribed or achieved personal change. It may also be that the possibilities for religious change come from the highly specialised class of literates in all world religions who have created a predisposition to expect personal changes but they need not necessarily involve or lead to the development of new ways of thinking and practising.

Certainly Christian and Islamic leaders have stressed the importance of being able to read their holy books. The former have stressed the medium of translation into local languages while the latter have used local languages to explain what is in the static sacred Arabic text. There is always the distinctions between reading in order to memorise and reading in order to understand and to write. In Christianity there would appear the inevitable reinterpretations of words which do not have any implacable sanctity which is the case with the *Koran*.

In the end religious developments may come from a very low level of literate competence when the use of a word or phrase conjures up parallels to traditional concepts and provides possible new solutions to inevitable stressful situations. It seems unlikely that the written word from a non-traditional source is likely to have any specific impetus for a culture in which that type of thinking is not endemic. The translated words whether in print or not, carry over and catch on in alien cultural environments which usually do not appear to relate to the situations for which these sanctified words were originally written. The stimulus to change comes from the conscious or unconscious intellectual perceptions of those who want to innovate which is possibly a continuous process. Literacy like the uses of any other tool, enables new forms of control and dominance and the parallels have already been made to its use in government and economics. Of course, this brings about major changes in the form of religious practice which are visible enough but its principal effect has been to divide existentially the popular practices and personal perceptions from written theological ones with its institutional contexts.

The Iconic use of Religious Writings

It is perhaps too easy to regard literacy and the printed religious text as necessarily having significance for the unconscious or conscious empowerment of the mind. It seems more likely that the uses of religious texts are mainly iconic. The reading of religious texts in support of some personal pattern of belief and practice which is read into the text rather than what it actually contains. The written religious statement may originally have done its best to mean what it states as a guide to conformity and public affirmation. Most pre-literate peoples have never thought that it was ever possible to know what people were thinking and their systems of customary adjudication are based on what actually happened rather than what personal intentions may have been.

Most people do not realise that its original meanings were from a long time ago and that the past is a foreign country, they do things differently there (Hartley, 1953). The reader may not be consciously aware of this disparateness which is the fact of any written text, but as Plato wrote 'anyone who leaves behind him a written manual or likewise anyone who takes it over from him on the supposition that such writings will provide something reliable or permanent, must be exceedingly simple minded'. (Plato, 1952). Even when a text makes positive unambiguous statements, they are always filtered through particular intelligence working in particular situations. What is read is turned into words in the mind and it is in this process that further changes occur on what the original writer and almost certainly the translator may have meant. Most of what is read for religious purposes has been read before, so it may well have mnemonic functions bringing out stereotypical responses.

What happens with the printed word in religious affairs is to create illusions of stability and provide the structure for institutionalisation. At the same time the mind will be working within a wider framework than the writing. Thus, the text may contribute to change which is being initiated elsewhere in a wider environment as a result of social experience; there is in any situation a proportional weighting in favour of the use of a text to the situation in which it is being contextualised.

Literacy as a Passing Stage in Religious Practices

It seems likely that even among the highly literate once literacy has been used in order to learn some religious texts, there is very little further reading as they already know enough for their own religious purposes. Once this stage is reached there is not much further use for literacy in a religious context. Literacy also exists as a stage into a form of specialised non-literacy in which it is no longer necessary to read or indeed to write as the necessary texts have been formally learnt. The Eastern religions and Islam in particular have always given a higher and indeed necessary status to those who have memorised large sections of sacred texts. Reading as a necessary precondition before Buddhist ordination, and for Moslems who have memorised the whole *Koran* as an act of particular piety. It is not unusual to find fundamentalist African Christians who know large sections of the Gospels by heart.

However, learning by heart has the function of regulating form in the mind and it would not usually lead to thinking about changes in meaning from thinking and discussion as the effort of memorising might often be taken as an end in itself. Indeed to discuss what may or may not be the meaning of a memorised text would undercut the primary purpose of the effort. A phrase from the *Koran* can be written on a board, washed off and the water drunk and the paper on which a particularly vital phrase has been written can be eaten. Writing the *Koran* or some other religious text is a means to a religious end and not part of some wider process of creating social and intellectual value.

The basic Buddhist phrase *Om mane padme hum* is written on prayer wheels which can be turned by hand, water or heat and the benefits of the printed word go to those who initiate its movements. The words can be carved onto a wood block, which is then repetitively printed on the water by someone sitting beside the stream (Ekvall, 1964.120-2). Much the same occurs in the basic prayers of Christianity which have been said aloud or in the mind so frequently that the sequence is mnemonic and the fact that it is printed has almost no relevance to these semi-automatic personal functions. It would appear, therefore, that on the one hand, literacy for religious purposes is for and by specialists for their own use and on other a step towards personal religious use for which it may have little continuing need.

The Elitism of Religious Writings

The original forms of most sacred texts have long since disappeared in a long process of repeated transpositions; whoever wrote them and under what conditions has long since been filtered through a continuing process of professional exegesis. The whole approach to religious writings whether in its possible original forms or in transliteration is elitist. It is either written by a professional elite in which assessments and understandings are aimed at fellow professionals with whom there is a constant dialectical relationship or the style is downgraded to the theoretical understandings of a particular market at a lower level to that of the professionals. It is of course a matter of practicalities rather than theoretical importance as to which can be regarded as the best or indeed correct form of writing.

It is noteworthy that only Christianity goes through this particular process of transcribing its sacred writings into some hypothetical simpler form for the understandings of wider markets that that of the professionals. It does not occur in Islam and it is doubtful whether it could even occur at all in the transliterations of classical Mandarin, Pali and Sanskrit. Whatever religious roles these specialised forms of literacy perform, they cannot stabilise religious ideas except mnemonically and this form of usage may have only linguistically and ideologically conservative functions. At the one end of this spectrum there are the dialectics of specialised discussion and change and at the other some constant inapplicability of fixed writings to the needs and understandings of part-time readers who thinking and behaviour is only religious in personal emergencies and for some part of their daily lives.

The mind in its religious usages is an amalgam of other less specialised practices and it is the religious specialists who attempt to isolate religious ideas and practices. It may be that this is a modern Christian way of thinking which ignores or at least side-tracks the interplay of these other and parallel factors. Traditional societies do not distinguish between social and religious activities, the society and its religion are one.

Literacy and Individual Religious Activity

Once literacy dominates religious activities, then individual creative religious activity becomes downgraded; the correct religious behaviour is the one that is written down and institutionally endorsed as the legitimate way to relate to 'the other'. This of course puts a premium on conformity but literate religious conformity covers a relatively small cross-section of individual and group behaviour. There has to be and will always be a range of religious behaviour or rather religiously acceptable 'conventions' which are not and indeed cannot be dominated by literacy.

Thus, the dominance of the literate theologian and the rule-making religious institution would tend to restrict religious participation but for two factors. Firstly, for a variety of reasons these writings are not read, of which the most likely is that it is not felt to be important enough to take up scarce time or that the writing is difficult to read and understand

and does not appear on the face of it to be relevant to the lives of potential readers. It is not just that the Prophet Mohammad may have held a rather poor view of the religious capacities of his fellow Arabians, and thus simplified the devotional practices required of his followers to ritualised prayer movements. All religions tend to simplify their devotional practices, particularly when they are printed and require generalised literacy beyond that of the specialists. Apart from the possible downgrading of prose style for popular use, it is hard enough to get theological and philosophical agreement to a single uniform series of devotions, how much more difficult it would be to agree on a much larger range of written variations.

It is possible that the more that is written in an understandable lowest common denominator style which is both clear and demanding, the less likely are individuals to find it useful and believable; if religious practices are concerned with the supernatural then bringing into ritual somewhat commonplace language may not attract. Thus, religious rituals which retain their popularity tend to have an ambiguous or virtually unreadable element in them allowing individuals considerable latitude or require such a small range of religious understandings that it similarly allows the individual this personal creativity.

Although both Christianity and Islam are intensely literate religions based on written records and putting a high but not an exclusive reliance on the ability to read their scriptures, neither demand literacy as a requirement for worship or indeed for attaining a successful relationship with God. It perhaps goes without saying that the involvement of literacy in the major religions has partly been used as a means of domination and encouraging participation within a narrow range of institutionalised acceptability. In the major religions the central celebrants are literate, but for most of the participants in their rituals which they have done many hundreds of times so there is no need to follow them in print. Core prayers, the *mantras* of devotion are probably better known and far more regular than anything else that they do.

Whereas religious speech does not necessarily have to have an institutionalised basis, writing for a religious purpose almost inevitably has such a background. The form of writing is 'deeply embedded in attitudinal, cultural, economic and technological constraints Reading and writing are socio-linguistic activities. People speak, listen, read and write in different social situations and for different purposes' (1980,15-6). Thus, the world of religious speech and more particularly religious writing whatever the public form it takes will always be as distinctive as that of other specialists groups be they farmers or lawyers. But because of its structural perspectives, the regular ways in which it is put together, it provides an 'illusion of a real whole world ' (Derrida. 1978).

The Fixing of Information in Writing

There is the mesmerizing effect of the existence of writing on which enquirers always tend to concentrate as religious data is there in its permanency ready to be analysed. This avoids all the inconveniences of having to find people willing and able to talk about their religious beliefs and practices. Thinking about the meaning of a text without the complications of any interpersonal relationship largely avoids the difficulties of trying to understand what is meant in cross-cultural settings which for most people is probably as much within their own households and neighbourhoods as in distant societies. There is in this methodological limitations, the bases of misunderstanding about ideal systems and their practice.

So we have researchers diligently filling notebook after notebook with records of what they have seen and heard. In this process what was once socially fluid becomes rigid and potentially independent of the person who put these understandings onto paper These writings are just understandings not reproductions of any exactness of what went on in the minds of the writers because once it is on paper even with the most illustrious of writers, it is no longer alive as it is an abbreviation of what has been thought about, seen and heard. As the researcher writes, what has been written becomes part of the professionalization of static information.

The language of reports, articles and books based on research is not often one that can be easily read by the people about whom it is written nor would informants recognise much of what has been written about them even if it had been translated back into their own languages from the texts in which it had become professionally embedded in the researcher's natal language.

The end of research writing is usually in a dominant international language needed for its professional use in universities, the governmental or non-governmental institutions sponsoring the project or the intellectual market at which the researchers are aiming. It is not in a form which is readily understood by outsiders with their own possibly simplified rather than simplistic understandings.

There are other simpler snags over considering what is written down as reliable data. We can be sure that these notes are abbreviations of what the researchers saw and heard; the writing records impressions filtered through the listeners or observers own ideas of what has been going on. An hour of observing any necessarily complex behaviour will be reduced to a page of abbreviating notes.

However, supposedly adequate the researchers may be in understanding what is said to them of which we can never have any proof, it will always be in some senses abbreviations. What they say to others, putting this into writing is always going to be an imperfect translation abbreviated in its extent and subject to handicaps which will have prevented it from being a quasi-mechanical record of what may and indeed may not have taken place once the echoes of spoken language or of the seen event have disappeared (Chafe, 1994).

The Impoverishment of Thought in Literacy

All languages are complex and speech and its written form may not fall easily into the finiteness of grammar which itself has been created by the fact that it has been committed to writing. This commitment involves two restrictive processes. Firstly, the multiplicity of sounds with cognitive meanings tied into body language, individual intellectual capacity and social environments is translated into a single set of symbols which even with the addition of accents, the upper and lower case in some languages and the additions of question and exclamation marks are certainly an impoverishment of the spoken language.

Secondly, the form of literacy which is put into writing and formalized by institutions such as organized religions is never a reflection of what is generally spoken in that society which will have different linguistic codes according to the roles of the speakers. Some of these will be permanent as the distinctions made in Japanese between men and women speakers and where and to whom they are speaking at any particular time. The form of language with which a Christian will address God, a particular saint, the parish priest and another parishioner will rarely be the same. Burmese involves status related personal pronouns related to the person addressed in which the monk is in a noun classification all on his own and to address him with pronouns assuming social equality is both ungrammatical and religiously incorrect.

It is obvious that how language is used inside and outside a religious ceremony will be different and that the documents issued by a religious institution are likely to have been filtered through committees and the opinions of elite colleagues. The translation of a religious text into what the writers consider to be everyday language which they do not use themselves, is a form of biased averaging out of meaning which will be impossible to validate except by imposition. It may be that it has no more and perhaps less validity in personal understandings than a specialised theological text which is probably what it is anyway.

What we get in writing connected to religion is a reflection of the semantic understandings of those who dominate this use of literacy, a very small number in any society who are to all intents a permanent professional elite. This is a two sided problem as on one hand there is the need for educational rather than intellectual excellence so that thinkers have consistent opportunities to produce ideas for the dissection of their intellectual equals within their professional competences. This contributes to the exclusion of most potential readers within any faith from taking on the laborious task of even attempting to read about their religion; it would possibly be a handicap to gaining any help about their immediate needs. It would seem probable that many gain religious value from the hearing of *mantra* like texts rather than the reading of lengthy documents when their reading is more related to newspaper headlines. An officer of the Guyana army was seen to be reading a comic strip depiction of some part of the New Testament with script in bubbles alongside simple pictures.

So on the other hand, there is the fact that in any functional sense literacy in a religious context appears to be a minority need for the operation of uniform liturgies. Most believers do not feel any overwhelming need to read about their faith and their needs are usually met by the commitment to memory of repetitiously repeated prayers, the *mantra* effect occurring in all institutionalised religions and behaviour generally.

Human cognition is typified by the ability to store in memory half understood information in meta-representational form accepted on authority (Sperber, 1996:71-2). This is to accept the intellectualist side of commitment to the writing of theological ideas and to suggest as Sperber does that half-understoodness is to ignore the range of uses for literacy of which even minimal rather than full understanding may be a small possibly attainable factor. It seems unlikely that any individual has a personal situation of half understanding some religious idea or practice whatever external observers may assess as they will always have a personal wholeness in their understandings. To suggest that they have partial understandings of what they are doing is an outsider evaluation which they might equally well apply to themselves.

Religious Writings

In some ways religious texts can be compared to music. The American musician Stravinsky composed a work which was called *The Rite of Spring* but he was adamant that such compositions had no meaning. The Russian composer Shostakovich's Eleventh Symphony is entitled *The year 1905* the year of the first attempted Russian revolution—but it cannot have had such specific meanings beyond his political obligations to produce works that were politically correct. Listeners to these compositions read into them what they will from mere appreciated sound to complex intellectual connections. It may be that for most participants in religious ceremonies there are parallels to going to a concert. They are hearing the sounds in a personal way and watch the musicians and this is put into a personal whole by the people who are there.

Misunderstandings arise from the simple fact that all except a few religious texts are translations and indeed probably repetitive retranslations by living people of what was written at another time by authors who are long dead. There is this repetitive frozen factor which has no parallels in verbal communications.

There are texts such as the *Koran* which are frozen from the moment that it was first written down with authority. Then there are texts which are relatively frozen because they reflect the corporate decisions of religious institutions such as creeds and canon law decisions of the major Christian churches and Muslim laws which are changed interpretations of the *Koran* to meet new situations. The Taliban government in Afghanistan abolished the Kabul zoo as zoos were not mentioned in the *Koran*.

Then there are the endless flow of documents produced by individual theologians, religious administrators and semi-secular commentators which have local and temporary relevance. These are flexible and probably have no long-term significance except to scholars.

Even if we assume that there was some clarity in the intentions of the original writer, we are still dealing with abstractions of their religious experiences and these require translation whether from one language into another or from the linguistic codes of one social category into that of another one. It is in this process that misunderstandings are inevitable. It may be that to think in terms of misunderstandings will always be no more than an outsider evaluation as each individual will always see their own understandings as a complete cognitive whole.

Whatever their inspired origins, the form they take in writing is the result of human translating. What is produced is the result of deliberate decisions which are usually meant to create intelligible communication. If they do not have this semantic intelligibility, then there are socially accepted translators of glossolalia and automatic writing. These translations are subject to both social and religious negotiations (Irvine, 1982) which Buddhists are advised to specifically avoid.

All religious writings have the potential and indeed a tendency to become frozen. The greater the importance to a religion a document has the greater the possibility that it will be written or become written or should we say enshrined in specialised codes or languages. These are bound to be elitist and have to be both translated and interpreted.

There is also the division between religious communication directed at a known universe of believers or interested persons as potentially visible interactions and communication directed at invisible readers about whom nothing is known or could be just presupposed. A talk in a religious setting to a specific audience will be designed with that audience in mind; a sermon to a congregation in church or mosque in so far as it has any meaning, can only see its possible listeners as guess work. A religious broadcast or television presentation can only have accidental meanings for it can have no known or designated audiences. Without a reacting audience much religious communication is tentative and falls back on authoritative and specialised linguistic codes. In such situations in which the assessable realities are one sided, the social sciences predominate in their interpretations of situations in which facts are elusive or need interpretation. The realities of religious communication are thought to be validated by this alone so researchers miss the point of the nature of religious convictions which may not be connected at all with the reading written documents.

The Diminishing Importance of Religious Literacy

Once religious information is available in print, it takes on some of the sacred qualities of its origin and value is often attributed to it from the fact of possession rather than from its reading which may have a low priority. There is a potency in the written word as in the Koranic phrases in the protective amulets worn by children. Almost always religious writing is in a specialised linguistic code and of course the fact that it is dealing with indefinable abstractions makes any form of agreement between readers and authors less likely. They do not read in order to believe or believe in order to read; the material identity of the amulet is enough.

It is only necessary to read the minutes of any meeting connected to religion to realise that it is the form of wording recorded is perhaps more important than what they are supposed to mean. The growth of scholastic literacy over the centuries has produced a theological elite, attaining and retaining a superiority over the laity which they have been able to retain up to quite recently.

Now this professional exclusivity has been challenged not only by the growth of an educated middle-class and the competition for their attention from the mass of religious media. There is also at least in Western world the recognised individualising of religious interests and New Age publications coming from private and less trained imaginings; a possible replication of the individualism of religious practices in non-literate situations in quasi-traditional societies.

It may also be that the dominance of an educated elite in religious affairs has passed its peak and that there is some reversion to religious activities based on personal experience and needs rather than literacy. It is not only so-called religious systems which existed and continued with no positive or popular correlations to literacy but the resolution of personal problems through religious experiences unmediated through time consuming literacy and its indefinable abstractions.

Chinese, Indians and Japanese flock to their temples and go on pilgrimages without any feeling that they have to prepare themselves by reading or enhancing their experience by reading. If there was such a need then popular and holy religious publications for these faiths would have been produced long ago as almost entrance tickets to religious experiences there. In fact one can visit these popular religious sites without seeing more than a very few reading rather than just holding what appears to be a religious document as a religious artefact.

The Influence of Literacy

Traditional faiths and the forms that they take are by their nature non-literate in much the same way as private spiritualities are in all cultures. They are immensely variable not so much in the paradigms within which they operate but in their constant variations to meet new situations of personal and collective anxiety.

The social scientist is preconditioned to seeing religion as a separate heading in the social behaviour of the people they are studying. In their notes they will have a heading for ancestor propitiation once they learn or assume that this is a factor in their thinking about the possible causes of their misfortunes. So having made their heading that is what they find; a category of religious behaviour, but this is imposed categorisation. It has little behavioural reality except in that written title.

Even if they see a hundred such ceremonies they will be all dissimilar in their individual creativity except for this categorisation imposed by their own writing. It is not that the Sukuma do not see or rather experience their behaviour in terms of social uniformity but it is not the form which is imposed on this social reality by writing. Their needs which they express in ritual are just too diverse for any such uniformities which are created by the use of literacy for liturgical uniformity.

Indeed there is some doubt among contemporary African social scientists as to whether there is such a traditional isolatable category as religion to parallel the cohesive ideological structures of Buddhism, Hinduism and Islam. Theoretically Islam has a structure which covers to some degree every aspect of social life so that it is possible to see such a society as one in which religion and secular life are indistinguishable paralleling traditional African or Asian 'tribal' systems.

Liturgies and the orthodoxies from which they are derived are enabled if not created by literacy and made even more uniform by printing. What is depicted with literacy comes in decided forms which must inevitably be pre-existing and currently viable so that it has within them inevitable functional differences.

Religions that have become institutionalised provide liturgies into which individuals are socialised and this provides the paradigm in which their individual religious thinking and behaviour operates in a constantly changing and varying social environments. The nature and extent of any compulsion to use these written liturgies is dictated by an ever-changing personal and social environments.

All the major religions have liturgies which are written but participants in these rituals may not pay much attention to the fact that these liturgies are written and their experience of the ceremonies is related to what they see and hear rather more than in the prayer books which they carry. The rare breakaway Roman Catholic Legio Maria sect in Kenya, not the Legion of Mary, use a Latin liturgy and paraliturgical procedures far more complex than what was used prior to the Vatican II changes, but participants are attracted to and experience these rituals without any use of explanatory literacy.

Once literacy and institutionalisation appears public religion becomes to some extent functionally separate from private spirituality as a disciplined 'ought to do' factor becomes prominent. This might be easy to follow if this institutionalisation of a faith occurs in a relatively homogeneous community as in the Scottish island of Barra which remained Roman Catholic after the Reformation or in the Muslim villages along the East African coast where religious literacy is left to an elite and is not seen as an important aspect of personal faith. On the other hand, one Sukuma chief in Tanzania had adult children belonging to five different denominations or religions each of which had provided them with socially divisive religious literature had they paid much attention to their contents.

The Limitations of Literacy

Human thought is complex at whatever level of intelligence is being considered and few are able to put this complexity into words which even partially cover this detail adequately as whatever is recorded will be experienced as inadequate. To go beyond this and to think that the complexities of thought can be put into writing using the limited number of available calligraphic symbols is a delusion except in the extent to which personal interpretations can create a parallel complexity. A religious experience is an emotional one and there are very few in any society who have the intellectual capacity to use their own natal language, much less its written forms, to adequately express what they feel.

Those who use writing in any sense of secular or religious emotional fulfilment belong to a highly literate minute minority whose lives probably pivot on their ability to put their thoughts into writing for personal fulfilment. Even these unusual men and women admit that what they have written is not quite what they meant to state in the range of words and their combinations available to them and they constantly change their drafts in order to achieve better approximations to their own emotional realities.

We can presuppose that the charismatic individuals who start new religions such as the numerous African independent Christian are acting upon personal convictions and they are not usually from any educated elite. The latter have largely excluded themselves from the possibility of having such innovative emotions by their prolonged secular education and the professional group to which they now belong. The attempt of the leaders and their close companions to put into writing their reasons for leaving Western influenced denominations has usually meant an extreme abbreviation of their complex thinking. Glossolalia in its unintelligible sounds may be a way of expressing emotion for which those persons do not have the language capacity to express what they feel.

Reading and writing for almost all those who are literate is a minority activity confined to some of the practicalities of living. For most reading and writing is considered to be very hard work and in excess likely to damage health so that its use in letters is usually confined to serious purposes and usually expected to be read by others beyond the person to whom it is addressed (Cannell, 2006). Overall literacy may be more a time consuming handicap and a requirement for employment than an aid to any uplifting of the spirit in religion or secular intellects.

For the rest of any society who consider themselves to be literate, the standards are much lower and the time spent in reading and writing is minimal. UNESCO defines literacy as the ability to send and receive a simple message. The headlines of popular papers, the pay slips for employment; they read little and write even less. To read a popular newspaper in Mandarin Chinese requires the enormous feat of memorising perhaps two thousand ideograms. The vocabulary of the average English man or woman is probably not more than a thousand words of which the majority will be job related.

Their homes may contain a few books chosen for their pictures and possibly some religious writings owned for some vague feelings of betterment that come from their possession nearby. The localisation of religious emotion. But even these people socialised by their permanent involvement in urban and industrialised ways of living in any time and motion sense are predominantly non-literate. Their lives are dominated by face to face interrelationships involving body language and television as well as the use of computer screens at work which similarly does not involve much writing.

For the rest of the global population literacy will have little significance except that writing will be as the means by which power holding secular and religious bureaucracies enforce their control dividing up societies by systems of examinations whose content may be little related to the realities of their lives. Any such community will always include men and women of highly natal intelligence which may not be reflected in their educational status. Religious writings are little used and even less understood as it is written in languages or linguistic codes into which most believers have not been socialised or particularly trained.

So it would seem that apart from its limited functional uses and for communication between geographically separated people who do not have mobile phones, literacy is predominantly used to discriminate in the examinations of educational systems. It may well be little used for initiating spirituality.

The Illegibility of Religious Experience

Religious institutions are no different to secular ones in wanting to get themselves regularised in writing. Civil services and churches all have their 'canon' laws. They conceive theological ideas and then because of their importance in order to make their institutions more stable and widely known than can be possible by word of mouth and personal influence, so down it goes into writing. The word 'down' in this context is significant.

Any relationship with the Divine cannot be an orderly pragmatic process as it is based basically on an indefinable and personal emotional rather than intellectual response to what must usually be an invisible stimulus. Koestler (Koestler, 1954: 352-3) describes a situation in which he was in solitary confinement during the Spanish civil war under sentence of death "when I was floating in a river of peace. It came from nowhere and went nowhere... then there was no river and no 'I'. The 'I' had ceased to exist'. It is extremely embarrassing to write down phrases like that...The meaning of meaning and ...logical positivism (aim) at verbal precision and dislikes nebulous gossip".

This was an unusual man in an unusual situation with an unusual literary ability but taken out of that context are such experiences unusual. We cannot know but can suspect that most people have periods of heightened liminal emotion which they do not wish and probably do not have the ability to put into writing.

Among an elite group there may be a compulsion to write down these key experiences and religious institutions wish to include them in the general understandings of their orthodoxies. It has to be accepted that such experiences do not go easily into the calligraphic abbreviations used by even the most talented of authors. Any abstract word has a fan of dictionary meanings and an even larger spread of personal understandings according to cognitive capacities and social environments. There is in the writings related to religion ample opportunities for working misunderstandings.

The Imposition of Literacy

Literacy is overwhelmingly considered to be beneficial by politicians and educationalists and a necessity for which all mankind should have the opportunity to benefit and in this there is some confusion in the implications of the categories 'illiteracy' and 'non-literacy'. Some are illiterate because of their own inadequacies while non-literacy can apply to whole communities which do not have the opportunity to learn or do not have much use for literacy including many people of high intelligence.

While writing on stone for religious purposes survive may distort our understandings of its more general uses, the ancient Sumerian clay tablets from the Fertile Crescent show that the main purposes of writing then as now was connected to taxation. For most people writing may not have happy connotations as it is the means through which governments impose their systems of control.

It is little recognised that in religious just as much as in secular writing once a matter is recorded in writing it has become detached from the social environment in which it was created. Further that in this process of recording it has diminished the 'wholeness' of what it was representing. The documents recording divorce in the local courts of the Tanzanian Sukuma require that the reasons should be given and this was always 'they did not get on' just as the reasons for homicide recorded by the Uganda police where the suspected killer was known usually stated that there was a quarrel. Writing in general is an abbreviation of social and personal complexities.

No writing tells us the social background or thinking of the writer nor will it tell even a fraction of the circumstances which went behind the writing. Negotiations and interpretations turn on the words recorded accepted as legally acceptable facts which have to be disproved. But this neglects the issue that the words are dated and inevitably socially detached and that definition may not have been part of the initiation of abstract thought.

So the individual being confronted with religious writing is likely to experience as something which invades their thinking from outside. It is largely an imposition and part of the contractual aspects of belonging to a particular faith which many feel that to read about it, is not necessarily a part of their spiritual needs nor something for which they have to budget time. It is rare to find a religiously minded community such as the Malagashi Seventh Day Adventists who set aside prolonged periods for the discussion of biblical meanings (Keller, 2006).

There are also the consequences of the static nature of writing that the readers and indeed the writers in any religious context are always in a constant process of change in how they react to their own social environments. Since anything written is an object in a varying social environment it can be treated as just that and can be just as easily neglected as used.

Writing and Religion

We have to accept in any approach to religious understandings and behaviour that we are considering behaviour that is intrinsically not only variable but unstable whether from a theological or secular point of view. It is not just something that can be related to abstract beliefs. We can be certain that anything about religious behaviour and understandings which has been recorded with great care and in detail, will be different in some respects to what may be recorded subsequently even after a few hours.

There is nothing in the workings of the human mind which stabilizes the consequences of social experience in ways that parallel the static nature of writing. Religious writings can have unlimited meanings attributed to them as is the case with any impersonal thought. It may even be that this rigidity makes writing unsuitable in some ways for any purpose that is not narrowly pragmatic.

The Limited Need for Religious Literacy

We can conclude that the vast majority of people in their fulfilment of their public religious obligations and private spirituality have no essential need to read and write. There are appeals from the heart in an emergency for which the reading of a prayer or the writing of a petition is unlikely to be a necessary part. For their regular devotions their repetitious nature makes reading unnecessary or involve complex documents which require the mediation of specially trained experts. The petitions on prayer boards in churches, temples and on the grave of the Rebbe of a Jewish orthodox sect (Heilman and Friedman. 2010:22) do not suggest that writing is a common activity or that it is easily used since the petitions do not often exceed ten words.

It is assumed by the writers and publishers of religious literature often at subsidised prices, that many will take advantage of these writings to enlarge their religious understandings. This is certainly so among the Seventh Day Adventists in Madagascar who are marginally educated and yet have carried out *Bible* study with the enthusiasm of scientific discovery (Keller, 2006) but this is rare.

This flooding of the media 'market' with religious literature raises complicated issues. These written texts are intended to provide specific meanings for what are basically metaphysical issues. There can be no realistic assumption that the readers will be understanding the text rather than just accepting as authoritative in the senses intended or indeed that it will be read at all.

Certainly an enormous amount of religious literature is produced particularly by Christians and to a growing extent by Muslims. We do not know the extent to which religious literature is read rather than just purchased because it is felt to be merit enhancing. This must certainly be the case in Eastern religions where religious literature is written in specialized languages no longer spoken or using ideograms which require specialised training and memorizing abilities. In many cultures most would prefer to have religious pictures on their walls than religious literature invisible in a box or cupboard and a worn amulet is better than both.

This is perhaps due to a misunderstanding of religious needs. Much religious need and its accompanying emotions are created and fulfilled in primary self-contained situations. While religious writing may for a small number initiate religious feelings, it is more likely to be read if at all after an event. It is not likely to augment or assist an emotion which has already passed into personal history. It may indeed be a gateway to profound understandings and an emotional experience but this depends on a very high standard of literary skill. The reality must be that for most reading is a tiring and laborious activity. To read a religious text and to get from it an emotional or intellectual reaction is likely to be unusual. There is always the plain fact that there is no knowing what the reactions to religious writing are or what the text and its socially hidden authors intended.

Nevertheless there may be *mantra* like situations in which a text is regarded as a sacred object as in the reverence for copies of the *Koran* or in the keeping of particular printed prayers which may not even be read as in those collected by pilgrims to temples in Taiwan or placed in prayer books..

Some pieces of religious writing may have been first read in emotionally laden situations but that is not likely to last. In most religions repetitively use prayers which they can recognise in print but repeat from memory. The Christian *Ave Maria*, the Buddhist *Om mane padme hum* which the devout might aim to say ten thousand times a day and the Muslim affirmation of belief in Allah as the first of the Five Pillars of Faith. In reality most religious practice is devoid of any need to read.

It would seem that the need to read religious literature is related more to what religious institutions consider a need rather than believers feel that it is a basic necessity. In general most purchase and retain religious literature for functions paralleling the traditional uses of protective amulets.

For whom is the reading of religious writing a need when religious practice is either a part-time activity or related to the immediacies of distress. Most believers can recite and get emotional satisfaction from the recitation of basic prayers almost on a Pavlovian basis triggered by a single word or gesture.

Literacy and the Autonomy of Religion

We can assume that whatever the specific origins of religion may have been, they developed in societies which had not divided people into the categories which are used today to describe societies and their functions used in the social, economic and political bureaucracies. On being asked his religion an elderly Sukuma replied that he was a Sukuma, a tribe that has generally been reluctant to convert to either Christianity or Islam despite the presence of these two faiths for well over a century. In traditional societies there are no specific and isolatable patterns of behaviour while in modern ones it is both isolatable and divisive. The Christian goes to church, the traditionalist has no parallel movement beyond the holistic home.

Social scientists working with communities which they classed as traditional found that their efforts to isolate religion there in the same way that it is isolatable in contemporary urban and industrial societies was impossible. The sacrifice of a bullock to the ancestors was an economic, social and political event. Even a cursory look at the ways that the Amish run their lives in the United States show that everything they do is linked to their elite's interpretations of the *Bible* from house-building to their use of horse transport as well as their reluctance to use personal telephones. In this impossibility to isolate religion there is little difference between Aymara Indians in Bolivia, the Amish in the United States and fundamentalist Ashkenazi Jews in Israel.

These people lead lives in which any such categorization would artificially divide up their behaviour and their unitary way of thinking. A ceremony reasonably enough to be classified as religious by an outsider trained in ways of analysis that owes more to Comte than to sensitivity to social situations in which they find themselves, because all activities are carried out around existing pervasive but latent presence of ancestors, ghosts and spirits.

In traditional or quasi-traditional communities religion may involve simultaneously any of a range of functions from segmentation, cohesion, status enhancement and so on. In whatever way it is analysed it works in some way or another. There is no misunderstanding as it is a creation of a particular social environment which has not been tied down to some requirement which has been set aside into writing.

Once religious understandings and requirements come to be written down from bases in which mythology is turned into theology (Pyyslainen, 1999) then the whole religious scenario becomes static information. From what are now objects rather than fluid behaviour a whole class of specialised operatives developed who pivot around this new isolatable factor which is no longer automatically a necessary and functioning part of any society in which it operates. "The whole idea of religion has been thus spread. This is due to the fact that only within literate religion is 'religion' seen as a distinct category. Only literate religions have autonomous boundaries and their adherents are defined by their attachment to specific scriptures and a specific credo in addition to their practice of certain rituals". This is one of the aspects of religious practice being a working misunderstanding because a religion tied to writing has acquired a rigidity which it could never have had in non-literate communities and does not have in even more literate contemporary societies.

Once religious ideas and requirements have been put into writing and become a core element in how the religious institution functions, their status becomes independent of its composers and the immediate needs of those who are thus compelled by orthodoxy to give public preference to these written forms. Of course, this writing was at one time related to particular needs and environments but even then it would have represented the restricted views of the writers. However, insofar as it is specific in creating rules, regulations and interpretations considered necessary by religious administrators, it would become more and more difficult to apply because those involved and their social environments have already changed.

Much religious writings are attempts to stabilize behaviour into institutional orderliness which is intrinsically unstable. This may be a form of hopeful thinking which is part of the underpinning of religions of the book and which is absent from Eastern religions with their absence of definitions and their recognition that all human behaviour has no more than momentary stability.

There is also the factor that the writers within and about religion are socially distant from almost all the believers other than their professional colleagues with whom there are ongoing negotiated agreements. Literacy in practice is a factor that does not unite societies and communities but socially divides them as it is used in all professional and utilitarian groupings.

On the other hand, much religious writing is ambiguous because it is related to metaphysics and thus is very much a matter either for personal interpretation or disinterestedness as it is accepted as revelation filtered through authority touched by its institutional rather more than personal charisma.

In both these areas of literacy there is a split between highly literate professionals who interpret what has been written under different circumstances from the points of view of their specialised understandings and the understandings of those who have little use for such productions except as part of the accepted authoritative shadows surrounding their own religious realities.

The whole process of committing religious thought and requirements into writing is a minority exercise in which a very small number of people actually write, read and use what has been written. This well-meaning professional elite are by definition world's away from what inarticulate or disinclined to read believers actually want and do intermittently within their personal private faiths.

In quasi-traditional communities or in contemporary urban industrial societies most public religious and private spiritualities are activities free from the use of literate liturgies as in many urban sects, cults and groupings (McGuire, 1988). What is carried out is in a constant process of unpremeditated and probably unrecognised change. While there will be paradigmatic themes within a culture which continue over a series of social generations, there will be only the more striking ones easy to remember which are likely to be carried forward.

The Understanding of Religious Writings

It is debatable whether the original documents of the Eastern religious in their obvious complexities and their widespread use of ambiguities meant to be understood by any generality of believers or were they produced as the bases for discussion and thought between and within circles of religious elitism? Has Christianity just created the need for religious literacy and the obligation to read as a way round the seemingly popular passivity of the Roman Catholic faithful under the dogmatic authority of its religiously educated priesthood.

It does seem that the majority of religions which in population terms must be predominantly non-Western retain their popularity in the use that people make of their religious ideas either in terms of regular worship, irregularly in pilgrimages or in response to personal or communal misfortunes. They do not find it necessary to read as part of their emotional commitment and those that write petitions are possibly in a small minority. One does not notice prayer books being carried at Lourdes or the *Bhagavad Gita* at the Kumbh Mela. There are several contributory factors for this rather conspicuous absence of any commitment to reading the available documents about their religion. For most the performance of a ritual is a return enough and thus for most believers reading and writing is not a necessary prerequisite.

Firstly, there is the fact that the majority of believers cannot read to the necessary level of intellectual capacity to get a cognitive return from reading-writing which are far from easy. In terms of intrinsic interest the *Bible* provides stories but the Hindu, Buddhist and Islamic documents provide no stories that can be easily linked to their own experiences or what they think may have been of others in mythological time. They are not easy reading. Even if they had this intrinsic capacity to enthral they are written in languages or ideograms unknown to them without prolonged learning.

Those who possess this knowledge in all the religions for which written sacred documentation is available other than Christianity have not shown any particular interest in getting translations available in everyday language, nor does there seem to have been any popular demand for readable religious literature except in relation to the recent Islamic fundamentalist resurgence.

Secondly, a written document is an object which can have the same material characteristics as an amulet or crucifix just as the Roman alphabet can be parallel to a box of tools which have both predetermined and imaginative uses which were never thought of by their creators.

All these religious objects have the potential to carry whatever meanings their owners want them to be. This potential rests not only on personal beliefs and needs which have an infinite number of individual variations but on particular meanings attributed to the interpretations of charismatic persons and the publicised ones of legitimate religious authorities. Writing stabilises certain information and fixes it in time and place but there can never be any assumption that it will be understood in the ways that the unknown and unknowable writers intended. The writers of the Hindu *Puranas* are unknown and the sayings attributed to the Buddha must be treated with some scepticism since they were written down several centuries after his death.

The Roman Catholic Church has its official system of stating before its publication that it contains nothing contrary to orthodoxy but much depends on the extent to which a religious institution has become centralised and thus able to produce authorised publications.

Thirdly, religious knowledge and understandings are very closely related to theology as a profession which could scarcely be described as an amateurish or indeed an activity which is quickly adaptive to popular activism. Theologians in their own way are as prudently sceptical of 'unusual' religious experiences as the interpretations of agnostic social scientists. Religious writings have rarely been written for popular consumption and in general people find the ceremonies of their faith adequate. For writers on religion their professional prestige rests on the approval of their fellow professionals and the retaining of the need for long periods of preliminary training before their writings attain some measure of authentication. Translating a religious document into a more widely understandable language and the result may well be the occasion for a wider range of criticism from outside the circle of trained professionals.

Finally, much theological and institutionally backed religious writings have the characteristics of handbooks for insuring some degree of uniformity for administrative reasons. It would seem that this is more a Western Christian rather than Eastern characteristic. The efficiency with which the annual Hajj pilgrimage is administered is a secular imposition as there is little in the structure of Islam which could have provided for this nor indeed in Hinduism which has no institutions capable of preventing the Kumbh Mela with its seventy million pilgrims from becoming, a national demographic disaster and the occasion for devastating epidemics. It could be said that these Eastern religions despite their long standing use of writing are in practice functionally chaotic and not related to institutional unity at all.

We can conclude that much religious writing was never intended to be read and understood by the generality of believers. Beyond institutional needs, the 'getting to the church on time' factor, the creators of literacy in religious contexts saw little advantage for their beliefs of making literacy into a necessary widespread religious requirement. Their supporting institutions or indeed for themselves in widening any popular intellectual perceptions through the use of writing never seems to have caught on. There is also the factor that any widespread literacy can have the possibility of creating challenges to existing religious elitism. Literacy has largely remained an elite system for the use of an educated theological elite.

Then how in fact can it be established that believers or potential believers have had their faith enhanced by reading rather than listening or being personally influenced by another person or situational requirements. It is impossible to measure the personal profit of an asset that has only implicit material benefits, a return on a very substantial material and personal investment. A time consuming requirement from which there may be a limited emotional return.

Sooner or later there is the dead-end of pragmatism in matters of religious faith and there can be no certain way of enhancing religious commitment. It would seem that in some Protestant denominations the decline in faith as measured by attendance was augmented rather than reduced by making the *Bible* generally available in vernaculars. This provided the subordinate but perhaps intellectual and theologically ambitious to criticize without the balance of fulfilling prayer and ritual.

The Felt Need to Read Religious Writings

For some certainly written religious phrases, pamphlets or whole books have the characteristics of a cognitive prosthesis (Rubin, 1997:311) as would be the case of Taiwanese pilgrims who collect writings from the temples they visit without being able to read them or indeed without any serious intention of ever reading them. This applies equally to the Koranic quotations written in Arabic sealed in protective amulets.

Others make *Bible* and Koranic study the centre of their religious life treating the words there as facts which they can disentangle by processes which are allied to science without realising that the text that they are using is a translation of a translation so that their actions are as much acts of faith as prayer. The Seventh day Adventists offer *Bible* study for the basic questions of life as a scientific enquiry not simply as a means to an end in a utilitarian sense so that the core of local people's commitment is the intellectual process itself (Keller, 2006). This must surely be a rare use of literacy in any community of believers outside institutions of both secular and religious higher education in which learning is segregated from earning.

Certainly Christianity and more recently Islam have invested huge amounts of material and human effort in the printings of religious writings. Whether the laity want to spend time and effort in reading religious documents rather than just possessing them does not seem to have been considered. We do not know what the demand for religious literature would be if it was not tied to specific faith or promoted as a religious good. This is apart from the enormous effort put into translations of the *Bible*; the British and Foreign Bible Society has produced it in over three hundred different languages and the sale of *Bibles* in Western societies still continues at a significant profitable commercial rate.

In the Eastern religious there is an enormous potential market if we consider the number who go on pilgrimages and visit temples. It is not just the question of translations from esoteric languages but the plain fact is that in whatever languages they are translated into, what is written is rarely of much interest to people who are not intellectually inclined and for most people the buying of incense and votive candles is enough. The enormous demand in India is for religious pictures which effortlessly satisfy the mind and the eye.

The Theological Need for Literacy

Literacy appears to be a term with a firm pragmatic base but who sets the standards as to what is literacy. The UNESCO definition of the ability to read and send a simple message is clear enough but who decides the definition of simplicity. Most Western can read roads signs, train destination indicators, most but not all menus in restaurants and what is written in their bank statements if they have an account and farmers read grain and livestock prices. A rise in the fixed price for maize in Uganda flooded the market at the next harvest but it seems likely that this information was passed from ear to ear rather than from printed publicity. People only read what is pragmatically useful or which they have to read for their work and what gives them self-defined pleasure.

It is difficult to see the advantages in the reading of religious literature. The Seventh Day Adventists in Madagascar read the *Bible* in order to discover the truths which are waiting there for their discovery. The reading of the *Bible* in Kiswahili for an educated Swahili is a lot easier than for someone who has learnt that language in school but not to the standard required for reading the linguistic complexities of the Swahili *Bible* when he or she would prefer to spend the time improving their English, the language needed for professional advancement.

The influence of a document connected with religion has to be accepted through some understanding of social realities. There can be no doubt that the *Bible* and the *Koran* in one form or another have sold in billions of copies to be found in most Christian and Muslim households. Copies of Buddhist and Hindu scriptures have no such prolific presence or protected retention.

We know that the novels of Scott and Dickens had an influence on the social and political thinking of the power-holders in Britain in the twentieth century and the latter monumental *An American Dilemma*, study of the effects of racial segregation in the United States by Gunnar Myrdal coincided with changes in the thinking among the American power elite that the modern world much less a country with an egalitarian constitution could not sustain anything as pragmatically ridiculous as discrimination from physical appearance. The influence of this book was to support not initiate an existing change in public opinion (Myrdal,1944).

To what extent does literacy aid the reading of religious documents and with it the possibilities of understanding or misunderstanding a faith and the answer must surely be very little in any global assessment. The *Koran* is written in classical Arabic and this script is in current use so that not only Arabic speakers have access to that text but Muslims in Central Asia, the Philippines and Indonesia have to learn this script in order to read the *Koran* in the sacred language in which it was originally recorded. Indians and Burmese who are literate in their own national languages have no access at all to Hindu and Buddhist texts written in Sanskrit and Pali without prolonged learning. For the Han Chinese the reading of religious texts requires the learning of highly specialised ideograms. So for very large populations there is no easy access to religious literature on which these religions are based even if it were provided cheaply and locally.

Reading is a difficult and often tiresome activity and few would prefer it to watching television as the hugely popular Indian production in multiple episodes of the Hindu mythological classic the *Mahabharata*. The Cistercian monk Merton's Seven Story Mountain sold sixty six thousand copies but how many of these copies were read from cover to cover and understood in the senses suggested by the author (Merton, 1948). Almost inevitably such texts let alone the *Bhagavad Gita* have complex meanings which require explanatory interpretations by experts which are similarly not easy to understand.

So we can assume that many religious texts are required reading but they are not necessarily read but make people feel better by possessing them. They are part of the religious equipment which contribute to a sense of well-being much as do religious pictures and texts on the wall.

An Egyptian Muslim farmer's house at Assuan had a picture of a religious dignitary flanked by that of a popular singer.

We cannot assume that there is any necessary causal relationship between the reading of a religious text which has parallels to work and the creation of a religious emotion. Taiwanese pilgrims circulating the island's sacred sites buy religious reading material at each shrine which they cannot in fact read because of the specialised ideograms used. We have to conclude that the writers and publishers of religious books and pamphlets in Western societies over estimate the amount of reading which is done in proportion to the amount of 'spare' time available. In Eastern societies what religious publishing that is done is directed at small exclusive groups involved in high level intellectual practices and theological thought. For popular consumption there are films with religious themes or implications, highly coloured pictures and 'souvenir' purchases. It would seem reasonable to conclude that religious publications are as likely to cause as solve working misunderstandings.

Non-Literacy

While we tend to think of non-literate people as those who have not learnt to read and write in terms of their own shortcomings when education is available rather than in thinking about what literacy enables and the extent in which it would be used profitably and for what.

It is assumed that literacy is a moral or natural 'good' to which mankind should have access as much more than a political right rather than in time and motion terms of its actual utility. The profit from reading a reading a train time table as opposed to reading the Hindu *Mahabharata* epic in all its hundred thousand verses. For most people the conversion of what is read or available for reading into understanding in complex situations related to religion cannot rarely be seen in terms of binary ability to read or not which in most cases is a limited ability used for limited purposes. There is a sharply inverted pyramid between the numbers reading a grain price on a market stall and those reading a religious document however simplified its phraseology is intended to be.

Universal primary education was aimed at in Britain as a necessary part of rapid industrial growth and not so that the working man and woman could read Thomas Paine's Rights of Man published in 1791. Protestants have seen the reading of the *Bible* as being a necessary part of an active faith but for Roman Catholics less so. The Amish today still see education as no more than what is necessary to read the *Bible* and what helps their agricultural style of communal living. These devout and successful farmers think that to have standards of education and literacy beyond what is needed for their communal needs just leads to personal instability and to people leaving the community with its long-term success for the uncertainties of outside life. It was not introduced in Britain so that the people in general could read the classics and have theological understandings beyond reading the *Bible*.

In Tanzania the *lingua franca* of business and administration is kiSwahili and has been so since its introduction by the Germans at the end of the nineteenth century. It is now the language in which most Christian denominations produce their literature and it is the language into which the *Bible* has long been translated and cheaply available.

However, this is the natal language of the coast, a language with a long literary tradition made up from Arabic and Bantu roots often written in Arabic script with its Muslim associations. It is the language of an Islamic culture and there is a saying *wenyeji wa pwani washenzi wa bara* the civilised live on the coast and the uncouth live inland.

This means that for the majority of Tanzanians it is not their natal language and for those who speak languages which have no Bantu grammatical affinities it has to be learnt as a totally different second language. Thus, for Christians to read the *Bible* translated into kiSwahili by committees of specialists is hard work. The new kiSwahili dictionary was written by a specialised group of men and one woman of whom ten out of fourteen were highly educated natal speakers from this coastal culture. Most Tanzanians speak and understand a much less complex form of this language from its use in business, bureaucracy and the popular media, in many cases retaining their tribal languages for use in their primary relationships and their thinking.

The religious words in kiSwahili have connections with Islamic understandings such as using the Arabic word for religion 'dini' and we have no understandings of how the majority understand this and other religious words in kiSwahili. This problem is not one confined to 'missionary' contexts and is just as likely to occur where there are not so much dominant 'official' languages as literary forms of Burmese, Urdu, Farsi, French and English.

It is not just that religious writings whether as translations or original productions are not written in the linguistic codes of everyday use, but that writing and reading is always hard work and is not often used as a means of self-expression and emotion. Humans are speakers and except for specialised vocabularies and linguistic codes of communities and occupations, their use of language is not seen as the medium for ideological and idealistic potentials. Most reading is related to sport and novels and most writing to business. It is a time consuming process and most would see the reading of religious texts in time and motion terms as not worth the effort in lives that are always short of time.

Mere literacy does not provide access to a new world of understanding as the forms of literacy which comes their way introduces them to new forms of discrimination in and derived from education. This is always against the background that most intercommunication is verbal and visual and that the literacy which they use is an inadequate methods of communicating anything more than simple facts.

We can conclude that those who write their prayers and petitions have rarely thought that any high standard of literacy is necessary to get the hearing of the Divine entities which they are addressing. These 'spirits' will understand the needs of the petitioners however poorly it has been written. We can also assume that those who put their petitions into writing are a very small minority of those who are petitioning through their prayerful thoughts.

It is easy enough to see that there is a limited use of literacy even in societies which have generally effective educational systems. Of course, there are those who have intellectual difficulties in accepting that literacy has a value worth the effort of learning and an even greater number perhaps even a majority who feel that their religious needs can be more than adequately met in thought than going through the time consuming efforts of reading and writing.

In every aspect of their religious commitments believers are confronted with the fact that their literacy and the literacy needed for the reading of documents of their religion come from different social worlds. This is very clear in non-Western languages where the basic documents of Buddhism and Hinduism are written in specialised literacy forms unknown to the commonality of believers. Well-educated men and women in hotels in Beijing and Shanghai cannot read the ideograms in popular religious pictures.

Taiwanese going on tours combining temple visiting with shopping collect religious texts which they cannot read. Much the same applies in Japan where temple visitors shake out numbered divination sticks for which they collect printed results which have to be read for them by religious experts. A well educated Japanese woman banker said that she could perhaps read some fifteen hundred specialised ideograms, a very small proportion of those that are available..

While perhaps the majority of the world's adult population cannot read and write much beyond simple messages and even urbanised ones working in industry may not use this ability for more than a minute or two in any day. What they do learn from their standard of literacy is their own personal comparative social and religious inferiority and that it is an inadequate method of expressing their feelings.

Religious language is not something specifically Eastern which keeps such knowledge within a specially trained religious elite. To some extent it is characteristic of all specialisations whether electricians and theologians. It would be much the same in Amharic the language used by the Ethiopian Coptic Church which has its own theological vocabulary which is unintelligible to the many thousands attending its religious festivals. The key requirements and understandings of Islam are written in classical Arabic script in the Holy *Koran* which millions of children learn by heart without having any literate understandings of what they are reciting from memory particularly if they are not Arabs.

We can perhaps conclude that for the fulfilment of religious needs most people in almost all religions whether those of quasi-traditional tribal types or in the imposing sophistications of Eastern religions, literacy is a specialised form of religious elitism which in general believers have not felt any great need to be involved in what would be a laborious and time consuming activity. This in the absence of any sense of religious collectivism dependent on reading and writing and some imposed understanding, most believers are to some extent free to interpret the requirements of the faiths to which they ostensibly belong according to their culturally restricted personal and situational requirements in what are working misunderstandings.

12
The Divisiveness of Language

In hard science it is reasonable to assume that as far as possible the data expressed in one language can have this exactness translated into another but this is far from the case when they are dealing with fringe evaluations as to the effects of hard information on human behaviour. A statement in one language such as the Chinese medical distinction of the human pulse may be recognised in Western medicine as on the debatable fringe of science. So exactness in translation of soft information particularly when it is over the linguistic boundaries of particular language groups which have few semantic affinities is rare if not impossible.

In religious translation as in anything other than hard science, something new is introduced into the receptor language which will now be comprehended by means of and in terms of the pre-existing language and its conventions. The receptor language has a dynamic of its own and takes the new material to realms it never touched in the source language (Walls, 1990).

Yet orthodoxy is overwhelmingly dependent on what religious organisations and theologians have written and the form which this takes will rarely be from the original languages in which the divine message was transmitted or whatever came out of the fog of history to receive subsequent religious veneration.

Translating in any behavioural sense cannot be anything more than intuitive transcription of any words and phrases that are not tied to the exactnesses of hard science or simple interpersonal commonsense. "When a speaker of language *A* labels a specific perspective of the world which the speaker of language *B* does not label but also does not share then translation cannot proceed by simply supplying a suggestive circumlocution". This is perhaps possible within a linguistic group but not between languages which have no cultural affinities.

"By contrast to understand what the Chinese speaker means by 'li mao' with its moral and natural law implications and by contrast what he means by its roughly English equivalent 'etiquette' with its social and conventional implications or to understand the highly subtle distinctions covered by the more than ten Chinese terms which divide up the semantic range of the English word 'reason' or the highly subtle distinctions in level of the formality signalled by the various terms that serve in the place of the English 'you' (Bloom, 1981:85).

"The rare bilingual person, the person thoroughly grounded in two distinct conventions, is the person most likely to be struck by the utter differences of the same text in his two languages becoming more heavily aware of the distinct value structure implied by the languages and the subversive force of whatever differences from convention that these established" (Parks, 2000 : 54).

The transfer of beliefs in personal communication much less writing or in translation is always difficult even in the closest of associations. The distinguished English novelist Nabokov (Nabokov, 1981) in writing about translations from Russian to English, stated that there are three grades of evil that can be discerned in the strange world of verbal transmigration. "Ignorance and misguided error which is excusable. The next step to hell is for the translator to shape words and phrases that he did not bother to understand or seemed obscure. The worst crime is that of the translator who aims to improve on the original".

Translation into print is a burden which Christianity alone among the major religions has inflicted on itself because it has gone out to others to convert them to this faith. In order to do this it has always had to put its message into languages which have no relationship at all to those in which its message was originally written. The message has been that 'we' have provided you with the original message in your own language for you to read, learn and believe.

All other religions have taken the position that our beliefs and practices are enshrined in documents tied to languages with their own inimitable sacred meanings. If you want to understand and believe then you come to these sacred documents as we are not going to diminish their sacredness by providing translations which will always be semantically and theologically inadequate.

There is always the factor of the probable impossibility of translating concepts from within one language group to another disparate one.

Richards has commented on the possible transfer into English of Chinese philosophic concepts that 'we have here indeed what may very probably be the most complex type of event yet produced in the evolution of the cosmos' (Richards, 1953 : 150). So it could be said that Christianity has within its practice of universal translating into print, the elements of working misunderstandings which other religions have avoided in these contexts.

The Inaccuracies Built into Translation

Translation cannot be seen as an impersonal exercise with parallels to mathematical equations. Indeed the language used can be seen as the impersonal medium in which individuals interpret a document in terms of their personal understandings for the transmission of these words to others; crudely it can be seen as a marketing exercise in which the translation is being carried out for a particular section of society even if it is ostensibly addressed to a culture wide universe. The finished work is not a commodity with limited uses such as a tool but one in which there are infinite numbers of alternatives in how the finished product can be presented.

There is as we have seen not only the difficulties of translating the complexity of Chinese thought which have developed in millennia of elite thinking committed to writing but the possibility of straightforward mistakes. This is probably common enough when those from a literate cultural background try and put into words the equally complex thoughts of people who have no literate backgrounds of detached abstract thought.

The Italian Catholic priests who originally to put their Christian thought into the language of the northern Ugandan Acholi, had problems. They had wanted to put the Christian concept of God into their catechetical work but the Acholi do not have an independent concept of creator or creation. So it was interpreted as 'who moulded you' which the answers of the elders consulted as obviously 'mother'. When pressed further they came up with the answer that hostile spirits created disease so what came to be translated as the Christian God, these well intentioned priests used the term *Hubanga* which for the Acholi was a supreme hostile spirit (Okot, 1970:62. 85).

In these semantic environments it is easy enough to find such mistakes but the "act of translating was not to erase linguistic boundaries but to reinscribe them within a framework of divine transactions which was most lucidly expressed in Latin. The codification of oral traditions as text often impoverished indigenous genres and privileged the creativity of the author over the audience. It rendered the written word more canonical" (Jolly, 1996).

There is always the difficulty of directing a translation at the users of a particular language who are never a uniform group in terms of their intellects, knowledge and uses of their own language and their literate competence. Indeed it may be that the cognitive processes in one culture cannot cope with the metaphysical ideas which have been produced by another culture. Even within a single culture with a single dominant language spoken by almost all there are many situations in which the receiver of a message has no understanding of its meaning which is a common situation in medical consultations even within a single society.

The usual situation is for the translators to produce a version which is acceptable to their knowledgeable colleagues and the small helping group of natal speakers of the language with whom they have worked over a long period to produce translations. They are usually middle aged men who are assumed to have the necessary level of theological understandings to give seemingly accurate interpretation of how it might be expressed in the language from which translation is undertaken. This puts the translation into a frame of high intellectual understandings which is unlikely to be that of the average worshippers for whom the translation is being made.

When the language into which translation is being made has no literate form it would seem that the translators work would be easier but this is not so. Non-literate languages are just as complicated in their semantic intricacies as languages with long literary traditions which are usually elitist in their forms and do not reflect commonplace semantic usages. In such situations the translators are always imposing a new form of understandings into an area which has already complex ones of which the translators may be only partially aware.

The translation of religious works is usually in the context of Christian practices or in the agnostic environment of universities. Hindus and Shintoists would see no purpose behind translating their works into the languages of people who would be unlikely to want to change their own faiths to these Asian ones. Since Muslims regard the *Koran* in Arabic as being the actual words of Allah, they regard any translation with deep religious suspicion. Sunni authorities wanted to buy up and burn all the copies of the Ahmadiyya translation of the *Koran* into kiSwahili as the impious production of Islamic apostates. So the translation of major Asian religious works has usually been done by academics for secular rather than for any specific religious reasons. The fields of religious translation is largely a Christian undertaking.

Where the translation is into a language which has a long literary tradition as would be the case with Mandarin, Hindi and the East African *lingua franca* kiSwahili, the translators are faced with three alternatives. A form imitating the literary style for liturgical use in churches which would support the importance of what is being said even if few worshippers would understand this form. There are plenty of parallels to this form of exclusivity in the classical Arabic of the *Koran*, the Hindu use of Sanskrit and the Buddhist of Pali as well as the highly specialised ideograms of Mandarin Chinese.

Then a further type of translation to be used in theological discussions of theologians and those teaching Christianity as catechists. Finally, translations for popular use of which there are several examples in English. However, few religious organisations would have the personnel or the financial resources to produce such different documents. There is always the issues of whether religions can be or indeed should be simplified since their theology is based on metaphysical mysteries.

Translation and the Limits of Adjusted Meanings

Translation is not just the exchange of words from one language to another but the constant process of adjustment which occurs in communication between people or groups of people who belong to different social and intellectual categories. The most difficult of these processes of translation will be between languages of different linguistic groups and which involve the metaphysical issues in religion and their commitment to the permanencies of writing.

One-to-one communication allows opportunities for negotiating a solution to apparent misunderstandings which are inevitable in matters that are not clear in the first place; a translation which is not understood is often shown in the face of the recipients. However, with written communications there can be no negotiations and the receivers are faced with the fact of print about which they may have very little background knowledge about the author(s) or institutions involved of what was on sale or provided free by Christian organisations or just there to be picked up in Taoist temples as part of their fortune telling system.

The people who get hold of these religious documents are not decoding machines processing the text in any rigid and anticipatable way. A religious document may be printed in large numbers but there can be no assumed uniformity of understandings as the social universes at which these translations are directed are indeterminate. It would be safer to assume that any coincidences of meaning are likely to be statistically minimal.

Firstly, the documents may be written in languages or scripts which the potential readers cannot understand who are then put into a forced dependency on an elite for an interpretation. Certainly there would be an immediate need in reading the interpretation of what has come up from the use of fortune-telling sticks in Taoist temples in Taiwan.

Then possessing a religious text and reading it are two different social processes. To get hold of a text may not involve any use of time but to read it involves the cost of using up time and paying for such interpretations and thus it becomes a question of priorities; what return are potential readers going to get from using up such a scarce commodity as time. If someone laboriously reads a religious text there is no reason to suppose that they are going to come to the interpretation intended by the writers or the promoting institutions.

Just Getting it Wrong

When it comes to translating metaphysical ideas from one language to another even within the same linguistic group of languages bilingualism is an illusion. Unless they are investigating and translating the commonplaceness of cooking and carpentry, the social scientist is looking at the religious practices and ideas from the perspectives of an inquisitive and concerned outsider. They are attracted to and pursue the exotic in the cultural situations which they encounter. Even nationals researching their own culture are going to prefer the discovery of some unusual event or perspective because they have not come across this in their own cultural settings. Similarly, cultural foreigners have not come a long way with much inconvenience and time and motion expense just to record or translate the commonplace. They search for the exotic and this is what they find (Beteille, 1986).

Most researchers in a culture which is alien to them even within a part of their own social environment will be prone to exaggerate in their own minds their competence in the language or linguistic code which they have acquired. Even with some preliminary study of the language academically prior to starting their research, we are looking at the competence which comes from less than two years emersion in this new language and which is not usually refreshed by continued association with that particular part of the society which speaks that linguistic code.

From the effort they have used to learning a new language, there comes the conceit which leads them to make more of their interpretations of the religious ideas of these people than the data which they have collected justifies. There is also the fact that their entry into these different metaphysical ideas is through informants who are from the start and throughout their research are similarly interpreters.

So they are using interpreters not only in the linguistic sense but also in explaining what the researchers want to know and to provide information supporting this; they know the general goal towards which these outsider men and women are directing their enquiries. They may even downgrade the language which they use to match what they see as the simplistic language knowledge of the researcher to whom they are talking with whom they may want to have a continuing relationship.

The researchers have had a prolonged education in their specialities and they are rarely getting information from anyone of the equivalent efficiency in the use of the language from which and into which they are translating with seeming confidence. However, these interpreters are usually self-selected persons who are intellectually more or less equal with their researchers and they may even contribute to the accumulation of exotic information and interpretations which are not the commonplace ones of the community from which they come. There is here a bilateral process of guesswork in which each interprets the other's specific hopes rather than understandings.

Social scientists of whatever national origin are seeking a linear logic in the behaviour which they record, a professional necessity, a cohesion which stems from the legacy of Comte. Western theologians also share this need for linear consistency. Both these professional groups find it difficult to accept that there may be no identifiable linear cause for some behaviour and that the predetermined factors are lateral according to the processes of Parallel Distributive Processing (Rumelhart and McClelland, 1986), an instantaneous conclusion from innumerable lateral factors.

Head-hunting has attracted the attention of many anthropologists who have inferred that there was a causal link between this practice and the benefits of fertility which was the transfer of a 'soul substance'. Needham explains that the use of scientific idioms to explain this practice was caused by the need for certain facts to be causally accounted for but that there is in fact no causal connection between these two complex ideas and practices.(Needham, 1977).

Much the same elaborations of occurred in the use of the Oceanic-Melanesian words 'taboo' and 'maana', which anthropologists have turned from relatively simple words relating to specific social prohibitions into nouns of great metaphysical importance (Keesing, 1989).

An anthropologist translating the religious ideas of the Fatalika of the Solomon Islands stated that during a certain ritual the truth becomes an illusion but it seems that the key word used means a coming into view according to latter informants, "What faith are we to have in philosophical explanations of the mystical depth of the Fatalika mind when they rely on linguistic misinterpretations and errors of transcription and translation" (Keesing, 1989). Turnbull's celebrated study of the Ugandan Ik states that their soul flew past the moon and that it is round and red but the word used is heart which a latter anthropologist found *Ik* informants unaware of such metaphysical ideas (Heine, 1985).

Such very questionable interpretations would seem to have been caused not only by the anthropologists search for exotica but their reading much more into metaphor than the understandings of the people using them. Conventional ways of talking whether by educated Indians or the uneducated members of an Orissa tribe are full of metaphors which have no corresponding beliefs of any metaphysical importance; they are not folk models of any deep thought any more than the English phrase that a person puts their heart into their work has any deep meaning (Keesing, 1985).

The Target of Translators

Whatever may be the stated religious objectives of translators of religious documents the background will be more pragmatic such as who has the time to do this prolonged work and how much is it going to cost. Disagreements over the translation of certain phrases in the *Bible* whatever the agreement which can be agreed on, comes down to the costs of reprinting and negotiated agreements rather than theological necessities. In these compromises there are another form of what are working misunderstandings.

The translation of the Hebrew in the *Old Testament* into English was systematically altered to make it acceptable to early modern English norms (Tadmor, 2010). A semantic shift from the Hebrew word for amity to neighbourliness. There is no single explicit stipulation in the Hebrew *Bible* of a marriage procedure in which the consent of the woman is given, but there were numerous accounts of women coerced into sexual and personal subordination. The English versions explicitly explain that the 'giving' and 'taking' of women in this context was in fact an act of monogamous not polygynous marriage. The word for women in this was 'she', one who has been mastered, but the English translation this woman which in the Hebrew occurs 569 times is designated in the English as 'the wife' 312 times and 'husband' for man 81 times. There is the similar change from slave to servant. So it would seem that the translation of the Hebrew *Bible* into English for the much appreciated King James version has substantially and deliberately ignored the Hebrew meanings of key words in order to make its message conform to what was then and continues to be English law. This would be a working misunderstanding at all levels of believers who use an English translation of the *Bible* from its Hebrew origins.

The effort to translate the classics of Buddhist and Taoist thought has come from those whose livelihood is assured through secular institutions. The bilingual intellectual elite in China and India have not seen the effort to translate justified in terms of the needs of their own believers. Foreigners who have translated these classics will no doubt be told that they have missed certain important aspects of the phrasing because they have no natal or sufficient acquired intellectual religious understandings of these works. The Westerners seeking their own enlightenment or qualifying for some examination are no doubt another form of working misunderstanding assessed to exist by Asian intellectuals. There is often the conclusion that certain words in Chinese philosophy can be explained but that they cannot be translated into equivalent phrases and words.

Important religious documents are frozen in the format in which they were written and as such readers come to them and have to conform in their minds to an alien form of cognition and often by specialist training to what has been written; they have self-created obligations which have to adjust to what has been written there. A translation outside the frame of their cognitive socialisations is a creative act in which specialists in languages in which the original documents were written, interpret what has been written without any direct help from the original writers. We have seen what happens in translation from biblical Hebrew into English.

There are also problems from the fact that the translators work from the foundations of their own natal language about which they may know very little beyond the uses into which they have been socialised particularly by prolonged education. The second language into which they are translating will have been learnt grammatically. So it may be that when dictionaries are available for both languages, the natal one is used more frequently because the translators have never previously had to look into their own understandings of a language which they have used from birth.

These translators are intellectually separate from the average speakers and writers of either of the languages involved, that of the documents to be translated which are soundless and the language into which translation is to be made, can only be heard in the mind. Bilingual men and women are usually confined to special areas of need and those connected with religion are few and highly specialised.

There is always the difficulty of the form in which these translations are made. The translators first direct their work at their own specialised understandings and the members of their religion who are assumed to have the same high level theological understandings of what is being translated. The result is usually a document which is itself difficult to understand because of its abstract nature ends up in another document which is equally abstract and difficult to understand.

The result is usually that the interpretations of the original document has been produced by the religion's own professionals and this is in a shared language so that these translations are open to the interpretation of anyone who can read in that language and cares to make their own conscious or unconscious interpretations. It would seem likely that any simplification of the second language to enhance its popular appeal may lead to even further misunderstandings between orthodoxy and complex socio-religious activities.

However, this is not a simple division between two languages of equal semantic understandings. The translation of Christian documents into kiSukuma, the language of perhaps five million is relatively simple because the translators are not in competition with any literary tradition of which there is none. The translators of the *Bible* into Burmese which is spoken by some twenty million, were probably not aware and certainly may not have used literary and religious Burmese with its Pali connections in their translation work. There is always the intellectually stressful process of forcing into translation ideas which have no current available usage in the receiving language. What words can be used for a monotheistic caring God when this receiving language carries the concept of a disinterested ultimate power which if anything the Tanzanian Sukuma wish would keep out of their lives.

Even a language which has no written literary background may still have something which parallels such sophistications as in the poetic form of Sukuma chorus singing similar to the complex brevities of Japanese *haiku* poems. Thus, any translations even from a language which seems related to the simplest of social and religious organisations is faced with three alternative approaches each of which will carry within it its own range of possible misunderstandings.

Firstly, a form which imitates the literary or special occasions semantic style of the receiving society which would be suitable for liturgical use. Few if any address the spirit world in the language of ordinary life; special honorifics are required as there is no equality in such relationships. A specialised style is needed which would support the importance of the occasion. Only Christianity in its translations appears to have gone down market in this respect in producing liturgies in modern English replacing the more sacralised earlier version with its specialised phrasing.

Secondly, there are translations for use in instruction. It is a particular feature of Christianity that people have to learn to be Christians by a special and prolonged form of training for which special handbooks are produced. In some cases there are simple productions for children or catechisms in English of many hundred pages which can only have intellectual appeal. The procedure for becoming a Muslim is a simple affirmation of faith in Allah and Muhammad as his Prophet in front of witnesses.

Finally, there are the translations produced for popular use and for people in particular difficulties which are on sale in the entrances to many churches; instructional do-it-yourself handbooks which seem to be a feature of Christian evangelisation.

In even the societies which have material simplicity, the thinking of their intellectuals about relationships with the supernatural is complex. It seems unlikely that there has ever been anywhere a deliberate policy of simplification and if there were it would seem that it degrades the complexity of the thought of even the most intellectually simple believers.

Translations can be produced for particular markets but most are intended for a mass market in which the people who will actually read these documents is unknown; who can know whether these simplifications have added to the readership and in what terms of understanding.

The Translation of Sacred Documents

Only Christianity seems to have considered it necessary to translate the *Bible*, the basis of their faith into the natal languages of the people whom they wish to convert and to enable existing believers to have a better understanding of the bases of their religious commitment. The enormous extent of this consumerist effort is not much more than a century old.

Other religions such as Islam have the basic objection to the translation of the *Koran* that the actual wording and its calligraphy was part of the original sacralised message and that translation must inevitable change these necessary meanings. Ahmadiyya sect which orthodox Muslims do not regard as Islamic produced a kiSwahili translation of the *Koran* which was widely condemned. This objection was related to translation as such rather than the presence in this work of mistranslations.

Whatever the theological justification for this dogmatism, there is certainly a real sense of pragmatism in this approach. Leaving aside the question as to whether any language can semantically express the ideas used in another from a different linguistic group, metaphysical translations are almost by definition bound to be inaccurate based as they must be on theological pragmatic uncertainties and ambiguities.

Most Christians especially Fundamentalists forget or do not wish to accept that the *Bible* to which they refer with reverential conviction are in fact sequential translations from the original Greek and Hebrew editions. The contemporary *Bible* published in American and English are as much translations as the earlier so-called King James edition much loved by British Protestants. Biblical scholars may well be able to argue that these translations are exegetically incorrect or that meanings are not fixed as they change with historical progression. Few early surviving documents pay much attention to Christianity. There is always the same tautological netting in which theologians use these historical fragments to prove Christian issues.

Chinese sacralised documents have their key words depicted in specialised ideograms. Their translation would mean the translations into a further set of specialised symbols which would similarly require specialised learning with no easy way out of this tautological network.

Eastern religions have regarded religious texts as the bases for the study and reflection of those who wish to go further in their religious progression. However, eschatological understandings and learning is one pathway but not a dogmatically necessary one. This required prolonged specialist study under monastic conditions or at least social isolation. There does not seem to have been any effort to make these Buddhist, Confucian, Hindu, Shintoist and Taoist texts available in any language other than that in which they were originally written which always required prolonged specialist study for even introductory understandings.

Those who could read these documents probably realised that from a intellectual point of view most of the metaphysical terms and phrases used could not be translated perhaps without turning even a single word or phrase into a further explanatory text. The translation of Saint Ignatius's Spiritual Exercises into kiSwahili with a shared script still involved lengthy explanations of these difficulties (Mkinda, 2008). The reading of this translation requires substantial intellectual effort which may not have much connection with the aim of any generalised religious enlightenment; in effect it is a Jesuit production for the use of Tanzanian Jesuits and their affiliations.

Thus the reluctance to translate into more commonplace language or did they never even consider it as a necessity, was the result of several factors. Hinduism has never centralised religious authorities who might underwrite such projects so it would not have been clear who would gain from such work other than the sect producing such translations. There would have been little agreement between Sanskrit readers as to the meaning of words antedating the era of English literacy by many centuries. The nature of sectarian Hinduism would make agreement on any metaphysical words and phrases impossible.

Buddhism has always had monastic libraries but agreement on what the Buddha said and meant in documents that were created several centuries after his death, is extremely unlikely. Indeed the Buddha is reputed to have said that arguments on metaphysical issues were to be avoided and that such disputants should each go their own way even to splitting monastic communities rather than reach compromises which would break the understandings of all disputants.

Only Western secular scholars rather than peripherally involved missionaries for these religions, produced translations into their own languages and which were published in specialised publications such as the Pali text series. These religions never considered that the popularising of these sacralised texts was theologically and socially necessary. In practical terms these religions were always and indeed remain theologically elitist; you come and work for understandings, we do not come to you.

So Christianity is alone in putting an enormous financial and intellectual effort into translating the *Bible* not so much as without reflection but seeing the proliferation of the Christian message to all mankind as a moral necessity in whatever form it took. The *Bible* was a manual for attaining salvation and conformity. There was never any doubt not only that the *Bible* should be translated but that it could be.

Whereas other religions were similarly 'frozen' in antique texts which were kept segregated from popular influences, Christianity was unique in making enormous efforts to put this 'frozen' text into these hands of any contemporary person who could read; faith and literacy enabled doubt to become more formally available and with it working misunderstandings; the necessity of ignoring the written text in the face of personal difficulties.

The translators were usually missionaries who had long experience of what were usually the languages of cultures with no literate records with the help of 'native' intellectuals. They produced texts for which the agreement of other missionaries was a prime necessity. Latter changes in these translated texts brought about by local clergy and ecumenical efforts implicitly hinged on the cost of producing new editions (Tanner, 1973).

In general it seems that no religion other than Christianity has produced translations with the aim of global coverage. It has done so on the basic and rather bland assumption that it is possible to translate metaphysical doctrines from one language to another. Perhaps there was also an element of the biased thinking that the complications of Western major languages with their literary manifestations could be translated into what missionaries and theologians considered to be the relative simplicities of what were largely unwritten languages without regard to the cognitive differences in which these people thinking in totally different languages regarded their metaphysical issues.

It is perhaps only recently that theologians as much as translators have come to realize that there are no simpler languages and that even the languages of small once largely self-contained communities as the Papuan Arapesh and Mundugumor are enormously complex as reflecting the thinking behind their use. The language of the several million Tanzanian Sukuma contains more verb tenses than English and is in fact tonal (Batibo, 1985).

These 'lesser' historically unwritten languages are not only grammatically complex but will vary internally to an even greater extent than languages which have been subject to centuries of imposed literate uniformities from universal primary education. Even the most 'primitive' of languages will have differences between the linguistic codes of diviners, and those for addressing the spirits, formal and informal forms, intersexual communication, that used for joking relationships and for family use (Nida and Taber, 1982 : 94). It may be particularly difficult for translators coming from societies with long traditions of bureaucracy and institutionalisation, to recognise the 'local' nature of dialogue. There are reputed to be no less than twenty different linguistic codes of the spoken English within a few miles of the northern British city Newcastle on Tyne.

People who consider themselves bilingual are often surprised by the repeated finding of complications of their natal languages in which they consider themselves to be reasonably conversant. They also find that the fluidity of the spoken language is rarely if ever reflected in any writings regardless of their literary traditions and competence.

The earlier translators tended to gloss over the complexities and philosophical backing of the languages into which they were translating and to look back into the Greek editions of the New Testament and the Hebraic Old Testament. They would not have been considering the implications of the Sapir-Whorf hypothesis that the grammatical categories of languages lead their speakers to think about things in particular ways (Whorf, 1956). The grammatical structure of Greek and Latin confines and enables certain forms of expression and understanding. We should consider the effects of Mandarin in how the Analects of Confucius were expressed. It would have been difficult for those earlier translators to accept the possibility that the comparatively uneducated thousands surrounding them might have contained theological thinkers of importance whose thoughts would have been structured by the ways in which the languages they used had been put together. If spiritual forces have to be grammatically expressed with impersonal pronouns, what forms do you use in addressing God who has the human form of Jesus Christ. Whichever forms are used fractures either the theological understandings of traditional or Christian speakers and thinkers and the modern expressions of feminism.

The Invisibility of Meanings

Translators want meanings for the words and phrases which they have to use in the crossover from one set of linguistic understandings to another and the difficulty here is that in finding these meanings they have to use one language to explain another or to use that language to explain itself; a tautological situation.

Until recently history is silent about how words were used and our knowledge is confined to interpretations of the formalities in inscriptions and honoured manuscripts; in comparison very little is known about the everyday use of language except for some graffiti, message scraps found in Egyptian and Roman rubbish dumps. In our understanding of language and in particular its metaphysical correlations we are left with modern uses without knowing all that much of how it came to have their current meanings.

There are thus very clear differences between all languages whether they are spoken by large or small populations. Whatever the grammatical differences there may be between English as the major language with cross-cultural usages and Mandarin Chinese with the largest number of natal speakers, there is also the possibility of cognitive differences in how the natal speakers of these two languages put or can put their thoughts into words. While it may or may not be possible to prove or disprove the Whorfian hypothesis, it must surely be self-evident that certain languages find it difficult to express certain ideas of which speakers of other languages are not aware and that while in theory a language may be able to express any idea, in practice their structure makes this difficult to achieve and it remains a serious problem for the translator.

A problem has been thought to exist about whether there are conceptual differences in how these languages are used. Particularly that English rather than Mandarin allows for counterfactual reasoning "to invite the reader or listener explicitly to shunt aside reality considerations in order to consider a state of affairs known to be false, not for the purpose of simply pretending but for the express purpose of drawing implications as to what might or might not have been the cause of that state of affairs were in fact true" (Bloom, 1981:14). We cannot be certain that 'if' is a difficulty for bilingual Chinese when they think in Mandarin or English or whether the conclusions come from the inadequacies of the methodologies used.

Once a speaker gets outside the linguistic and, therefore, the cultural perspectives in which the communication takes place, counterfactual difficulties arise. The translators are then faced with statements made from within one culture which in any real sense they cannot accept as true; how can a Western theologian accept as anything more than imaginative contemporary Chinese festivals based on devotion to the Black Dragon King for whom capitals are used in view of the extent of that belief but which do not exist in Mandarin.

At a personal level conversations between Christians and Taoists about their beliefs can avoid difficulties by the polite use of circumlocutions. Translators can only fully succeed if the communication involves the sharing of the same parameters of thinking which is not too difficult in everyday affairs. So in communication it may be that "languages differ not so much in what can be said in them but rather as to what is relatively easy to say in them... The impact of inherited linguistic patterns is least important in the most practical contexts and most important in such purely verbal goings on in story-telling. religion and philosophy" (Hockett, 1954:106-23).

But once this translation of ideas gets into upper levels of communication the possibility of any exactitude is probably minimal. In the case of China translators in or out of Mandarin are confronted with a culture whose foundations antedate Christianity by several millennia. The Kiangsi Emperor's reaction to Clement XI 1715 decree that it was impossible to reason with Westerners as they did not understand larger issues as they understand them in China and their remarks are often incredible and ridiculous and that he had never seen a document that contained so much nonsense (Li, 1969 : 22). This ruler's outspoken comments would have been shared by the contemporary Chinese intellectual elite. It is not difficult to see that such difficulties in understanding are likely to be just as current now as then. From the Chinese point of view the kind of thinking that leads one to accept for the sake of argument that a triangle is a circle...is a kind of thinking...personally debilitating...and in fact an amoral perspective on the world (Bloom, 1986:57). Modern Christian thinkers if they were not restricted by the politically motivated necessity of ecumenism would write in much the same vein about a Hindu document which stated that Hanuman, the monkey God with his allies had built a causeway between Sri Lanka and India.

The Jesuits in China when they were originally confronted with the ritual expression of the Chinese devotion to their ancestors, worried as to whether this constituted worship and thus could not be included in the Christian patterns of worship. Worship in their thinking was a Christian term and the problem was only resolved by thinking that worship in the Christian sense did not exist in Chinese thinking and what was involved was veneration. This theological conflict over several centuries was only resolved in the middle of the last century so that now there are altars to the memory of ancestors in American churches in which the congregation is predominantly Chinese.

Attempts to resolve such differences cannot be achieved by committees going over the texts phrase by phrase so as to reach what can be no more than compromises over fundamental differences in thinking. There is no reason to suppose that such difficulties do not occur in all languages in their cultural foundations. It is perhaps best to admit that such basic differences are unlikely to be resolved and that the best solution is to introduce appropriate words for the required meanings and not to attempt the impossible of translation so the Christian translators in Eastern Africa have introduced for religion the Arabic derived word '*dini*', despite its origin in the Islamic faith and to just use the English word for sacraments.

The Translators Approach to Religious Texts

The translators are in general translating for people of the same social and intellectual level and usually of the same religious susceptibilities as themselves; in such situations much can be assumed about those for whom they are translating as there would be some shared religious interests and understandings.

Communication is mostly within a person's own social circle. It is less common between people of different status, occupations, ethnicity, education and possibly religion. In such situations communication even within a society is likely to involve a measure of perhaps unconscious translation over wide ranging and largely unknown cultural barriers and for narrow social purposes.

Where there is not this assumption of some measure of intellectual equality, translators are in practice down marketing their translations for the use of people who are thought to be less clever than themselves. In such situations we can assume that there will be substantial opportunities for misunderstandings. Of course, in verbal communication misunderstandings can always be corrected as the speaker can see in the faces of the people to whom they are talking that they have not been understood.

Translation from one written language into another rather than just with the linguistic codes of a single language is a much more complex process. There is rarely particularly in religious translation the straightforward translation of any isolatable facts with clearly defined meanings into another language with similar clarities. There are not likely to be any difficulties over translating the phrase 'open this book', but 'open this holy book with care' is much more difficult.

A comment on the interpretation of a Shakespeare play for a new edition which is in effect a translation 'embodies a sum of personal judgement, textual probability and scholarly and editorial precedent. It is a recension which seeks to gauge the needs and resources of the educated reader of the mid-twentieth century. It is different from the original printings in punctuation, line division, spelling and capitalisation'(Steiner, 1975:2).

We can see in this quotation the difficulties of updating a text from an historical form of English to a contemporary form of the work of a playwright about whose work thousands of books have been produced. Producers and actors are always in the process of reinterpreting Shakespeare and in this respect they are not much different to the theological interpreters of religious texts and those who endeavour to put explanations of these texts before people who want to believe or on behalf of whom they want to enable belief to occur. We can see here that the translator has been faced with the task of not so much using an existing text but the translations of others which are similarly biased as being out of date as they have used their own culturally judgments.

The *Bible* which is the basis for all Christian translations, has itself been subject to a continuous process of updating so that the contemporary translator is using what their predecessors consider to be its proper even though it is not the language in which it originally gained its contemporary local form. The English translation which is much liked by English speaking Protestants is an example of with its avoidance of such loaded words as slave and concubine; it is a translation tailored to the moral preferences of its potential contemporary readers.

Unless the translators are aware of the extent to which their thinking and choice of words and phrases are culturally tied, translators are bound to produce work which is as much a reflection of their own thinking as that of the cultures into which they have translated.

Languages as the Bearers of Ethical Biases

Social scientists whatever the length and extent of their professional learning are born into particular cultures and with this comes linguistic understandings which are not the result of any teaching process; it is the result of socialisation not the distinctive process of scholastic learning. This is the way I express myself, it is natural even if intellectually I know that this understanding may have no pragmatic validity outside my personal realities; one language can no more be natural than any other. There may be affinities in thinking patterns within certain language groups such as within the Romance languages, but it seems unlikely that there can be any equivalences in the structures of thought between languages which have no shared semantics at all such as between Burmese, Bengali and the Bantu group of which the last has speakers of similarly structured languages from Kenya to South Africa.

Indo-European languages have exclusive personal pronouns that carry with them no social categorization other than their connection with persons or groups. Other languages are more complicated than this since they carry specific social categorizations from which they cannot be separated (Suzuki, 1978). The irreducible 'I' in Western thinking and social practices makes it a difficult inter-relational barrier in Japanese where speech is always relational (Smith, 1982). The construction of sentences can provide meanings which are not available in English. The end particle of a sentence in the Venezuelan Gualca language states whether the information is related to a person seeing the speaker, heard from a reliable source or the product of myth and imagination (Nida and Tabor, 1982 : 116).

The use of the major languages has inevitable problems as in Japanese "it is utterly impossible to form a sentence without commenting on the relationship between oneself and one's interlocutor. This language teaches one that as human being is always and inevitably involved in a multiplicity of social relationships" (Kondo, 1995 : 31). This would apply as much to relationships with spirit identities with whom there will always be a contractual element.

This is just one example in which by using one of the major languages, the social scientists would be conveying social facts beyond that which they are intending to convey. The national user of their own languages would know what their language was intending to convey and of course in doing so restricting the use of their research results to those in the same language group or the limited group of social scientists who have acquired a similar standard of linguistic syllabic signs and intellectual competence with which ideas can be expressed allowing an individual the opportunity for substantial creativity.

Then there is the question of the symbols used to express languages and in which English has the advantage of 26 only whereas Mandarin Chinese has well over forty thousand different symbols. To read a popular newspaper in English requires a knowledge of just these 26 and to read at the same level in Mandarin probably requires a knowledge of two thousand. Translation in terms of complicated Western social science hypotheses is probably an impossibility, hence the point that Eastern and Western scientists are only comfortable in the shared use of mathematical and chemical symbols which have no social component.

Translation is always difficult if not impossible when the language to be translated does not have the same ideas as that of the receiving language. Social scientists researching religion have particular difficulties when they use pejorative words such as 'magic' or 'witchdoctor' or the language does not have an indefinite future tense. Few would want the word 'magic' to be applied to the illogical aspects of their own beliefs and behaviour nor would they apply the term 'witchdoctor' to the conductors of European séances. In general whatever words the social scientist and theologian uses from their own languages their minds will carry the meanings of their own culture and tend to interpret them in those usages in the cultures which they are studying. They are sceptics or at least pragmatists by profession and they can have no instinctive understandings of the peoples in other cultures use of magic anymore than an Englishman or a Bengali woman can understand the sophisticated implications of the winning *haiku* in national Japanese poetry competitions.

There is an even more basic difficulty in translations from languages relating to cultures which have for reasons that can scarcely be called religious have separated that activity into a distinct cultural box semantically separated from economics and politics with which it is intrinsically mixed in every traditional society and in Islamic states.

In kiSwahili, the Arabic derived word 'dini' is used for religion but kiSukuma spoken by some five million has no word for religion which separates it out from other activities. Without using the Sapir-Whorf hypothesis, it must surely be obvious that the Sukuma are unlikely to think of religious beliefs as a way of coping with certain problems that could be separated from economic cost and the social power of those involved. They have rather obviously seen no need to categorize certain activities as separate from what they see as predominantly social. It is not that such a language cannot express certain ideas but that these people have not seen or developed the need to create certain words and phrases which the English over what may have been a similar period of time, have created.

But what happens when there is no easy way round such issues as it is obvious enough that modern Western Christians do have a circumscribe activity which they call religion while Islam also has such a linguistically separate category of behaviour which directly involves virtually all social activities.

In kiSukuma it is possible to say 'I love God' but not that 'I am loved by God' and in both phrases the verb tense is passive; it just does not exist in an active form. Thus, it would seem that the theistic reciprocity built into Christian theological thinking is not available to these people and moreover never has been as far as we can estimate. How do you translate into a language a basic religious principle in the language from which translation is required when it is not possible to say it in the other.

What do we do in translating to and from the language of the Hopi American Indians who distinguish between events that exist or have existed, into English which has past and present tenses and events which may or may not happen, and the English future (Whorf, 1946). The Portuguese has also the same uncertainty about considering the future. There are semantic differences here, a built-in uncertainty may be connected to subsistence farming. But then there are in the pre-Columbian Mayan society lineal time cycles of great length, thousands of years in a cycle which see the future as far from epistemologically uncertain.

Some languages such as Kenyan kiKamba have no indefinite future tense and their three future tenses are related to specific time spans tied to nearly now, next month and next agricultural season. Japanese has no future tense but gets round this by saying 'coming next Monday we are meeting so there are practical ways round such difficulties. But then how do we translate the certainties of the Second Coming and the Paradise to which Islamic suicide bombers consign themselves. Even colours which are of liturgical importance do not translate easily between cultures and the Sukuma in identifying plants for their religiously related ethnomedicine do not have words to describe the colours of purple, blue and orange flowers.

Such metaphysical intricacies are not just tied to the thoughts of a few intellectuals who can go theoretically beyond the thinking boundaries of their own cultures of whom proportionate numbers exist in all societies whether they are literate or not; they are part of the everyday thinking of average men and women.

There are also problems from the existence of key words in one language which may not have equivalences in other languages. The Sukuma have the abstract noun *busebu* which refers to anyone with unusual secular and religious charismatic qualities such as the killing of a lion or having a permanent relationship with the spirit world. Would this be the correct word to use for what people accept as possession by the Holy Spirit in glossolalia when it is used for ancestor possession.

There are also difficulties in which the calligraphy imposes confusion. In Japanese the normal term for ancestor *hotoke* is written with the same Chinese ideogram as *butsu* meaning Buddha (Smith, R.J.,

1974:50). The series of Shinto rituals by which a child is turned into an adult parallel the series of Buddhist rituals by which a dead person is turned into an ancestor (Ooms, 1976).

What these difficulties make necessary is an understanding of the basic meanings bound into languages as part of cultures which may be easy enough when there are some cultural consistencies. The concept of invisible spirits with powers would appear to be almost universal (Boyer, 2000) but on the other hand, Christianity is not geared to monsoon and annual floods but to pastoralism. The individualism of worship in Islam moves easily into the thinking of city people and factory workers. Metaphysical translations are environmentally constrained by the societies in which they prosper and by individual intellectual capacities. Early Christian meanings just as those in Buddhism and Hinduism are long gone into the lost contexts of history. Some sacred Hindu *Puranas* refer to horse sacrifices for which there is so far no archaeological evidence and not even the vaguest of folk memories among the devout.

The Pseudo-Democratisation of Translation

Certainly the early Christian writings as much as the historically earliest of the chapters of the *Koran* message were intended for ordinary people with a variety of everyday preoccupations rather than for any contemporary elite. However, with time writing religious texts became an elite occupation and with this concentration of thought going into what would be propagated by printing; it became an elite profession perhaps feeding itself with obscure thinking committed to writing; a continuous process of increasing complexity rather than simplification.

Now with the new thinking of the theological elite resulting from the resolutions of the Vatican II Conference and the reawakening of Islam, there is a new effort going into translation both within and beyond the major texts to translate their religious message into more ordinary language so that the range of hearers and readers might be increased.

The translators instead of being satisfied with their work in terms of their own intellectualism have begun to use back translations in which less intellectually able people have provided their own understandings of what they have been provided with.

The *Bible* translated into the kiSwahili would still not be an easy read for those for whom it was their natal language and these people were almost all coastal Muslims. It was difficult reading for those who learnt it as a second language as the official national language. For the new generations for whom kiSwahili is more their natal language it is still not written in the linguistic code intelligible to most of the population who are subsistence farmers and slum dwellers.

Thus, there are at least two factors working in combination contributing to straightforward misunderstandings. Bilateral misunderstandings which will always occur over cultural and demographic social boundaries. They are more likely to occur with increases in social distance and the extent to which metaphysical issues are involved so that there are built-in misunderstandings. When people are about to have a ceremony to propitiate annoyed ancestors there will be less occasion for misunderstanding than in attempts to explain the Christian or Hindu notions of sacrifice.

Secondly, what might be called the intellectually 'heavy' nature of translators who are not working just as translators but as theologically committed and segregated intellectuals. There is also the factor that where there is a hunger for reading materials so that the subsidised *Bible* is usually the best buy on the book market containing as it does a large number of interesting and understandable stories about pastoral life which fit into the lives of keepers of livestock rather than of subsistence farmers

The Historical Bias of Translators

Translators are looking at the languages with which they are working in terms of what is already semantically established and for one of the languages formally available in printed documents and dictionaries with all their historically well-established meanings. Outside this circle of professionally committed translators, these same languages are involved in further secular formalisations in print are under processes of constant change. These changes not only involve those which come from economics and politics but certainly from metaphysical issues as well and these changes are far from being homogeneous.

It seems likely that in many cultures the concept of ancestors will have changed from the large numbers involved with extended families to the much smaller numbers in the history of Japanese nuclear families. A similar change has occurred in the Shinto concept of *kami* attached to all natural objects has now extended to machines and the annual blessing of cars. There will be a constant dialectic between the personal and narrowly environmental understanding of spiritual forces and the wider social dominances as well as cross-cultural uses of the same terms.

The thousands of urban diviners in Delhi and Dar es Salaam will certainly have developed contemporary linguistic codes supporting their professional standing which brings in customers depends on their being up-to-date in what goes on around them. Social scientists tend to think in terms of discrete and ostensibly static social units but these men and women who may be restricted geographically will always be taking ideas increasingly from a global universe. Most will have access to computers, mobile phones, newspapers and books from which they will be taking ideas. Whatever their cultural and religious affiliations the range within which working misunderstandings can occur may well increase proportionately to their use of mass media stimulations.

The intellectual world of the translators may not change so quickly and always for these major religions there is the major handicap of what has already been written and defined about metaphysical issues. The Roman Catholic translator has always to remember the decisions of the Council of Trent *circa* 1545 and other meetings which the secular translator may not even know about. The contemporary Shinto or Taoist translator or interpreter is not tied to such authoritarian institutionalised theological landmarks.

The Dominance of Major Languages and Translation

Social science researchers are under a professional obligation to write up their fieldwork and to gain progressive credit in their careers as well as to fulfil their own personal ideas of success. The issue most often be the languages in which this process is inscribed and there is a triple stage process of translation. The language or linguistic code in which the research was carried out, the national or natal language in which the researchers think and finally the language used in their reports and publications. If language is the vehicle within which thought is expressed, then the researchers' linguistic understandings are the hinges round which their conclusions are expressed; this is bound to be a filter which creates differences in meaning as the information goes through these processes of successive translations.

For the national researcher the language in which their research work is done is likely to belong to the same language group as their natal language and cover a range of shared understandings and practices. Nevertheless the final work will usually be in one of the internationally dominant languages which is usually not one that has been learnt by these researchers through socialisation or one in which they have been professionally trained. Chinese social scientists and theologians publishing in Mandarin will have a readership that will be almost exclusively Chinese. If the topic has wider relevance, then it would have to be translated into English and through this process there are bound to be difficulties over meanings. These are important linguistic hurdles which are made more difficult to pass by the dominance of these international languages in which most professional publication is carried out. Proportionately only a minute number of Westerners are learning Mandarin while there are thousands of Chinese learning English beyond the graduate level.

For the non-national researcher the barriers are different as there is little possibility of anything more than limited sharing of linguistic and social understandings. They probably feel that the most important understandings can be more adequately and professionally expressed in a major international language in which English leads followed by other less important but still dominant European ones. If Arab, Chinese, Japanese or Russian social scientists and theologians publish their thoughts in their own languages, they are not likely to receive the international recognition which their intellectual content and their national reputations might justify; the script alone must restrict their readership to their own professional colleagues.

More importantly the wording used in these European languages becomes what the original field sources are accepted as saying although the discontinuities between the languages used would make it impossible for this to be so; they have been semantically dominated out of consideration to what may actually have been meant (Asad, 1986). In addition the process of translation into print will systematize the thinking of people who are essentially if not entirely non-literate (Douglas, 1966; 91) and may not have any such society wide cognitive rigidity.

An Indian writer has summarised these issues in the preface to one of his novels written in English (Rao, 1938) "The telling (of the story in this novel) has not been easy. One has to convey in a language that is not one's own the spirit that is one's own. One has to consider the various shades or omissions of a certain thought-movement that looks maltreated in an alien language. I use the word 'alien' yet English is not really an alien language to us. It is the language of our intellectual make-up-like Sanskrit or Persian was before—but not our emotional make-up. We are all instinctively bilingual, many of us writing in our own language and in English. We cannot write like the English. We should not. We cannot write only as Indians. We have grown to look at the large world as part of us. Our method of expression, therefore, has to be a dialect which will some day prove to be as distinctive and colourful as the Irish or American. Time alone will justify it." The modern world with the instantaneous availability of information makes it much more difficult to contain religious ideas in any particular social environment; there is always the handicap to this that interested men and women have the time to look for this unknown information as it may not be addressed to them and be under other headings than religion.

The Decisions Enforced by Print

The Laws of Gortys inscribed in Greek on a block of stone in southern Crete are in continuous lettering without punctuation or line distinguishing although we can presume that those who read it were able to put appropriate intervals into their speech because the divisions were self-evident. The putting into print the words of a language for which the translators have no long standing literary tradition from which they can get clues, is a handicap to interpretation and involves translators in decisions for which they may have had little prior social awareness.

Almost all languages exchange the complexities of innumerable sounds into a limited number of symbols. Any Mandarin speaking Chinese can exchange what they hear for over forty thousand ideograms of which they will know only a limited number but for most people the complexities of meaningful sound are exchanged for a limited number of symbols in both Roman and Arabic script.

There is also the difficulties of pronunciation which in some languages is formalised in tones. Cantonese has six tones so that seemingly identical sounded words can have multiple meanings which can only be identified by the surrounding sentences, social environment or body language. KiSukuma is a tonal language which has not been shown at all in its written form. The accents in written French are probably a simplification of its spoken form.

So translators into or from languages using the Roman alphabet have to decide on formal punctuation rather than the intervals for breathing, the use of capital letters which do not exist in Arabic and also tonal differences. The readers thinking in terms of their own cultural and linguistic understandings will expect these to be available in these new texts or they will have to be created in the minds of these new readers.

The translators have to accept that whatever they personally know or learn about the language into which they are translating is bound to be in some degree inadequate in comparison to those for whom it is their natal language. Whatever they do learn will increase the complexities of what they are doing and will certainly not lead to any simplification of their work. So what goes into writing are complicated social and psychological events which have been simplified or rather constricted into a limited number of symbols. Even with the most talented use of these symbols, they probably have only exact meanings when they refer to inorganic materials. In religious and spiritual matters there can never be more than temporarily acceptable and inadequate theological and social equivalences.

We have to accept that 'each language has its own system of symbolized meaning and has a distinctive way of segmenting its experience by means of words. A phrase may appear to have one to one meanings but in reality there will be an almost endless chain of related meanings' (Nida and Taber, 1974:20-1). Whether a language was designed with such obscurities in mind, the fact remains that ambiguity will always be a factor in religious communication and it should remain a constant element in whatever translation are achieved. It seems doubtful that translators ever have any intention of reproducing such ambiguities as they aim at as accurate transposition of meanings as possible. A survey using thousands of respondents in Tanzania asking "what was wrong with the Christian Church today" which was intended to bring out theological questionings, produced virtually none. Respondents did not distinguish between 'Church' and 'church' and most of the replies were of the 'leaking roof' and too much concerned with collecting money varieties (Tanner and Morgan, 1976).

Print unlike speech has no elasticity so that it is a frozen symbol forcing readers to make their own interpretations over which there can be no negotiation. If a language in its literary form print does not have capital letters or punctuation then the translator has to interpret the significance of certain words and phrases and how sentences are to broken up according to breathing possibilities, This will involve major theological issues. In ecumenical dialogues Muslims would have no difficulty over discussions that Jesus was the son of God but when this is printed as the Son of God, the possibilities of ecumenical dialogue becomes difficult (Tanner, 1979).

This would be ignoring the fact that such languages as Arabic and Mandarin have seen no need to mark their thinking in this way and thus the Western thinker using a Romanized script is creating categories with this and the punctuation which those cultures have not seen as necessary to develop. We cannot do this in writing except with personal idiosyncrasies, ritual behaviour and the illumination of initial letters.

This raises the whole issue as to how far a translator should allow themselves to interpret what they are hearing or seeing in other languages except when they are working to spread another pattern of thought. How does one write the word G(g)od when the people for whom the translation is being written have no such concept. Not to stress the fact that Christians consider Jesus to be the Son of God would be undercutting one of the purposes of translation. Similarly an Islamic translation into English would want to highlight the fact that they hold the Prophet Mohammad was the Messenger of Allah. The Sukuma have no clear word for their Highest Divinity and use words that are different within their cultural area between dry zones and nearness to Lake Victoria and it would seem that their concepts of this power are more aligned with the Hindu concept of Brahma than the Christian God.

Punctuation is a lesser issue but it will always be imposed on poetry and recitations. Perhaps all translations should be read aloud rather than just in the head to find out if they sound right because the understanding of written texts will always be slower that the translation of sound.

Ambiguity

Despite the efforts of theologians to clarify religions ideas and to produce definitions they remain metaphysical and thus always retain doubtful and uncertain meanings. Indeed it is never a simple issue of double meanings and binary choices, a particular feature of Western thinking. A single abstract word in one language may have a dozen alternatives in the language into which translation is made. Of course in reverse a word in the second language may have an equal number of alternatives in the first natal language of the translators. In making such choices the translators are guided by their own cultural and indeed moral understandings.

With material objects there may be few difficulties except when a language is tied into a particular physical environment such as semi-desert pastoralists who would have no knowledge of snow and whales. Nida and Taber (Nida and Taber, 1974:7) refer to the Gospels in Greek as containing some 700 grammatical and textual ambiguities of which a high proportion are resolved by the linguistic context but "these languages employ words which have meaning in terms of the cultural contexts in the languages used". It may be possible to find this out with languages which are currently spoken but what may have been their meanings historically can only be enlightened guesswork.

Thus there are built-in difficulties in any attempt to resolve these ambiguities which are cultural as much as linguistic. Firstly, we cannot know the situations in which these ambiguities emerged; and secondly, it is almost inevitable that since then these words and phrases will have developed new meanings with new ambiguities.

Finally, the translators whether they are religiously committed or not are faced with choices in these metaphysical contexts which are moral ones. An example of such moral choices would be the translation of customary behaviour which those involved would assess to be the result of spirit possession or the influence of the Devil which the translators might want to describe as psychiatric distress (Nida and Taber, 1974:14); a cultural interpretation rather than one that might have some more universal application. Many African Christians accept the Devil as a reality and spirit possession in such cultures could be described as just as commonplace as marriage. In a 1987 lecture at Harvard by a distinguished ex-communist Polish professor of philosophy, chose as his topic the Devil in history to the mystification of his audience; it took some time for them to realise that he was talking not about the idea but about the reality of just that (Judt, 2009:6-8). What does the translator do when Western theology would exclude the Devil as a reality but not many of those to whom their translations are directed would accept this.

Western or Westernized translators are socialised into a system of thought which prefers a meaning to meanings and indeed the Oxford English Dictionary numbers meanings in descending order of importance. Should we not assume that any metaphysical word or phrase was never intended to have a single meaning and indeed it could probably never have one without preceding definitions which minimally require the created legitimacies provided by literacy and the creation of dictionaries.

It may be that the individual mind in its complexities is basically non-literate in its functions in most environments even in the context of Eastern religions with their long history of literacy and an absence of metaphysical definitions. They have rarely if ever seen any value in abstract metaphysical words having a single meaning. In getting Sukuma non-literate or semi-literate intellectuals to assist in the creation of a customary law handbook they would agree on a definition probably thinking without verbalising of particular examples but then would change their definition for another case. A further illustration of this cultural dislike of binary choice occurred when Sukuma church elders were asked to choose from a paint catalogue what they wanted for their chapel but they chose all the colours available for use in downward stripes. Similarly, Hindu religious pictures contain so many strikingly different symbols that it would be impossible to create any single meaning from such a mass of illustrated ideas except that any particular picture was intended to illustrate devotion to Krishna or Kali.

It may be not so much that ambiguity was intended, a difficult assumption to substantiate but that ambiguity is a built-in characteristic of all metaphysical words and phrases perhaps contributing to the longevity of the major religions. Fixing a religious obligation to some particular social activity makes such religious formalisations look foolish when the social environment of such activities change. But translators have to physically choose one word or phrase for its supposed equivalences and they cannot put into the physical form provided by literacy in the series of alternatives which they know or suspect exist; they can think laterally but print is always linear. So they make choices and hope that what they put into writing conforms to the potential understandings of the majority of readers.

If the translation is important it is less likely to be the choices of an individual but of a committee of elite translators with some sort of institutional awareness of both secular and theological implications. Religious translation is unlikely to be done by agnostics who might not have the necessary theological and linguistic expertise. Even if the *Bhagavad Gita* is translated by a secular orientalist or philosopher, such people are not likely to be examples of semantic detachment. Thus the choices made where ambiguity has to be resolved are likely to be very much the result of the socialisation of those involved. Further, it would seem likely that translators of religious texts would be working for connected institutions which would want meanings on important issues to be conformist to established understandings rather than retaining their ambiguities.

Consistency

Religious practices in quasi-traditional societies can have no narrow consistencies without the imposition of literacy even though practitioners will often assert that they are conforming to historical patterns. They keep within the broadly understood varying paradigms of their culture in which religion was not a segmented and socially isolatable activity.

The translation of a religious document not only requires that religiously related words should have specific meanings but also throughout that document there should be consistency in the use of key words and phrases as well as conformity to how they have been used in associated important texts. Human behaviour cannot have consistency in any narrowed sense and where religious activities are not linked to writing, it is quite possible for nominally similar ceremonies to change from one day to the next as memory is always unreliable. A Hindu ceremony which goes on for a week is unlikely to be following a text even if the celebrants state that they are doing so.

There is a natural tendency of translators to reject repetition and to use richer and more literary vocabularies where the original text was lean and simple and above all to return stylish transgressions to convention. Most translators obey another authority, that of the conventional versions of good French or whatever language is being used (Kundera, 2000).

Much translation involves the use of words which either have no fixed meanings in the dictionary sense of definition or have several alternative words which have varied situational uses. Meaning may be a requirement of the translator while the actual users of a language may always find meanings in how the words are used than in any detached abstract situation. They may like the sound of the words so their attributed meanings are allied to the abstractions of music.

This is a difficult achievement even for those who are highly literate as before the arrival of computers, it would have been extremely difficult to achieve with the translation of lengthy documents. There is also the factor that the writer may not have intended that their sayings should have any such consistency. The Ayatollah Khomeni is alleged to have remarked that there was no reason to suppose that what he may have said last month would conform to what he might say subsequently.

Perhaps one can suggest that in the social realities of language use, there can be little other than general consistencies because words and phrases will always have differential uses according to any number of situational factors. So consistency is an objective enabled by literacy and the institutionalisation of religion but there are unlikely to be parallel consistencies in their readers understanding of their own natal language.

Would the original writers of these religious documents have in mind the creation of consistency as if they were arguing a legal case or providing an idea for scientific development. The four Christian Gospels were produced by four different men and while they may have intended consistency as a necessity in furthering their faith, it would not seem to be a rational possibility. It would seem somewhat ridiculous to read the *Bhagavad Gita* in terms of consistencies perhaps because it has varied purposes; it is an imaginative evocation and not a manual.

To go even further consistency is a relatively recent practice which historically has been related to law and taxation. Western religious institutions through the medium of literacy have imposed consistency on their definitions of metaphysical ideas which can have no such social and behavioural rigidity. Eastern religions with a far longer history of literacy have avoided this trap of using literacy to define the objects of belief.

Are there not parallels between the Sukuma propitiation ceremonies for their annoyed ancestors and those Christians in all cultures who attend the Catholic Mass. The former ceremonies are invariably different one to the other if indeed anyone of the anthropologists will attend more than one or two well separated in space and time. It seems likely that those who attend or perform a repetitive ritual will 'read' into these ceremonies the meanings which suit them individually if they go through any cognitive processes other than just attending the ceremony.

On the other hand, most Catholics will have attended a thousand celebrations of the Mass which will have been liturgically similar. This theologically backed consistency enabled by writing will not alter the fact that those attending will be taking out of what is going on what they individually need which is unlikely to have any consistency. A feature of Sukuma and Swahili informants who were asked to write down what they understood by the meanings of key words related to religion found that they were in general uncomfortable with abstract words. They tended to view than in terms of actual events rather in terms of generalities which might have come from long-term literate consistencies; not 'love' but 'what they liked'.

Whatever consistency comes from literacy a more imposed factor is the bureaucracies within which it is used. There are also the additional factors that consistency is correlated to those with higher education and intellectual skill who will be using religious texts in the assumption that it should exist. Certainly for most denominational believers consistency is assumed to exist as a fact and that it will exist in the documents which their faith produces.

13
The Communication of Religious Understandings

While translation is usually taken to be the transfer of messages from one language to another, the definition is much wider beyond 'turning (word, book etc.) from one language into another, express sense of other words, and to infer or declare or convey significance of messages (Oxford English Dictionary). We take it to mean the social and psychological processes by which information related to religious matters passes between individuals and within and beyond related institutions.

In these processes there are a series of stages which we have already enumerated. First, there are the senders of messages, then the methods by which these messages are sent and finally the receivers of these messages. This is a complicated circuit whenever it goes beyond simple primary instructions between two people in face to face contact. The basic factor in all communication whether religious or secular must be that the verbal communication has no longevity and whatever understanding have been reached they can be forgotten or altered minute by minute in order to fit into new environmental situations. On the other hand, the written communication is always in the background as an historical fact to the new social situations which will always be occurring. Face to face misunderstandings can always be rectified but written ones require explanations which can always involve even more misunderstandings.

Religious Communication and Social Reality

Whatever communication has been initiated and even religious pronouncements which have been formalised in writing, it is part of a process of negotiated behavioural adjustment. It has no stability other than what may be agreed and that itself can be no more than a momentary coming together of individually different and temporary behavioural needs.

Communication in religious activities takes three forms; word of mouth, print and religious experience which is the individual sense of an out of this world reality. So firstly there is the passage of religious information from one person to another and there are differences between two social equals talking together and the imparting of information by a person of higher status to those beneath them.

Communication between people who are more or less social equals is not likely to involve doctrinal matters but in matters of gossip. An educated Madeiran family with a seriously ill child took the advice of their long serving servant that prayers at the shrine of a particular saint on the mainland were known to be highly efficacious and so it was when these parents took their child there. Gossip carried the information that a particular woman Bibi Kalembwana in Ulanga, Tanzania was able to rid individuals and communities of witchcraft and her activities prospered (Green and Mesaki, 2005).

The larger the number of human links through which items of information pass, the greater the proportion of inaccuracies in what has been understood. It seems likely that very little doctrinal information is ever likely to be passed in this way as theological discussion is not a common or popular activity outside professional circles although it was so in mediaeval Byzantium. Personal communication is likely to be opinions about the social side of religious activities rather than about personal feelings and involvements; it is just not an area of human behaviour in which there is much interpersonal communication between equals.

Communication there may be in which individuals consult priests, pastors, rabbis, *imams* and diviners in which there is the factor of social distance between people who are both conceptually and socially unequal. As regards its contribution to the possibilities of working misunderstandings, this would appear to be common or subject to conscious or unconscious negotiable resolution. It is nevertheless face to face attempts to find solutions to difficulties or misunderstandings. Attempts have been made to cope with psychiatric problems by enabling them to phone into specially trained social workers (Cullen, 1995) in which the dynamics of face to face are missing even though it avoids the difficulties of personal confrontations which are as common in religious as secular situations. Communication to a divine figure to whom the petitioner assumes a benign involvement has more potential for success than a secular consultation.

When priests, monks or *imams* address congregations they are certainly attempting to pass on religious information or advice legitimated by their status and the religious authenticity of the occasion. However, we know that even information passed on in university lectures is not well remembered by a more or less uniform audience seeking information on a subject and it has been found experimentally to be a poor way of passing on necessary information to students committed to learning. Believers attend religious ceremonies for emotional reasons and the satisfactions from regularity and the accumulation of merit but not usually in order to accumulate religious knowledge. The sermon is accepted as a part of this, being washed over by holy words but they may not be listening in the sense of putting this knowledge into their personal memories. Many of those listening to the words of a Buddhist monk at a day of spiritual renewal in Katagarama, Sri Lanka were asleep. It seems unlikely that those listening to an Indonesian *imam* who stated at Friday prayers that the recent tsunami was the result of sexual irregularities in the Muslim community were accepting this as authoritative information on which they should act.

It seems likely that where authoritative religious statements are made orally they are likely to be heard and remembered by relatively few of those who have listened to these religious sounds. Others will continue to worship relatively unaffected by what are personal working misunderstandings which are irrelevant to their well-being.

Secondly, there are the printed words produced by religious writers and institutions in which Christianity has exceeded all other faiths in the quantity of its written productions and indeed made the ability to read as almost a precondition for adult baptism. Islam has more recently started publishing on a large scale beyond the long standing printing and distribution of the *Koran* in its original classical Arabic. It remains doubtful whether this will have involved any changes in basic religious understandings which have a cultural bases (Carmody 1988).

The Eastern religions have never developed popular publications and indeed the vast majority of Buddhist, Taoist, Hindu and Shinto believers and practitioners have no felt need to have access to the basic documents of these faiths which would require special learning. The continuing popularity of these faiths in what are in effect non-literate religious environments makes literacy a questionable religious necessity.

In Islam there is an intrinsic religious value in being able to read the words of the *Koran* which are defined as holy and this reading is perhaps independent of the readers orthodox understandings.

Finally, religious experiences in which individuals have a direct encounter with some supernatural element. It seems likely that very many more people have had such experiences than they are prepared to admit publicly and that they occur at many levels and in many situations. These are below the religious status of the peak events recorded in the lives of specially endowed people who have written authoritatively about these occurrences and which have been the subject of critical or at least explanatory analysis by agnostic psychologists.

In many if not most societies such encounters are accepted as a matter of course in spirit possession and glossolalia and that the supernatural is a reality to which anyone can attain access or be the unwilling subject of such interventions. Christian institutions have often been reluctant to accept these personal experiences as religiously valid. The Roman Catholic authorities have yet to accept the appearance of the Virgin Mary at Medugorje as a real event despite the fact that the site is the centre of devotion for some million pilgrims annually.

Overall it seems unlikely that the spread of communication electronically will have widened religious involvements but not necessarily theological understandings as it is not just a question of the propagation of information but the ability and the wish to read or listen. Sitting in an Assuan, Egyptian coffee shop during the time of the Friday prayers when a sermon was being loudly broadcast by the state controlled radio, it was obvious that no one there was listening except to the extent of talking more loudly as it was a handicap to conversation.

While of course there are pious individuals who have the spare time or make time to read and listen to religious productions because they are unable to get to public ceremonies. It seems more reasonable to assume that religious needs are usually met largely independently of formalised theology printed in what are the productions of and for their profession.

The Categories of Interpersonal Language Communication

The most important issues, perhaps the most fundamental are those raised by language in religious communications and the variations in what is used in language. A language can be divided into four schemas of which only the last is the most important for those seeking the nature of working misunderstanding in religion,

Firstly, there is the language of the people from whom religious information is received. No matter how many people use a particular language, there is no overall homogeneity and every person uses that language in such a way that it is both individual, situational and polyphonic so each individual is speaking to the recipient in a form of their language which is founded in a particular cultural environment and individualised (Aartz & Aartz, 1982). Within even a limited vocabulary which the people use in their religious thinking and verbalisation, the words and the spaces between them will be put together in the mind in a particular personal order.

Then there is the linguistic and cultural understandings of the researcher and in this the natal speaker with any degree of shared language and cultural understandings has an advantage over almost all non-natal ones regardless of their degree of absorption and intellectual understandings of their host society. It seems certain that what the individual understands of the meanings of religious communication will largely coincide with their natal understandings of the language which are held in the mind unconsciously. It was the English author Somerset Maugham, an agnostic, who said that he could never rid himself of the implications of the bell ringing in the Catholic Mass signifying the present of Christ on the altar.

But then no society or indeed no religion have any wide ranging social and religious uniformities except what is created within the static factors of print. However, theoretically possible it may be to become a full member of a culture other than their natal one as an adult, it has to be accepted that no one can make or subculture this psychological and social transfer from one culture to thinking and communicating correctly in another. In the uses of language the odds are heavily loaded against the non-national and more so or non-believer using or understanding any language correctly in religious circumstances to which they can never obtain complete behavioural access.

A national believer can often establish a reciprocal relationship by using as vernacular relationship term such as brother or sister. It seems doubtful that a diviner in such circumstances would regard such an outsider as lineally connected to him. Many anthropologists have been adopted by their American Indian hosts to regularise their relationships in terms that they could understand (Kan, 2001). but that did not entail any cultural transformation. Whatever is established by such behaviour it will not cancel the personal and situational reasons for such attempts.

Then there is the language understandings of the person who is receiving the communication. We know that this is unlikely to be more than marginally shared with that of the communicator. The situational factor makes it even more unlikely that situational feelings at the time of one communication will be the same at another even between closely related and socially involved persons. It is rather more likely that the proportion of coincidences will not be high even between adjacent sentences.

Finally, there is the language in which theologians and religious office-holders communicate their understandings to their colleagues and fellow believers and in the end the abbreviated and probably foreign language in which any of these communication are formalised in print.

Talking to Another and Understanding

In any vocal or written communication whether participants see themselves as one or not as fellow believers or outsiders, the question of language and meaning arises. A prominent feature of rapidly changing societies and the creation thereof provincial, federal or unitary states, is that these people grow up into and using layers of different languages, not just the local and professional differences in how spoken English is used which exist in Britain as in the use of Hindi in India and Mandarin in China.

An older East African priest may have had to move himself theologically through five languages prior to his ordination; tribal, the national *lingua franca*, English, Latin and French because he studied in a North African seminary. It seems likely that any Chinese, Indian or Tanzanian who wishes to be upwardly mobile in secular or religious environments will have to learn three languages or indeed those who have commercial and political relationships at the simplest level at least two. So at whatever level of understanding information is being passed whether from the communicators to the communicated or in reverse, there are complex issues which need to be discussed. The language used between believers in a particular religion or between them and the Divine is not likely to be the language of the street, their homes or work-places. No one experiences the Divine as in any way equal to themselves. So languages such as Burmese and Japanese which are used to illustrate the relationships between communicators may find it easier to express religious ideas in those languages than in English which has no grammatical distinctions illustrating reciprocal status because the devotional requirements are already available in that language.

The Layers of Language and Religious Communication

There can be little doubt that in the use of language the natal speaker of a language has advantages over anyone learning a language as an adult in a grammatical but not in a social framework; language teachers do not instruct their pupils in the use of their hands and eyes. This advantage continues as theology and the decisions of religious institutions are written and presented in one of the major languages when the advantages may in some degree turn against the natal speaker of a lesser known language used by smaller populations who may now be using a language into which they were not socialised.

The nominal sharing of a single language does not necessarily mean a semantic understanding across the whole range of social and philosophical issues, but it does make for an ease of entry into any community. But the theologians or highly educated priest or pastor's speech is going to be the linguistic code of those educated in that specific field as would be the case within any profession. The religious understandings and abilities to vocalise them will be very different between the person who has left school in adolescence or even earlier and those who left full-time education in the early twenties and even later for a Jesuit priest who might be ordained in his early thirties.

In talking and writing an educated Chinese Mandarin speaker might have the ability to recognise and use ten thousand ideograms, while a literate working man might not know as many as a thousand. The educated in their natal languages may always tend to over extend their presumed linguistic understandings and usages and it is indeed too late for them to reassume the relatively simpler understandings of the less theologically educated believer. Even within an ostensibly homogeneous culture the professor's understanding of peasant behaviour will be filtered through layers of differently acquired knowledge so that their cultural sharing will be largely illusory.

Thus, the most important issues in religious communication arise around the uses of any language, perhaps even the most fundamental one that in practice in any community there are always languages involved rather than a single language. The result so that it is an immensely varied scenario into which those wishing to understand the religious beliefs and practices of others will undertake this with their own natal language and its social meanings already fixed in their minds.

In the situation of trying to understand the religious understandings and behaviour of others there is the language used by informants but no matter how many people are alleged to use a particular language and this is usually within a conscious or subconscious religious and political allegiances, it has no homogeneity. Every individual uses that language in an individualised way so it is both idiolect and polyphonic.

The listener has to understand the phonetics, the sounds which are broadcast into their ears, how the words are constructed and the set rules which have been found to exist in the formal understandings of the language which may be known only thought the formalities of learning a language. The non-natal speaker in learning a language which is not their own learns these things. The natal speaker who has spoken this language from birth will have no knowledge of the formalities of syntax and certainly does not possess or feel that he has to buy a grammar (Aartz and Aartz 1982;6-7). Nevertheless under almost every social category the language of one natal speaker is different to that of another.

There is always the linguistic and culturally acquired understandings of those wishing to understand the religious complexities of others and in this the national enquirer with any degree of shared language and culture has an advantage over almost all non-nationals regardless of their degree of absorption in and intellectual understandings of the people with whom they are working. It should be remembered that religious communication outside the range of their own social involvements may have characteristics of social foreignness as the social distance between them is too great to be bridged by goodwill and effort.

Learning A Language to Understand the Religion of Others

During World War II in India it proved possible to produce Japanese speakers or readers in eighteen months under school conditions in order to interrogate prisoners or to read captured documents but not both and any wider understandings might be learnt by accident. More recently the same language has been taught by total emersion at some expense and in six weeks it proved possible to learn reasonable commercial Japanese by using it ten hours a day on the basis of no Japanese spoken, no food; a harsh process. The language used in religion is likely to be much more complicated and varied than that used in these two fields of use. As there will always be the minor but personally important differences between what communal or institutional orthodoxy may be and what each person personally beliefs and actually does perhaps almost by accident under constantly varying social environments.

Social scientists even if they are nationals with a shared faith will still have to learn the local linguistic code and its personal behavioural ramifications. However, religious communication has the complication of being directed at the spirit as well being overheard in a particular social environment and it has none of the relative simplicities of interpersonal communication. All their research work is against the ticking of the clock; the length of time they expect to be in a community which is foreign to them in social and religious terms and the practical cost in financial terms and the amount of time for which teachers and teaching is available. More importantly do they assess the learning of a specialised foreign linguistic code to this depth of understanding as a worthwhile personal investment within hoped for careers. An old style missionary might expect to live his or her working life in a single social environment with perhaps one leave after twenty years. No priest would be empowered to hear confessions until he had mastered the local language to a high standard. Now no missionary would make this commitment and similarly no internal expatriate with job changes would make this investment unless perhaps they were academically committed to one area as Kumar was for her work in Banaras (Kumar, 1992). There is also the factor that learning a new language in the twenties is much easier than attempting to do the same at the age of forty.

In the time available what is learnt is likely to be idiomatically restricted and probably reflects the social status of the teacher. This is particularly so with language use which reflects social status and the teacher being older than the learner so that the phraseology and grammatical forms would be inappropriate for a non-national or internal expatriate in the mid-twenties. All these factors make for complications in religious communication in situations that can never be linguistically and socially homogeneous. There is usually the hope that such communications have some general homogenising value whereas in fact whatever form it takes, it is unlikely to have any general applicability. It will always be understood in the individual's own understandings of a particular social and religious environment.

Also language learning is often at first restricted to everyday affairs rather than its idiomatic use for the specialised needs of anyone working within or practising a religion. It is probably more valuable and more impressive for any cultural or religious outsider to be able to say with confidence 'when was the last time that you propitiated your patrilateral ancestors' or 'how do your commitment to keeping free of pollution affect your daily life' than to be able to ask the way to the temple.

Learning a language must always be related to how much time is spent in using it each and everyday. Notes are rarely written in the acquired language so that their understanding of the religious behaviour and ideas of others starts with this personal translation. It may be difficult for these cultural and religious outsiders not to consciously translate. A Polish missionary who has worked for many years amongst the Bolivian Aymara does not use that language in talking with his fellow missionaries.

However, there are additional handicaps in the transfer of knowledge from one person to another. Whether the religious communicator is a national or non-national there are always additional changes in understandings as information is received from the people with whom they are talking; what did they intend to say or avoid saying and what was accepted into the minds of these researchers.

While the Apache reluctance to speak to someone who is socially unknown may be unusual in the clarity of this reluctance, have we not to accept that any communication about any matter in which there is an emotional commitment is not going to be communicated with any openness to someone about whom they know little and who is speaking to them in a form of their language which they will instantly recognise as different to their own understandings. Certainly the Apache have this reluctance but so do the English and the Mahrattas.

So whatever the efforts put into becoming linguistically competent to communicate religious matters, it will vary between communication within a narrow social environment or when it is aimed at a larger more universal audience about which little is known. There will always be the extent of their involvement within a community, and it seems unlikely that non-natal speakers of any language can become fluent however long they stay in a culturally different environment to the one in which they have been brought up and perhaps more specifically in which they have undergone prolonged education. Grammar can be learnt externally for the major languages but there is no published material available for many languages on the behaviour connected to language use and even less for linguistic codes which may have no one available who is competent to teach them. Even national researchers such as Kumar working in the Hindu holy city of Banaras will have taken some time to gain competence in the local dialect of the community in which she was interested in which they have to conduct conversations with the people from whom they hope to gain information.

The Religious Understandings and Levels of Translation

In any social situation there are continuous processes of translation going on from the simplest conversations with passers by about their food taboos to that of the language used in the printed declarations of religious institutions. Even if the social and psychological background is known about these enquirers into religious behaviour and ideas whether they are benign or hostile to manifestations of religion will be reflected in what informants provide. The researchers make their observations or even their descriptions from the photographs taken and recordings made, in their natal language and then possibly translate them again into the professional language used in print.

In the commonest situation, religious communication is face to face and that is formally communicated is inevitably an abbreviation of a complexity which is only partially understood and this is likely to be revealed later as a working misunderstanding. Few enquirers use shorthand for what they hear and see so what they record is a translation of some lengthy activity into a fraction of what they see and hear. A propitiation ceremony for ancestors in Tanzania or Hungary ghosts in Vietnam may take several hours or a perfunctory few minutes but both are translated into a limited number of words, essentially an inadequate representation of what has occurred. These are unscripted rituals which would necessitate detailed descriptions for every occasion but most formal religious communications are the translations of religious ideas into prescriptive forms which attempt to impose meanings on people whose thoughts on such matters are either unknown or thought to be in need of changing.

However, often the major process of communicating from one language to another and in fact into an internationally recognised language of which the commonest is English, it is a process of translation from a lesser language of much more local use. Even if those involved share the same natal language which is the official language or *lingua franca* of the enclosing society, there will usually be the need for a translation into an internationally acceptable language in which notes are taken or which are later translated into that language. There is no reason to assume that there will be shared understandings of what are likely to be indefinable metaphysical abstractions at several different levels of communication.

The natal speaker of the language to be used in religious communications has the advantages of being aware of the social environment involved in the language and its social and religious uses. They will still have the problems of learning the linguistic code of these particular people and indeed of their religious specialists for a fuller understanding of their social and psychological behaviour in local religious settings which may be sporadic rather than regular.

Learning to use a language for an understanding of the everyday activities of those being researched is not and is never likely to be adequate for understanding of their metaphysical ideas whether this is of a Nuer leopard skin 'chief' or a Hindu *sadhu*. Fishing and forms of spirit possession involve very different and complex linguistic understandings which will be as different as the speech patterns of lawyers, librarians and labourers. The Sukuma diviner and herbalist will have knowledge of hundreds of plants used by them in their diagnoses of their clients and it will be just as complex as that of the national lawyers about the legal processes in which they are involved.

So we see that whatever the language or languages involved in communicating enquiries about religious ideas and practices, there are always more than one process of translation from what may have happened to what is finally taken as the 'official' viewpoint of those involved. There are mutual processes of filtering in and filtering out information through the minds of the enquirer and the enquired about.

Languages as the Bearers of Ethically Disputable Biases

Communicating religious ideas and behaviour whatever the length and extent of their professional learning, researchers are born into particular cultures and with this comes linguistic understandings which is not the result of any teaching process; it is absorbed. This is the way I express myself, it is natural even if intellectually I know that this is nonsense; one language can no more be natural than any other. There may be affinities in thinking patterns within certain language groups such as within the Romance language group, but it seems unlikely that there can be any sharing in the structures of thought between languages which have no shared structures at all.

In Burmese personal pronouns refer to the relation of the speaker to those spoken to and the Western liberal social-scientist would be uncomfortable using a superior set when talking in general and for a woman to use the inferior ones in talking to men of the same age or older than herself. There is only one culturally and grammatically correct way in which anyone should speak to a monk and that is one of personal inferiority. To use such languages correctly is to use biases implicated there which may conflict with the researchers alleged moral and professional neutrality.

A congregation receiving a uniform pastoral message can never be a uniform receiver; some never collect the message, some collect and never read it and the few that do in fact read it will vary according to almost every possible intellectual and social dimensions. The advertiser, the theologian and religious administrator are all representing different employers who are trying to further their own specialised interests. In the case of the advertiser their task is relatively easy as they are presenting material products which have some visible qualities, but every adjective they use even colours have ambiguous meanings as would be the case with Coca Cola and Marlborough cigarettes. Black to the Sukuma is a good colour as it does not show dirt and white to the Chinese is the colour of mourning and indeed in some cultures some colours do not exist at all.

The religious message comes from a source which is much more complex and carefully considered but is received according to very divergent patterns of thought and in different social environments (Eco, 1994:90.98). "There exist depending on socio-cultural circumstances a variety of codes or rather of rules of competence and interpretation.... So the suspicion grew that the sender organised the television image on the basis of his own code which coincided with those of the dominant ideology, while the addressees filled it with 'aberrant' meanings according to particular cultural codes ....One thing we do know is that there does not exist a mass culture in the sense imagined by the apocalyptic critics of mass communication".

The average congregation in its reception of a printed message cannot now nor can ever have received it uniformly. Looking at any religious gathering it is so obviously mixed that the possibility of misunderstandings which will always exist, has to be seen in individual terms. Any religious gathering contains a social mixture; the mother of two children, a divorced and lonely man, the mentally handicapped young man who takes the collection, the bored adolescent and the millions who plunge into the polluted Ganges at an astrologically determined time for the Kumbh Mela. Everyone is reacting to their own understanding of a religious message however simplistically presented which can have either some narrowly restricted interpretation or quite indeterminable.

The Range of Misunderstandings

All humans are individually different not only from their genetic inheritance but from the fact that they each have social experiences that cannot be reduplicated. It is also difficult to differentiate in behaviour as to what may have a genetic element from what may have been based on ethological predispositions. Even identical twins will have a whole range dissimilar experiences such as an accident and hospitalization happening to one and not to the other.

Whatever the intellectual capacity and physical ability of the individual, he or she will be subject to biological change as they age as well as by the diseases or accidents to which they may have been subject such as giving birth or being circumcised. An endless variety of experiences which will certainly affect their public religious and private spiritualities.

We can thus appreciate that however we interpret the relationship between individuals and religious orthodoxy, misunderstandings are inevitable. The categories which are imposed on what social scientists observe and record do no more than obscure the individuality of all religious experiences. Everyone at whatever level of understanding experiences their own relationships with the Divine or whatever category of the supernatural which they have had access to, so that there is little chance of agreement between the halves of any behavioural equation.

It may be that those who are brought up together or who have institutionally similar experiences as soldiers, students, age-grade initiates or cattle keepers have surface similarities in their devotional practices. All social scientists are likely to be overly impressed by the ranks of Muslims praying together but that is as far as the similarities can go. They cannot obscure the individuality of any experience and with that the inevitability of working misunderstandings between what is done and what should have been done.

14
Contemporary Religious Ritualism

In whatever way we look at contemporary religious behaviour it should be accepted as a predominantly individual and private activity in many societies. It is only in Western Europe that there has been a decline in institutionalised religion but not necessarily in private spirituality.

The decline in religious beliefs and practices anticipated by social scientists as the inevitable consequences of the extension of education, economic development and the successes of science has just not occurred even in Russia and China and other Communist states where there has been prolonged suppression and indeed persecution of public religious activities. Certainly a change in the forms shown in public religiosity and private spirituality but certainly no decline in the pervasiveness and persistence of religion in which humans relate to the supernatural.

The seventy million who were estimated to have attended or participated in the last Kumbh Mela, was no more than an enormous collection of individuals who would have had conscious and subconscious reasons for being there. Since only a small proportion of that number of pilgrims would have any comprehensive knowledge of Hindu doctrines, it would seem that the main reason for their presence there was related to belief in astrology. Their satisfactions of being there at this auspicious date means that in relation to this and the religious factor of orthodox Hinduism this is a working misunderstanding.

There would have been Christians and Muslims and thousands taking advantage of the commercial opportunities in such an enormous gathering. Sellers of food and religious pictures, banks, journalists and tourists. Similarly the small group of Chinese who held their Bible classes in a branch of McDonald's fast food restaurant to avoid the attention of the police was a coming together of individuals with different motivations and personal returns on the effort and dangers involved.

Religious practices are usually thought of in collective terms because that is the easiest way to collect information on any human behaviour. We see and conclude from these primary and surface activities and the reality that a religious institution has to plan on what their believers actually do or are anticipated doing in entirely secular terms. The authorities at Lourdes are dominated by the secular needs of the anticipated one million pilgrims who can be expected to arrive each year. The Saudi-Arabian authorities have to make secular arrangements for sudden road overloads and accidents, lavatories, the disposal of enormous quantities of meat from sacrificed animals and the prevention of epidemic diseases. We can only guess at the reasons why Muslims from Beijing, Belfast and Banaras went last year on the Hajj except that the common factor is that the increase in numbers is related to the invention of aeroplanes and the use of oil; a diminishment of secularisation, not its increase.

Thus, there is a scale of religious involvements most of which cannot be observed and we are forced to rely on what individuals say about their inner thoughts and the extent that they participate in what their orthodoxies require; there is no reason to suppose that this will have any accuracy even if these men and women have a genuine intention to be accurate, the intellectual capacity and wish to express themselves on such private matters to strangers. Some studies have shown the persistent tendencies to over estimate the extent of their own private and private devotions. When these ideas and practices are put into writing there is even less hope of accuracy as most people have neither the vocabulary, the wish nor the intellectual capacity to report on themselves in these specialized ways.

It seems likely that the whirlwind of religious ideas is mostly within the head and this only connects into a small amount of actual behavioural activity which is likely to have been initiated by secular as much as religious events influencing individuals in many different ways. Then it is necessary to recognise that in time and motion terms religion takes up only a small proportion of the daily lives of even those who are committed full-time to religious life as an institutionalised vocation. It may be that individuals are prepared to spend a fixed amount of time in religious involvements so Christians becoming involved in ecumenical worship must mean a replacement of one form of worship by another or the less likely doubling of the time spent in worship.

In terms of the whole field of human behaviour only a small range of activities can be defined as being exclusively religious with only small secular elements. The taking of communion as part of the celebration of the Mass and blood sacrifices to the Hindu Goddess Kali at her Kolkota temple are exclusively religious activities. No one can suggest that these activities are not religious in intention even if participants may not know the orthodox reasons behind what they are doing and have been defined which only occurs in the so-called religions of the book.

In many other activities the religious element is in practical terms no more than a valuable and valued veneer. Hospitals run by Jewish or Roman Catholic foundations are probably to all intents and purposes functioning in similar professional and secular ways. Patients have the satisfaction of being among their co-believers and have rabbis and priests available to help them. It is only in such matters as terminal care and the possible treatment of the dead and defective foetuses that there may be differences to the practices of secular hospitals. Monasteries have designated members who run their secular affairs and other members have predominantly cooking and cleaning secular obligations.

It may be that Buddhist monks and Hindu *sadhus* come the closest to full-time religious involvements as far as can be observed as they are permanent mendicants who live by begging and who have little institutional support but even then we do not know what goes on in their heads. The monk is meditating or is that Buddhist monk thinking of what food will be given to him on his next morning's begging round and the Benedictine postulant who admitted to having learnt to sleep standing up during some night-time devotions. Sleeping in a religious environment may be considered more meritorious than sleeping in a bed as can be seen in some mosques and Ethiopian churches.

The Individualism of All Religious Practices

The primary impulses to religious thinking and practices has always been within the individual mind and that is not just a modern development created by the conditions of urban and industrial living. In fact it may be that this is likely to have been more dominant in the historical past. In the absence of widespread literacy and institutionalisation of religion every individual, family or community were in practice creating and doing their own 'religious' thing. We have already described the Sukuma ceremonies to propitiate troublesome ancestors are inevitably all different in every detail except the intention to propitiate.

Contemporary Western societies ostensibly base their political and secular philosophies on the value of the individual but in terms of religious options there may be far less overt individuality than exists for Hindu and Chinese subsistence farmers who are provided in their temples and popular religious art with innumerable visual alternatives to which they develop their own individual but culturally confined interpretations and uses.

The modern denominationalised Christian, Shia or Sunni Muslim are provided with restricted options. They do not have the range of options which are available as a matter of course to the quasi-traditionally minded Sukuma and Hindu. In order to follow such religious options which are not related to denominations of belief they would have to move into New Age systems of devotion or join a Sufi sect or get into serious social and religious difficulties by becoming an Ahmadiyya which orthodox Muslims do not even recognised as a valid faith. A modern Roman Catholic can ask for a Mass to be said for their special intentions which they do not have to specify but the liturgy is largely the same.

If there is any individuality in religious thinking which might distinguish various societies and the overt religious options available it will be inaccessible in the individual mind. It may be that theologians and social science researchers into religious thinking and covert and overt behaviour, overdo this assumption of cognitive rather than active similarities in investigating the individuality and identifying how it shows itself in any secular or religious activity. It is a time consuming and expensive as well as methodologically difficult exercise requiring great patience and the humanity to relate to a small number of individuals from whom they are socially distant.

The Reactive Nature of Religious Involvements

Religious practice is largely reactive in that a menu of options is provided by socialisation. There is no reason to suppose that modern men and women are faced with greater distress and disturbances than African, Americans, Asians and Europeans two centuries ago. There have always been natural disasters, devastating wars and destructive epidemics East Africa may still be suffering the effects of the Rinderpest epidemic of the 1890s which allowed the tsetse fly to spread just as it is now suffering from widespread AIDS. The recent tsunamis in Indonesia and Japan will only have been duplication of what must have happened many times in history. Modern men and women suffer just as much from economic fluctuations created by surpluses of copper and shortages of oil as well as the inevitable failures of scientific medicine.

Merton has suggested that individuals faced with change react in five different ways (Merton, 1957) and of course individuals may react in different ways to successive and different changes as they change themselves. The possibility of behavioural similarities may have some limited possibilities but psychological ones are far less likely even if such mental processes were readily accessible to evaluation. Very generally people react by conformity to what they have been habituated to doing and they choose from a religious menu of limited options. Tied to this is that globally people are conforming ritualists; orthopraxis is virtually universal with people in all large and small faiths, sects and cults feeling that they get direct benefits from the performance of overt and covert rituals for which they may have no theological or religious institutional support at all.

There are many who retreat into the avoidance reactions to the change which has affected them. The isolation of the Ethiopean hermit as well as those who take refuge in secular alcoholism and religious drugs, Then there are those who adapt creatively and manipulate the existing religious system for their personal needs by making up their own ways of religious thinking and practice as in the household shrines on Cuban refugees in Florida, Puerto Ricans in New York and the descendents of Yoruba ex-slaves in Brazil. Every person in their individual non-literate religious environment has always manipulated their own available symbols creatively even if their cultures have been inundated with mass media symbols. Finally, there are the revolutionaries of religious thinking of whom most become extinct as their ideas and practices do not catch because the charisma of the founder does not occur in their successors. All of these reactions to the situations in which people find themselves by the accidents of their personality and the environments in which they find themselves are individual responses. Overall those involved in religion get their needs fulfilled by overt conformity to socially or theologically authenticated rituals to which they attach their own interpretations.

These primary reactions which can only become grouped responses by the accidental cohesion of overt activities which have similarities from the definitions of the institutions providing these types of active fulfilment or by the social scientist excluding individual religious behaviours which are too difficult methodologically to handle or just not available for scrutiny.

So far we have only touched on overt religious practices which are reactions to what is affecting the individual and which only secondarily become grouped in the relative simplicities of collective action. What need in which we can almost conclude from the universality of religious activities that it is some part of the human constitution and a significant and effective contribution to the survival of the individual and the group.

Religious Needs and its Fluctuations

The practice of religious in its enormous variety seems to be a constant in its attractions but without any overarching parameters in how it is expressed. Indeed the complexity of the factors that initiate religious thinking and its materialisation is probably inaccessible to rational investigation and comprehensive conclusions and is likely to remain so. To implicate rationality into metaphysical issues which range beyond religion is probably a waste of intellectual effort on both sides of these insurmountable philosophical and theological barriers.

Once we exclude regular religious behaviour which are similar to all regular activities such as the Saudi shopkeeper who covers his goods prior to the midday prayers which is more than religious conformity since there are religious rather than secular police on duty to ensure conformity to the requirements of Wahabi orthodoxy, religious behaviour becomes more individualised. It seems likely that much if not most religious activity is related to immediate needs but there are nevertheless religious processes which are detached from these such as the spiritual exercises of St. Ignatius and the meditation manuals of Buddhism and Hinduism. These have all come onto the scene of religious experience comparatively recently and are not tied to any specific situations as they are not reactive but enabling provisions. They are there for humans to use and they are provided in the abstract for people to make of them what they will and to get from them what they need. No exact system of spirituality can provide for all the situations which believers are likely to encounter as they are abstract systems. They do not have the individualised reactive capacity which must surely have existed in the preceding non-literate millennia in all its cross-cultural variety.

The need for religious involvement whether it comes from the development of some psychological need or is the result of reacting to some external events, Maslow has provided a scale of needs providing a pyramid of increasingly sophisticated consequences (Maslow, 1970). At the lowest level there are survival needs, food, the safety, togetherness, individual development and at the highest level events such as the complicated religious and aesthetic accompaniments to a religious event such as the writings of the mystic Khalil Gibran, the symphonies of the Japanese composer Ochi or the American abstract painter Jackson Pollock.

The subsistence farmer on the edge of starvation from crop failure is unlikely to be involved in any religious rituals involving effort but his mind is likely to have religious thoughts. They may clutch the protective religious symbols which have been in use in their community for as long as they can remember. It is difficult to see that religious sensitivities within the mind can be related only to their physical expression. A serious need in a wife who has the physical and material means to express it externally may be no different in the extent to which she is mentally involved in religious thoughts about starving compatriots, Maslow's hierarchy of needs would appear to be a scale in which physical expression may be evaluated. Certainly wealth and spare time and a general absence of subsistence tensions allow the individual to express him or herself in a wider range of rituals than the impoverished. This is not a developmental process as an individual can reverse or progress as their environments change.

A more important consideration is that this scale implies not so much uniformity but persistence. In practice needs are likely to vary even perhaps over very short times as and when tragedy strikes the individual from an accident or there is a massive disaster such as the Haitian earthquake. The Indonesian tsunami soon led to the radical secular and religious reorganisation of the coastal Muslim communities affected which had resulted in a shortage of women who had been drowned as their husbands had been at sea when it happened and were unaffected and unaware of the disaster ashore.

At top end of this scale there is the factor of intellectual and social capacities and it may be that only a small number in any society may be able to react in this way. An individual with Down's Syndrome can become depressed at the realisation of their own incapacities and have religious needs which cannot be fitted into such a comprehensive universal scale.

We have little means of knowing the extent of individual religious needs and how they are expressed in the mind and it is only when these needs are externalised that we have some clues. In any event the vast majority of people are permanently clustered at the bottom of any such scale around the need for survival and safety. The remainder enter these categories when on their Asian holiday they experience a tsunami or when going to work they become involved in the terrorist destruction of the World Trade Centre in New York.

The Institutionalisation of Religion

Once worship takes on a public appearance tied to writing and timing in the organisation of personal life because it is provided by specialised personnel in special buildings, there is the split between public religion and private spirituality. Whether this institutionalisation has effects beyond the personnel directly involved depends on the surrounding society needs a complex evaluation which would involve every facet of social behaviour. Time keeping depends on the prevalence of clocks and being within the sound of bells or the muezzin calling to prayer which is now broadcast loudly and competitively from every minaret and thus loses the stimulation of audible isolation.

The fact that a religious process has become institutionalised does not necessarily mean that believers will keep to what this system requires. It may mean no more than a form of availability so that a reasonable harvest may lead to more religious ceremonies just as the previous year's shortages would have diminished them in a culture which would expect serious food shortages for one year in five. The economic success in Taiwan has led to increases in religious expenditure and activities. Institutionalisation makes orthodoxy a realistic possibility as it can produce what in secular life would be described as job specifications. Communities can know from this who is a 'good' Muslim or Roman Catholic because it has been defined by conformities to visible orthodoxies.

Whereas in quasi-traditional religious situations actions are taken when they are needed or when people remember to practice them so there is only a difference in scale between the rituals of family and neighbourhood, the range of misunderstandings are limited by the fact that much religious activity is imaginatively individualistic. A hundred Sukuma ancestor propitiation ceremonies would be analytically different as would spirit possession ones in Bali and the picture and flower arrangements of Hindu or Buddhist domestic shrines.

Once religious activity becomes institutionally controlled it creates a distinction between what has been regularised and what is not. In this distinction participants tend to over estimate the extent of their regularity and to forget the nature and extent of their private forms of spirituality. They may be reluctant to disclose as too trivial in comparison to what they know or at least suspect would be acceptable to orthodoxy. The non-regulars to a faith into which they have been socialised appear to retain a residual commitment whether as Christians, Hindus or Muslims rather than to actively disassociate themselves from what may have been at one time a more active commitment; they often keep to participation in rites of passage.

The geographical institutionalisation of religion in the form of the Christian parish, an adjunct to local government does not appear to be duplicated in other religions. Mosques and temples proliferate wherever individuals wish to build them and their survival depends on their use. Myanmar is littered with decaying pagodas which have served their constructors' need for accumulating merit and have not acquired any continuing public appeal. The parish provides opportunities for groups to be created with this locus which in other religions form their own locii. The parish can provide a range of potential services, liturgical, para-liturgical and social. Each parish creates engenders its own idiocentric cultures which are localized expressions of a broader meaning system that in turn becomes the source of new collective shared meanings (Baggett, 2001:42) In the United States the urban parish in the larger cities tend to cater for special needs almost by accident such as ones that appear to be sympathetic to 'gay' needs, Latin Americans and the Chinese with a side altar dedicated to the ancestors in general.

Archaeology provides ample evidence of the extent that religious activities in the past must have required institutionalisation, The temples at Karnak in Egypt and the European megalith sites at Carnac in Brittany and at Callenish in the Outer Hebrides require substantial institutional organisation and investment over long periods. We can presuppose that these were centres to which people came for their special needs and for major festivals. Their religious usefulness operated at several levels coincidentally. They were not systems of religious involvement which could be extended outwards to the invasive control of individual religious activities.

In contemporary practices Western Christianity has developed complex institutions overtaken by secular developments in which both are dependent on financial viability. Generally the faithful provide this financial support sufficient to maintain the religious personnel that they need but the maintenance of the physical plant is not so easily related to individual religious needs. The maintenance of religious institutions and specialised personnel requires substantial support on a semi-permanent basis or the diversion of plant and personnel to intermittent mixtures of part-time secular and religious involvements. To develop a need to worship indoors in specially created buildings put up to impress the Divine with their organised devotion rather than for large congregations imposes a burden on subsequent generations if they see it as a necessary obligation.

In sub-Saharan Africa the one-time missionary dioceses have gradually erected a substantial physical plant supported by overseas donations and personnel. The local financial support was and is now minute in comparison to the aim of those dioceses to be self-supporting. These dioceses have been taken over by local clergy as a by-product of nationalism no doubt with some pride that these buildings and projects are now 'ours'. However, the situation has not worked out as they may have planned as both financial support and shortages of missionary personnel from a general decline in vocations for the religious life, have scaled down their involvements. These churches as branches of an 'overseas' faith are inevitably wanting money to run the institutions which they have inherited rather than paying to the religious needs of the faithful. The situation is made worse in such Roman Catholic dioceses as Ulanga in Tanzania where these repetitive requests for money come from well-dressed and well-fed local clergy with cars (Green, 1995). The local subsistence farmers see this and its association with substantial buildings as evidence of hidden wealth which should be used for believers benefit. In this situation working misunderstandings exist in an environment in which orthopraxis dominates because the institutional Church has not created a system of reactive rituals (Green and Mesaki, 2005) leading to the increasing popularity of quasi-traditional rituals.

In these parishes there will be overt conformity to what the particular Church promulgates and a covert working misunderstanding through which these regulars feel at home because there is no open confrontation between what they covertly want from their participation and what their Church provides liturgically. A study of East African breakaway Churches (Welbourn, 1961) makes the point that a motivating factor was that these new Churches provided a place to feel at home. The conscious and unconscious needs of those involved were liturgically expressed through the innovations of a charismatic leader.

The American development of multiple churches and parish patterning with the positioning of clergy with particular aptitudes and sense of specialised commitment with no great stress on orthodoxy suits both regulars and those who use their religion mainly for rites of passage and for social services unavailable elsewhere such a computer learning group contained by a bounded prayer. They provide non-religious benefits just as the coming together for a propitiation ceremony does for the Sukuma.

If a religion provides in this way for a generality of alternative ideas and practices with a not too specific commitment to orthodoxy, it will retain its followers.

It is only in urban environments that there will be enough churches to allow for an element of choice. In rural areas a faith may find it easier to survive where there are dispersed and irregular opportunities for worship and no obligatory religious foci. The shortage of priests in Roman Catholicism was already the subject of worry for bishops in East Africa before World War I. The Bishop of Shinyanga once commented that wherever he built a church, there would be a thousand converts but there would not be the priests to service their needs except on an intermittent basis.

Islam has no priesthood and there are no orthodox objections to their being financially independent. Muslims can pray wherever they want such as public places on the pavements outside crowded mosques or in the first class cabin of an aircraft while it is on auto-pilot. Buddhists in Thailand have no such problems with the proliferation of shrines so that staff can pray in the early morning at the hotel's shrine. Faiths which are polytheistic in practice have few problems over religious foci.

The narrowing aspects of Western Christian institutionalisation obscures the fact that contemporary societies provide individuals with a wide range of alternatives to orthodoxies if not geographically near with the intermittent unavailability of transport, then through the electronic media. There are thousands of so-called independent Churches in southern Africa and enormous numbers of quasi-religious alternatives are available just round the corner in Delhi, Moscow and Tokyo. This is not too different to the quasi-traditional situation in tribal societies where those in difficulties have always been able to find religiously motivated help within walking distance; there may be scepticism but it is muted by immediate needs and the potential availability of people providing possible solutions. All modern cities have large numbers of healers who combine elements of the surrounding religious thinking and practice with commercial and social opportunities for these people to attempt the resolution of problems for which national governments do not have the personnel or revenue to provide.

A Church that has become heavily institutionalised does not have this adaptive capacity and has to depend on the attractiveness of its liturgical ambiguities. The need to recognise that the existence of 'Sheilaisms'(Bellah *et al.*, 1985), individual systems of belief rather than conformist practice is not something new but the universal pattern which preceded the regularities imposed by institutionalisation and literacy which could be seen historically as a form of deviance from normality.

The predominant uses of religion have always been demand centred which we can see in the successful survival of Eastern religions and it is not as if these have deliberately marketed themselves this way but have responded to observable needs as in Buddhist and Shinto temples providing profitability in both religious and commercial spheres by providing for the needs of the Japanese elderly increasingly isolated by the small size of their families and for the priest caretakers who have to provide for their own survival and the maintenance of each shrine. The priests at many Japanese temples survive by what they can sell as much as by donations related to their religious ceremonials.

However, the development of institutionalisation which seems to have been an economic and administrative burden to contemporary Christianity does not seem to be inevitable when religiously motivated individuals are market oriented in much the same way that super-markets have to be who would avoid telling their clients what they should buy. We have pointed out the contrasts in Tallinn, Estonia on a weekday which was not a religious festival the Roman Catholic cathedral was more or less empty except for a table with details about donations whereas the Orthodox cathedral was full of people kissing an icon and being blessed by a seated priest with whom there appeared to be no verbal communication at all and seemingly an example of orthopraxis. Heathrow, London airport, has two resident chaplains with the Protestant one working from an office with involvement on committees, usually in secular dress and low attendance at weekly services. The Roman Catholic one has no office and wanders about in clerical dress advertising his role with direct availability through his mobile phone and good attendance at Sunday Mass from airport staff rather than passengers (Tanner, 1974). The only institutional commitment of this airport chaplain was to fix the times of Mass on notice boards. In these cases whether by accident or design the 'successful' priests have responded the occasional nature of religious need such as hearing confessions in a canteen and giving blessings to those who just happen to come off the street.

The availability of Eastern religious seems to come predominantly from the idea that the God(s) are there in the temples and in the case of Japanese are made aware of petitioners as they are alerted by ringing the temple bell or striking its drum. In the case of Hinduism with its concept of *darshan* the ritually empowered statues actually see those who petition them who get benefits without requiring priests to be present.

It is not the case that Eastern theologians have directed Hinduism, Taoism and Shintoism in particular directions which have resulted in the sustained popularity of these faiths. The principal element in these faiths is the absence of definitions and the lack of authoritative institutional centralisation which has allowed individual believers and believing communities to develop their own systems of belief and practice.

Hinduism operates on two theological levels in even the smallest of villages and in individual households. A level based on documents written in Sanskrit and dominated by Brahmin priests and an alternative rather than a lower level with priests who are not Brahmin and operate independently of Sanskritic texts. These two systems are permanently intermingled and whether one is or is not superior to the other is a matter of coincidental viewpoints (Babb, 1970).

The Illusion of Regularity in Religious Behaviour

Contemporary men and women at least in Western societies tend to think that they are more in control of their own behaviour than what actually happens which is habituated perhaps but not regular. This illusion comes from time keeping and conforming to this supposed regularity does not extend to a wide range of spiritual behaviour.

Without clocks or a social system that enforces conformity religious ceremonies start when enough people turn up to validate its performance and when there is cloud cover everything will start later. Insects possibly but the higher primates are only regular in vague terms.

Most people will carry out religious rituals if they feel that there is social and religious return from such performances in relation to the effort involved. Eastern theologies hold that there is merit in these performances and this accumulates with repetition. However, this is discouraged by contemporary Christian theologians despite the fact that orthopraxis is probably as common among all varieties of Christians as it is currently among Buddhists, Hindus and Muslims and has always been the background to traditional religious practices. In terms of Christian theology it is not what orthodoxy hopes to be encouraging but it is universally a working misunderstanding. The performance of the rituals is an end in itself.

It seems regularity may be largely the creation of observers who wish to see in religious behaviour refractions of ideal systems and social scientists who do not have the time or the methodology to cope with such varied activities related to individuals and constantly changing social environments. Individuals may aim at regularity in their religious involvements but that will always depend on factors over which they have limited control such as their health and the ease with which a ritual can be carried out as a personal ritual or one that depends on others such as the presence of a priest. Regularity in any phenomenological sense in religious practice as in any other activity remains a supportive hope rather than an existential reality in any meaningful sense.

The Growth of Religious Institutionalisation

Prior to widespread literacy and a cultural impulse to extend the necessary economic and political systems to religion, religious needs have either been necessities responding to personal anxieties or general occasions celebrating events in which in reality the religious element is not exactly dominant. Some churches in Crete are unused for most of the year but which have annual feasts dedicated to that saint attracting hundreds from the rubbish left behind. In contemporary China the annual festival in honour of the Black Dragon King and his temple attracts thousands with its food and goods stalls and an opera performance combined with a visit to the temple largely taken up by queuing to get in for a cursory bow to the statues and a donation to keep the good nature of the God(s) on their side. At whatever level we look at such occasions they can be seen to work as everyone seems to be having a satisfying time. In what senses is there any understanding of what is going on beyond the obvious pleásure that people have in being thereunder the nominal heading of a temple festival. It is certainly a very active misunderstanding of Taoist theology.

Historically Christianity with its premise of loving others has always stepped in to provide social services for which there were no other provisions. Commentators on the plague in Alexandria in

AD 263 remarked on the altruism of Christians looking after victims to whom they were not related and this has continued down history in specialised institutions. Care of the dying has been a religious obligation for some time but the hospices in Britain are now largely secular perhaps because there is no longer enough people with religious vocations for this kind of exacti ng work. However, Mother Teresa, a teacher of history to middle class girls in Kolkata, distressed by the neglect of the dying in India, started a new religious order with this objective which now has several thousand Indian nuns with international commitments. India certainly has a long tradition of self-abnegation for personal ends in *sadhus* which in this case has been diverted to contemporary social distress.

With the growth of secular education as a necessity for social and professional advancement there was a growth of a movement for more special Islamic schools 'darasas'. In Pakistan there has been a significant growth in their numbers but as the public educational system has progressively failed to provide an efficient nationwide service, these 'darasas' have started to teach secular subjects which have nothing to do with Islam as both a commercial opportunity and as a response to public need and for those who have the means to pay. Should the public secular system become efficient then they might return to their specifically religious role.

In sub-Saharan African so-called missionary hospitals are felt to be less corrupt that the public service ones but providing a medical facility is a lot more expensive to provide help than providing a minimalist educational one and regular religious ceremonies. Without substantial external support they are finding that having the religious motivation to help others is not enough and they need substantial material help that cannot be provided locally.

It seems to have been the case that that religious institutions have held on too long to institutions which are in any practical sense secular; why should religious personnel be involved in teaching secular subjects or nursing in hospitals where their work practices are laid down and controlled by secular authorities. Moreover, they have taken on modern obligations which are tied to financial backing and to the availability of specialised long-term personnel.

The Eastern religions do not seem to have involved themselves in activities which became legally secular. Contemporary secular wealth in Buddhism and Hinduism seems to have gone to furthering individual merit and thus to have little impact on the surrounding societies except in the using up of resources such as the running of special institutions for preserving the lives of unwanted cattle which uses up scarce grain supplies in the drier regions of India.

The Security of Conforming Idealism

Most people live within their own circle of ideas of which part are individualised conformities to partially misunderstood external ideal systems. It seems likely that most contemporary religious behaviour is thought to be conformist if only because being too behaviourally individualistic is an isolating process. Not too much thought goes into religious behaviour in any society and individualism is shown in varieties in which the elements of performance are put together and in what people hope to get out of what they do. If we look at the amulets worn by those involved in quasi-traditional practices we see that they are all different and thus very personal. However, when we look at the amulets sold in Thai Buddhist temples there are limited choices and even fewer in Roman Catholic shops attached to their larger churches. It would seem that contemporary believers are pushed into a manufactured conformity in how they can express their individual beliefs materially.

In what might be called the non-literate areas of religious practices conformity to the generalities of cultural orthodoxies is likely to be high and few East Africans would deny the existence of witchcraft with its ability to transmit evil effectively. What they do in furtherance of their beliefs can be individualised such as the use of Coca Cola bottle tops in divination rather than local bits and pieces and in what the local diviner and herbalist puts into the medicines they are prescribed and how they interpret the patterns when they are thrown down.

In how this seemingly disorganised system works when each practitioner and patient has no culturally enforced connections with anyone else, there is a working understanding of its effectiveness. In Taiwan the island's premier Goddess Ma Tsu to whose shrines a very large number of Chinese make annual pilgrimages, reasoning quite logically that if prayers to her for help were not answered, then she would not be the subject of such mass devotion. The fact that this is a tautological argument is irrelevant in a society in which economic success has proportionately increased time and motion expenditure on religion.

In this area of quasi-traditional beliefs and practices, these men and women practitioners provide a service in areas not covered by any social welfare systems. Just as medical private practice flourishes because it is both personal and readily available, so at the other end of the scale subsistence farmers and urban workers find these quasi-traditional healers much more satisfactory to consult than any social service facility in which they are not treated as persons. They live nearby, they are available at times more convenient for those that consult them and they treat their patients as active participants in solutions to their difficulties. More importantly there is some culturally shared understandings; these practitioners believe or at least accept that ghosts and malevolent ancestors exist. Psychologists trained in Western understandings rarely share what may be the religious beliefs and cultural practices of those that consult them. Their long professional training has alienated them from much of their cultural sympathies for those who consult them. An Indian psychiatrist and a Taiwanese doctor spend not much more than a few minutes with each patient. The quasi-traditional healer has no such rush and indeed it is not in his or her interests to do so.

As religions become more institutionalised and dogmatic individualism become more restricted in how it can materially express their beliefs and difficulties they still have the pre-existing ability to read into rituals their personal needs. This seems to have resulted not so much as orthopraxis which has always been the main theme in traditional understandings but orthopraxis for a much more restricted range of provided rituals. This comforting conformity provided by legitimated practices is more confined to the religions of the book and proportionately absent in Eastern religious systems.

The Comforts of Religious Conformity

It does seem that the Eastern religions in their contemporary practices have no more than conformities to the broadest of religious understandings such as *karma* and rebirth. Beyond this there are endless social as much religious variations which often makes it difficult to sustain the nomenclature of Hindu for individuals and their practices. Literacy has not had any noticeable effect on the generalities of religious behaviour except perhaps as visual decoration in popular art. If religion there provides personal comfort it is more from their enormous range of visibly obvious non-conformities within the context of merit, rebirth and ritual performance.

Religions of the book are much more restricted in their religious activities. Both Islam and Judaism have restrictions on what can be materially expressed and Christianity provides little scope for personalised inventiveness. It may be that most people unless living in exclusive communities in which there is little if any distinction between the secular and religious as with the Amish, would find orthodoxy somewhat emotionally arid and which is compensated by the creation of personalised complexities in their own rituals. A small Christian group in northern England has a meeting room which has been sanctified by the spiritual manifestation of St. Paul according to a plaque on the wall. Its book of prayer requests for their mid-weekly meetings is noticeably connected to the welfare of pets.

In the religions of the book personal security may come from restricted but not too difficult conformities to the Five Pillars of the Faith which are a feature of Islam's particular attraction. The station staff at Wembley near London which has few stopping trains can pray in Arabic on the platforms which are aligned to Mecca without obligatory work interruptions. Governments which are worried over fundamentalist interpretations of the *Koran* may reinterpret religious doctrines for their secular usefulness. The Egyptian Government sees in Islamic regularities for prayer and the required preliminary washing valuable lessons for civil discipline and public health.

Roman Catholicism with its concentration on the one centralising ritual, the celebration of the Mass, is an obvious parallel when globally the liturgy was said in Latin. This is less so now with the use of vernaculars but most believers will have heard this same ritual thousands of times. Their participation is perhaps cognitively and intellectually automatic, leaving the mind free to involve itself in whatever thoughts it wishes.

In these conformities there are definitions attached to the obligations of performance but their success comes from the ways that modern people just as those in medieval Europe and contemporary Arabia get their comforts from this absence of overt meaning into which each person can insert their personal needs; the comfort from reciprocal silence.

Conformity to an accepted orthodoxy should rarely be accepted as the position of those who do not have the intellectual capacity to seek out solutions to their difficulties through personal reasoning. Modern religious participation as it has always been in every culture historically, remains an individual experience; the bunching together of these individual experiences in large scale categories imposed by researchers are demeaning to this reality and are the creation of the intellectual elite who have distance themselves from these emotional personal needs (Spickard, 2002).

Most people lead disturbed lives with individually different anxieties not only because of the demographic fact of ageing but because all personal relationships are irregular affairs in which smooth running is inevitably uncommon. Thus, they would be inclined to seek stability in religious participations provided by acceptably authenticated religious authorities, their own ritual creativity as well as new opportunities as in the expansion of pilgrimages where in the degree of conformity which they define for themselves, provides psychological stability.

At whatever eschatological level dictated by the parameters of their faiths, conformity provides not only self-assessed and experienced stability but progress towards the reduction of their difficulties. Most of those who are practising a recognised religion believe that they are conforming and that what they are thinking is theologically valid. Conditionality is not something that people would seek from their religious practices as they would see in its uncertainties the replication of the pragmatic uncertainties of their existing lives.

Much might depend on the degree that the individual is incorporated into the sub-groups of a society rather than into the macro-society itself. Most people find it difficult not to participate in the regularities of what is going on around them but conformity need not have an either or binary quality. Most people are quite able to believe in contradictory propositions provided that their coincidence does not involve overt choice. The Cheeta-Merats of Rajasthan (India) have both Hindu and Muslim names and functionally would appear to belong to both faiths at the same time so that their marriages would not have the categorization of being inter-faith; an ecumenism of necessity. In the 1911 census some 200,000 declared themselves as Mohammadan-Hindu (Nandy, 1990:45). Many shrines in India have both Hindu and Muslim devotees and in villages there would be mutual participation in the festivals of local divinities. Not to conform in a village festival in Vietnam would be making a political issue out of something which need not be interpreted as having any religious exclusivities. One may document a householder helping hungry ghosts by leaving food on the doorstep but these spirits are everywhere and these people do not know what might be their reaction from neglect.

How does one conform or not conform to Buddhism when the rules really apply only to monks who have made the first necessary step to the dissolution of self. The laity have developed their own systems of ritually coping with their immediate difficulties and who would tell them that these activities are not Buddhist since the local monks have no supervisory role. It would appear that in the Eastern religions there is nothing normatively orthodox to which believers in the mass could conform. Whatever inclusive qualities there are in sub-group memberships are likely to be predominantly social rather more than the religious thinking.

It may be that modern man and woman just as their ancestors and the generality of subsistence farmers and the seasonally employed move in and out of their religious involvements on a demand basis and in this there can be only the vaguest conformist trends. Conformity in any persistence sense may be both the creativity of the social science categorisations and the preoccupation of those who have time to spare within the time specifications of industrial life. Roman Catholic attendances at Mass which fitted into a single shift factory system dropped dramatically when this changed to a continuous three shift one, just as cattle keeping in Chad makes day-time conformity to Islamic rules reasonable but not for the night time care of cattle.

Some of the underlying issues in the possibility of conformism are shown in the semantic changes from the use of 'we' as in stating that someone is 'our' wife or these are 'our' fields, common enough in traditional societies to 'I', this is 'my' husband and this is 'my' car in more modern social environments. Nevertheless the fact that opportunities for regularity have always been available if not so obvious with the absence of time keeping and persisting institutions. The Manus islanders when they decided to go 'modern' ran their new villages according to mechanical not social timing by the ringing of a bell for the start and ending of the working day.

As far as can be assessed conformity has always been as it is now as much social as religious and predominantly within the individual mind. There is probably an ongoing individual process of conformism to what is considered appropriate at any particular time and in any social environment in which each person will be regarded their participation holistically. There is a subliminal adjustment to personally experienced change which believers may think is conformity to a particular set of beliefs and practices which itself has been constantly changing as in the prevalence and acceptability of glossolalia which can be interpreted to conform to any social situation.

Glossolalia: Talking in Tongues

Spirit possession is common enough in many rural societies as it occurs in the open and social scientists are attracted to behaviour which is bizarre by their standards. It certainly occurs in most urban societies whether in Japanese and American cities and is a frequent feature of Protestant fundamentalism.

Those who become possessed whether by the Holy Spirit, by a disapproving ancestor or by an angry ghost, speak sounds rather than words which have no immediate meaning. These sounds which do not have any semantic or syntactic structure except for the theological motivations which have been attributed to what is classified as speaking in tongues. It appears to be not much different to the babblings of children and these sounds have received substantial analytical attention from social scientists. Their conclusions are that these sounds have no identifiable meanings that could class them as part of linguistic communication but they are composed of the phonemes from the natal languages of these speakers (Francis and Robbins, 2003; Goodman, 1972; Hine, 1964; and Samarin, 1972).

These sounds are not from the languages of any other society and come from the minds and mouths of the speakers and cannot, therefore, be part of any explicit social communication between speakers and listeners but they may be interpreted by religiously committed third parties. These somewhat bleak conclusions come from studies which are mainly based on its Christian forms and have tended to see such manifestations in psychoanalytical and, therefore, secular terms. It must have a wide variety of functions.

If speaking in tongues and that is a particularly Christian descriptive phrase, is a rare activity in Western religious ceremonies then it would be reasonable to see it as a purely personal aberration from what the majority consider to be religious normality. It would appear to be too widespread and numerous to reach conclusions based on individual psychology alone. It also occurs in secular situations such as young people reacting to the performances of pop stars, the productions of abstract art, free-form poetry, writings such as James Joyce's novel *Finnegan's Wake* and indeed music are all acceptable culturally as having functions rather than meanings. Their origins are just as inexplicable as the external signs of spirit possession. This would suggest that it may be a combination of social and religious factors working together in particular public religious environments which existentially has been seen to be socially useful.

It occurs in the Christian New Testament, Acts 2:4-11 and Saint Paul letter to the I Corinthians:12-14 appears to accept it as an incoming of the Holy Spirit while seemingly restricting its occurrence to the

Apostles. The Roman Catholic Church views its occurrence with caution without necessarily prejudicing its possible genuine religious possibilities (Hellwig, 1994. 34:6-7).

Beyond these conclusions it should be assessed in relation to two further aspects. The social and functional distance between speakers and hearers and that in terms of frequency it occurs almost universally in non-Christian religious contexts. There are few social scientists researching religious activities outside the Western world who have not seen spirit possession and glossolalia in many different forms in a variety of societies. The writer has seen it occurring in Ssonjo, Sukuma, Kikuyu and Swahili contexts in Tanzania and Kenya.

We do not know whether people practise glossolalia in private and apart from the weakness of data produced by people describing their own religious activities, it seems unlikely that anyone would speak aloud to the Spirit world in an empty room although American Indians might speak aloud in the solitude of a sacred mountain top.

So we are assessing sounds which are produced when there is an audience as the publicizing of some personal need. If this is the case it is a behavioural inter-relationship; he or she wants and expects to be heard, but even in this there are likely to be a variety of audience. In some cases speaking in tongues could be seen as the accepted way of illustrating commitment to a Pentecostal worshipping group. The student from a Kenyan Independent Christian Church in a cross-denominational Protestant seminary who in the regular morning service started to talk in tongues whenever the Our Father prayer was recited, was in a more or less tolerant environment for a denominational outsider from which the only reaction from the congregation was a single suppressed giggle.

Its occurrence need not be the result of the speaker being in personally or environmentally induced trance because of music, incense or lack of oxygen. It seems more likely to be responses to socio-religious expectations in particular situations. In the generality of such behaviour, the sounds are produced not just as an end in themselves and are self-explanatory to the speaker. For the listeners it provides the opportunity for interpretation and self-satisfaction as might be the case for listening to music which has no predetermined social correlations.

Even though in the Christian context and in some African ones talking in tongues appears to be a predominantly female activity, averages in any behavioural context are unwise. While this is often attributable to mental shortcomings, there is little evidence that this is so. It appears more to be a personal expression of their individual religious feelings in much the same way that people are overcome by emotion from music, the performance of plays and the reading of poetry as well as in the creations of abstract art.

It is difficult for theologians within the pragmatics of Western thinking to accept spirit possession and the social groupings within which it occurs as a reality which it certainly is to those involved. In Christian literature there are numerous examples of men and women who have reached states of religious ecstasy which have been accepted as divinely inspired. The Christian churches are perhaps not just cautious but right in withholding judgement as to their authenticity but the principles by which to evaluate the genuineness of Christian mysticism has a long history (Scaramelli, 1754).

Religious phenomena in any cross-cultural sense are on a sliding scale from the enlightenment of the Buddha, the reception of Allah's teachings by the Prophet Muhammad and the mystical ecstasies of such Christian saints as Saint Francis of Assisi and Saint Catherine of Sienna. At the other end of this scale are the obvious cases of psychiatric disturbance such as the three mental patients at Ypsilanti who all considered themselves to be personifications of Christ (Rokeach, 1964).

Eastern religions with indistinct but pervasive concepts of spirituality there are fewer reasons for disallowing the general possibility of spiritual forces crossing the dividing line into the behavioural world of which they have always been an acceptable part as in the experienced realities of hungry ghosts and ancestor intervention. Since Eastern theologians have been reluctant to reach any definitive conclusions as to the elusive nature of reality in Buddhist and Hindu thinking, it is certainly a working element in global religious behaviour. In the absence of its exclusion from what orthodoxies there are it seems reasonable to describe the generally accepted spirit possession as possible misunderstandings within some orthodoxies.

The Changing of the Parameters but not the Paradigms of Faith

Any individual is not only the centre of their own thinking but usually assumes that they have some consistency and indeed are likely to be surprised at the frequency of changes in their thoughts which have been written in their diaries. Nearly a century ago an American advertising agency wrote that the public were just not aware of how quickly they made up their minds to change their minds (Calkins and Holden, 1927), There is no reason to suppose that pre-industrial people would have been any less ready to change their religious ideas and practices of which they have no more than the memories of their old people to assume and ensure consistency. The elusive nature of Eastern religion such as Hinduism in which the nature of gods and goddesses change with the circumstances in which they are involved, mirrors the changeableness of the human retention of specific religious ideas. Change in how individuals see matters which are not tied to pragmatic facts, is a constant feature of personal religious understandings and behaviour.

It seems likely that in both Vietnam and Virginia there are beliefs in active ghosts and God. There is also the need in China and Japan to feel that their ancestors are part of their current lives but how they relate to these enduring concepts is immensely varied and varying. The Chinese have retained the concepts of 'yin' and 'yang' but in comparison to the pre-Communist period and the succeeding period of atheist persecution, they have created new localised less obtrusive systems of great popularity. The state only reacts when a new system overarching the popularity of communalism such as the Falun Gong appears to have the capacity to challenge the state's assumed monopoly to control the expression of thought. It is difficult to hold onto any concept of misunderstanding when what is alleged to have been understood is not only ill-defined but subject to as many changes as individual interpretations.

The Continuing Use of the Unintelligible

A basic factor in religious ideas and behaviour is the permanent background of unintelligibility. The prime factor for Hindus as much as for Christians is faith in the supernatural which can be explained but not proved. An enormous amount of intellectual perhaps rather more than experiential effort has gone to the theological justifications of belief. There is little doubt that what has been written in this context is beyond the understandings of almost all believers in the faiths about which they have been written. Most are aware that such elaborations and explanations of their faiths exist, but they do not see any need to know more about their beliefs when orthopraxis fulfils most of their religious needs. Thus, individuals and communities with this distant but authoritative backing, develop their own ways of coping with their religious needs within the boundaries of what to them are unintelligible parameters. Hindus spend much time and effort in covertly circumventing these distant ideological restrictions. This is not a conclusion which denigrates the religious understandings of anyone, however, their perceptions are assessed. No one uses weed killer in a field in which it is growing satisfactorily and no one would use orthopraxis unless they are reasonably certain that it would be useful in terms of the effort and material involved.

If there is a religious hierarchy as in Hinduism in which greater social and religious privileges go by birth to the higher grades there has been a long standing system of inching up the sub-caste grades by the hypergamous provision of dowries, buying husbands for daughters of a higher sub-caste than her family, so that the children would belong to the higher sub-caste of their father. This is indeed a long-term and expensive process when many families are impoverished anyway by the expenses of providing a status enhancing marriage rituals. Only families benefit and this is always circumscribed by the jealousy of others.

Some groups have created two processes getting way round these blocks to the aspirations of individuals and sub-castes to rise in their own and other people's estimations. Firstly, away from their own village or neighbourhood temple the ceremonies are conducted by a Brahmin in Sanskrit for a negotiated fee which gets round the difficulty of conducting their own status enhancing rituals. Thus, by migration to cities and by emigration to another society they have freed themselves from some of their religious restrictions and create opportunities new ones.

Then most Hindus go on pilgrimages away from their homes and indeed India is criss-crossed by this religious traffic made possibly in the first instance by the network of railways (Bhardwaj, 1973). At these centres ceremonies are again performed by Brahmins in Sanskrit and these occasions have provided opportunities for the spread of Sankritic ideas and beliefs (Srinivas, 1967:74). In much the same way the Legio Maria, a rare breakaway Roman Catholic Church in Kenya uses Latin in their ceremonies as it had once been the sacred language of global Catholicism as many there had disliked the celebration of their rituals in understandable local languages which lacked this sacred quality.

The second process has been for a group to take on certain ritual practices associated with higher sub-castes. The gradual reshaping of local beliefs and practices in the direction of Brahmanical ideals using Sanskrit formulas in their rituals (Veer, 1994:166). The *mantras* which are taken into the rituals of these groups are phonetically correct and thus audibly carry with their performance the reality of divine power (Bakker, 1986:72); yet another example of orthopraxis.

This learning of Sanskritic sounds can be no more than the use of simple phrases and to go further than this is beyond the capabilities of most people wanting to climb the sub-caste ladder of religious preferment.

A socially easier way to gain status is to take on some of the attributes of higher caste ways of behaving such as greater stress on vegetarianism. So in these socio-religious practices of circumvention, it would seem that believers feel that they are conforming to what their faiths require without paying too much attention to what it is; it is an example of working misunderstanding.

The Continuing Value of Sacralised Objects

Religious practice revolves round the use of objects and their manipulation. The latter may not always be available, unsympathetic to use as well as being too emotionally detached and expensive to maintain and use. Believers want a personal inter-relationship which is not too difficult to use and is immediately available for their needs.

A theme running through contemporary Western Christianity as shown in the major denominations is the development on the one hand of a required intellectual understanding and explanations of faith so that to follow what is required of believers is going to require a substantial amount of literate determination among the minority who may have the time and the ability to do this; an elite preoccupation. The Eastern religions have no such requirements and leave it very much to the individual as to whether they attempt further and deeper understandings of their faith through the serious handicapping of specialised literacy.

This has been combined with the rise of the involvement of the laity to direct the clergy and then to take over clerical roles as the clergy diminish in numbers or fail to continue their institutionalised charismatic roles to some extent hiding from their professional commitments by wearing lay costume. These men and women may not be representative of the generality of those who want an emotional return from the practising of their faith.

So it would seem that many Western churches have become both institutionalised and intellectualised into a form of elitism not all that different from the structures of most voluntary organisations which are minority rather than popular ones. This has taken the necessary ambiguity out of these religious practices and replaced it with forms of confrontation. This has also occurred in Hinduism with the dominance of Brahmins, a superior caste with elastic functions, some of whom are full-time priests while others are full-time cooks which allow people of all castes to eat in these restaurants without dangers of religious pollution.

One alternative is the use of objects which in Hinduism involves the concept of power *darshan* from seeing and being seen by something or someone which or who is considered to have some spiritual power. This Eastern concept of *darshan* would seem to apply to some extent to Christian and other religions objects of devotion, such as religious pictures, rosaries, amulets, statues and icons.

In orthodox Christianity there is the continuing popular need to relate to icons in their liturgy and particularly so with ones that have charismatic value. Recently in St. Petersburg there was a short visit of a such an icon from America and on its last day in the cathedral late in the evening the queue three deep was perhaps half a mile long. In India the proliferation of cheap highly coloured Hindu religious pictures is the extension of the Hindu concept of *darshan* in which not only does the believer have a religious benefit acquired from seeing the picture or other religious object but the object actively sees back to the viewing believer.

While Christians refer to the 'Holy' *Bible* there is little actual reverence for the actual words of God in an actual book except for the Roman Catholic priest's kissing it during the celebration of the Mass. The Muslim actively reverences the *Koran* as the Words of God even in is mass-printed editions. It is often kept in an embroidered cover and other objects would not be placed on it.

Western churches have been progressively emptied of religious decorations which testified to the personal devotions of believers but this is not so in Orthodox churches where icons are surrounded with silver tokens as testimony to the ways that it has been efficacious. A Western observer would describe most Latin American churches as filled with almost irrelevant religious clutter.

There has often been a rise in popular devotions as in Dutch Roman Catholic churches with ancillary shrines which are alive with a mass of burning candles. In Dutch Brabant where monastic ceremonies have held their popularity which has dropped elsewhere (Bax, 1985), particularly in relation to Saint Gerlach, a little known saint of no great ecclesiastical importance if indeed he ever existed. The monks have connected the generality of personal needs to his veneration and his shrine as a place of pilgrimage to which they have added the blessing of vehicles to their pastoral obligations. In New York there has been the filling of car radiators with sacralised water from a water hydrant which has become connected to the Virgin Mary and in Japan a manufacturing firm has an annual blessing of its vehicles and of a department in which there was a greater possibility of accidents.

It is easy enough to take the intellectualist and dismissive approach to this form of practical and personal devotion but if these devotees can be seen as consumers in a market place filled with anxieties for which rationality can provide little successful relief. The shrine with personally lit and placed candles has a cumulative and responsive appeal which relates back to the petitioners. Many religious objects are portable and thus provide persistent support. Few are not affected emotionally by music and yet there is nothing there but ephemeral sound.

The Touching of Sacred Places

Historically in all cultures there has been the visiting of sacred places by enormous numbers of people over long periods of time. A mediaeval pilgrimage site in Wales in which pilgrims knelt before a natural feature in the rock has the kneeling place granite worn away by these devotees. Many have walked to Mecca sometimes taking years to get there as they earned the resources to go on and suffered known privations and dangers in the process. In this there may be little difference between authentic places associated with a venerated figure and at Medugorje in which the connection with a sacred apparition is disputable and the debatable sacredness of Ayodha for Hindus as the reputed birthplace of Rama, an entirely mythical God. Other places such as the Christian pilgrimage centres of Compostela and Assisi have retained their sacredness from medieval to modern times.

Although we tend to see pilgrimage sites as religious centres because that is their social designation they have certainly in the past served other secular purposes; Mecca was a trading centre and market associated with a religious cult before it became the centre of Islam, the 'navel of the world'. For the pilgrimage month there will have been an invasion of people with secular reasons for being there, police, hospital staff, drivers and the providers of livestock for the obligatory sacrifices in an inhospitable place of volcanic rock and sand. Lourdes has grown from an insignificant village to a town in which the provision of accommodation for an annual intake of a million pilgrims is a major industry and the town authorities will be doing all they can to increase the drawing power of its religious meaning; the feet of believers touch this sacredness.

In all societies there will have been the growth of travel agencies to assist pilgrims and in India the provision of special buses to take Hindu corpses for cremation at Banaras and in Europe ambulance buses to take the sick to Lourdes. The growth in Japan of companies providing temple tours for the increasingly isolated elderly combination religious needs and companionship.

Other pilgrimage sites have developed political and religious power in tandem. The Ma Tsu veneration in Taiwan has made her cult into a national focus so that a high proportion of the adult population visit her shrines annually. The shrine of Our Lady of Guadalupe in Mexico city has the characteristics of a national devotional figure. Katagarama is a increasing focus for annual Buddhist pilgrimages in Sri Lanka with its processions of gaily decorated vehicles. While we tend to denigrate religious tourism such as those to Assissi and indeed by animal lovers to the shrine of their patron saint, Taiwan has always had island wide tours combining temple visiting with shopping opportunities.

It would seem that people have always had a tendency to sacralize places which have taken on a tinge of sacredness and which have grown into major sites for as multiplicity of reasons. In Pangani, Tanzania small rock outcrops have been treated as the tombs of Muslim saints, and piles of stones on Himalayan passes for the mountain spirits which is just the use of sacralised by passers by. On a scale of involvements there are the pilgrims approaching Guadalupe, the Mexican national shrine on their knees, climbing Croagh Patrick, the sacred mountain of Ireland in bare feet and the circumambulation by Tibetans by caterpillar like movements around temples and sacred mountains.

The point must be that the going on pilgrimages in all religions has not faded with or without economic success or education but has increased both in the numbers involved and in the number of places which have become the centre of such visiting devotion so it cannot be accounted for solely by the ease of religious tourism. Pilgrimages further illustrate the inevitable combination of secular factors in all contemporary religious activities just as much as it did in the past.

From whatever perspective taken in considering contemporary social life, religion has not faded away as was so confidently anticipated by social scientists. The form has changed in every society as has its political, social and economic significance ranging from religious terrorism to increased expenditure on religious activities and the religious uses of cyberspace. Its basis has always been individually creative and to some extent its group manifestations are collectively observable but still individually utilised and interpreted.

At the back of this persistence there is the enduring fact that science and pragmatism may diminish certain difficulties and anxieties but they still persist and have replaced by others just as distressing such as the prolongation of old age. Religion provides emotionally and in practical terms portable answers or reductions to the persistent uncertainties in the lives of every individual (Tanner, 2009). In this context its ability to adjust or be adjusted to human needs and issues, it certainly works for the benefit of mankind no matter how tautological these explanations may be. As to whether this is a misunderstanding would seem to depend on who is making such evaluations. Those who do so are either theologically elitist or social science agnostics who are both perhaps professionally detached from the realities of individual life for which religion continues to be of persistent practical need or are philosophically committed to a system of thinking that is far from neutral.

15

The Nature of Working Misunderstandings in Religious Practice

The social sciences and theology share a basic characteristic that their thinking and the data on which this is based is one of inference. The social scientists cannot see roles, lineages and societies but they infer that they exist just as the theologian can see spirit possession but they have to infer what has been the cause of this and all the behaviour which they class as religious and irreligious. Religious persons and those that act religiously infer from their socialisation and personal experience that their rituals are reciprocated. In crude terms they act on silence which they infer is reciprocated. What those believe is a reality supported by inference.

Explanation and theory may be connected but not necessarily in the minds of the people about whose behaviour such thinking occurs. Societies have paradigms within which their people think as a matter of course, and since these ideas do not have the rigidity which can be applied for a time to so-called scientific facts, they have a plasticity while being considered at that time to have a personal binding cultural authenticity.

Most if not all communities have at least a minority of intellectuals, the apex of religious understandings and behaviour in which there will be an element of working misunderstandings but below them in this pyramid there will be an increasing proportion of people who will know little of this elitist thinking and who will practice a religious faith in which there is a wide divergence from these understandings and requirements and who continue to believe and practice within working misunderstandings. Most will accept the rationality of explanations provided in a culturally acceptable linguistic code, which do not go too far outside the paradigms into which they have been socialised.

Prayers to a spirit or a statue with non-human characteristics have a situational social reality and it is usually outsiders who apply theoretical explanations which amount to doubts which have little approval or even understandings among worshippers. Explaining away of religious practices is the privilege of outsiders which still leaves the reality of personal experiences intact.

There is no such thing as primitive thought in any identifiable community and whatever may have been its theoretical characteristics, it is just as likely to occur in individuals who have spent their lives in Stockholm as Sikkim. Humans are clearly overwhelmingly logical in how they live their lives or as a species they would have largely disappeared long ago. Certainly some communities have deliberately destroyed themselves such as the Jonestown Christian and York Jewish communities mass suicides. Mankind works out solutions to their problems by their culturally cause and effect understandings. The Swedes and the Sikkimese by their own standards are no more or less logical than each other. Logic is socially layered according to the situations in which it is applied. Planting seeds according to the phases of the moon may be as logical in one cultural setting as the consequences of ancestor irritation or hungry ghosts in others.

These theories which support their holistic interpretation of their existence have a reality which the agnostic social scientist in their professional isolation defines as illusionary. However in the understandings of religiously active people and their subtended behaviour, religion may and indeed actually work despite the fact that their bases are misunderstood. A kind of situational holistic placebo.

A group of Sukuma elders who at best would have been marginally literate when provided with anthropological explanations in their own language about mother-in-law avoidance and joking relationships as well as the unity of alternate generations as not necessarily correct but at least plausible. They should be assessed as likely to have the same and indeed perhaps a higher intellectual level than social scientists who have no experience of such realities. The same group when provided with Freudian explanations such as the Oedipus Complex agreed intuitively that it was just plain ridiculous and saw such ideas as possibly some sort of European joke which had not been adequately explained in translation.

The conclusion might well be that social science theory if it has to have any reasonable chance of acceptability has to tie itself to at least the fringes of popular understandings. A theory which has a professional appeal can rarely have any holistic value because those who create them probably cannot and indeed would not apply it to the totality of their own lives; the looking glass test of applicability. Theological theories and popular understandings are each the bases of working misunderstandings while at the same time may be the substantive bases within which people live at least most of their lives reasonably content. These concentric circles of understanding only symbolically overlap irregularly in socio-religious situations in which particular thinking and behaviour may only occasionally coincide.

The Processes of Theorizing

The social scientist in producing a theory supporting or altering an existing one, is involved in an isolating exercise from the objects of his or her research and aligning themselves to their professional colleagues; they are looking over their shoulders for that support and not so much from their transitory informants. These men and women in reality are not as important as their departmental head or that of the foundations supporting them who are linked to researchers' professional careers.

At the same time they are not looking in the mirror of their own lives and what they may have done in similar situations when they have been distressed and euphoric. The theologian endeavours relate to the object of their thought, the social scientist would seemingly endeavour to detach themselves from it. Theorizing is a dehumanizing process as however much it may be based on personal interrelationships, it is almost always based on wider ranges of explanation than personalised case studies which possibly and inevitably end up as either too complex or too situational to provide explanations beyond individual. Of course, they recognise that what they are theorizing about is based on information obtained from individuals who are never very reliable informants about their own behaviour. The result must be except in the possible cases of identical twins for certain behavioural traits, that there will be no binding fit between the theory and particular individuals. Every single factor is involving constantly changing interrelationships and environments.

Social science and theological theories are often based on imposed categorizations into which people are fitted for the convenience of explanations with little regard to the fact that people cannot be treated in this way without losing their basic individualities. Theories based on these aggregates when presented to those about whom it has been written, may well respond by saying that this may be your opinion but it does not apply to me and the situations within which I am now thinking. The conclusion is that there is no theory can coincide to an exact fit. In the terminology of the social sciences it might be seen as ignoring social reality in exchange for the possible rather than probable profits of scientific hope. Societies and individuals base their behaviour on combinations of inaccurate memory and reactions to contemporary social situations which cannot be tied to any theory which suggests any narrow overall stability in behaviour.

Most theories of Western origin have binary characteristics, that the explanation of some behaviour is either this or that so that any theory whether it is positivistic or inter-actionist has to be one or the other. The Western system of logic holds that we cannot state that something which has pretensions to be correct which is contradicted by some other logically determined factor. However, it seems to be better to assume that the individual may be unaware or more likely uninterested in such logical contradictions which they do not think are related to their current thinking which is lateral rather than lineal.

Their processes of thinking is so instantaneous and all embracing that it irons out these logical contradictions in an instant as not relevant to the issue about which they are now thinking and making decisions. The thinking in the parallel distributive processes theory is that the human mind moves much more quicker than even the most powerful computer. The fact that there are logical contradictions can be determined by an outsider isolating the issues while any individual including social scientists can retain any number of these contradictions without giving them even any conscious passing thought.

Whether we are New Age Californian Americans, nuclear physicists or Bangladeshi rice farmers, we act personally on circumscribed thinking. Whatever may be the degree of illogicality in our thinking as decided by the assessments of outsiders of which we have no necessary need to be aware, logic has little part in our metaphysical thinking and actions because it is not necessary for personal fulfilment. What has metaphysical bases cannot be related to pragmatism whether in religion or in artistic appreciation.

Do individuals in any cultural environment or at any level of intellectual understandings adhere to a pattern of behaviour which is so persistent and so exclusive that we can say with some assurance much less with scientific rectitude that it can be explained by positivism or whatever to the exclusion of other theories. Positivism indeed may be a figment of statistical opportunism in which the assessors have created their form of socially isolated reality.

It seems more likely that in religious thinking and behaviour there are fields of relativity which form a cohesive whole for each individual who will have little interest in its logical composition even if they consider this to be a relevant issue which itself is unlikely. This field of religious emotion and commitment has the composition of a picture in which the relevance is its perceived wholeness. The dissection of a poem or a prayer is to lose its perceptual wholeness which is held in the individual mind for particular circumstantial reasons.

A popular Hindu coloured print of Krishna or Parvati is appreciated as an enabling whole although it will contain such a mass of symbols that would be beyond the analytical powers of any social scientist to explain as there is always perceptual variability. We have little evidence that any individual has more than limited primary consistency in their public religious behaviour and probably no evidence at all as to this in private spirituality. The individual may be no more than minimally aware of the extent to which their religious thinking and behaviour varies and indeed may think it inconsequential in terms of the hypothetical continuing wholeness and immediacy of their understandings.

Abstract Thought and Religious Practice

In recent discussion involving Tanzanians and a Swedish academic who had spent his childhood among the Sukuma, it was suggested that non-literate pre-industrial peoples did not have an automatic cultural ability to think abstractly which was felt by educated Tanzanians there to be an imputation against their overall intellectual capacities.

It is reasonable to consider at what stage in linguistic development of an individual or a culture a factual noun has an abstract form. Certainly Sukuma asked to write or draw what they considered to be their understandings of key words such as love *upenzi* rather than *upenadaje*, what do you like, explained little beyond listing what they 'liked' such as a full stomach after a good meal.

It would seem that it is not so much an incapacity to think abstractly but that most people do not have any need to do so. It has been shown that in the language of the Kenyan Meru it is not possible to express a belief in God as that would imply the possibility of disbelief and that for them was an impossibility. Most people do not require a theoretical background for their religious beliefs and behaviour. Some presumably more traditional Roman Catholics in Liverpool when asked for their view on the change from Latin to English in the celebration of the Mass, said that they had no views since this is what the Holy Father had ordered.

In much the same line a Sukuma knows that their ancestors are influential on their current lives and a Vietnamese knows that there are hungry ghosts which have to be appeased; these are facts not abstractions. There is no need for any theoretical background to their beliefs. From such backgrounds it is easier to understand that that they are orthopractical in how they understand their religion. It is not what you believe that is important but how you practice its rituals.

Many theoreticians approach the religious behaviour of others on the assumption that there must be underlying abstract reasons as much as pragmatic causes for what is being done. Indeed it is possible to create these out of the data with which they are presented. By careful questioning and the understandings which would come from prolonged association with this 'other' culture it seems likely that the reasons are primary under such phrases this is what we have always done or just do or that is what we do as a result of or in anticipation of misfortune. The Italian footballer who crosses himself as he runs onto the field or the bystander who throws flowers onto the hearse containing the coffin of a British serviceman killed in Afghanistan have causes to do so but there is no conscious reasoning. It was just the right thing to do at the time.

If there are no such abstract frameworks in the thinking of so many people cross-culturally there would seem to be at least two possible explanations. Firstly, that this codification of abstractions have been the creations of these theoreticians because this is how they were professionally expected to conclude. The complex thinking produced about the religious understandings of the Sudanese Nuer (Evans-Pritchard, 1956) can be criticised on the grounds that it seems reasonable enough to suggest that no Nuer consciously can have had such beliefs, much less expressed them through a marginally bilingual interpreter. Similarly, the elderly Navaho probably did have even the glimmerings of the moral code attributed to him in Ladd's comprehensive study (Ladd, 1957). Possibly such complexities of thought may exist departmentally rather than cross-departmentally in the universities of Oxford, Delhi and Beijing but not as a universal feature of all thought from high individual intellects which often enough will be in people without education or from all those in a tribal culture. Schools of thought which aim at comprehensive understandings are more likely to exist in academic surroundings than in the cultures from which these attributed ideas are said to come. The assumption that a community has a pattern of religious thought and practice might come from the fact that the research do not have enough information to create theories which start from the inevitable differences with any community.

Thus, these interpreters of other people's unconscious rather than conscious thinking are producing the results of their own creativities which we often read with committed excitement as we want these people to have these complexities. As Alan Bennett wrote about psychoanalysis that people who are dull when they are sane are equally dull when they are mad and that if you thought your wife was a hat you would never suffer from lack of medical attention (Bennett, 2005:34). We are excited by the possibility of finding the creativity in others which we hope to have in ourselves. Social scientists knit together the odds and ends of information from the people they intermittently associate with and create polished frameworks of their thought. A process of elevating the purported background thinking of rather ordinary people doing ordinary things in ordinary ways whether in London or in some distant part of south-west China.

It is also necessary to recognise that these enquiring intellectuals are educated to find these abstractions and in this they may be isolating themselves from the 'ordinariness' of the lives of most people. Everyday activities like cooking and personal cleanliness are relatively unknown because they are less intellectually attractive than the abstract thought of those who are socially unknown to researchers. They are perhaps as much the products of their professional environments as any subsistence farmer. Victor Turner may have seen in Muchona the Hornet, an Ndembu diviner, a fellow intellectual with whom he could share speculations in confidence and Muchona may have felt the same thing. In much the same way Turner saw in a series of photographs of the initiation ritual of the Sukuma Buchwezi society several points unnoticed by the anthropologist photographer and of course irrelevant to the functional needs and understandings of the participants. Photographs of this ceremony taken ten years apart showed little similarity but the participants stated that this was the way that the ceremony was always carried out.

These interpreters of behaviour of socially and geographically distant peoples both from each other and those social scientists have missed the fact that those whose behaviour they have recorded and analysed would not recognise the interpretations of these outsiders when they translated back their conclusions for the people from whom they got their data.

The Intellectualism of Theological Understandings

The study and understandings of religious thinking and behaviour is usually an intellectual exercise in social detachment. It is not done in the immediate environment of those about whom it is written because it is done away from such distracting personal involvements. Certainly among the intellectual elite in any society there are metaphysical speculations or at least we can presuppose that this is so. Such people are not going to expose themselves as being too deviant to the more simplistic assumptions of a community. Social scientists and theologians are more likely to discuss their ideas and interpretations with their colleagues than to go back to their informants to get their reactions for which they do not have the time or financial support.

In order to study religious behaviour researchers usually start with the reading of the sacred texts on which theological thinking is based rather than the observation of behaviour; they are starting at the wrong end of what most people would consider religion. There is the assumption that in order to understand Buddhism and Hinduism, there has to be the reading of their texts in Pali and Sanskrit which either involves the long segregated process of learning no longer spoken sacred languages or reading them through the semantic contaminations of translation. The pinnacle approach which may leave less time for actual contact with Buddhist and Hindu related behaviour which may have no discernible relationship to what is locally considered to be their orthodoxies; it is a dehumanizing process of detachment from behavioural realities.

It is reasonable to suggest that the social scientists approach to their research is a search for a working hypothesis to explain what they are observing and that this is always a working misunderstanding. Without the creativity of these working misunderstandings they would have difficulty in describing any behaviour.

Even the educated Chinese finds it difficult to read the specialised calligraphy on a popular religious poster. If we recognise that any approach to religious thinking and behaviour is more than anything else an intellectual exercise in abstracting this from its entanglement in a mass of behaviour in which the dominant theme is secular. A Buddhist monastery has to be seen in this wider context because the monks have to be fed as the monastery has no kitchen and they go out daily on a begging round which intersects with secular life and involves them in always eating cold food.

The average Buddhist and Hindu has little interest in sacred literature and if they had any such need they would go to a specialist who is thought to have the necessary knowledge to answer their questions. Of course, there is a do-it-yourself element in this as with some of the Seventh day Adventists in Madagascar and the members of the small Remnant Church in the Solomon Islands studying the *Bible* (Burt, 1985) but these are exceptional cases involving a few people who have the interest and find the time to do so. The average believer in all religions is orthopractical so they follow the performative requirements of these faiths in the contexts of their individual and immediate circumstances and within their personal understandings.

The complicated theological and philosophical thinking behind the major and indeed minor faiths which the writers tautologically define as important have no peripheral wider understandings. Any general understanding of these abstractions must be doubtful because they have all the understandings that they need in their orthopraxis. Any such wider understandings must rest with the interpretations of the religious elite who have both personal and professional charisma and these have little functional reality to social environment of religious behaviour.

The Need for Multi-level Theologies

Historically and in contemporary religious behaviour orthopractice predominates. There is the belief that performing rituals is enough because they are believed in and these acts have a combination of both passive and active positive effects. Through this same period theological thinking as committed to writing has tended to concentrate on metaphysical abstractions and to place orthopractice, the physical performance of even core rituals into a status of theological inferiority. This may receive greater attention in monotheistic religions than in Eastern faiths, in which individuals have an endless succession of lives in which their metaphysical status can be altered. Eastern thinkers have not made any such derogative distinction in their predominantly karmically based orthodoxies.

Over time theologians have worked and thought in social situations in which their audience was mainly the elite in their own communities. A degree of conformity and interdependence combined with some evolution of thought not entirely uninfluenced by the views of the surrounding secular elite and general political, social and economic changes. A film of the current Dalai Lama undergoing some religious examination showed him physically addressing a crowd of monks underlining his points with demonstrative body language. It could be that theological thinking has been and remains a professional form of discourse not much different to that of lawyers and doctors, theoretically open to the understanding of all but not directed at them; a closed intellectual world fenced in by their own linguistic codes and prolonged 'endogamous' cognitive training.

Beyond this elitist restriction thinkers might have very limited influence as religious operatives unless they belonged to self-sufficient religious communities, where they would have been too dependent for survival on their local community or them on their ritual services to have gone too far beyond local understandings and practice. The Buddhist monk and Hindu *sadhu* lead by visual example rather than by vocal direction and admonition. In this sense the Christian priest or nun in lay dress has lost the major part of their ministry of leading by visual demonstration of their dedication. A religiously dedicated person in lay costume has a range of personal influence restricted to social distance. On the other hand, those who wear the distinctive costume of their calling whether Buddhist monk, Hindu *sadhu* or Christian nun are mobile reminders of religious involvement.

Whatever religion is being analysed there has always been a two level area of activities in which theological thinking has systematic intentions. At other levels which perhaps should not be thought of in hierarchical terms, there are common activities of those whose personal needs dominate the rituals of any religion. These are much less part of any system in their individualities whether in pilgrimages, prayers and physical prostrations which operate without much attention to theological thinking because such activities are largely both individually motivated and self-fulfilling.

Both sides of this divide function under the same titular cover which is perhaps easier with Eastern religions which have no overarching institutional structure and which people pay more attention to practices than beliefs. In all cases involving major faiths which have survived significant social, political and economic as well as theological changes, believers know that these 'great' thoughts exist should they need them. Few have the time and ability to relate personally to this background but they remain a shadow force behind the immediacies of religious need and day to day practices.

Theological thinking is inevitably committed to writing and except for dedicated individuals, such reading is both time consuming and tiring and indeed isolating and in comparison to the carrying out of a ritual, it provides no immediate emotional return. Reading about their faith is not a primary preoccupation of those who are not professionally committed to religion. The fact that the assumption of religious literacy motivating and supporting belief is more a hope than a reality makes working misunderstandings all the more likely. The ideas of this elite have survived because they have been written down, even inscribed on stone and we know more about this and their hypothetical influence than we do about the current common practices of 'ordinary' Buddhists and Christians. The seventy million pilgrims who were estimated to have attended the last Hindu Kumbh Mela on the river Ganges passed into history virtually unnoticed although this was the largest religious gathering ever known to have occurred.

Because of the survival of writing we know more about the potential orthodoxies of charismatic individuals in history such as Asoka and his edicts than we do of the religious practices of the millions of their social subordinates. Archaeological guesswork certainly but contemporary theological thinking has certain similarities as to what these specialists know of the thinking of Bengali peasants and Berlin factory workers do in their popular religious practices.

As the Christian Churches and Islamic legalisms became institutionalised and bureaucratically organised, written rules became the networks through which these denominations were run, it became less possible for branches to be run theologically idiosyncratically which did and still does occur in Eastern religions. On the other hand, there are still opportunities for liturgical differences to which people covertly attach their individual understandings.

Non-Christian religions have the same two levels but with the possible exception of Islam and Judaism, there is not the administrative machinery for the one to invade the other. The Tanzanian Yao are both Muslim and matrilineal and as to how these two systems interrelated, they have worked out for themselves without any direct outsider interference.

So we have to ask ourselves in what social and religious situations do these two levels influence each other. There is the overwhelming fact that individuals interpret their theologies in personal as much as institutional terms. In contemporary Japan in Kyoto the participants in annual festivals combining social as well as religious factors from the concept of acquiring *kami* values for their religious understandings. This is a term allied to charisma which can be applied to outstanding individuals as well as to natural phenomena and mythological gods and goddesses and this comes from a sense of reciprocity at the local shrine. There is a very limited knowledge of sacred texts seemingly seen as irrelevant to the immediacies of irregular practice (Roemer, 2007).

On the other hand, if success is measured globally in the number of people who participate in public religious activities as in the enormous growth in the numbers going on pilgrimages or the millions who log-on privately to religious websites. It seems clear that very large numbers indeed are involved in forms of religious activity which are not susceptible to the statistical formalities of mere regular or guess-estimates of attendance. The key to what appears to be success is that a religion offers non-specific and indeed has ambiguous guidelines.

The Layering of Religious Needs

Children and perhaps theologians share a separation from the wider aspects social living and while they are experiencing this, they are largely separated from the crudities of much personal anxiety and it is this that gives rise to the immediacies of much religious behaviour.

There would appear to be not only a pyramid of religious thinking and behaviour in which the pinnacle is dominated by socially detached theologians. Below this there is a predominance of commonplace religious involvements that are tightly integrated into the political, social and economic lives of individuals and communities and the surrounding macro culture; a horizontal conception of religious thinking and behaviour.

There is a parallel here to the modern 'do it yourself' procedures which will have always predominated in non-literate religious practices. The Sikkimese and Swedes as well as the Swazi will attempt to solve their problems and satisfy their metaphysical needs with the means they have to hand. When their problems and needs are too complex, they move to a different layer of expertise; the Chinese will call in a Taoist professional ritualist just as the Westerners will go to rabbis and priests or psychotherapists.

The Split between Religious Practice and Theological Theory

Each individual has their own floating idealism which relates to their conceptions of the 'good' life and this has an immediacy related to what they consider to be a reasonable return to what they are now doing. It is much the same in all societies; steady partners, pleasant friends, a reasonable job and return on their farming, neighbours who do not interfere except in reciprocal terms, adequate health and an easy death.

Many theologically based systems pay little exact attention to short-term personal needs which dominate personal behaviour and if they do it tends to regard them as less important than long-term metaphysical and eschatological contexts. Believers may accept these as part of their religious coverage while keeping to their own individualised immediate practices.

Buddhism is a case in point in which its basic teachings were written down some centuries after the Buddha's death. This required his followers to accept that both pleasure and pain made life difficult and that the only way to avoid this was progressive detachment from all earthly involvements and to do this over an almost unlimited succession of lives. It is no part of this system to make the Lord Buddha into a divine being who can intervene on behalf of believers to ensure a benign life. It is hard to think of a system of belief which is both pragmatically realistic so alien to self-expressed and exsperienced human needs.

It is indeed a harsh doctrine. It is scarcely surprising that nominal Buddhists have turned this arid philosophical system into a religion with its hierarchy of divine figures to whom petitions are made and who reciprocate by helping their petitioners to get through the difficulties of their current lives. Certainly there are consistently unpleasant aspects to living which most people both anticipate and experience quite regularly. It is altogether another thing to accept that the pleasures of eating, companionship and providing for their family should be avoided as preludes to the sufferings which come from not being able to have these enjoyments. Many men become monks for a while but few would admit to becoming ordained as an ambition because such a personal wish would be a pleasure to be disallowed under Buddhist aims of progressive detachment from any personal identity.

Among the Burmese certainly (Spiro, 1956) very few actively pursue this process of progressive detachment from all that most Burmese could consider to be their reasonable expectations for their lives. Those who are widowed tend not to remarry, some keep account books in order to check on whether their behaviour in Buddhist terms has earned them positive or negative merit for their next reincarnation although it is not at all sure what is the 'essence' which is passed from one life into the next one.

The Burmese then accept which is perhaps too strong a word, that there is a metaphysical background to their religious ideas without being too concerned as to what it actually is since the basic documents are written in Pali of which they have no knowledge unless specially acquired with all the expenditure of time and effort necessary for learning a second language for which there would be few material returns except status.

They more or less say to themselves that these teachings are all very well and are no doubt correct for those who know about such matters but we have personal problems over which we need help. Anything specifically required of us as Buddhist might perhaps wait for our attention at our next reincarnation. In the mean time they treat Lord Buddha as a divine figure who can be petitioned for help.

In addition they create a whole range of activities which have short-term aims and a large number of ancillary spirits of home, field and forest to whom they perform devotional acts. While the density of pagodas and monasteries in Myanmar and Thailand may be no greater than the churches and chapels in Britain or mosques in Egypt. In Thailand and Japan the devotion to spirits is widespread and it is possible to see innumerable shrines and indeed factories that produce them. There are shrines under isolated forest trees and outside urban garages as well as concrete ones outside hotels, houses and offices. It would seem that in Burmese Buddhism there is a working misunderstanding which is not covert at all. It is clear that these people needing help have created a religious system which has little to do with Buddhist orthodoxy. It has little of the attempts in the religions of the book to eliminate or at least minimize the overt practices.

So it seems that in the practice of religion whether in the major religions, sects or cults or in personal systems of devotion there are clear differences between what people do whether immigrant Italians in New York, Bavarians in Austria or Kachins in northern Myanmar in reaction to their immediate needs and their long-term religious understandings. It is probable that most pay no more than nominal attention to these distant and complicated theological and philosophical issues which they accept in some vague way as part of the belief package about which they know very little because it has little to do with their immediate needs and understandings. They acquire satisfaction from what they do ritually and this is a working misunderstanding of the doctrines of which they are supposed to be believed. It is certainly not the case that they have evaded definitions as impractical. The whole basis of their theological thinking is the reality of interminable impermanence, an inching backwards and forwards in processes which have no beginning and no end.

The Unattractiveness of Defined Religiousness

All religions have the characteristic of dividing themselves into innumerable denominations, cults and sects but in this there is a difference between the religions of the book and the Eastern faiths. The former define themselves into theological exclusivities and to frown on orthopraxis, the performance of religious rituals as more or less ends in themselves. The latter on the other hand seem to have avoided the pitfalls of seeking definitions and to have accepted the validity of orthopraxis. This was not caused by any aimed conscious decisions which have resulted in the retention of their popularity or the popularity of orthopraxis avoiding theological definitions and any attempted exactnesses in religious practices an exercise that has little popular support is impossible to decide. It would seem that theological thinking has worked up from the commonality of suffering rather than top-down abstractions.

While this top-down approach is an invariable characteristic of all groups however hard they try to enforce or at least retain their public uniformities, they are always segmenting as a response to new circumstances and the demographic inevitability of new leaders and new needs, and literacy has made this adaptability more difficult. The retention of unity may be due as much to the ambiguity of doctrines as to their definitions in religious law.

It is no longer the case of points of theological argument being matters of public rather than elite group debate as may have been the Byzantine situation, Christianity does have a record of frequent defined denominational division. A study of South Africa prior to the abolition of Apartheid (Barrett, 1968) found over six thousand Christian groups which had defined themselves as distinct enough by theological definition to have themselves registered with the civil authorities. Almost the first thing that a Kenyan independent Church did when it had acquired a social identity was to write its own constitution and beliefs possibly in the hope of wider theological recognition.

Religions that tie themselves to sacred writings have the difficulty of accepting that they were written for their own contemporary needs and understandings. Jesus Christ was a rather geographically static figure while Saint Paul was a compulsive traveller. The Prophet Muhammad started as a local religious visionary and ended up as a secular ruler in an emerging state fortunately stuck between the existing regimes of Byzantium and Baghdad. So little is known of the Lord Buddha that what is alleged to have been said by him cannot be related the contemporary conditions in which he lived; an archaeological problem rather than a theological or philosophical one which can fit into contemporary life.

Now theologians are stuck with sacred documents written for reasons which can have little clear relationship to modern issues of electronic communication and organ transplantation and unavoidable international relationships, made more difficult by successive translations and the politics of interpretation.

In other religions there are and have been no centralising institutions other than the temporary popular influence of charismatic personalities. Hindus are so loosely categorized that in crude terms they can more or less believe what they like when they like in some form of spirituality without creating intra-religious tensions. Inter-caste tensions are in violent existence more as a political issue than a religious one as a consequence of a one person one vote political system with groups wanting a larger share of economic advancement opportunities. Castes get the benefits of exclusivity without the confinement of defined and administered religious inclusivity.

Buddhism is not so much concerned with defining what the individual should do as detachment is the aim of all behaviour. It is difficult to see Taoism and Shintoism as having any institutional cohesion from which it might be possible to isolate theological deviance, much less the entanglements of disbelief and disunity. These are religions with a multiplicity of divinities with ephemeral influences, and disorganised systems in which parts become activated by need. The Japanese define themselves as not committed to any religion but yet use religion whenever they feel that it is appropriate in contexts that are as much secular as religious.

It seems doubtful whether theological definitions are attractive to those attempting to solve or reduce their day-to-day problems. There is only the personal feeling that their beliefs have some systematic wholeness which may always have been part of idiosyncratic understandings and practices. Theological definitions have an arid and depersonalizing quality about them which may subliminally encourage the covert individuality of religious understandings and practices.

Working Misunderstandings

It seems unlikely that any individual except for the improbable existence of an introspective theologian who is on the verge of leaving his or her previous religious commitments, is likely to see their beliefs and practices as a working misunderstanding. Such a cynical and detached evaluation must be rare indeed.

Human individual variability and the ever changing social environments in which they live always has the potential for and an ongoing reality of misunderstandings in which there is a combination of cooperation and the satisfying illusion that it does not occur.

Just as human interrelationships are based on direct or attenuated reciprocities, the real or anticipated pay-offs which keep societies going, so we have the same approaches in our relationships with the supernatural in whatever cross-cultural situations it is observed. The differences between social reciprocities and supernatural ones, is only the silence with which it is received and responded.

So what might be the purposes of such an evaluation that large numbers of believers in terms of the orthodoxies of their faiths, have a subconscious working misunderstanding over what they are practising from which they covertly benefit in a whole range of behavioural consequences.

The difficulty here is that the social sciences and pragmatism generally apply their own standards of evaluation to understandings for which they cannot apply. Just as it cannot apply these standards with any measure of success to the appreciation of art, music and literature, it cannot do so with religion which is just as much a reality to believers as in any other abstract appreciations. So we end up with an enormous amount of predefined secular intellectual effort being used to explain away rather than however tentatively explain in these socio-religious realities. The Christian believing and acting on the assumption of the divine humanity of Jesus just as the Vietnamese woman place placatory offerings on her doorstep for hungry ghosts, are quite unmoved by these secular explanations of what the social scientists assess as their intellectual shortcomings.

There is also the difficulty that orthodoxies in some form or another in all religions differ from what is supported by popular religious opinion in societies which are predominantly non-literate as regards the reading of the written complexities of belief and practices in institutionalised religions to which they consider themselves to belong. It is an almost inevitable result for a faith which has become institutionalised and successful in retaining within its field of a large number of believers over successive generations that it will put its beliefs and regulations into writing. This has occurred in the Roman Catholic Church and in both the Shia and Sunni branches of Islam as well as such newer religions as the Zairean Church of Christ on Earth by his Special Envoy Simon Kimbangu with its estimated five million adherents.

It would seem that the use of the word 'popular' in this context prejudges the importance of this religious reality in uplifting the lives of those involved. The Londoners who recently had visions of the Virgin Mary did not think that this had happened to them, it did happen and in every sense of the word it was a personal reality. It is indeed verging on the ridiculous to evaluate this enormous range and persistence of religious thinking and activities as motivated by imagination and defective pragmatism. This assessment within the limited range of agnostic thinking is not widely held outside this professional circle.

Misunderstandings in the Context of Change

Human social, physiological and psychological life is always in the process of change as innumerable variables come together in influencing human behaviour to which individuals react in various ways. Religious behaviour is part of these reactions and if this is related to what has been written it is always in the process of catching up with what people are already doing. Thus, there is the reality of what are the working misunderstandings in religions which attempt to achieve conformity through institutionalised writings.

When the religious practices have not been institutionalised, there is a constant process of adjustment and since nothing has been defined and put into writing the question of misunderstanding cannot arise. Where the religion has become institutionalised there are probably five ways in which believers can overtly react while the covertly rearrangements are likely to be even more complex and hidden within the inaccessible individual mind.(Merton, 1957).

Firstly there is ideological conformity to what has been changed and this is well documented for Roman Catholicism where the disapproval of orthopraxis in the externally motivated Reformation (Duffy, 1992) led to the creation and maintenance of parallel systems which coped with believers emotional rather than intellectual needs. Much the same thing happened again with the changes instituted internally in the Vatican II Council which led to enormous numbers of dropouts in Western Europe as again attention was focused on ideological aims rather than responding to the personal needs of their members.

While conformity in an all embracing sense may only apply to members who are professionally committed to their faith, the other possible reactions to change whether inside a faith or not, have to be seen in the context of a worldwide availability of alternatives which if not available nearby are available electronically. The enormous numbers of people who use the Jesuit spiritual website is just the modern form of what has been available for much longer on the wireless from the Vatican Radio and the Voice of Prophecy from Addis Ababa and a number of West African stations.

Religions whether they are institutionalised or not provide approved rituals and even if the religion changes the meaning of particular ceremonies, believers can still use it for their own personal needs and covert interpretations. In this the rituals work according to those involved independently of what may be their intended theological meanings. Whether the aims of a faith have been narrowly or vaguely formalised, it seems likely that orthopraxis, the performance of rituals being an adequate end in itself is so prevalent that this means that theological understandings in all religions are largely irrelevant. This is the persistent and nearly universal working misunderstanding if viewed from theological assumptions but not of course from the feelings perhaps rather more than the thinking of participants.

Individuals can of course create their own personal rituals as a response to change but while they may be satisfying in the short term they lack the authenticity of a ritual which is known or thought to be of great antiquity; it has the patina of the divine which can only come from the millions who have done the same thing over the centuries in many different societies. The burning of incense before images, the Roman Catholic Mass and the Muslim collective prayer procedures on Fridays and the almost universal popularity of pilgrimages to sacred places.

Then there are the few who retreat into mysticism and meditation well recorded in the religions of the book but probably more numerous in Eastern religions in which these patterns are accepted as the way forward towards total detachment from selfish and futile individualism.

There are also those who initiate change which will always be happening in the combinations of theological and secular involvements of religious thinkers. But individuals are always in the process of changing their own systems of religious practice so innovation is perhaps personally universal. There are always dissatisfactions within anybody of thinkers which are not working misunderstandings as they are facilitators of improvements rather than rectifiers of what is going wrong. Lastly, there are the charismatic individuals in their thousands who create new religions which catch on such as the founders of Kimbanguism in Zaire and the Latter Day Saints in the United States.

Reciprocal Silence in Religious Realities

The most important part of individuals lives is not their intellectual understandings of their faith but the range of religious experiences which occur to them. Of course, there is a scale in this but to restrict it to the peak elevations of the spirit experienced by Hindu *sadhus* and Christian mystics cuts out the generalities of religious experience, the everyday perhaps peripheral and perfunctory acknowledgement of the supernatural; the passing momentary elevation of the spirit from the view of a religious statue, the hearing of a bell, the smell of incense and the touch of the charismatic gaze which establishes a relationship (Argyle and Cook, 1976:149).

All of these events establish a relationship however tenuous between two realities of equal social and personal importance. In all societies there are many certainly in their hundreds of thousands who have had occasional experiences of the supernatural and of these thousands who have maintained such personally productive relationships with a spiritual entity throughout their lives.

This belief in a supernatural reality is so strong that it cannot be assessed as purely imaginary. It has apparently caused contemporary people to economic, social and political extremes of devotion involving the violent persecution of other believers and personal martyrdoms as well as dedicated lives of personal self-denial. Yet the most striking aspects of this enormous range of behaviour is that it is carried out in anticipation of reciprocity and this return of reciprocal silence is valued as an adequate response.

Memory and Working Misunderstandings

Apart from the situation in which there are clearly defined religious orthodoxies as in Islam and some Christian denominations in which it is relatively easy to identify working misunderstandings, learning and memory are important factors. The wholesale conversion of communities of Hindu Untouchables to Buddhism and to Christianity in Indonesia so as to have a religion on their identity cards, cannot have involved any understanding of theological and philosophical requirements so that in their conformities to their new faiths there are clearly misunderstandings that work for these converts in a range of both secular and religious issues.

Whether we are considering religions with written orthodoxies or ones in which the individuals either do not keep to what is written because it is too much trouble and unnecessary for their personal needs or do not have written texts as a background for their ceremonies, most consider that they are doing religiously is what they have always done.

For individuals who base their religious activities on what they state to be traditional practices, they are almost always quite firm in stating that what they are doing now is what they or their communities have always done. We have shown that this is not true with photographic evidence from the initiation rites of the Sukuma Buchwezi cult. Memory of even the details of key personal events will always be suspect.

Indeed how could there be any conformity to more than an idea when there are no written records and what they do, whether they are Mishmi or Manipuris depends on a combination of memory, environmental pressures and individual creativity. It is always the illusion of accurate memory on which believers rely in their religious practices.

Memory about what may or may not have happened in even the quite recent past, has no stability and is always adjusting, unnoticed by the individual, according to their current needs. It is certainly persistently unreliable for anything beyond the immediate past and of course when what is being remembered is the collective property of a group of celebrants which is likely to be even more unreliable as the individual reacts to the others involved. So individuals are likely to think that they are conforming and consistent which allows them to continue within a working misunderstanding in the comfort of their own inexact memories.

Secular Necessities in Institutionalised Religiosity

All systems of belief and practice whether they are cult, sect or denomination once they can write or have access to writing, put their orthodox thinking into printed form and this seems to limit its personal appeal. There is now a barrier between the believers reciprocal relationship with the supernatural and these temporarily fixed impersonal directions and explanations. It is not only a theological but an administrative necessity for the reasonable functioning of the various branches whether churches, temples, mosques, schools, shelters for the dying or orphans or hospitals. There has to be order but it seems likely that order is more a secular than a religious necessity. This automatically leads to ideological and secular clashes between the realities of running an institution for a religious purpose and the health and safety regulations. More importantly it leads to a functional dichotomy between orthodoxy and what believers actually do and believe in. These foundation religious principles can only be vague guidelines for the solution of administrative issues. The feeding in the New Testament story of the five thousand crowd as a singular occasion has little relevance for the feeding of staff and patients in a religiously motivated hospice for the dying or hostel for the homeless. A constant process of reinterpretation.

No organisation which copes with more than a limited small scale range of interpersonal contacts and needs, can function effectively without regulations which they construct for their own use or are imposed on them by supervising governments. Just as certainly once these regulations are in place, the constant variety of human individuality and the social environments in which they live means that those involved whether priests, pastors or petitioners will have to work round these regulations to enable the organisation to work and to conform to their religious needs. They all know that the regulations of the system exist and agree that they are an administrative necessity.

Similarly, they all know that there is a parallel way of behaving which for them is a personal necessity in the situations in which they find themselves. This is certainly a working misunderstanding if only because a substantial amount of behavioural if not cognitive duplicity is involved in order to keep the personal individual need and the impersonal religious system in a binary cohesion when each is working for different proximate and distant objectives.

While these modern administrative requirements are largely followed so that places of worship can be built and the participants whether practising members or not, are adequately serviced according to legal as much as administrative standards, as well as what believers and participants actually want and do according to public opinion have to be maintained or these institutions go out of 'business'; it is a marketing situation. These institutional practices are based on secular realities rather than on bureaucratic requirements. Monks, nuns and patients whether Buddhist, Christian or Hindu have to be fed and housed adequately or otherwise provided for by society as in the begging rounds of Buddhist monks.

The bigger the institutional commitment, the bigger the need for financial support even if there are adequate numbers of personnel working without salaries. Most groups of believers who may not have any communal cohesion, will keep their priests or imams in a reasonable standard of living but beyond this there is the need for large amounts of money. This is needed to keep the training institutions for their personnel running, homes for the deprived and abandoned which are left out of governments calculations and financial abilities to support; the school for the blind in Nairobi run by the Christian Salvation Army would have to shut down very quickly if it depended on local donations. The weekly donations in Asian and African churches would not keep their priests alive and it is usually up to them, to organise their own survival.

So Christian churches are thought to be over-interested in money and they are forced to give this impression by the realities of any religious system. This is certainly a not too efficient working misunderstanding of religious institutions which attempt to provide more than short-term priest to person help which would parallel the client-diviner relationship in quasi-traditional situations.

A village monastery or temple can be built in Cambodia with the agreement of those who live there but for a Hindu temple to be built in London requires planning permission from secular administrators and elected secular authorities. This itself is a costly time consuming process in which the religious factors are secondary.

This institutionalised rationality seems to be the creation of Western thinking which imposes regularities on all secular and religious activities. Eastern religions do not have these regularities which they themselves have created. When there are enormous religiously motivated gatherings we have secular rather than Hindu authorities doing their best to organise them. Without this the last Kumbh Mela with its seventy million pilgrims would have become a demographic disaster from water born diseases. In the same way it is secular authorities which are responsible for the efficient organisation of the annual Muslim Hajj pilgrimage to Mecca. Insofar as it is possible these are secular requirements which are generally seen as reasonable and followed if only because their performance is visible and administered by power-holding secular authorities. The religious authorities with their over-riding theological concerns do not have the wish nor the ability to be involved in sanitation and crowd control.

These public activities which are often quantifiable form a minority of religious activities and it is in its private and personal aspects of all ceremonies that working misunderstandings are more likely to occur as all individuals will always be able to create their own rituals which will move between secular and religious necessities and motivation. The orthodox requirements of their faiths for a variety of reasons often do not fit in with the primary needs of these men and women who develop parallel systems of belief and practice without any overt clash as they do not think that their activities are schismatic. Middle class American (McGuire, 1988) as much as Vietnamese practice multiple belief systems without seeing any religious conflict in what they do.

Theological Orthodoxies

It would be reasonable to assume that printed theological orthodoxies are statements of aspiration, hopes of conformity and there can be no assumption that how they are interpreted behaviourally will necessarily coincide. Some conformities to these orthodox requirements can be quantified. As attendance at obligatory ceremonies but public conformity need only be nominal and cover a multitude of private conscious and unconscious variations. These visible rigidities such as attendance figures for being present at a ceremony have little more analytical reality than can be obtained from knowing the numbers who pass through a turn-style to watch a football match.

Certainly believers can aspire to conform to these orthodox requirements and probably think that they are more or less doing so, as a basis for accepting the inevitability of working misunderstandings. In reality they are likely to reach these standards infrequently if at all because of innumerable environmental factors which will affect their ability and need to do so. What is required of believers in the majority of modernised religions are still as long-term as when their ideologies were first committed to writing.

It has also to be accepted that theological statements are almost always top down intellectual, professional and committee determined productions which have little overt connection with the common behaviour when it is definable as religious. On the other hand, non-literate and quasi-traditional religious behaviour is down-up with the consumers ensuring that their religious needs are met by those to whom they go for help and whom they materially support.

The term 'popular religion' is ill advised for any religious behaviour when the converse 'unpopular religion' might just as well be applied to theologically determined religious requirements. Orthodoxies may also vary in what they require from believers and the ease with which conformity can be fulfilled and in this they are not constructed from the results of market research. A Sukuma, Thai or Vietnamese with contemporary beliefs in the powers of ancestors, house spirits or hungry ghosts are likely to see these systems of beliefs adequately fulfilled by occasional celebrations and the placatory offerings of food in feasting which they eat themselves, or by throwing a scrap of food into the ancestors hut in the compound or throwing some food on the road outside the house or shop to appease hungry ghosts. The fulfilment of these obligations are either pleasant to do or trivial which are done with little or no preceding thought as would be the case in the way that Roman Catholics frequently cross themselves with their right hands. In such contexts the spirits could be seen as easily placated. It is much more time consuming and difficult to go to a Christian ceremony in a special building on Sunday or much more so to go on the obligatory pilgrimage to Mecca but less so now that pilgrims can go by air rather than walk.

What believers actually think and do is often assessed in relation to what is required by orthodoxy. In this there are very clear distinctions between what is required from a Muslim and what a devout Buddhist needs to do which in social terms can be clearly assessed as psychologically and socially impossible.

Islam can be assessed in this same pattern of commitment and attainment when the Five Pillars of the Faith are clear enough; to believe in Allah, pray five times per day, fast between sun up and sun down in the holy month of Ramżān, give alms to the poor and go on the pilgrimage to Mecca. These can be completed without the difficulties of compliance with the beliefs and practices of interior faiths such as Buddhism and Christianity in which their exterior forms are ancillary to self-control in the mind. The committed Muslim who fulfils these obligations is not unusual, while lapsing in the terms of praying five times per day must be relatively commonplace outside the towns of Iran and Saudi Arabia patrolled by religious police overseeing that shops shut for the midday prayers. The amount of charity can often be partially assessed through national bureaucracies which oversee and supervise wakfs charitable trusts in such countries as Egypt.

The possibilities of working misunderstandings are limited in Islam by the comparative simplicities of its basic requirements for overt ceremonial behaviour. However, when it comes to Islamic law in which rulings are made by interpreters of the Holy *Koran*, they are no more likely to be followed than any other set of regulations which do not fit into the surrounding social understandings and conveniences. When these rulings become national law and become both invasive and extensive as restrictions on clothing and the charging of interest in commercial transactions, then parallel systems working round these restrictions are inevitable as stimulated by inconvenience and dislike of such restrictions.

Just as with secular restrictions imposed on religious institutions these parallel systems are not so much working misunderstandings as the result of ignorance and the feeling that these religious requirements have become too invasive and, therefore, have to be worked round.

Buddhism in its orthodoxy is a philosophical rather than religious system which holds that an individual can only achieve release from the wheel of suffering and the miseries of reality by the progressive detachment from all desires over innumerable rebirths. Buddhism is characterised by little or any concern with the mundane problems of everyday life which could have been avoided by detachment. None of its goals or instruments involve the aid of any supernatural being or saviour. Salvation is achieved by the unaided efforts of the believer without any assistance from either the gods or the Buddha (Spiro, 1971:140). It is hard to envisage any Buddhist going even a fraction of the way to fulfil this orthodoxy when even enjoying the view or a successful harvest is a form of desire to be avoided because of its potential absence.

We can see, therefore, that in the case of Buddhism and to almost parallel, extent, with Jainism, Hinduism and Taoism, the vast majority of practitioners are only marginally if at all acting within the ill-defined soft orthodoxies of the faiths to which they belong. Indeed Buddhism to all intents and purposes has been turned into a religion so that it could be described almost totally as a working misunderstanding.

So there is an initial division between religious commitments that can be carried out and those that clearly cannot be fulfilled such as the abolition of self in Buddhism or the requirement to love one's neighbour as oneself and not to covet other people or their property. Indeed Hegel described Christianity as an impossible religion (Hegel, 1807) because of its inhuman aspirations.

There is seemingly a sense of fulfilment which may be as much social as religious from the carrying out of rituals which require no deep spiritual commitment beyond the fact that by carrying out these obligatory performances they are personally acting within the parameters of their faith. It has been ticked off as compliance for that activity.

The dividing line would appear to be whether the carrying out of rituals is regarded as an end in themselves and of instrumental value to put something right or to reduce anxiety which is certainly the predominant view of the generality of religious people whether they are

Muslims, Moravians or Melanesians. This does not have much to do with what the theologians of cult, sect or major faith have ruled as to the long-term purpose of ceremonies as a necessary part of orthodoxy. It is immediate needs that predominate.

However, there are major faiths such as Buddhism, Christianity and Hinduism in which their orthodoxies may accept that ritualistically performed activities are better than nothing, but their aims go far beyond mere ritualism. The fact remains that these aims and their related behavioural requirements are realistically beyond any social possibilities for any individual. In single life faiths such as the religions of the book. On the other hand, successive but innumerable reincarnations give everyone in Eastern religions the opportunity to achieve this annihilation of self required by Buddhism. This is a matter of dogma among southern Mahayana Buddhists that only the Lord Buddha has achieved this. On the other hand, northern Hinayana Buddhism has an unknown number of Boddhisattvas, individuals who have delayed Enlightenment in order to help those who have delayed their detachment. So we have here an enormous and continuing gulf in which almost all believers find their religious satisfactions in what are clearly in orthodoxy terms, theologically inadequate which are unconsciously working misunderstandings.

In behavioural terms there is probably no other alternative for those who want their primary experiential realities to be provided by some aspects of religious faith and commitment without going too deeply into what are the fundamental requirements of the faiths to which they feel general affiliation from socialization or conversion.

There are two contrasting aspects to consider. Whenever religious thinking or orthodoxies provide certainties, the more likely it will be that the vast majority of believers will feel that the carrying out of rituals or participation in their performance will be adequate enough to conform to the requirements of membership and to get desired results without feeling any need to find out the religious bases for what they are doing.

Then there are religions such as Buddhism and Christianity which set behavioural objectives for which there are no set and dominating rituals such as the dissolution of self or to give up all and follow Christ and to love one's neighbour as oneself which are in practice impossible objectives. So involvement can be seen rather too clearly as failure and that degrees of personally accepted fulfilment are working misunderstandings.

The Thai Buddhist putting flowers on their domestic shrine or changing the costume on their statue of the Buddha as the season's change or the Burmese one with his account book working out his balance of earned merit may be subscribing in very vague terms to Buddhist objectives of personal extinction. The fact that they are practising a religious system for the reduction of their immediate difficulties means that Buddhists benefit from what they have created which has little to do with its philosophical reasoning which is not religious.

It is in this interrelationship between philosophical and theological ideals and the basic immediacy of human behaviour whether it is secular or religious, that working misunderstandings not only exist but become a fundamental human necessity. A pattern of aspirational thinking which is thought to be religious which provides hope and the rules for its achievement. This institutional and personal acceptance of what they know to be inadequate in terms of what their faith requires, allows them to feel that they are within their natal or converted faith and to get some at least of the hoped for benefits.

The Limitations of Categorization

As religious behaviour and thought is individual any attempts at grouping must inevitably result in abbreviating this personal complexity most probably because it is just too difficult and expensive in time and money indeed as well as the personal difficulty of recognising and identify this complexity in others.

To what extent is it reasonable rather than rational to apply categorizations to religious beliefs and practices and recording for any activities which are not a matter of public record and even that is no more than a record and not an explanation or guarantee of accuracy. The fact that someone states that she is a Hindu is no more than what is carried in the wording and it tells us nothing more than the biased speculations created by the word Hindu.

It is possible to find out in general terms what are the broad cultural bases of religious thinking and behaviour. Bantu cultures have a general belief in the reality of witchcraft and in the influence of ancestors on the living, Islam has the Five pillars of the Faith and Christians have the Ten Commandments and so on. These are useful for categorization but certainly simplifications of individual social and religious realities. When it comes to Hinduism, Confucianism, Taoism and Shintoism, any attempts at categorization are on much shakier ground when these faiths have no defined foundations.

It may be that the Western or Westernized observer from the restrictions built into the European Enlightenment, have always looked for narrowly definable factors. We have to recognise that all these created boundaries are penetrable by the influences of individuality and changing social environments. The contemporary ideas and practices of Muslims living in Riyadh may be just as penetratable electronically and socially as those living in New York and Lagos. For those that live in social environments in which there has been no fixing of beliefs and practices in any written form, it must be a doubtful assumption that there can be any categorized uniformities as a basis for the understanding individual behaviour.

The basis for any understanding of religious behaviour should not start from any group categorization as the individual will unconsciously rather more than consciously pick and choose from what is available which may be as much archetypical as socially created. Even at the level of the simplest material environments such as that of the hunter gathering Kung Bushmen of the Kalahari desert there will always be choices involving their marginal pragmatics and differences in intellectual capacity. For the urban Hindu in the sacred city of Banaras with its large Muslim population, the Muslim in Cairo who is living in a graveyard and the Taoist living in high-rise apartments in Hong-Kong, there is not the remotest possibility of anyone duplicating the religious beliefs and practices of his or her neighbours and relatives with their thinking confined to situational specifics.

The conclusions of social scientists will be based on their own personal intuitions and choices of the data to be used rather than on the detached methodologies currently available to them from their professional understandings and the restrictions of linear thinking.

The Limitations of Linear Thought

Whether we can establish and retain religious understandings in any evolutionary and logical form, it may prove unwise if not impossible to see such complicated and individual behaviour in any linear form without involving the crudities of quantification (Sanderson and Roberts, 2008). There may be a form of evolution among literate thinkers but as with other abstract conclusions there may be little evidence that they have broad influence beyond the intellectual community with their thinking confined within situational specifics in which these thoughts arise. The correlation of mass religious themes which would only have writing as a provable connection and which would then have some evolutionary momentum of its own creation. It would be even more unwise to commit available and very limited data from large and individually varied populations to the simplification of any single pattern of belief and practice to what is basically just abstracted quantification.

Certainly there are broad patterns of social change which may have Darwinian elements but in supposition of linear religious change as it may have affected communal patterns of behaviour remains unproven as this field contains many interwoven and inconstant complexities. Even monotheistic faiths appear to be functionally polytheistic as in devotions to the Virgin Mary and Saints in Western Catholicism and in the Islamic devotion to their Saints. Perhaps not so extremely diverse as Hinduism but nevertheless a broad frame of devotion whatever distinctions made be made by theologians. The innumerable sub-divisions in Eastern religions make any linear approach impossible except by distorting the data obtained from observation.

It seems reasonable to suppose that the individual nature of religious ideas and the permutations of religious behaviour have always existed without any cultural means of insuring conformities. Modern societies with its urban nature and the observable proliferation of cults has perhaps placed individuality into the forefront of theological and social science understandings. The even more limited data of what may have occurred historically has made it inevitable that the researchers would tend to reach group conclusions. It is a big jump to conclude that the surviving writings of Greek philosophers and those of early Christian much less those who emptied the churches after the Reformation had an effect encompassing whole societies in which individuals would have had their own dominating needs.

The growth of highly personalised religions in modern societies may be individualised but possibly not nearly so much as the Sukuma subsistence farmer who now as previously largely makes up his own form of religious behaviour as occasion demands. The modern range of choice in Western societies may in fact be less innovative that among the Tanzanian Sukuma because so many of the ideas are visually presented in picture and print. An all powerful God in the background below whom there is a lower order of supernatural availability; my needs are listened by my saint. What we see as the collective forms of Western religiousness may turn out to be a relatively short-lasting form in a continuing pervasive varied individuality.

Any understanding of a religion as having some mass uniformity is quite against most if not all theological understandings and the results of social science investigations since the unit of concern and comprehension must always be the individual except at the lowest of partially analytically useless common denominators.

Even Dumont's distinction between individual's religiousness as outer worldly or inner worldly (Dumont, 1982) fails to recognise that for both these forms of epistemological understandings, the person is still the centre of their own thinking and behavioural patterning whatever the levels of religious detachment they may aspire.

Among the Tanzanian Sukuma and urbanised Chinese their communities will be equally diverse and individualised irrespective of any connection to intellectual capacity and education. There will always have been as now a range of religious understandings from the sophisticated to the simplistic. There are the Sudanese Nuer who were found by the Catholic convert Evans-Pritchard to be essentially monotheistic while the new Roman Catholic cathedral in Liverpool as a number of seemingly polytheistic side chapels dedicated to different saints.

16

The Reciprocities in Religious Ideas and Practices

It is important to realise and accept that the study of religious behaviour and what this discloses has built into it a fundamental assortment of working misunderstandings in assessing its realities. Firstly, the social scientist does not accept religious understandings and practices as having a comparable reality to what can be expressed about inorganic materials or indeed scientific validated medicine. Whatever the reality of agnosticism it is not cognitively similar to the thinking behind inorganic chemistry; it is just as much a biased evaluation as religious beliefs.

As bias deprives the social scientists of the detachment which is their principal methodological legitimation they should start their evaluations with the admission that religion works. They have misunderstood this reality as they are involved in explaining away rather than supporting the religious ideas and practices which they observe whether from the viewpoint of simpler intellects in societies from which they are socially distant or grudgingly or from that of the professional theologians and philosophers.

We live and usually more or less prosper on the personal realities of inferences so it seems intellectually awkward to exclude the reality of religion based on inferences when we use these all the time not only in our emotional perceptions but in how we make many of our rational decisions.

The Reality of the Supernatural

If the reality is that virtually all people regularly or intermittently relate to some form of the supernatural, it seems rather naïve to disallow its reality when we accept many other invisible concepts as real. We know that whatever a belief is, it has the potential to be real in its consequences. This has to be accepted in proportion to the minute number who throughout their lives not just take up an agnostic intellectual stance as social scientists and philosophers but behave agnostically.

The Universality of Prayer

Some people pray as a preoccupation in an orderly life, others do so as an accompaniment to important events and rites of passage and some in a response to crises. These attempts to relate to the supernatural and to establish their intervention is to all intents and purposes universal.

This universal procedure to get help for their material and spiritual difficulties has evolved because more than just a substantial majority of their prayerful hopes have been assessed as successful by those involved in a psychological rather than material sense.

However, it is analysed this practice is so universal that it could be described as a human characteristic and that it has been so not only in historical circumstances but is the dominant religious characteristic of all people in all contemporary in an indefinable variety of situations and forms. No amount of scientific analyses of primary causation can avoid this conclusion that from its proportional success rate it seems rational behaviour.

The Nature of Experienced Reciprocity

There can be no experiential proof that the supernatural does or does not exist but human beings as far back as records go and contemporary attitude surveys show, have acted not on the assumption of but on its reality. Human experience has shown that this entity responds benignly not only in occasional miracles and appearances but in an enormous numbers of general experiences.

Human beings have a practical rationality in how they conduct their personal lives which can account for their successful biological survival. This survival has been characterised by a social system based on reciprocities. They have used this same reciprocity to create and cement their successful relationships with the supernatural.

The Ambiguity of Silence

The reality that the supernatural can have no experiential proof allows believers of whatever persuasion to have their own personal satisfactions within the interpretable best of the agnostic and believing world views. The silence of the supernatural is not definitive but ambiguous.

Our conclusions must surely be that religious beliefs and behaviour, however defined and however created, are an essential part of human ability to survive and change. To this end there is a continuing and necessary working misunderstanding between the ideological pronouncements of theologians and charismatics and the corporate necessities of religious organisations and the ways that individuals put them into practice.

Bibliography

Aarts, F. and J. Aarts. 1982. *English Syntactic Structures. Functions and Categories in Sentence Analysis*. Oxford. Pergamon Press.

Aberle, D.F. 1966. *The peyote cactus of the Navajo Religion*. New York. Wenner-Gren.

Abrums, M. 2000. Jesus will fix it after awhile. Meanings and Health. *Social Science Medicine*. 50:89-105.

Ackerman, S.E. 1979. The language of religious innovation. Spirit possession and exorcism in a Malaysian Catholic Pentecostal movement. *Journal of Anthropological Research*. 37(1):91-100.

Al-Nagar, S.A.H. 1980. Zar practitioners and their assistants and followers in Omdurman. In V.G. Pons. (ed). *Urbanization and Urban Life in the Sudan*. Khartoum. Khartoum University Press.

Amin, S. 1995. *Event, Metaphor. Memory. Chauri Chaura*. 1922-1992. Berkeley. University of California Press.

Anagnost, A.S. 1987. Politics and religion in contemporary China. *Modern China*. 13(1):46-61.

Appadurai, A. 1981. Gastro-politics in Hindu South Asia. *American Ethnology*. 8(3):494-511.

Argyle, M. and M. Cook. 1976. *Gaze and Mutual Gaze*. Cambridge. Cambridge University Press.

Asad, T. 1986. The concept of cultural translation in British social anthropology. In J. Clifford and G.E. Marcus. (eds). *Writing Culture—The Poetics and Politics of Ethnography*. Berkeley. University of California. Press. 141-164.

Babb, L.A. 1970. Marriage and malevolence. The uses of sexual opposition in a Hindu pantheon. *Ethnology*. 9(2):137-148.

Badone, E. 1990. *Introduction. Religious Orthodoxies and Popular Faith in European Society*. In E. Badone.(ed). New Jersey. Princeton University Press. 3-23.

Baggett, J.P. 2001. *Sense of the Faithful. How American Catholics Live Their Faith*. New York. Oxford University Press.

Baker, T.L. 1998. *Doing Social Research*. New York, McGraw-Hill.

Bakhtin, M. 1981. *The Dialogical Imagination*. In M. Holquist and C. Emerson (trans). Austin. University of Texas.

Bakker, H.T. 1986. *Ayodha*. Groningen. Egbert Forsten.

Barrett, B. 1968. *Schism and Renewal in Africa—An Analysis of 6000 Contemporary Religious Movements in Africa*. Nairobi. Oxford University Press.

Barret, J.L. 1998. Cognitive constraints on Hindu concepts of the Divine. *Journal of Scientific Study of Religion*. 37(4):608-619.

Basso, K.H. 1970. To give up on words. Silence in Western Apache culture. *South-Western Journal of Anthropology*. 26(3):213-228.

Batibo, H. 1985. *Le keSukuma. Langue Bantu Tanzania*. Paris. Editions Recherche sur les Civilisations.

Bateson, J.H. 1911. *Creed (Buddhist) in Encyclopaedia of Religion and Ethics*. Edinburgh. T and T Clark.

Baumann, G. 1986. Introduction to G. Baumann. (ed). *The Written Word. Literacy in Translation*. Oxford. Clarendon Press.

Bax, M. 1985. Popular devotions, power and religious regimes in Catholic Dutch Brabant. *Ethnology*. 24(3):215-227.

Behrend, H. 1999, Power to heal, power to kill. Spirit possession and war in northern Uganda. (1986-1994. In H. Behrend and U. Luig. (eds). *Spirit Possession. Modernity and Power in Africa*. Oxford. Currey.

Behrend, H. and U. Luig. 1999. Introduction to Behrend, H. and U. Luig. (eds). Spirit possession. *Modernity and Power in Africa*. Oxford. Currey.

Bell, C.M. 2002. The Chinese believe in spirits; belief and believers in the study of religion in N.K. Frankenberry. (ed). *Radical Interpretations in Religion*. Cambridge. Cambridge University Press. 106-116. 1-19.

Bellah, R. *et al.* 1985. *Habits of the Heart*. Berkeley. University of California Press.

Bellwinkel, M. 1979. Objective appreciation through subjective involvement—A slum in Kanpur. In M.N. Srinivas *et al.* (ed). *The Field Worker and the Field*. Delhi. Oxford University Press. 141-151.

Bennet, In S.t., A. 2005. *Untold Stories*. London. Faber.

Bernardi, L.B. 1959. *The Mugwe—A Failing Prophet*. A study of a religious and public dignitary of the Meru of Kenya. London. Oxford University Press.

Beteille, A. 1986. Individualism and equality. *Current Anthropology*. 27:121-134.

Bhardwaj, S.M. 1973. *Hindu Places of Pilgrimage in India*. A study in cultural geography. Berkeley. University of California Press.

Bishop, G.V. 1971. *Witness to Evil*. San Francisco.

Blackmore, S. 1993. *Dying to Live. Near Death Experience*. Buffalo. New York. Prometheus.

Blau, P.M. 1965. *The Dynamics of Bureaucracy*. Chicago. Chicago University Press.

Bloch, M. 1990. Language, anthropology and cognitive science. *Man(ns)*. 26:183-198.

——, 2004. Ritual and deference. In H. Whitehouse and J. Laidlaw. (eds). *Ritual and Memory: Toward a Comparative Anthropology of Religion*. Walnut Creek. Altamira Press. 65-72.

Bloom, A. 1981. *The Linguistic Shaping of Thought*: A Study of the Impact of Language on Thinking in China and the West. Hillsdale. Erlbaum.

Boddy, J. 1989. *Wombs and Alien Spirits. Women, Men and the Zar Cult in Northern Sudan*. University of Wisconsin Press.

Bourguignon, E. 1976. *Possession*. San Francisco. Chandler and Sharp.

Boyer, P. 1990. *Tradition as Truth and Communication: A Cognitive Description of Traditional Discourse*. Cambridge. Cambridge University Press.

——, 2000. Functional origins of religious concepts: ontologies and strategic selection in evolved minds. *Journal of Royal Anthropological Institute*.(ns). 6:195-214.

Brandes, S. 1990. Reflections on the study of religious orthodoxies and popular faith in Europe. In E. Badone. (ed). *Religious Orthodoxies and Popular Faith in European Society*. New Jersey. Princeton University. 185-199.

Brook, T. 2009. The politics of religion. Late Imperial origins of the regulatory state. In Y. Ashiwa and D.L. Wank. (eds). *Making religion, Making the State*. Stanford. Stanford University Press. 22-42.

Brown, F.C. 1972. *Hallucinogenic Drugs*. Springfield. C.C. Thomas.

Browne, D.G. 1986. Umbanda. *Religion and Politics in an Urban Setting* Brazil. Ann Arbor. University of Michigan Press.

Buddha—the Dialogues of. 1931. Pali Text Society. London. Oxford University Press.

Burke, J.F. 1992. Research in a post missionary situation among Zairean Sisters of Notre Dame de Namur. *Journal of Anthropological Society* Oxford. 23(2):157-168.

Burke, K. 1981. *Permanence and Change—An Anatomy of Purpose.* Berkeley. University California Press.

Burt, B. 1985. The Remnant Church—*A Christian Sect of the Solomon Islands*. Oceania. 53(4):334-46.

Calkins and Holden. 1927. *The World has changed. Advertising and Selling*. 29 June:12.

Cannell, F. 2006. Reading as gift and writing as theft. In F. Cannell.(ed). *The anthropology of Christianity*. Durham. Duke University Press. 134-162.

Carmichael, E. and C. Sayer. 1991. The Skeleton at the Feast. *The Day of the Dead in Mexico*. Austin. University of Texas.

Carmody, B. 1988. *Conversion and School in Chikuni.* 1905-1939. Africa. 58(2):193-209.

Castells, M. 2004. *The Rise of the Network Society*. Oxford. Blackwell.

Chafe, W. 1994. Discourse, Consciousness and Time. The Flow and Displacement of Conscious Experience in Speaking and Writing. Chicago. Chicago University Press.

Chan, W.T. 1953. *Religious Trends in Modern China*. New York. Columbia University Press.

Chatley, H. 1917. Feng Shui. In S. Couling.(ed). *Encyclopaedia* Sinica. Shanghai.

Chau, A.Y. 2006. *Miraculous Response. Doing Popular Religion in Contemporary China*. Stanford. Stanford University Press.

Chen, G. 1996. The old tradition in a new setting. A preliminary study of mortuary rituals in a Chinese village. *Journal of Ritual Studies*. 10(2):41-57.

Chi-Cheung, C. 1984. *The Chinese Yue Lan Ghost Festival in Japan*. A Kobe case study. Royal Asiatic Society (Hong-Kong Branch), 24:230-263.

Ching, J. 1993. *Chinese Religions*. London. Macmillan.

Chitando, E. 2005. The Phenomenology of Religion and the Study of African Traditional Religions. *Method and Theory in the Study of Religion*. 17:299-316.

Christian, W.A. 1981. *Local Religion in Sixteenth Century Spain. New Jersey*. Princeton University Press.

Clark, J. 1992. *Madness and Colonialism: The embodiment of power in Pangia*. Oceania. 63(10):15-26.

Cohen, M, 1988. Souls and salvation. Conflicting themes in Chinese popular religion. In Watson, J.S. and Rawski, E.S. (eds). *Death Ritual in Late Imperial and Modern China*. Berkeley. University of California Press. 180-203.

Coker, C. 2008. Review of Chris Patten. *What next? Surviving the Twenty-first Century*. London. Allen and Unwin. 5 December. Times Literary Supplement. 31-33.

Colby, B.N. 1969. Izil country. *A Plural Society in Highland Guatmala*. Berkeley. University of California Press.

Comaroff, J. and J. Comaroff. 1993. *Ethnography and the Historical Imagination*. Boulder. Western.

Comstock, G.W. and K.B. Partridge. 1972. Church Attendance and Health. *Journal Chronic Diseases*. 25:65-72.

Corin, E. 1979. A possession psychotherapy in an urban setting. Zebola in Kinshasha. *Social Science and Medicine*. 138(4):327-8.

Cory, H. 1953. *Sukuma Law and Custom*. London. Oxford University Press.

Cribb, R. 1990. The Indonesian killings 1956-6. *Studies from Java and Bali*. Victoria. Monash Papers on South East Asia.

Cullen, D.L. 1995. Psychotherapy in Cyberspace. *The Clinician*. 26(1):6-7.

Daniel, C. 1996. The Story of the Eyam. *Plague—Eyam*. Privately printed.

Davies, R. and Ikeno, O. 2002. *The Japanese Mind*. New York Tuttle.

Davis, K. 1946. *Moral and Pastoral Theology*. 4 Vols. London. Sheed and Ward.

Dean, K. 1995. *Taoist Ritual and Popular Cults of South-East China*. Princeton. Princeton University Press.

Denzin, N.K. 1984. *On Understanding Emotion*. San Francisco. Josey Bass.

Derrida, J. 1978. *Writing and Difference*. A. Bass.(trans). New York. Cornell University Press.

Dillon, M. 1999. China's Muslim Hiu Community. *Migration, settlement and Sects*. Richmond. Curzon.

DiMaggio, P.J. and W.W. Powell. 1983. Introduction. In P.J. DiMaggio and W.W. Powell. (eds). *The New Institutionalism in Organisation Analysis*. Chicago. Chicago University Press. 1-38.

Doom, N. and K. Vlassenroot. 1999. Kray's message. A new koine. The Lord's Resistance Army in Northern Uganda. *African Affairs*. 98:5-36.

Douglas, M. 1966. *Purity and Danger*. London. Routledge and Kegan Paul.

Dronen, T.S. 2006. Scientific revolution and religious conversion. A close look at Thomas Kuhn's theory of paradigm shift. *Method and Theory in the Study of Religion*. 18:232-253.

Dua, V. 1979. A woman's encounter with Arya Samaj and Untouchables. In M.N. Srinivas *et al.* (eds). *The Field Worker and the Field. Delhi*, Oxford University Press. 115-126.

Du Boulay, J. 2009. *Cosmos, life and liturgy in a Greek orthodox village*. Limni. Denise Harvey.

Duffy, E. 1992. The stripping of the altars. *Traditional religion in England*. 1400-1580. New Haven, Yale University Press.

Dumont, L. 1982. *A Modified View of Our Origins; The Christian Beginnings of Modern Individualism Religion*. 12:1-27.

Eck, D.L. 1981. Darsan. *Seeing the Divine Image in India*. Chambers Burn. Anima.

Eckensberger, L.H. 1994. Moral development and its measurement among cultures. In Lonnrer, J. and R. Malpass. (eds). *Psychology and Culture*. Boston. Allyn and Bacon. 71-78.

Eco, U. 1994. *Apocalypse Postponed*. Bloomington. Indiana University Press.

Eickelman, D. 1978. The art of memory. Islamic education and social reproduction. *Comparative Studies in Society and History*. 20:485-516.

Ekvall, R.B. 1964. *Religious Observances in Tibet—Patterns and Functions*. Chicago. Chicago University Press.

Evans-Pritchard, E.E. 1934. Levy-Bruhl's theory of primitive mentality. Cairo. *Bulletin Faculty of Arts*. University of Egypt.

1956. Nuer Religion. Oxford. Oxford University Press.

Fan, W. 1992. Village feng shui principles. In R.G. Knapp.(ed). Chinese landscapes. *The Village as Place*. Honolulu. University of Hawaii Press.

Fetherstonhaugh, D. *et al.* 1997. Insensitivity to the value of mass life. A study of psychophysical numbing. *Journal of Risks and Uncertainty*. 14:283-300.

Feierman, S. 1990. Peasant intellectuals. *Anthropology and History in Tanzania*. Madison. University of Wisconsin Press.

Feng, G. and L.Yi. 2005. What if Chinese had linguistic markers for counter-factuality. *Language and Thought Revisited*. 27th Annual Meeting of the Cognitive Science Society:1281-6.

Ferguson, J. 1999. Expectations of modernity, *Myths and meanings of urban life in the Zambian Copperbelt*. Berkeley. University of California Press.

Fernandez, J.W. 1965. Symbolic consensus in a Fang Reformative Cult., *American Anthropologist*. 67:02-929.

——, 1966. Unbelievable subtle words. Representation and integration in the sermons of an African reformative cult. *History of Religions*. 6(1):43-69.

——, 1980. Edification by puzzlement. In I. Karo and C.S. Bird. (eds). *Explorations in African Systems of Thought*. Bloomington. Indiana University Press.

Fields, K. 1985. *Revival and Rebellion in Colonial Central Africa*. New Jersey. Princeton University Press.

Francis, L.J. and S.M. Robbins. 2003. Personality and glossolalia. A study among male evangelical clergy. *Pastoral Psychology*. 51(5):341-346.

Fraser, G.E. *et al*. 1991. Diet and lung cancer in California Seventh day Adventists. *American Journal of Epidemiology*. 133(7):683-93.

Fuller, C. 1992. The camphor flame. *Popular Hinduism and Society in India*. Princeton. New Jersey. Princeton University Press.

Gambie, V.N. 1997. Under the shadow of Tuskegee. African-Americans and health care. *American Journal or Public Health*. I7(11):1773-1777,

Gardet, L. 1981. *La cite Musulmane. Vie sociale et politique*. Paris. Vrin.

Geertz, C. 1973. *The Interpretation of Culture*. Chicago. Chicago University Press.

Gennet, J. 1985. China and the Christian Impact—A Conflict of Culture. Cambridge. Cambridge University Press.

Giel, R. *et al*. 1968. Faith healing and spirit possession in Ghion, Ethiopia. Social Science *Medicine*. 2:63-79.

Glass, L. 1985. The changing of things. *Memories of Burma*. 1934-1949. London. Owen.

Gluckman, M. 1962. Les rites de passage. In M. Gluckman. (ed). *Essays on the Ritual of Social Relations*. 1-52. Manchester. Manchester University Press.

Gombrich, R. and G. Obbyeskere. 1988. Buddhism transformed. *Religious change in Sri Lanka*. Princeton. Princeton University Press.

Gomperz, J.J. *et al*. 1984. Cohesion in spoken and written discourse. *Ethnic Style and Transition to Literacy*. In D. Tannen.(ed). Coherence in spoken and written discourse. Norwood. New Jersey. Ablex.

Goodman, F.D. 1972. Speaking in tongues. *A cross-cultural study of glossolalia*. Chicago. Chicago University Press.

Goody, J. 1977. *The Domestication of the Savage Mind.* Cambridge. Cambridge University Press.

Gopnick, A. 2009. The philosophical baby—*What children's minds tell us about truth, love and the meaning of life*. London. Bodley Head.

Goudsblom, J. 1989. Ecological regions and the rise of organised religion. In J. Goudsblom *et al.* (eds). *Human History and Social Process.* Exeter. Exeter University Press.

Green, M. 1995. Why Christianity is the religion of business. Perceptions of the Church among Pogoro Catholics in Southern Tanzania. *Journal of Religion in Africa.* 25(1):25-47.

——, 2000. Participatory development and the appropriation of agency in southern Tanzania. Critique of Anthropology. 20(1):67-89.

Green, M. and Mesaki, S. 2005. The birth of the 'Salon': Poverty, modernization and dealing with witchcraft in Southern Tanzania. *American Ethnologist.* 32(3):371-388.

Gronewold, S. 1972. Did Frank Hamilton Cushing go native. In S.T. Kimball and J.B. Watson. (eds). *Cross-cultural Boundaries*—The Anthropological Experience. San Francisco. Chandler.

Haider, H. 1985. *A Banquet of Seaweed.* Cairo.

Hall, G.R. and Galanter, M. 1984. Gone from the promised land. Jonestown in American Cultural History. New York. Sage.

Hall, G.S. 1904. *Adolescence.* Its psychology and its relation to physiology, anthropology, sociology, sex, crime, religion and education. New York. Appleton.

Hannerz, Ú. 1990. Cosmopolitans and locals in world's culture. *Theory, Culture and Society.* 7(2-3):237-51.

Harvey, G. 2000. Introduction. In G. Harvey. (ed). *Indigenous Religion.* London. Cassell.

Hatfield, C.R. 1968. *The Nfumu in tradition and change.* A study of the position of religious practitioners among the Sukuma of Tanzania. D.Phil. Washington. Catholic University of America.

Hartley, L.P. 1953. *The go-between.* London. Hamish Hamilton.

Hayward, C. Madill, A. 2003. The meanings of organ donation. Muslims of Pakistani and white English nationals living in North England. *Social Science and Medicine.* 57:389-401.

Hegel, G.W.F. 1807. *The Spirit of Christianity and its Fate in Early Theological Writings.* Philadelphia. Philadelphia University Press.

Heilman, S. and M. Friedman. 2010. The Rebbe. *The Life and Afterlife of Menachem Mendel Schneerson.* Princeton. Princeton University Press.

Heine, B. 1985. *The Mountain People*. Some notes on the Ik of north-east lUganda. Africa. 55:3-16.

Hellwig. M.K. 1994. Glossolalia. In M. Glazier and M.K. Hellwig. (eds). *The New Catholic Encyclopaedia*. Dublin. Gill and Macmillan.

Hermann, E. 1992. The Yali movement in retrospect; rewriting history, *Redefining Cargo Cults*. Oceania. 63(1):55-78.

Hine, V.H. 1964. Pentecostal glossolalia. Toward a functional interpretation'. *Journal Scientific Study of Religion*. 8(2):211-226.

Hinfelaar, H.F. 1991. Women's revolt. The Lumpa Church of Lenshina Mulingo in the 1950s. *Journal of Religion in Africa*. 21(2):99-129.

——, 1994. Bemba-speaking women of Zambia in a *Century of Religious Change*. 1892-1992. Leiden. Brill.

Hinton, W. 1983. Shenfan. *The Continuing Revolution in a Chinese Village*. New York. Random House.

Hockett, C.F. 1954. Chinese versus English. An exploration of the Whorfian thesis. In Holster, H. (ed). Language in culture. *American Anthropological Association Memorandum* 79. Chicago. Chicago University Press. 106-23.

Hoehler-Fatton, C. 1996. Women of fire and spirit. History, fasith and gender in Roho religion in *Western Kenya*. Oxford. Oxford University Press.

Hordes, S.M. 2006. To the end of the earth. *A History of the Crypto Jews of New Mexico*. New York. Columbia University Press.

Hostetler, J.A. 1974. *Hutterite Society*. Baltimore. Johns Hopkins University.

——, 1993. *Amish Society*. Baltimore. Johns Hopkins University.

Hostetler, J.A and G.E. Huntington. 1971. Amish children. *Education in the Family, School and Community*. Philadelphia. Harcourt Brace Jovanovich.

Hsieh, E. 2006. Interpreter as co-diagnostician. Overlapping roles and services between provider and interpreter. *Social Science Medicine*. 64(4):924-37.

Humphrey, N. 1981. Four minutes to midnight in R.J. Lifton and M. Humphrey. (eds). In a *Dark Time*. Camb. Mass. Harvard University Press.

Houtman, D. and P. Mascini. 2002. Why do churches become empty while New Age grows. Secularization and religious change in the Netherlands. *Journal of Scientific Study of Religion*. 41(3):455-473.

Humphrey, C. and J. Laidlaw. 1994. *The archetypal actions of ritual—A theory of ritual*. Illustrated by the Jain rite of worship. Clarendon Press. Oxford.

Hutchins, C. 1980. *Culture and Inference*. A Trobriand case study. Cambridge. Mass. Harvard university Press.

Icaza, R.M. 1987. *National Pastoral Plan for Hispanic Ministry*. United States Bishops Conference. Colorado Springs. Colorado.

Ileto, R.C. 1979. *Pasyon and Revolution*. Manila. Atheneo de Manila.

Irvine, S.T. 1982. The creation of identity in spirit mediumship and possession. In D. Parkin. (ed). *Semantic Anthropology*. London. Academic Press. 241-60.

Ivy, M. 1995. Discourses of the Vanishing Modernity Phantasm, Japan. Chicago. Chicago University Press.

Jaschok, M. and Jing Jun. 2000. The history of women's mosques in China. *A Mosque of Their Own*. Richmond. Curzon.

Johnson, J.M. 1975. Doing Field Research. New York. Free Press.

Jolly, M. 1996. Devils, Holy Spirits and the swollen god. Translation, conversion and colonial power in the Marist Mission, Vaniatu. 1887-1934. 231-62. In P. van der Veer.(ed). *Conversion to Modernity*; the globalization of Christianity. London. Routledge.

Jordan, D.K. 1976. *The Jiaw of Shigang (Taiwan)*. An essay in folk interpretation. Asian Folklore Studies. 35(2):81-107.

Joshi, P.C. 1979. Field work experience relived and reconsidered. In M.N. Srinivas *et al.* (ed). The Fieldworker and the Field. Delhi. Oxford University Press. 73-94.

Judt, T. 2009. *Lessek Kolakowski*. 1927-2009. New York Review Books. 56(4):6-8.

Juergensmeyer, M. 2008. *Global Rebellion*. Religious challenges to the secular state from Christian militias to Al Queda. Berkeley. University of California Press. Review in Economist. 3 May1962.

Jung, C.G. 1959. *The Archetypes and the Collective Unconscious*. London. Routledge and Kegan Paul.

Kakar, S. 1983. *Shamans, Mystics and Doctors*. A psychological enquiry into India and its healing tradition. Boston. Beacon Press.

——, 1999. Some unconscious aspects of ethnic violence in India. In V. Das. (eds). *Communities, Riots and Survivors in South Asia*. Delhi. Oxford University Press.

Kamalkhani, Z. 1997. Women's Islam. Religious Practices among Women in Today's Iran. London. Kegan Paul.

Kan, S. 2001. Strangers and natives. The adoption and naming of anthropologists in native North America. *Introduction*. Lincoln. University Nebraska Press. 1-27.

Keesing, R. 1985. Conventional metaphor and Anthropological metaphysics. The problem of cultural translation. *Journal of Anthropological Research*, 31:201-7 1989. Exotic readings of cultural texts. *Current Anthropology*. 30(4):459-79.

Keller, E. 2006. *Scripture Study as Normal Science*. Seventh day Adventist practice.

On the east coast of Madagascar. In F. Cannell. (ed). *The Anthropology of Christianity*. Durham. Duke University Press. 277-294.

Kendal, L. 1995. Shamans, Housewives and Other Restless Spirits in Korean Ritual Life. Honolulu. University of Hawaii Press.

——, 1996. Korean shamans and the spirit of capitalism. *American Anthropologist*. 98(3):512-27.

Kenyon, S.M. 1999. The case of the Butcher's wife. Illness, possession and power in Central Sudan. In H. Behrend and U. Luig. (eds). *Spirit Possession—Modernity and Power in Africa*. Oxford. Currey.

Kessler, C. 1977. Conflict and sovereignty in Kelantan spirit sequences. In Crapanzana, V. and V. Garrison. (eds). *Case Studies in Spirit Possession*. New York. Wiley.

Kirsch, T.G. 2004. Restaging the will to believe. Religious pluralism, anti-syncretism and the problem of belief. *American Anthropologist*. 106(4):699-709.

Koestler, A. 1954. *The Invisible Writing*. London. Hamish Hamilton.

Knutsson, K.E. and R. Selinus. 1970. Fasting in Ethiopia. An anthropological and nutritional study. *American Journal of Clinical Nutrition*. 23:956-9.

Kondo, D.K. 1990. *Crafting Selves—Power, Gender and Discourses of Identity in a Japanese Workplace. Chicago. University of Chicago.*

Kramrisch, S. 1976. *The Hindu Temple*. Delhi. Banarsidas.

Krings, M. 1999. On history and language of the European 'bori' spirits. In Behrend, H. and U. Luig. (eds). *Spirit Possession—Modernity and power in Africa*. Oxford. Currey.

Kuiper, J.C. 1990. *Power is Performance*. The creation of textual authority in Weyewa ritual speech. Philadelphia. University of Pennsylvania Press.

Kumar, N. 1992. *Friends, Brothers and Informants*. Field work memories of Banaras. Berkeley. University of California Press.

Kundera, M. 2000. Quoted in T. Parks. The Perils of Translation. New York Review of Books. 20 January:54.

Ladd, J. 1957. *The Structure of as Moral Code—A philosophical analysis of ethical discourse applied to the ethics of the Navaho Indians*. Cambridge. Mass. Harvard University Press.

Lai, W. 2001. Dao. In Leaman, O. (ed). *Encyclopaedia of Asian Philosophy*. London. Routledge.

Laitin, D.D. 1977. Politics, language and thought—*The Somali experience*. Chicago. Chicago University Press.

Lambert, M. 1993. Knowledge and practices in Mayotte. *Local Discourses of Islam, Sorcery and Spirit Possession*. Toronto. Toronto University Press.

Lambert, T. 2006. *China's Christian millions*. Oxford. Monarch.

La Saga, J.L. 1980. Death in Jonestown. Techniques of political control in a paranoid leader. *Suicide Life Threatening Behaviour*. 10:210-213.

Lattas, A. 1992. Skin, personhood and redemption. *The double self in West New Britain Cargo Cults*. Oceania. 63(1):27-54.

Lawson, E.T. and R.N. McCauley. 1993. *Rethinking religion: Connecting Cognition and Culture*. Cambridge. Cambridge University Press.

Le Comte, L. 1896-1900. Nouveau memoires sur l-etat present de la Chine. Vol 2. Paris.

Le Hong Ly. 2007. Praying for profit. The Cult of the Lady of the Treasury. *Journal of South East Asian Studies*. 38(3):493-513.

Leinhardt, R.G. 1980. Self, public and private. Some African representations. *Journal of Anthropological Society* Oxford. Xi(2).

Lewis, C. and R.E.S. Tanner. 1998. Head or Heart. *Should Christians be educated*. Parson and Parish. 151:14-18.

Lewis, I.M. 1971. Ecstatic religion. Harmondsworth. Penguin.

——, 1986. *Religion in context. Cults and Charisma*. Cambridge. Cambridge University Press.

Lewis-Williams, D. 2010. *Conceiving God*. The cognitive origin and evolution of religion. London. Thames and Hudson.

Littleton, C.S. 1995. *Understanding Shinto*. London. Duncan Baird.

Liu, W.T. and Leung, B.F.K. 2004. *The Chinese Catholic in Conflict*. Florida. Universal Publisher.

Livingstone, D. 1857. *Missionary Travels*. London. John Murray.

Loizos, P. 1988. *Intercommunal Killing in Cyprus*. Man(n s). 23:634-53.

Lubeck, P.M. 1985. Islamic Protest Under Semi-Industrial Capitalism. Africa. 55:369-89.

Luig, U. 1999. Constructing local worlds. Spirit possession in the Gwembe valley, Zambia. In Behrend, H. and U. Luig.(eds). *Spirit Possession—Modernity and Power in Africa*. Oxford. Currey.

Lurie, A. 2008. The message of the school-room. New York Review of Books. 4 December. 31-33.

Macdonald, C.F. 1997. *Plato's Cosmology*. The Timeaus of Plato. Indianapolis. Hackett.

Maslow, A.H. 1970. *Motivation and Personality*. New York. Harper and Row.

Mayaram, S. 1996. Speech, silence and the maskers of violence in Mewat. In S. Amin and D. Chakrabarty. (eds). *Subaltern Studies IX*. Delhi. Oxford University Press. 126-163.

McGuire, R.B. 1988. *Ritual Healing in Urban America*. New Jersey. Rutgers University Press.

McLuhan, M. 1962. The Gutenberg Galaxy. *The Making of Typographic Man*. London. Routledge and Kegan Paul.

Mead, M. 1956. New lives for old. Cultural transformation. *Manus* 1928-1953. New York. Morrow.

Mehta, S. 2004. Maximum city. *Bombay Lost and Found*. Delhi. Penguin India.

Mennell, S. 1989. Short-term interest and long-term process. The case of civilisation and decivilisation. In J. Goudsblom *et al.* (eds). *Human History and Social Process*. Exeter, Exeter University Press.

Merton, R.K. 1957. *Social Theory and Social Structure*. Glencoe. Free Press.

Merton, T. 1948. *The Seven Story Mountain*. New York. Harcourt Brace Jovanovich.

Mesaki, S. 1992. The preponderance of women as victims in Sukuma witch killings. In Foster, P.G. and S. Mughimbi. (eds). *The Tanzanian Peasantry—Economy in Crisis*. Aldershot. Avebury.

Meyer, B. 1994. Beyond syncretism. Translation and diabolization in the appropriation of Protestantism in Africa. In C. Stewart and R. Shaw. (eds). Syncretism/Anti-Syncretism. *The Politics of Religious Synthesis*. London. Routledge. 45-68.

——, 1996. Modernity and Enchantment. The image of the Devil in Popular African Christianity. In P van der Veer.(ed). *Conversion to Modernity—The globalization of Christianity*. New York. Routledge. 199-230.

——, 1998. Making a complete break with the past. Memory and post-colonial modernities in Ghanian Pentecostalism. *Journal of Religion in Africa*. 28(3):316-349.

Micklethwait, J. and A. Wooldridge. 2009. God is Back: How the Global Rise of Faith is changing the World. London. Allen Lane.

Mills, M.B. 1994. Attack of the widow ghosts. Gender, death and modernity in North-East Thailand. In A. Ong. M. Peletiz. (eds).

Bewitch Women, Pious Men and Body Politics in South-East Asia. Berkeley. University of California Press. 244-273.

Miner, H. 1939. *St. Denis—A French-Canadian Parish*. Chicago. Chicago University Press.

Mkenda, F.L.M. 2005. *Mazoezi ya Kiroho ya Mtakatifu Inyasi wa Loyola*. Nairobi. Paulines Press.

Moberg, D.O. 1967. The encounter of scientific and religious values pertinent to man's spiritual nature. *Sociological Analysis*. 28(1):22-33.

Molho, S. 2001. Mask for Kippur, Mask for Passover. A sociological look at the Belonante Marranos. *Proceedings Twelfth World Congress of Jewish Studies*. 265-6.

Murphy, J.M. 1993. *Santeria—African Spirits in America*. Boston. Beacon Press.

Myrdal, G. 1944. An American Dilemma: The negro problem and American democracy. New York. Carnegie.

Nabokov, V. 1981. *Note on Translation in Lectures on Russian Literature*. London. Weidenfeld and Nicolson.

Nandy, A. 1990. The politics of secularism and the recovery of religious tolerance in Veena, Das. (ed). *Milieu of Violence: Communities, Riots and Survivors in South Asia*. Delhi. Oxford University Press.

Naquin, S. 1988. Funerals in North China: uniformity and variation. In J.C. Watson and E.S. Rawski. (eds). *Death Ritual in Late Imperial and Modern China*, 23-33. Berkeley. University of California Press.

Needham, R. 1977. *Belief, Language and Experience*. Blackwell. Oxford.

——, 1977. *Skulls and Causality*. Man(ns). 11:71-78.

Nida, E.A. 1958. 'Analysis of meaning and dictionary making'. *International Journal of American Linguistics*. 24:279-92.

Nida, E.A. and C.R. Taber. 1974. *The Theory and Practice of Translation*. Leiden. Brill.

Nisbet, R.A. 1969. *Social Change and History: Aspects of the Western Theory of Development*. Oxford. Oxford University Press.

Obeyesekere, G. 1978. The firewalkers of Katagarama. The use of bhakti religiosity in Buddhist Sri Lanka. *Journal of Asian Studies*. 37(3):457-476.

O'Dea, T.F. and O'Dea, J. 1983. *The Sociology of Religion*. New York. Basic Books.

Ohnuki-Tierney, E. 1984. *Illness and Culture in Contemporary Japan*. Cambridge. Cambridge University Press.

Okot p'Bitek. 1970. *African Religion in Western Scholarship*. Nairobi. East African Literature Board.

Ong, A. 1985. The production of possession; spirits and the multinational corporation in Malaysia. *American Ethnologist.* 15:28-42.

Ooms, H. 1976. A structural analysis of Japanese ancestral rites and beliefs. In W.H. Newell (ed). *Ancestors.* Paris. Mouton.

Orta, A. (2000). Syncretic subjects and body politics; doubleness, personhood and Aymara catechists. *American Ethnologists.* 26(4):864-889.

Ortner, S.B. 1999. Life and death on Mount Everest. *Sherpas and Himalayan Mountaineering.* Prinçeton University Press.

Parkin, D. 1971. Language choice in two Kampala housing estates. In W.H. Whiteley. (ed). *Language Use and Asocial Change—Problems of Multilingualism with Special Reference to East Africa.* Oxford. Oxford University Press. 347-363.

Parks, T. 2000. *The Perils of Translation.* New York Review Books. 20 January, 1954.

Parry, J. 1980. Ghosts, greed and sin—The occupational identity of the Banaras funeral priests. *Man* (Buena Aires) (ns). 15:88-120.

Pastor, F.A. 1994. Popular religion. In R. Latourelle and R. Fisichella.(eds). *Dictionary of Fundamental Theology.* Slough. St Paul's. 849-51,

Patimokkha. *The 227 Fundamental Rules of a Bhikhu.* 1966. Bangkok. Maha Makut.

Philips, L. and M. Jorgensen. 2002. *Discourse Analysis as Theory and Method.* London. Sage.

Plato. 1952. *Phaedrus.* 277c. P. Hackforth.(trans). Cambridge. Cambridge University Press.

Poloma, M.M. 2006. Glossolalia, liminality and empowered kingdom building. In M.J. Cartledge. (ed). *Speaking in Tongues: Multi-Disciplinary Perspectives.* Bletchley. Paternoster. 147-173.

Poloma, M.M. and Gallup, G.H. 1971. *Varieties of Prayer. A Survey Report.* New York. Trinity Press International.

Porter, L.C. 1920. Feng Shui or how the Chinese keep in tune with nature. *Chinese Recorder.* 12:837-850.

Pyyslainen, I. (1999). Holy Book. A treasury of the incomprehensible. *The Invention of Writing and Religious Cognition.* Numen. 46:269-290.

Ramabai, S. Pandita. 1977. *Correspondence.* Bombay. Maharashtra State Board for Literature and Culture.

Ramirez, R. 1985. Hispanic Spirituality. *Social Thought.* 11(3):6-13.

Ransome, A. 2008. *Russia in 1919*. Quoted by C. Coker. Times Literary Supplement. 5 December: 31.

Rao, R. 1938. Preface to 'Kantapura'. *New Directions*. New York.

Rapoport, D.C. 1992. Terror and the Messiah and ancient experiences and some modern parallels. In D.C. Rapoport and T. Alexander (eds). *The Morality of Terrorism. Religious and Secular Justification*. New York. Pergamon Press.

Rappaport, R.A. 1976. Liturgies and Bias. *International Yearbook of Sociology of Knowledge and Religion*. 75-104.

——, 1979. Ecology adaptation and the ills of functionalism. In R.A. Rappaport. *Ecology, Meaning and Religion*. Berkeley. North Atlantic Books. 43-95.

——, 1979. Adaptive structure and its disorders. In R.A. Rappaport. Ecology, Meaning and Religion. Berkeley. North Atlantic Books. 145-171.

Rawski, E.S. 1988. A historian's approach to Chinese death ritual. In J.C. Weston and E.S. Rawski. (eds). *Death ritual in Late Imperial and Modern China*. Berkeley. University of California Press.

Reader, I. 1991. *Religion in Contemporary Japan*. Stanford. Stanford University Press.

——, 2000. *Religious violence in contemporary Japan—The case of the Aum Shirikyo*. London. Curzon.

Redfield, R. 1956. *Peasant Society and Culture*. Chicago. Chicago University Press.

Reynolds, V. 2005. The chimpanzees of the Budongo forest. *Ecology, Behaviour and Conservation*. Oxford. Oxford University Press.

Reynolds, V. and Tanner, R. 1983. *The Social Ecology of Religion*. New York. Oxford University Press.

Richards, A.I. 1953. Towards a theory of translating. In A.F. Wright. (ed). *Studies in Chinese Thought*. Chicago. Chicago University Press.

Robb, G. 2007. The Discovery of France. London. Picador.

Robinson, G. 1995. The dark side of paradise. *Political Violence in Bali*. Ithaca. Cornell University Press.

Rodriguez, A.P. 1994. Spirituality. Hispanic. In M. Glazier and M.K. Hellwig. (eds). *The Modern Catholic Encyclopaedia*. Dublin. Gill & Macmillan. 828-30.

Roemer, M.K. 2007. Ritual participation and social support in a major Japanese festival. *Journal of Scientific Study Religion*. 46(2):185-200.

Rokeach, M. 1964. *The Three Christs of Ypsilanti*. New York. Vintage.

Roseman, M. 2001. Engaging the spirits of modernity. The Temiars. In L.H. Connor and G. Samuel. (eds). Healing Powers and Modernity. Traditional Medicine, Shamanism and Science in Asian Societies. Westport. Bergin and Garvey. 109-129.

Rouch, J. 1978. Talking about his films. *American Anthropologist.* 80;1005-22.

Rubin, D.C. 1997. *Memory in Oral Tradition.* New York. Oxford University Press.

Rumelhart, D.E. and J.L. McClelland. 1986. Parallel Distributive Processing. Explorations in the Microstructure of Cognition. Cambridge. Mass. MIT Press.

Saiyid, A.R. 1984. Idea and reality in the observance of Moharram: A behavioural interpretation. In I. Ahmad. (ed). *Ritual and Religion among Muslims in India.* Delhi. Mandhar. 113-142.

Salamone, F.A. 1977. The methodological significance of the lying informant. *Anthropological Quarterly.* 50(3):117-129.

Samarin, W.J. 1972. Tongues of men and angels. *The Religious Language of Pentecostalism.* New York. Macmillan.

Sanderson, S.K. and W.W. Roberts. 2008. The evolutionary form of religious life. A cross-cultural quantitative analysis. *American Anthropologist.* 110(4):454-466.

Scaramelli, G.B. 1754. 2005. *A Handbook of Mystical Theology.* D.H.S. Nicholson (trans). Berwick. Ibis.

Schull, W.J. *et al.* 1962. Kuroshima. The impact of religion on an island's genetic heritage. *Human Biology.* 34:271-98.

Scolen, R. and S. Scolen. 1979. Linguistic convergence. *An Ethnography of speaking at Fort Chipewyan,* Alberta. New York. Academic Press.

Scribner, S. and M. Cole. 1981. *The Psychology of Literacy.* Cambridge. Mass. Harvard University Press.

Sherlock, P. and E.O. Rothschild. 1967. Scurvy produced by a Zen macrobiotic diet. *Journal of American Medical Association.* 198:794-8.

Shuming, L. 1929. *The Civilisations of the East and the West and their Philosophies.* Shanghai. Commercial Press.

Smith, R.J. 1974. *Ancestor Worship in Contemporary Japan.* Stanford. Stanford University Press.

——, 1982. Japanese society Tradition. *Self and the Social Order.* Cambridge Cambridge University Press.

Southworth, F. 1978. On communicating with the masses. A linguist's view. In L.A. Mahadev. (ed). *Mass Culture, Language and Arts in India.* Bombay. Prakasian.

Sperber, D. 1996. *Explaining Culture*. Oxford. Blackwell.

Spickard, J.V. 2002. Disciplinary conflict in the study of religion. Anthropology, sociology and lines in the sand. *Method and Theory in the Study of Religion*. 14:141-169.

Spiro, M.E. 1971. *Buddhism and Society: A Great Tradition and its Burmese Vicissitudes*. London. Allen and Unwin.

Srinivas, M.N. 1967. The cohesive role of Sanskritization. In P. Mason. (ed). *India and Ceylon: Unity and Diversity*. London. Oxford University Press.

Stark, R. *et al*. 2005. Exploring spirituality and unchurched religions in America, Sweden and Japan. *Journal of Contemporary Religion*. 20(1):3-23.

Steedy, M.M. 1993. *Hanging without a rope. Narrative Experience in Colonial and Postcolonial Karoland*. New Jersey. Princeton University Press.

Steiner, G. 1975. After Babel. *Aspects of language and translation*. London. Oxford University Press.

Stephen, M. 1976. Dreams of change. *The Innovative Role of Altered States of Consciousness in Traditional Melanesian Religion*. Oceania. 50(1):3-22.

Stromberg, P. 1981. Consensus and variation in the interpretation of religious symbolism. A Swedish example. *American Ethnologist*. 8(3):544-559.

Stubbs, M. 1980. *Language and Literacy*. London. Routledge & Kegan Paul.

Suinn, R.M. *et al*. 1992. The Suinn-Lew Asian self-identity Acculturation Scale. Concurrent and factorial validation. *Educational and Psychological Measurement*. 52:1041-46.

Suzuki, T. 1978. *Japanese and the Japanese: Words in Context. S. Miura*.(trans). Tokyo. Kodansha.

Tadmor, N. 2010. The social universe of the English Bible. *Scripture, Society and Culture in Early Modern England*. Cambridge. Cambridge University Press.

T'ai-Li, H. 1986. *Gods, Ghosts and Gamblers*—The influence of folk beliefs on the Everybody's Happy Lottery. Paper. Taipai, Second International Conference on Sinology. Academia Sinica.

Talbot, M. *et al*. 2003. *Language and Power in the Modern World*. Edinburgh. Edinburgh University Press. 9-13.

Tanner, R.E.S. 1956. Introduction to the northern Sukumas' idea of the Supreme being. *Anthropological Quarterly*. 29(2):45-56.

Tanner, R.E.S. 1963. Dancing and hysteria among the Sonjo. *Illustrated London News*. 18 May.

——, 1973. Economic factors in East African ecumenism. *Ecumenical Studies*. 10(1):51-69.

——, 1974. A Sociologist at Heathrow. *The Clergy Review*. 59(9):596-605.

——, 1975. A note on Christianity and traditional religious practices in Ngara. *Journal of Religion in Africa*. 6(3):151-166.

——, 1979. 'Word and Spirit in contemporary African religious practice'. *Journal of Religion in Africa*. 9(2):123-135.

——, 1993. East African ethical ideas and translation; a bilateral process. *Anthropos*. 88:29-37.

——, 1997. Cognitive development, socialisation and cognitive mutations, A critique and elaboration of Boyer, s Naturalness of Religion. A case study of the Sukuma of Tanzania. *Journal of Social Sciences*. 1(2):91-98.

——, 1999. The reluctance of the Sukuma to convert to Christianity and Islam in contemporary society. *Tribal Studies, Vol* 4. New Delhi. Concept, 183-193.

——, 2009. *Spirituality and Well-being*. New Delhi. Concept.

Tanner, R.E.S and J. Morgan. 1976. *Opinion Survey of Attitudes to Church and Education in Tanżania*. Nairobi. East African Publishing House.

Tanner, R.E.S and F. Wijsen. 1993. *Christianity in Usukuma: A working Misunderstanding* Nouvelle Revue de Science Missionnaire. 49:177-194.

Thien, D. 2007. Unjust death deification and burnt offerings. Towards an interpretive view of popular religion in contemporary southern Vietnam. In P. Taylor. (ed). *Modernity and Re-enchantment in Post Revolutionary Vietnam*. Singapore. Institute of South-East Asian Studies. 161-193.

Thomas, W.I. and Thomas, D.S. (1928). *The Child in America*. New York. Knopf.

Toren, C. 1993. Sign into symbol, symbol as sign: Cognitive aspects of a social process. In P. Boyer (ed). *The Cognitive Aspects of Religious Symbolism*. Cambridge. Cambridge University Press. 147-164.

Troyer, H. 1988. Review of cancer among four religious sects. Evidence that lifestyles are distinctive sets of risk factors. *Social Science and Medicine*, 26(10):1007-17.

Tsing, A.L. 1987. *In the Realm of the Diamond Queen*. New Jersey. Princeton University Press.

——, 1987. A rhetoric of centres in a religion of the periphery in R.S. Kipp and S. Rodgers. (eds). Indonesian Religion in Transition. Tucson. University Arizona Press. 187-210.

Turner, H.W. 1967. *African Independent Church.* Oxford. Oxford. University Press.

Veer, P. van der. 1994. Religious Nationalism. *Hindus and Moslems in India.* Berkeley. University of California Press.

Walls, A.F. 1990. The translation principle in Christian history. In P. Sting. (ed). *Bible Translation and the Spread of the Church.* Leiden. Brill. 24-39.

Warren, C.A.B. 1980. Data presentation and the audience. Responses, Ethics and Effects. *Urban Life.* 9(3):282-308.

Watson, B. 1963. *Hsun-Tżu Basic Writings.* New York. Columbia University Press.

Watson, R.S. 1988. Remembering the dead. Graves and politics in South Eastern China. In J.C. Watson and E.S. Rawski. (eds). *Death Ritual in Late Imperial and Modern China.* Berkeley. University of California Press. 207-216.

Weber, M. 1978. *Economy and Society.* Berkeley. University of California Press.

Weil, O.M. *et al.* 1965. *The Psychedelic Reader.* New York. University Books.

Welbourn, F.B. 1961. *East African Rebels: A study of some Independent Churches.* London. SCM Press.

Wheatley, P. 1971. The pivot of the four quarters. *A preliminary enquiry into the origins and character of the ancient Chinese city.* Edinburgh. Edinburgh University Press.

Whorf, B.L. 1946. The Hopi language. In O. Osgood. (ed). *Linguistic Structures in Native America.* New York. Viking Fund. 158-183.

——, 1956. Language, thought and reality. Cambridge. Mass. MIT Press.

Whyte, M.K. 1985. Death in the People's Republic of China. In T.V. Sathyamurthy. (ed). Region, Religion, Caste, Gender and Culture in Contemporary India. New York. Oxford University Press. 300-1.

Wijsen, F. 2007. Seeds of conflict in a haven of peace. *From Religious Studies to Interreligious Studies in Africa.* Amsterdam. Rodopi.

——, 2009. *Discourse Analysis in the Study of Religion: The Case of Interreligious Worship in Friesland.* Spring Conference of the Netherlands Association for the Science of Religions. Radboud University. Nijmegan.

Wilson, B. 1952. *Religion in Sociological Perspective*. Oxford. Oxford University Press.

Wilson, P.J. 1962(a). *Status Ambiguity and Spirit Possession*, Man(ns). 2(3):366-78.

——, 1962(b). *Spirits and the Sex War.* Man(ns). 2(4):629-39.

Woodstock, G. and Avakumuvic, N. 1977. *The Doukhoburs*. Carleton Institute of Canadian Studies.

Woss, F. 1993. Pokkuri temples and aging. Ritual for Approaching Death. In M.R. Mullins *et al.* (eds). Religion and society in modern Japan. Berkeley. Humanities Press. 191-203.

Wuthnow, R. 1998. After heaven. *Spirituality in America Since the 1950s*. Berkeley. University of California Press.

Yang, F. 2005. Lost in the market, saved at McDonald's. Conversion to Christianity in Urban China. *Journal of Scientific Study of Religion*. 44(4):423-441.

Yeh, D. and Gentner. D. 2005. *Reasoning Counterfactually in Chinese*. 27th Annual Meeting Archives of Cognitive Science Society:2410-15.

Ying, F. and K. Leung. 1996. *The Three Self-Patriotic Movement in the 1950s*. Hong-Kong. Alliance Bible Seminary.

Younger, R. 2002. Playing host to deity. *Festival Religion in the South Indian Tradition*. 26-40. New York. Oxford University Press.

Yovel, Y. 2009. The other within. The Marranas. *Split Identities and Emerging Modernity*. Princeton. New Jersey. Princeton University Press.

Zaman, M.Q. 1999. Religious education and the rhetoric of reform. *Madrassas in British India and Pakistan*. 41(2):294-323.

Index